European History

An Enthralling Guide to the Story of Europe, the Renaissance, and the Enlightenment

Free limited time bonus

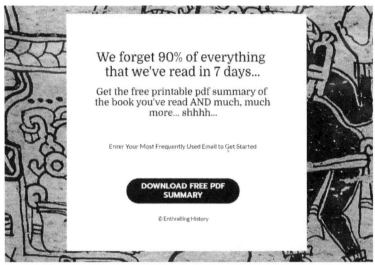

We forget 90% of everything
that we've read in 7 days...

Get the free printable pdf summary of
the book you've read AND much, much
more... shhhh...

Enter Your Most Frequently Used Email to Get Started

DOWNLOAD FREE PDF
SUMMARY

© Enthralling History

Stop for a moment. We have a free bonus set up for you. The problem is this: we forget 90% of everything that we read after 7 days. Crazy fact, right? Here's the solution: we've created a printable, 1-page pdf summary for this book that you're reading now. All you have to do to get your free pdf summary is to go to the following website: https://livetolearn.lpages.co/enthrallinghistory/

Or, Scan the QR code!

Once you do, it will be intuitive. Enjoy, and thank you!

Table of Contents

Part 1: History of Europe

An Enthralling Overview of Major Events and Figures in Europe's Past

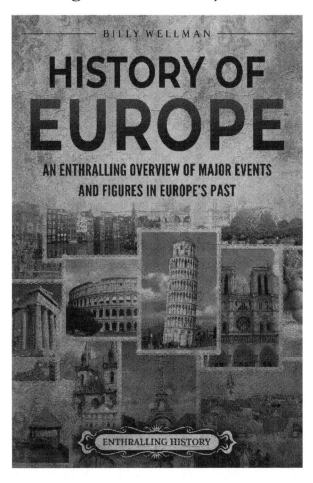

Introduction

What exactly is Europe? Is it just a continent, a landmass just like any other in the world, or is it something more? Who are European people? What does it mean to be European in the broader sense of the word? What do European ideas represent? What is it to be European?

The answers to these questions have always changed throughout history. It is undeniable that Europe, however people may interpret the meaning of this word, has played a crucial role in the development of the human species. Some would argue that Europe, its people, and the ideas they have produced are central to how we view things today, and that is certainly true to a large extent.

Still, to find answers to the above-mentioned questions, we must dig deep into the history of Europe—the continent, the people, and their ideas—since that is exactly where they lay. In fact, the answers to these questions may still be evolving and changing, as Europe continues to be an important part of the world's political, social, and cultural life today.

The history of Europe is complicated and long. It is full of struggles between peoples and nations, constant wars and bloodshed, deceit, backstabbing, manipulation, and everything in between. It is also a history of development and flourishing civilizations, of vibrant, distinct, second-to-none cultures, of wholesome instances and hope, and, above all, of the progress that we all have undergone. As we will come to see, it is, in part, this diversity that has led to the blossoming of the main principles we consider a part of life on a daily basis.

This book is going to tell the history of Europe, from prehistoric times all the way to the 21st century. It will tell the story of this magnificent entity and try to make sense of what transpired in the past and what we all, collectively, have learned from it for the future. Although it is almost impossible to fit the whole of such a complex history inside a single book, we will look at the most vital developments that have greatly affected the course of European history— and best believe, there is quite a lot to cover.

The opening chapter of the book will focus on the general makeup of Europe, describing the physical geography of the region and the spreading of the peoples who inhabited it during the prehistoric age. We will talk about the signs of the earliest Europeans and the archaeological evidence we have of their existence in various regions of the continent. We will also talk about why the first Europeans chose where to live and what was, generally, the structure of their primitive (or more advanced) societies up until roughly 1000 BCE.

From there, we will move on to the discussion of perhaps the two most vital ancient European civilizations—ancient Greece and ancient Rome. We will cover the amazing social and political transformations of these two cradles of European civilization, such as the concept of the city-state in ancient Greece, the birthplace of Western philosophical thought, the political transformation of Rome and its subsequent domination of most of the known world, and some of the main actors that were involved in the rise and fall of these two civilizations.

The next chapters of the book will talk about the transformation of the European continent after the fall of the Western Roman Empire in the 5th century CE. We shall explore the period that is usually dubbed the Middle Ages, a dark and tumultuous thousand years or so for Europe but nevertheless crucial in constituting the sociocultural makeup of the continent. During this period, Christianity spread all throughout Europe, emerging as the main pillar upon which European society was based. In the turbulent times of the Middle Ages, Christianity provided some stability to the people. The religion was respected by all European kingdoms, which were undergoing a process of formation in the lands formerly occupied by the Romans.

Then, we will move to the early modern era of European history, which began with the Renaissance and ended with the start of the Industrial Revolution. In the eyes of many, this period was fundamental in providing the moral and cultural basis of what we now perceive as

European values and ideas. The Renaissance saw the bridging of the ancient world with post-Middle-Ages Europe. Scholars brought back some of the principles that had shaped classical antiquity. Indeed, it is due to this all-encompassing cultural, artistic, social, and political movement that society saw the re-emergence of the best of ancient Greek and Roman thought, with early modern scholars developing early forms of humanism, which underlined the best qualities of humans and put it in a contemporary context.

The revolution the Renaissance caused was carried on by changes in religion, namely the Protestant Reformation, which significantly altered the cultural makeup of the continent. Thanks to the advances in political thought and the emphasis on the centrality of humans in the world, Europeans were able to arrive at vital conclusions about what kind of system would be best to live in, resulting in the rise of progressive, liberal, and nationalist ideas that once again transformed Europe and the world. These changes persisted for about five hundred years, never slowing down and eventually leading to a never-before-seen tense situation in Europe at the turn of the 20th century.

The final part of the book will discuss the history of 20th-century Europe; although it is a timeframe of only a hundred years, there is quite a lot to unpack. The social and political processes of the past centuries led to the moment when the nations of Europe were ready to go at each other. In 1914, a struggle began to determine who was truly the most dominant of them all after such massive transformations.

The Great War (the "war to end all wars") would fundamentally shake up the balance of power in Europe, but it would also have far-reaching implications for the rest of the world. The war would come to be later known as the First World War, as the unstable situation and the power vacuum the war created would eventually lead to another war, which would overshadow its predecessor.

The Second World War was a clash of good against evil, and it would redefine Europe and the world.

The book will finish by summarizing the effects of thousands of years of development and the most recent events that have affected Europe.

Chapter 1 – The First Europeans

The peculiar detail about Europe is that different people interpret what it actually is. Of course, we all have a general idea of what "Europe" is and where it is, lying to the west of the larger Eurasian continent and bordering Africa from the north through the Mediterranean Sea.

It is the eastern boundary of Europe that is often thought to be open to interpretation; we need cultural and social barriers in addition to clear geographical markers to distinguish between Europe and Asia. Today, it is largely perceived that the easternmost boundary begins northeast along the Ural Mountains and comes south along the Ural River, which flows into the Caspian Sea, the body of water that is attributed to neither Europe nor Asia. West of the Caspian Sea, namely the Caucasus region with its three modern-day countries of Georgia, Armenia, and Azerbaijan, is also a part of Europe, although it is a part that is often forgotten by many Europeans and non-Europeans due to the region's remoteness in comparison to the otherwise tightly-packed continent.

The Caucasus is an interesting region since the three countries that make it up are a blend of Asian and European cultures, having long served as the gateway between the two different continents. It is where social and cultural markers come into play in order to recognize one's "Europeanness."

The eastern border of Europe follows the Caucasus and also includes the Anatolian Peninsula, home of modern-day Turkey, which has historically been a part of the Greek or Hellenistic culture. Thus, the eastern boundary of Europe lies far more east than one might think.

Earliest Human Life in Europe

Africa is rightfully considered the cradle of human civilization. From there, our species migrated for tens of thousands of years, settling in different parts of the world. Much of Europe's geography and climate is similar to how it was about ten thousand years ago when the first *Homo sapiens sapiens*, or, in other words, us, made their way there. The earliest evidence of *Homo erectus*, the ancestor of *Homo sapiens*, has been discovered in the modern-day country of Georgia in the Caucasus and is dated to about 1.8 million years ago. It was the first hominid species to inhabit Europe.

Evidence of the early *Homo sapiens* activities is more widespread throughout the continent. France's Rhône Valley is one of the primary examples of European life in the Upper Paleolithic era, which happened about twenty thousand to thirty thousand years before the last ice age.

By then, the distinct physical features of Europeans had developed, thanks to tens of thousands of years of evolution from their African ancestors. These humans are thought to have already possessed some of the vital skills that distinguished *Homo sapiens* from the other hominid species. Primitive tools were already in use, primarily for hunting.

Homo sapiens also seem to have replaced the Neanderthals, who had inhabited mostly western Europe, by the year 40,000 BCE. Although it is not exactly known what happened, archaeologists' best guess is that the Neanderthals went extinct after regular encounters with the *Homo sapiens*, who were far more advanced than them. In any case, by the year 10,000 BCE, humans lived and roamed freely in continental Europe, preferring to settle in the low-humidity areas, such as the plains, where there was an abundance of water.

We cannot confidently say much about these early humans when it comes to their cultures or beliefs. We know from the evidence of paintings in caves and little wooden figurines that they did express themselves, although there is no evidence of any writing systems. Their relationship with the natural world was what mattered the most to them, and Paleolithic weapons made from bones and wood show that they were organized in simple hunter-gatherer societies.

A pivotal development came about in the year 7500 BCE: the Neolithic Revolution. This term was first used to refer to the appearance of stone tools, which replaced the more primitive tools used by the earliest humans. The development of stone tools was accompanied by cultural advances, opening up new opportunities and means of expression for the earliest Europeans.

The first evidence of pottery and even metalworking can be dated to this period. Humans learned to place more emphasis on the durability and efficiency of their tools, preferring newer materials to the old ones.

Most importantly, the Neolithic Revolution produced something that would revolutionize human life forever and become a staple or a must-have for all societies that wanted to be considered "developed." That something was agriculture.

The "invention" of agriculture was what really separated the Neolithic Age from the Paleolithic Age. Agriculture helped the hunter-gatherer groups organize themselves into more cohesive entities. They could enjoy an abundance of food supplies, which led to more stability and population growth. Agriculture meant that the food supply was more guaranteed, opening up "jobs" in early societies. People had been solely focused on gathering food, but now they could focus on other things.

We are not exactly sure how agriculture came to be, but by the year 4000 BCE, most of Europe was already engaged in primitive farming. Agriculture likely spread from Mesopotamia. In fact, the earliest Neolithic sites in Europe are considered to be those found in the Balkans, perhaps due to the region's close proximity to the cradle of civilization. Still, many theories exist about whether or not agriculture, much like many other inventions of prehistoric times, was something brought by cultural exchange and diffusion or if it emerged independently on its own.

Around 4000 BCE, Europe experienced its first large-scale migration since the development of agriculture. The newcomers have been identified as being part of the linguistic Indo-European family, a huge conglomeration that includes, as its name suggests, almost all of the languages spoken in Europe, the Middle East, and India. Through the diffusion of the Indo-Europeans into the existing populations in Europe and their gradual settlement of various regions inside the continent, later ethnolinguistic distinctions would arise, notably in the forms of the early Slavic and Celtic peoples. Also, gradually, the "first" Europeans would migrate more to the west, dominating western France and Iberia, as well as penetrating into Britain. Such a large demographic change eventually led to more technological developments in Europe, with people utilizing copper as their primary material in making tools.

By about 2000 BCE, metalworking had become more widespread, and pure copper tools were gradually replaced with bronze tools— an alloy of copper and tin that was far more durable than its predecessor. This became especially common in regions like the Balkans and Iberia, where there was an abundance of raw materials due to the mountainous terrain.

One example of cultural development is the huge megalithic structures scattered throughout the continent. They are most prominent in western Europe, parts of Britain, northern Germany, and Denmark. Thousands of huge stone monuments were carefully carved and organized in shapes like circles. They are believed to be some of the earliest cultural sites in prehistoric Europe.

Just like many other aspects of prehistoric Europe, various explanations have been suggested regarding how and for what purposes these sites came to be built. Stonehenge, of course, is the most prominent example of a prehistoric megalithic site. It still baffles archaeologists and historians to this day and attracts tens of thousands of visitors each year. Its sheer size amazes everyone who has the chance to see it in person, instantly clouding their minds with questions about its mysterious origins.

The Aegean Civilization

The inhabitants of central, northern, and western Europe are interesting to consider. They organized themselves into mostly agriculture-based small-scale societies by the year 1000 BCE.

However, the civilization that attracts the attention of historians and archaeologists first popped up in the southern and southeastern parts of the continent around the shores of the warm waters of the Mediterranean and the smaller seas. Thanks to the region's constant contact with the more advanced civilizations of North Africa and the Levant, Mediterranean civilizations took off around the year 1000 BCE and developed at a faster pace than societies in other parts of the continent.

One such location where a more complex form of ancient civilization was born was near the Aegean Sea, located between the Anatolian Peninsula and modern-day Greece.

Again, it is logical to assume that the geographic makeup of the Aegean was what caused the region to develop quickly and shape the future of Europe's civilized future. It was a meeting place of cultures, with warm weather and many small islands and sea crossings, which made it easier to establish links than, say, the dense forests and inhospitable climate of northern Europe. Due to the Aegean having far more connectivity, commercial and cultural exchange was facilitated, and the nice climate made it possible for the region to be agriculturally advanced.

We have to remember that by the year 1000 BCE, civilizations in the Middle East, Mesopotamia, and Egypt already had a developed social, economic, and political structure, with large city-states, kingdoms, and empires constantly at war with each other. Multiple dynasties had risen and fallen, and trade had flourished long before Europe had anything similar to be proud of. The Aegean, as the closest and the most connected region to these places, was the first region in Europe where similar developments would take place.

The island of Crete is a great example. By 2000 BCE, the island had towns with stone and brick buildings, and the societal makeup was rather diverse, with many different classes like artisans, metalworkers, and merchants. The Minoan civilization, named after a legendary king who ruled Crete, had all of the attributes of a thriving civilization and is rightly considered to be one. Its influence on subsequent civilizational advances in Europe is massive. For example, Crete is where the earliest form of writing was found, as the Cretans engraved clay tablets to use for administration. It is likely they adopted this method from their Asian neighbors since clay tablets had already been used there for many centuries.

Olives, grapes, and wheat were the main crops that were harvested and traded with neighboring societies. Animals like cattle and sheep were also domesticated. In addition, due to its geographic location, shipbuilding and other activities related to maritime life were very advanced. The Minoan civilization had a prosperous society that lasted for about six hundred or so years. Eventually, it would be destroyed, most likely due to a powerful earthquake that struck the neighboring island of Thera.

The decline of the Minoan civilization came approximately in the year 1500 BCE, but it would not be long before Crete became the homeland for a new people who took over what the Minoans had started. We know of this "replacement" thanks to administrative tablets that appear to be written in a completely new language after about 1450 BCE, suggesting that they were created by new people. Evidence of the same language has been discovered in southern Greece in the area known as the Peloponnese and has been identified as a form of ancient Greek. So, what exactly happened to this civilization in Crete?

The people who came from Greece introduced their own language and took over the remnants of the Minoan civilization. They were most likely part of a larger migratory wave in the 2nd millennium BCE. The Aegean saw the migration of Indo-European people from the north and northeast crossing, for example, to Anatolia, where the Hittite Kingdom was eventually established. These people were not only the first Greek speakers, but they were also fierce warriors and invaders. History has come to know them as the Achaeans after they had settled mainly in the archipelago of the Aegean Sea.

The Achaeans were far more advanced than the Minoans. Their military technology, for example, included chariot warfare, an innovation that allowed them to triumph over their enemies. Settling in fortifications that would later become ancient Greek cities, the Achaeans built up places like Athens and Mycenae on mainland Europe around 1650 BCE before they crossed to Crete. They possessed great administrative and governing skills, and the Achaean culture prospered for a few hundred years, building up the core of the Greek cities and having close contact with the Mediterranean world.

The Hittites mention Mycenae in their records. The legendary siege of Troy, which occurred around 1200 BCE, is evidence of the prosperity of the Achaean civilization. The Achaeans, who were most likely divided into several city-states and small kingdoms, united their forces and organized a large-scale attack on the magnificent ancient city of Troy, something that is seen as one of the last great Achaean successes.

Needless to say, the Mycenaean period, which lasted roughly up until the year 1000 BCE, was very influential in the development of the ancient Greek civilization. The Mycenaeans laid the foundations for the large-scale Iron Age transition, which started during their time but mostly took place after their decline. It is unknown what exactly caused the Mycenaean civilization to perish, but it is clear that its decline coincided with an overall, more general decline of the Bronze Age in the eastern Mediterranean.

We are not exactly sure if the Mycenaeans were destroyed after a series of devastating earthquakes or if they fell to invaders like the Minoans before them. What we do know is that their heyday was also the heyday of prehistoric Greece, and their demise set into motion a period that would be known as the Greek Dark Ages—a transitory period that lasted for a couple of hundred years and eventually led to the emergence of one of the most culturally advanced European societies ever.

Chapter 2 – Ancient Greece

The Greeks

The Minoan and Achaean civilizations were the two predecessors to a civilization we now refer to as ancient Greece. Historians have identified this highly influential period to have lasted from roughly 800 to about 300 BCE—a span of five hundred years or so. Despite this, the importance of ancient Greece, with its rich and vibrant culture and the immense social, material, and philosophical heritage it has left us, should not be understated.

Rising from the ashes of the Mycenean civilization, the Greek world of the Aegean would eventually become significant in almost all aspects of society and would play an important role more than a thousand years after its decline in the Renaissance.

There are few periods in Europe's history that deserve as much detailed attention as ancient Greece, and we certainly will not be able to cover it fully here. Instead, this book will touch on the main aspects that made ancient Greece what it is remembered for today.

Ancient Greece was by no means a united political entity, nor was it confined to the territory that is occupied today by the modern-day sovereign nation of Greece. Instead, what we now call ancient Greece refers to a distinct culture that served as a unifier of several cities and city-states. The ideas and institutions that were built during this period have stood the test of time and continue to influence everyday matters in ways that are very subtle, such as through language.

For many centuries, the Greek language was a staple of European languages, alongside Latin. It was one of the first languages that every educated person knew, much like how English is regarded nowadays.

Yet, Greek influences lay far beyond the semantic implications of certain words and phrases we use. They are rooted in every aspect of our lives. The ancient Greeks made significant breakthroughs in art, politics, and science, revolutionizing their own worldview and, later on, without perhaps intending it, revolutionizing the world.

The people who inhabited the Aegean at the time of the Mycenean civilization's collapse called themselves Hellenes. Ethnically, they were mostly the same, although they did live in separate societies, mostly in thriving, advanced cities with a couple thousand inhabitants. Sparta, Corinth, and Athens are the most well-known examples of ancient Greek cities, and they would eventually transform to become the first European city-states.

Still, despite the people's allegiance to their own city or region, they all shared a larger identity, something that was manifested in their language and beliefs. When a person from Sparta met a person from Corinth, they could converse freely with each other, understand each other's outlooks on the world, and agree on core religious beliefs. This was because they were all Greek and belonged to an overarching entity, which they referred to as Hellas.

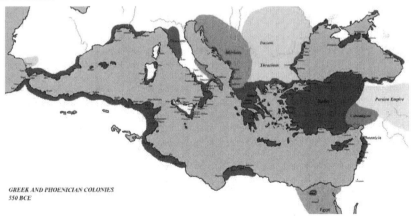

Greek and Phoenician colonies in 550 BCE.
https://commons.wikimedia.org/wiki/File:Ancient_colonies.PNG

The Hellenes distinguished themselves from other peoples, whom they considered to be non-Hellenes. Non-Greek speakers were barbarians, even if they possessed power and wealth that rivaled or eclipsed the Greeks. And despite the Hellenes' petty quarrels, countless wars against each other, jealousy, and competition, when it was needed, they moved against the barbarians based on their joined identity. For instance, in the 5th century BCE, they united to fight the Persian invaders, the non-Greeks who wished to take over their lands and destroy the rich heritage they had constructed. In short, the ancient Greeks, as a people, were very much self-conscious of their own identity.

The collapse of the Mycenean era and the beginning of the Greek Dark Ages meant there was great social and economic upheaval in the Aegean. The Greek Dark Ages resulted in a complete restructuring of the old hierarchies and led to the constant movement of people in regions that were already very interconnected. Many large urban centers were abandoned, and a large part of the population began to live in more modest villages and pursue pastoral lifestyles. Some tried their luck overseas, utilizing their maritime skills and sailing away to explore the Mediterranean. They founded several colonies.

The Greek Dark Ages were, by all means, a transitional period from the Bronze Age collapse to the Iron Age. The migration of peoples and the demographic changes that followed it slowly stabilized; by the 8th century BCE, things were starting to move forward once again.

For example, one pivotal development that distinguishes a "Dark Age Greek" from an "ancient Greek" was writing. The Mycenean language was almost fully put out of use during the Greek Dark Ages, so reading and writing had to be "relearned" from scratch. A new alphabet came into use in the 8th century BCE. Legendary epics like the *Iliad* and the *Odyssey*, which were written by an equally legendary man named Homer, are both thought to be dated to the 8th century BCE. They serve as foundations for ancient Greek and, to a larger extent, ancient European literature. They are also the first to use the new alphabet style the Greeks adopted from the Phoenician people. This cultural and social revival of the former Mycenean people eventually led to the birth of what we now call ancient Greece.

While Homer's epics are a good marker of the beginning of ancient Greece, there is an even better one: the first Panhellenic Olympic Games held in Olympia in 776 BCE. Greeks from all over came to participate in the games due to their love of sports and to join in a sense of community. The first games played a big role in the cultural revival of Greece. Other developments, such as the new alphabet and new monetary system (which was introduced first in the Anatolian Kingdom of Lydia and later adopted by the Greeks), help us to mark the beginning of ancient Greece.

Around this time, colonization really took off. The Hellenes colonized the Aegean islands to make the region more interconnected but later moved to other horizons, first in the western Mediterranean and later even into the Black Sea. Greek colonies were founded by Greek sailors as trade outposts.

Due to similar living conditions, it was relatively easy for the Greeks to establish themselves in far-off places like Crimea, Sicily, Iberia, and southern France. The Greek colonies in south Italy, most prominently Syracuse, were so connected to the heart of Greek culture that they were referred to as Magna Graecia (Greater Greece) in Latin.

The harbors of these colonies became an exchange of not only valuable goods, like iron and wine, but also knowledge and customs of ancient Greeks. They thrived, emerging as Greek overseas outposts, something that would become celebrated down the line.

The Greek City-State

Perhaps what best encapsulates the essence of ancient Greece is the Greek city-state, a political entity that dominated the Aegean after the end of the Dark Ages and before the eventual conquests of Alexander the Great. The Greek city-states were very important in shaping ancient Greek life and giving their inhabitants a strong sense of identity. A city-state's location, relations with neighboring city-states, and relative size were good indicators of a city-state's strength and the type of political system that was in place. As the Greeks started to come out of the Dark Ages, they chose to gradually abandon the rule of kings, replacing it with polities that were more representative of the inhabitants of a certain city-state.

By the 7th century BCE, powerful urban hubs like Athens were the centers of the political entities we now call city-states. These urban centers were usually surrounded by smaller towns, ports, and villages, and they served as "protectors" to those lands that surrounded them. The united political entity rarely contained more than one large urban center, and if it did, it was only temporary due to success in war. Therefore, these centers acted as de facto capitals of the lands they surrounded, hence the name city-state.

The structure of the city-state, on paper, is very similar to the structure and makeup of a small kingdom. The essence of a kingdom is a large center that presides over the affairs of less important areas, making up a cohesive political entity. The main difference between a kingdom and a city-state lies in its political system. As we mentioned, Greek society transformed gradually from one reliant on a king's supreme rule to one that was ruled by more than one person. Mainly, this was exercised through the rule of the aristocratic elite—men who owned property and were, therefore, the wealthiest and the most powerful. There seemed to be a natural tendency from the people to give the elite the ability to rule, and the transition to aristocratic councils that replaced the kings' rule came about as something natural, although to varying degrees of success at first. This system resembles what we would today refer to as oligarchy—the rule of the rich.

We can say that ancient Greece invented politics. The word itself comes from the Greek word *polis*, which means "city." Although the boundaries of what politics encapsulate may be blurry at times, at its heart, as the ancient Greeks envisioned it, it meant the recognition of public interest (in their case, of the city-state) and the exercising of activities (governance).

The city-state's political course was hardly reliant on one single individual, although there was certainly a period where tyrants rose in prominence in several city-states. They were considered strongmen who brought prosperity (this was before tyranny was ultimately condemned after the 5th century BCE). Tyrants led to the development of aristocratic councils and eventually to the development of a political system that we now call democracy, another word whose origins come from ancient Greek.

"The rule of the people" as a tangible, long-term method of governance was most successfully put in effect in the city-state of Athens in the 5th century BCE, though forms of democratic representative rule were present in ancient Greece before that. It was a system built on discussion, stressing public opinion and thought of the many rather than orders from one person with a "God-given" right to rule.

The purest form of Greek democracy envisioned the complete participation of all citizens since everyone had something to say about public affairs. Of course, the biggest criticism of democracy in ancient Greece was the fact that it was not representative; it was just more representative than other systems elsewhere in the world at that time. Only property-owning free men were considered citizens in ancient

Greece, and they constituted a minority of the entire population, which included women and slaves. Despite this obvious flaw, the political system of the Greek city-state, a system built on discussion and participation, reflected the overall way of life of the ancient Greeks. Greek city-states flourished with their vibrant cultural and commercial centers and dominated the region for many centuries.

Aside from social and economic matters, the prosperity of the Greek city-states relied on the development of a unique military system, which would later be perfected and emerge as one of the strongest in the world. This is evident in military technology and strategy. The transition to the Iron Age meant that better weapons and armor were available to those who had access to iron, something the Greeks were happy about due to the abundance of iron in the region and through the various trade routes they had established with their colonies.

The armies of the city-states were made up of citizen-soldier hoplites, who were typically armed with spears, short swords, and shields and wore heavy armor. Disciplined and professional hoplites constituted the core of the army. They marched alongside cavalry, archers, and artillery corps.

By 500 BCE, the emphasis on physical well-being, the Greek love of sport and competition, and general military education at a young age led to the development of a coherent military tradition in ancient Greece. The city-state of Sparta is a great example, as it is known for its amazing elite troops and a lifestyle that was fully concentrated on "producing" citizens capable of warfare.

Ancient Greece's main challenger came from the east. The Persian Empire expanded far beyond its origins in Iran, conquering much of the Anatolian Peninsula and threatening an invasion of Greece. The Greeks and Persians had long maintained contact with each other, but by the 5th century BCE, they had become antagonistic due to the latter's aggressive expansion and oppression of the peoples they conquered. Among the conquered were the Hellenes, who occupied the shores of Anatolia in the region of Ionia; they would eventually become the reason why a war erupted.

The Ionian Greeks revolted against the despotic rule of the Persians in the early 5th century BCE, getting support from other city-states, most prominently from Athens and Eretria. Although the revolt would be put down in 493 BCE, the involvement of the city-states made the Persians launch their first invasion of Greece in 492 BCE, resulting in the capture of Macedon and Thrace. The expedition continued for two more years before the Greeks finally crushed the Persian army in the Battle of Marathon in 490 BCE.

According to legend, after the Greeks' decisive victory, a Greek messenger ran a distance of approximately forty kilometers (twenty-five miles) from the site of the battle to the city of Athens to be the bearer of good news. Upon delivering his message, he died of exhaustion. Although this story was likely fiction, this messenger was never forgotten, as the marathon race was modeled after his race to Athens.

The Persians launched a second invasion of Greece in 480 BCE, with Emperor Xerxes personally leading the force to mainland Greece. Xerxes was in charge of one of the largest armies assembled in ancient times, with tens of thousands of men marching under him.

Xerxes ran over most of the initial Greek resistance. At the famous Battle of Thermopylae, King Leonidas of Sparta led a small allied Greek force. He stationed his men in a narrow mountainous corridor and halted the Persian advances to the main Greek cities, allowing the population to evacuate. Leonidas and his three hundred Spartans, along with hundreds of Thespians and helots, took a final stand but were eventually overwhelmed after being betrayed by one of their own.

However, their effort would not be in vain. About a month after Thermopylae, the Greeks achieved a decisive naval victory at the Battle of Salamis, where they destroyed most of the Persian forces and forced them to retreat. The victory at Salamis was followed by a couple more successes for the Greeks.

For the next few decades, a confederation of Greek city-states called the Delian League, led by Athens, continued the Greek campaigns against Persia before the invaders were completely expelled and the city-states regained their independence.

The struggle between the Greeks and the Persians in the first half of the 5th century BCE was perceived by the Greeks as a general struggle between good and evil or between the civilized and barbarians. In many regards, it can be considered the first instance of the Western world coming into conflict with the East, a clash of values and cultures that ended in a Greek victory. Their success opened the way to the most prosperous period in ancient Greek history, something we will discuss later.

Despite their united victory against a common enemy, the Greek city-states did not maintain peaceful relations with each other at all times. After the defeat of Persia, Athens and Sparta emerged as the two main powerhouses, each leading their own confederations against each other and struggling for dominance in the region. Their rivalry would culminate in a series of conflicts history now knows as the Peloponnesian War, which would dominate the second half of the 5th century BCE.

The Peloponnesian War is a very interesting conflict that helped shape ancient Greece before the conquests of Alexander the Great. The main thing we need to know is that the Athenian-led Delian League was counterbalanced by the Spartan-led Peloponnesian League. Athens was seen as becoming far too powerful, extracting tribute from weaker city-states. Sparta and its allies would emerge victorious by the end of the century, setting the stage for a very brief period of Spartan hegemony, although that never truly ceased the struggles between individual city-states.

Overall, it can be said that, in hindsight, the Peloponnesian War weakened the Greek city-states politically, making them susceptible to threats. Despite this, cultural, scientific, and social achievements occurred after the Greek victory over the Persians.

The Cultural Legacy

Although political history and wars can be very interesting to look at, they are not the main thing for which we now remember the ancient Greeks. Instead, it was their marvelous achievements in science, arts, and philosophy.

Their advancements in these fields were very important, but they were also largely the first ones to start engaging in them. The social and economic prosperity of the Greek city-states made it possible for many ancient Greeks to indulge themselves in activities that were not solely focused on survival or gaining power, as was the situation in most other places around the world at the time.

The European search for truth, for an explanation of the world besides religion, both scientifically and philosophically, originated in ancient Greece. In ancient Greece, the notion of the scientific method originated, although, admittedly, that concept has been advanced and adapted consistently throughout the ages. However, at the heart of the scientific method lies a profoundly ancient Greek idea of observing and making conclusions about the natural world through reason.

Still, that is not to say that observation and the study of the world could only be found in ancient Greek culture. The ancient Egyptians and Mesopotamians, among other civilizations, made a lot of developments in fields like architecture, mathematics, and astrology. They knew quite a bit about these topics before the golden age of Greece was ushered in around the 5th century BCE. However, we place a lot of emphasis on ancient Greek thought because of the Greeks' detached way of thinking about these topics and their conscious decision to differentiate between rational, material, and other worldly concepts for the sake of differentiating between them.

It is not exactly an exaggeration to say that ancient Greeks "invented" science, much like they "invented" politics. Anaximander and Thales, Ionian Greeks from the city of Miletus, were among the first Greek scientists. They distinguished themselves from other people, such as the Babylonians, due to their distinct ways of interpreting and understanding the phenomena they observed.

What is the origin of the world? What gives life its foundations? Is there a boundary to the natural world? These are the questions these 6th-century BCE scientists (philosophers, if you will) tried to answer. But it is not their discoveries that make them so interesting and important. Rather, it is the fact that they broke away from the traditional way things were conceived. They were one of the first people in history who speculated there was more about the world than gods and goddesses. Although they would be heavily criticized for these "radical" views not long after their lifetimes, they laid the foundations for what became Western thought and science.

Of course, no history of ancient Greece should omit Plato, a monumental Athenian philosopher who died in the mid-4th century BCE. It is difficult to fit into words the impact Plato, alongside the two other titans of ancient Greek philosophy, Socrates and Aristotle, had on the development of Western philosophy. An aristocrat-turned-thinker, Plato was concerned about the state of affairs, first in Athens and then more generally in the natural world.

Plato was a student of Socrates, the man often dubbed the "Father of philosophy," Plato wrote down much of what Socrates advocated for (how to acquire knowledge and the study of morals, or ethics), but he also greatly expanded Socrates's thoughts by introducing different concepts. For instance, Plato was the first to distinguish between the natural, observable world, where humans may be deceived by their senses, and the otherworldly dimension of "ideas," where abstract notions like justice and truth or material notions like cat and dog exist in their truest, most ideal forms. Plato argued that this immaterial form of life was what truly mattered but that it was only accessible by the human soul, which could get to it by employing reason.

Plato's idealism and the implied notion of human dualism—the distinction between the soul (mind) and body—became the basis for all schools of philosophy. In addition to his theory of forms and ideas, he wrote *Republic*, which is perhaps the most famous of his works. Written in the style of a dialogue, where the main character is Socrates, it explores the idea of what the best form of society is and how people can achieve it. This work shows the range of questions the Greek philosophers pondered on.

Plato's thoughts were later expanded by his student Aristotle in his writings. Aristotle was another giant of ancient philosophy and the tutor of Alexander the Great. Aristotle's writings on logic, rhetoric, ethics, and metaphysics were just as influential as his teacher's. Aristotle diverged quite a bit from Plato, arguing against his theory of forms. Aristotle was more about deriving general laws from physical facts that were present in the everyday world. His work set the framework for European thought for the next two thousand or so years, and it is still referenced today.

More importantly, Aristotelian philosophy, his science of deductive logic and his approach to matters of great complexity, would eventually be partially incorporated into the world's biggest religions—Christianity and Islam.

His attitudes regarding the city-state as the best possible form of societal structure would reinforce the ancient Greeks' pride, something that was increasingly present after they defeated the Persians.

Philosophy is just one part of ancient Greek culture that has stood the test of time. Constantly reevaluating life and inquiring more about it pushed the Greeks to explore other, more material or, if you will, factual disciplines, like mathematics. Platonian idealism played a role there. As a philosopher obsessed with the truth and the ideal form of life, Plato could not ignore that some truths existed and manifested themselves in everyday life, like mathematical numbers. Mathematics was something abstract but also something very concrete and true.

This semi-mystical aspect of mathematics was appealing to many, and much of Western mathematics was founded by ancient Greeks like Pythagoras. Perhaps it was not the discipline in which the Greeks excelled at, as they were overshadowed by Arab mathematicians about a thousand years later, but Greek knowledge of arithmetic and geometry was used by the Western world for many centuries. It was only after roughly the 17th century CE that Europe advanced the field of mathematics by introducing new concepts like algebra.

Literature was another field that thrived in ancient Greece. This seems obvious, especially since we have already talked about the Greeks' influential philosophical writings, but other genres were also popular. There were history books, such as the work of Herodotus. Poetry was also considered to have been notable piece, with poets being regarded as public educators. We have already mentioned Homer and his two great epics, both of which are still staples of classic literature. His works combine elements of ancient history and myth and tell the story of the Achaean conquest of Troy and Odysseus's subsequent voyage back home. These literary works provided the ancient Greeks with different models of people, including their exuberant personalities and behavior. They fused their legendary, godlike attributes with more humane details that made them relatable to the general public.

Literature and poetry gave birth to another famous aspect of ancient Greek culture: drama. Of course, the origins of the Greeks' love for theater, performance, and drama can be traced back to rituals and religious ceremonies. Key aspects of these rituals were fused with the literary genius of dramatists like Sophocles and Euripides, which led to the golden age of Greek drama. Theater would become an inseparable part of Greek life. The Greeks not only enjoyed great plays but also amphitheaters and stages that could fit hundreds of people at a time.

The Age of Alexander

By the end of the Peloponnesian War in the late 5th century BCE, a new force was emerging in ancient Greece located north of the city-states of Athens and Sparta: the Kingdom of Macedon. Macedonians were, by all means, Greeks, as they spoke the same language and had a vastly similar culture to that of the other city-states. They also participated in the Panhellenic festivals and games and claimed that they were the descendants of the legendary Achilles, the Achaean hero of the Trojan War and one of the most celebrated characters in all of Greece.

The main difference between Macedon and the rest of ancient Greece was its political structure. Macedon was a hereditary kingdom, a type of polity long considered to have been old-fashioned by most Greeks. Macedon had never switched to the oligarchic or democratic makeup of the traditional Greek city-state, something which aroused a sense of contempt in places like Athens, where the local form of governance was considered to have been much more noble. The Kingdom of Macedon, which occupied the territory in the northern mountains, was regarded as the inferior middle child of ancient Greece by many contemporary Greeks, but developments in the 4th century BCE would dramatically alter these attitudes.

Everything began to change after an ambitious king came to rule Macedon in 359 BCE. His name was Philip II. After deposing his infant nephew, the rightful ruler named Amyntas IV, Philip II sought to become the sole ruler of Greece. He had an eye for strategy and politics, and he recognized that the Greek city-states, although prosperous, had been weakened by the constant squabbles they had with each other.

Philip had received a great military education during his youth in the city of Thebes, and he came up with a new military tactic that would eventually help him assert his dominance over his enemies. Philip advanced the traditional Greek hoplite by introducing a new phalanx formation, where hoplites would wield pikes that were twice as large as the traditional spears. Organized in ranks of ten, the soldiers holding these pikes would be defended in the front by men holding large shields, resulting in a remarkable defensive and offensive machine. It was largely thanks to this military invention that he was able to trample over the Greek city-states, achieving a crucial victory against a united force from Athens and Thebes at Chaeronea in 338 BCE.

Before his assassination in 336 BCE, Philip managed to establish himself as the ruling hegemon of Greece, forcing the other Greek cities into a confederation known as the League of Corinth. The center of his kingdom remained the Macedonian capital of Pella.

Philip II singlehandedly put an end to the Greek city-states, emerging as the sovereign of most of Greece and laying the foundation for the great things that occurred after his death.

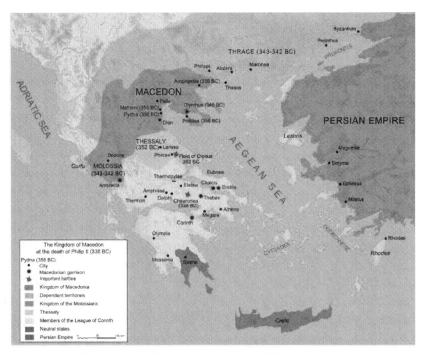

The Kingdom of Macedon at the time of Philip II's death.

Alexander the Great is one of the most widely known figures in history. A magnificent general and a wise ruler, he came to power after his father's assassination (there is speculation that he was even involved in the plot to murder Philip). Having been tutored by none other than Aristotle, Alexander had the zeal and ambition of his father but would manage to demonstrate it on a whole another level, unachieved by any European ruler until his time.

Personally leading his soldiers into battle, Alexander crossed into Anatolia in 334 BCE to begin his campaign against the Persian Empire, something Philip had planned to do in his lifetime. It is truly remarkable what Alexander was able to achieve in just the span of a decade before his untimely death in Babylon due to, most likely, typhoid disease. It is unsurprising that he earned himself the title of "Great" in the process.

Alexander never truly suffered any setbacks in his ambitious military endeavors. He started off with a decisive victory against the Persians in the Battle of Issus in 333 BCE in Anatolia. He shattered Emperor Darius

III's army and forced it to retreat. Alexander chose to march southward to Egypt through Syria after taking over the Persian possessions in most of Asia Minor. His next major victory was achieved at Gaugamela in 331 BCE, which led to a series of successful campaigns in the former Persian territories by the year 326 BCE.

Darius III would be assassinated during his retreat, and with him, the Achaemenid dynasty of Persia perished. This opened up a power vacuum in the Near East, something that was swiftly utilized by Alexander, who emerged as the ruler of the lands from Greece all the way to the Indus River, including territories in the Levant, Egypt, the South Caucasus, Mesopotamia, Iran, and Afghanistan.

This was a great achievement, but Alexander wanted more. In 326 BCE, he crossed the Indus River to launch a campaign against the Indian King Porus, something no other European had ever dared to do. Despite emerging victorious from this campaign, Alexander was forced to return home and give up on his conquest of India since his soldiers were exhausted and homesick after years of constant warfare. Alexander would die in Babylon three years later, in 323 BCE, at the age of thirty-two.

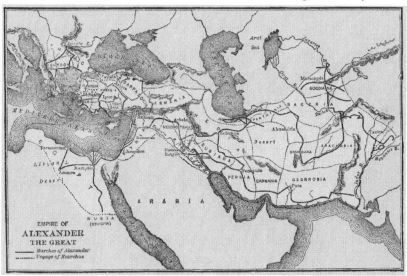

Map of Alexander's conquests.
https://commons.wikimedia.org/wiki/File:Map-alexander-empire.png

It is difficult to truly state the impact Alexander's conquests had on the ancient world. Expanding the borders of his empire to such an extent was remarkable on its own, although there were more far-reaching implications. Primarily, Alexander is hailed for spreading Greek culture in lands it had never reached before, such as throughout the Near East and Egypt. These places, while fundamentally different from ancient Greece, accepted the Greek customs and way of life, giving birth to a multicultural environment that would persist for centuries and whose traces can still be found today.

Alexander can also be considered the first European ruler with cosmopolitan views, something that is best demonstrated by his reliance on foreign, mostly Persian, troops during his campaigns in order to earn the loyalty and respect of the people he conquered. He paid a lot of respect to Persia himself, even though he knew Persia was the historical enemy of Greece. Alexander arranged a mass wedding involving his soldiers and Persian women. He married the daughter of Darius, which signaled that he wished to maintain strong relations with the Persians.

Alexander did not bring Greek officials to administer the unknown lands; he preferred local, more experienced advisors and bureaucrats, something that led to his empire being prosperous during his short lifetime. Sometimes, these choices provoked discontent among his soldiers, but Alexander was willing to compromise to achieve his goals and emerge as the most powerful man in the ancient world.

Alexander left no heirs, and the empire he had built through his conquests was divided by his generals soon after his death in 323 BCE. Ptolemy took over the Egyptian territories, while Seleucus established his Seleucid Empire, which stretched from Damascus through Mesopotamia to Iran. Anatolia was divided into several small satrapies, out of which Galatia and Pergamum stand out, while Greece remained nominally under the control of the Kingdom of Macedon.

The death of Alexander the Great ushered in a new era for ancient Greece, shaping and developing the concept of the Hellenistic world. In all of the territories that were taken over by Alexander and his successors, the Greek culture thrived in tandem with local cultures. The Greek language became an official language of the Near East and was widely used as the international lingua franca. New cities were modeled after the best Greek cities, taking elements from their architectural and infrastructural styles, leading to an eclectic mix found nowhere else in the world. Alexander himself founded many cities that bore his name, some of which still exist to this day.

The cultural and social overhaul of these places led to a population boom and a thriving lifestyle, with large urban areas like Babylon and

Alexandria becoming centers of the world. The people looked and spoke Greek and, to some extent, were ruled by the Greeks, although they were mostly inhabited by non-Greeks.

Eventually, what Alexander had conquered and what later became the Hellenistic successor states would be taken over by another rising European power, a culture that had many commonalities with ancient Greece. Another thriving, monumental civilization came into existence during the developments we just described in ancient Greece. This civilization was located just to the west, in the Apennine Peninsula. And this civilization was destined to take over much of the known world. You may have heard of it before: Rome.

Chapter 3 – Ancient Rome

Origins

Parallel to the developments in ancient Greece after the Greek Dark Ages, another magnificent civilization just west of the city-states in the Apennine Peninsula was slowly emerging. Ancient Italy was a very diverse place early on, as it was home to an eclectic mix of peoples and cultures by the time of the Bronze Age collapse. These people groups, much like everywhere else in Europe at the time, lived agriculture-dependent lives in small towns and villages and only occasionally had contact with the outside world. They were relatively peaceful, having no real tradition or history of warfare, and most of them spoke a type of an Italic dialect, like Latin, which belonged to the Indo-European language group.

Northern Italy was occupied by western and central European Gallic tribes, while several Greek and Phoenician colonies were established in the south, including in Sicily. However, one people group stood out among the rest. They mostly occupied the central-western region of Italy known as Etruria, what is now roughly Tuscany. They were even scattered thinly along the western coast down to Campania. These people were the Etruscans, and they were perhaps the most civilized people of early ancient Italy. Interestingly, they did not belong to the Indo-European language group; they spoke their own unique tongue and gave birth to a complex culture that would come to shape Europe in the coming centuries.

The Etruscan civilization was a very interesting one, predating the ancient Roman civilization. The Romans would eventually borrow quite a bit from the Etruscans, but to say they were Etruscan people is wrong. Lying on the border of the regions of Etruria and Latium, Romans spoke Latin, even though they were under the Etruscan dominion for a long time.

The exact history of how Rome came into being is shrouded in mystery. Despite archaeological evidence of the early period of ancient Rome from about the 8th to 6th century BCE, no real historical records of the time survive. The Greeks would be the first to pay attention to Rome, but that would only happen in the 3rd century BCE when Rome had already become a republic and was involved in many wars.

Due to this lack of attention, a well-known, although probably highly inaccurate, story about the foundation of Rome became popular. This story talks about twin brothers named Remus and Romulus. They were supposedly children of the Roman god of war, Mars. According to legend, they were raised by a she-wolf after being abandoned in the Tiber River. The brothers founded their own city on Palatine Hill, after which they would have a falling-out, resulting in Romulus killing his own brother and becoming the first king of Rome in the mid-8th century BCE, sometime around the year 753.

Of course, the legend of Rome's founding should not be considered to be entirely true. Many other theories exist, even among the ancient Romans themselves. According to another famous story, the Romans were descendants of some Achaean soldiers who had settled on the Tiber after the Trojan War. Still, the legend of Romulus and Remus is cherished to this day and is widely considered to be the "acceptable" version of Rome's founding.

Again, due to the lack of evidence and records, it is hard to say how Rome developed immediately after its founding. Romulus is often regarded to be the first king, but not much is known about him and his rule. Not much is known about what happened after his rule either. Seven kings ruled the city of Rome, although Rome was most likely not a fully independent political entity when it was ruled by these kings.

This line of kings would come to an end in 509 BCE when the unpopular twenty-five-year reign of Lucius Tarquinius Superbus led to a popular uprising. Before him, Romans had accepted the suzerainty of kings, mostly viewing them as just rulers who defended the city from other Etruscan kings. The reason behind the uprising against Tarquinius Superbus, which means "proud" in Latin, was not entirely due to his unjust rule. In one of the most infamous stories of the ancient world, his son Sextus Tarquinius raped Lucretia, a woman of noble descent, lighting the spark that led to the overthrow of the king. After the popular uprising, the people of Rome decided to get rid of the monarchy, implementing a republican rule.

Despite the convenience of this story about the last king of Rome, historians have recently challenged this view, suggesting that Tarquinius Superbus was actually forced out by a foreign king. According to this version, the king of a neighboring Etruscan city of Clusium, Lars Porsena, besieged and defeated the Romans. The already discontent population of Rome decided not to reinstall a king. Moreover, the story of the rape of Lucretia might have been adapted from a similar story of one of the Greek tyrants. Greek culture had a massive influence on ancient Rome. The Greeks' overall negative view of the tyrants and their keenness on the rule of the people might be the reason behind such a negative description of Tarquinius Superbus.

Whatever the case, it is clear that by the late 6th century BCE, Rome was no longer being ruled by a single king, instead having implemented a system that resembled the early Greek aristocratic democracy (oligarchy). So began a highly influential age in ancient Roman history: the age of the Roman Republic.

The Early Republic

Rome would stay a republic for around the next five centuries. This period largely shaped the institutions and the people of the ancient Roman civilization, laying the foundations for what was to come next. Rome would start its expansion, emerging as a dominant military force and engaging in many wars before finally capturing the Greeks' attention. But what exactly was the "republic" all about?

Much like the Greek city-states, the political and social concerns of the early republic revolved around the city of Rome itself, as well as the modest possessions under its jurisdiction. In the early years, contact with neighbors was limited, with the Etruscans being the only people the Romans were preoccupied with. Despite the fact the Roman Republic was, well, a republic and thus largely responsible for the development of the much later concept of republicanism, its political system was very complex and even subject to systematic power struggles in its early stages.

One thing that is clear is the fact that the Roman people were done with one person having absolute authority; they wanted to have more say in how they were governed. So, when the last king was overthrown, his immediate successors were two people called consuls, who were in charge of the Roman forces and basically acted as executives, executing the will of the people as determined by the Senate.

The Senate was comprised of the elite, often rich and prestigious men from the patrician class (the higher of the two social groups in ancient Rome). The Senate was technically only an advisory body to the two consuls and may have even existed in some form during the Roman monarchy. Senators would discuss pressing matters and come up with solutions, passing decrees that were respected and obeyed by the public.

In the beginning, as the people were getting used to the new kingless political system, the Senate's power was quite limited. However, as time passed, the Senate grew to become the most influential body in Rome. Eventually, plebeians, the lower social class of ancient Rome, would be admitted to the Senate. Every senator served for life, and the size of the Senate varied from time to time.

Interestingly, despite the Romans' evident hostility toward a sole authority, a common practice during the republic was the appointment of a dictator—a single figure who would assume absolute political power for a period of six months during times of emergency. For example, when Rome was at war and the Senate and the consuls were divided over executive decisions, the Senate would appoint a dictator who would have the ability to lead the republic however he wanted before his term was over. This way, the more drawn-out and discussion-based politics would be avoided, as the dictator would be charged with the responsibility to act.

This phenomenon is interesting since it provides evidence of the complexity of the republic's early political system while also underlining the fact that completely abandoning authoritarian rule was impossible for Rome.

There were also two primary popular assemblies, the Centuriate Assembly and the Tribal Assembly, which would discuss and vote on military and civilian matters, respectively. The assemblies allowed for even more public participation and sometimes even acted as courts in times of need.

In the modern sense of the word, the Roman Republic never truly became a democracy, largely because it was never fully representative. The patricians, who were the minority, had more say and power in the Senate. Yes, as time went by, the plebeians did gain more power, thanks to cooperation from the patricians, but they never retained control of the Senate for a substantial amount of time.

In the early days of the republic, a typical Roman citizen lived outside of the city of Rome or any large urban area and pursued agriculture. Despite this, he was an upholder and a developer of Roman virtues and fully believed in the rightness of the republic. He was ready to serve whenever he would be needed. Gradually, the Roman citizens grew their properties into humongous estates that would become especially prominent in the later period of the republic.

Expansion

Nowadays, people think of Rome as a mighty empire that dominated most of Europe and the Near East. However, before Rome could reach that level of dominance and develop the military tradition it is known for today, we have to understand its humble beginnings.

We have already said a bit about the Etruscan dominance of territories north of the city of Rome. It appears the Etruscan kings were organized into some form of a confederacy—the Etruscan League—but the borders between their dominions were rather unclear. They were more like warlords than actual kings. They were always at war with each other and other Italian peoples of the time, explaining the somewhat incoherent accounts we have of their actual power and the politics that dominated their realms.

What we do know is that the Etruscans were the first to clash with the Romans, likely because the city challenged their dominance in the region. The Roman kings struggled against the Etruscans but to no avail. This was largely due to the fact that Roman armies were nowhere near as powerful and experienced as they would become centuries later.

Roman expansion really began during the republic, but even in the early days, Roman gains were rather modest. The early republican Romans were not adamant about being aggressive and engaging in wars, unlike their future counterparts. In the 5th century BCE, Romans achieved military victories against some of their Etruscan neighbors. They seized control of the city of Veii and started a slow process of replacing the Etruscans as masters of central Italy.

The Roman armies were by no means powerful at this point. In 390 BCE, northern Gallic barbarians came down and sacked Rome, marking one of Rome's earliest defeats. This defeat meant that Rome had to become more powerful, and one of the ways in which the republic sought to achieve that was by waging wars against the Etruscan kings. However, instead of solely focusing on the Etruscans, who were arguably the most powerful people in Italy and were also being pressed by northern invaders themselves, the Romans decided to turn their attention south and subjugate the Latin cities, an endeavor that was far more successful. The Latins were no match for the Romans (who were Latins themselves), and much of mainland Italy was under Roman control by the 3rd century BCE.

The relationship between the conquered cities and Rome was not that complex. The cities would be subject to tribute, and the freemen would become citizens of Rome and could benefit from the privileges that status brought them. In the 150 years after the sack of Rome in 390, Rome managed to increase its dominance in the region by acquiring new lands and making allies in the south.

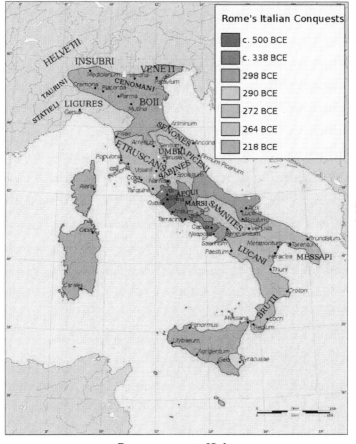

Roman conquest of Italy.
https://commons.wikimedia.org/wiki/File:Roman_conquest_of_Italy_en.svg)

One other thing Rome demanded of its conquered territories was manpower. The conquered cities would be allowed to retain their local administrators in exchange for supplying troops to Rome in times of war. Every property-owning male citizen had to serve in the army whenever it was needed, a system that made Rome superior to its neighbors. The recruiting system meant that more citizens became experienced warriors while also enjoying the material benefits of successfully returning from military campaigns. They provided the foundation for the military machine Rome would eventually become known for, and the increasing pool of recruits from Rome's allies made it so that the republic never had problems with manpower.

By the mid-3rd century BCE, Rome had defeated the Samnite peoples and fended off an invasion of King Pyrrhus of the Greek city-state of Epirus. In fact, Pyrrhus's campaigns would be so costly for him that the name "Pyrrhic victory" would forever be attached to a success that cost far more than it is worth.

The Roman successes against Epirus and the Samnites made Rome the most dominant force in Italy, but Rome's real military challenge was still ahead. The ambitions of the republic grew as it sought to expand its dominion beyond Italy, but an already established foreign power stood in its way. On the North African coast, in what is now Tunisia, there was a rich and prosperous ancient city that had basically monopolized maritime trade in the western Mediterranean. This city was Carthage, which was of Phoenician origin and a true successor of the Phoenician tradition of naval supremacy.

When Rome was squabbling with other Italian peoples, Carthage not only controlled the North African coast but also established itself in southern Iberia, Sicily, Corsica, and Sardinia. By involving itself in regional politics, Carthage managed to stave off the rise of a powerful actor, although the quick successes of Rome certainly caught the eye of those living in Carthage. The two were clear rivals of each other by the time they went to war for the first time in 264 BCE.

There were three Punic Wars between Rome and Carthage, which lasted from 264 to 146 BCE, but the conflict never truly ceased during this time. The first war would end in a complete Roman victory in 241 BCE, resulting in the expulsion of the Carthaginians from Sicily and an exponential increase of Roman naval power in the Mediterranean. Corsica and Sardinia were also taken over by the Romans, along with all of the riches and resources the islands had to offer.

Carthage licked its wounds after the humiliating defeat and assembled an even larger force. Its new invasion against the Roman Republic took shape in 218 BCE. The legendary Carthaginian general Hannibal Barca famously surprised the Romans when he led his forces into Italy, not from the south by sea but from the north. He started his march from the city of New Carthage in southern Spain, moving up the coast through France and crossing the Alps with his war elephants in one of the most daring military maneuvers of ancient history.

Thanks to this totally unexpected move, Hannibal managed to achieve a couple of victories against the Romans, but the Roman armies stopped his advance. And thanks to the military genius of Roman general Scipio Africanus, the Romans turtled up in their cities while the Carthaginian army had to retreat from Italy since it suffered from attrition and disease. Then, in an equally daring move, the Senate would grant Scipio Africanus permission to cross to Africa, chasing after the badly battered enemy and achieving a decisive victory at Zama against Hannibal in 202 BCE.

Carthage had to settle for another humiliating peace. It was not allowed to wage war without Roman permission, and its might was reduced to a shadow of its former self. Scipio was hailed as the most formidable commander, and the Romans enjoyed the spoils of war. However, the rivalry was by no means over. Many in the Senate had come to hate Carthage, and the senators feared the Carthaginians plotted the demise of the republic.

Finally, after about fifty years of peace, Rome decided to send a large army to punish Carthage for breaking the terms of the peace by raising its forces to fend off the invading Numidians. The Romans launched their final assault in 146 BCE, laying siege to the great city of Carthage. The Romans eventually exhausted the Carthaginian defenses after a long siege. Carthage, which had been one of the most prosperous cities of the ancient world, was looted and razed to the ground. The victorious Roman soldiers reportedly sowed salt in its fields to prevent it from ever rising up again. This marked the end of the third and final Punic War and the beginning of Roman supremacy in the Mediterranean and its surrounding lands.

The defeat of Carthage opened up new possibilities for Rome. Carthage had been the most powerful state in the western Mediterranean, and all of its colonies were very developed. With the fall of Carthage,

Rome became a natural suzerain of the colonies and came into possession of territories in Iberia. The riches and the slaves that flowed into Italy from the newly acquired lands made it possible to finance even more daring expeditions. Rome took out the former Carthaginian allies one by one.

By the turn of the 2nd century BCE, even before Carthage would be fully eradicated by the Roman legions, Rome had already grown interested in gaining more lands in the east and had its eyes set on the Greeks. The old Greek colony and an old ally of Carthage, Syracuse, was defeated, and Sicily was unified under Roman rule. Only after that did the Roman legions sail to mainland Greece, where the successors of Alexander the Great were engaging in constant squabbles with each other. The Kingdom of Pergamon, a Hellenistic state in western Anatolia, requested help from the Romans against Macedon, and Rome obliged, partially because Macedon had been on favorable terms with the Carthaginians in the past. Rome's prior successes motivated it to push for even more and to expand the horizons of the republic far beyond the limits of what had been conceived by its founders.

Roman and Carthaginian possessions before the First Punic War.
Harrias, CC BY-SA 4.0 <https://creativecommons.org/licenses/by-sa/4.0>, via Wikimedia Commons; https://commons.wikimedia.org/wiki/File:First_Punic_War_264_BC_v3.png

Throughout the 2nd century BCE, Rome managed to defeat and take over all of Greece, with the weak city-states being forced into a union with their new Latin suzerains. Infamously, perhaps to demonstrate their real power and instill fear in the proud Greeks, the Roman legions burned the great city of Corinth in 146 BCE, leading to the old Macedonian lands being divided into two administrative territories: Macedonia and Achaia. Pergamon submitted in 133 BCE as Rome made its way into Anatolia.

Meanwhile, Roman legions also campaigned in western Europe, crossing the river Po to the north and launching expeditions against the Celtic barbarians. The Celts, who had a complex, thriving culture and civilization, occupied most of western Europe and the banks of the Danube River, and their successors still survive in Britain, Ireland, and northwestern France. Skilled ironworkers and farmers, the Celtic people were also fierce warriors, and their infantry corps were always a thorn in the side of the Roman legions. The Celts used guerrilla tactics and often ambushed the disciplined Romans when they dared to venture into the European woods.

The Celtic territories were nevertheless conquered one by one, as the Romans pushed into northern Italy, Spain, and France, which they called Gallia, hence the name they gave to its inhabitants, the Gauls. Ultimately, factional and tribal differences and the lack of a single united political entity caused the Celts to suffer defeat at the hands of the Romans.

By the 1st century BCE, the Romans had made their way into western and central Europe. The Mediterranean was now almost completely under Roman control, with only its eastern shores outside of the Roman dominion.

The Dawn of the Roman Empire

In addition to material gains, the expansion during the later stages of the Roman Republic introduced a lot of cultural novelties for which ancient Rome is remembered today. This is especially true when it comes to the Roman takeover of Greece, something that produced a completely unique mix of the best of the two civilizations and led to, somewhat surprisingly, the Hellenization of Rome and, therefore, the rest of western Europe.

The Greek culture had always influenced Rome from its earliest days due to the close contact between the two civilizations and the existence of Greek colonies close to Rome, but after the Roman conquests of the 2nd century BCE, these influences could be seen much more clearly. Most importantly, Romans adopted and advanced the Greek practices of politics and government, in addition to incorporating many of the elements from everyday Greek life, like circuses, theaters, and public baths. The Hellenistic culture, although at first regarded to be barbarian, was by no means as barbarian as, for example, the Gallic peoples, who did not even have their own writing system when they were conquered by the Romans.

The complexity and beauty of the Greek civilization, including its culture, language, architecture, and everyday life, astonished Rome. The first Roman literature was translated Greek works. Greek language and classics were taught in schools. Greek architecture was hailed and adopted. Even the Roman religion came to largely resemble that of Greece.

Rome's expansion meant that significant changes had to occur in many aspects of Roman life. The institutions and makeup of early republican Roman society were no longer compatible when Rome came into possession of half of Europe, Anatolia, and North Africa.

For instance, changes were made when it came to Roman citizenship. In the old days, Roman citizens were all property-owning men, in most cases plebeian small farmers who inhabited the city of Rome itself and its surroundings. They had the right to vote, bring matters to court, and serve in Roman armies when duty called. But after the Punic Wars and as Rome engaged in more and more wars, these small farmers no longer continued their original agricultural activities. The constant wars took many men away from agriculture, resulting in the impoverishment of the Italian countryside and leading to many plebs moving to urban centers. Even those Romans who made money from wars no longer dwelled in the countryside; they decided to buy more estates and employ slaves to work their lands while they moved to the cities.

The migration of poor citizens to cities resulted in the emergence of highly polarized social strata. They would eventually be referred to as the proletariat. They owned little to no property and instead worked jobs in the cities. They still had citizenship, but they gradually became less important as slavery became more widespread. The hold of the patrician class over the Senate increased as a result.

This social movement also resulted in changes in the composition of the Roman armies. In the past, only men with property could serve; now, the proletariat, since they had no other apparent use, were encouraged to enlist in the Roman legions. They would often volunteer to join the army, sometimes overfilling the ranks and remaining in the army for most of their lives. This, in turn, led to the development of almost completely independent Roman armies, which became self-sustaining. The legions were far more loyal to their commanders and colleagues than, say, to the Senate, and they claimed most of the glory and the spoils of war from foreign conquests for themselves. Roman generals rose in prominence and gradually became powerful political actors who involved themselves in civic matters to gain even more power.

The expansion did not cease. The southern Black Sea shores of Bithynia and Pontus were conquered in 74 and 65 BCE, Cilicia on the southeastern coast of Anatolia was conquered in 67 BCE, Syria was taken over in 63 BCE, and Cyprus became a Roman territory in 58 BCE.

The year that would mark the beginning of the end of the Roman Republic is 59 BCE. That year, a young politician by the name of Julius Caesar was appointed as consul. Julius Caesar is one of the mightiest names in history, and that is for good reason. A year after his appointment, he became the commander of the Roman forces in Gaul and completely wiped out the remaining Celts in modern-day France over the next seven or so years. Caesar even crossed to Britain twice but chose not to remain there, instead focusing on consolidating his power in Gaul and gaining more respect and loyalty from his troops. Caesar's military successes and the exponential growth of his reputation coincided with an extremely troublesome period for Roman domestic politics that led to a civil war.

Prestigious and successful generals were becoming more independent and acting outside the interests of the Senate. In other words, they took matters into their own hands. Meanwhile, with more people becoming citizens and migrating throughout the Roman lands, popular governance and republican rule were beginning to lose their importance. Political intrigue became more common, with the senators trying to manipulate their way to the top. They wanted more direct power and influence than they had before, and the fear of a single authoritarian ruler returning became widespread among the population.

Interestingly, it would be none other than Julius Caesar who would make that fear come true. Having spent many years conquering the Gauls and claiming glory for his conquests, he had accumulated a lot of prestige and wealth. Plus, he could not be blamed for the instability in Rome since he had been away for quite some time. The Romans were more upset with many of the big politicians. In other words, the complex and chaotic political climate of the time made it possible for Caesar to swoop in and assume dictatorial leadership, filling the Roman power vacuum.

Caesar, the governor of Gaul at the time, was instructed by the Senate to return to Rome in 50 BCE. He had to leave his armies in Gaul since bringing them into Italy would mean that he was breaking the law. In January 49 BCE, Julius Caesar, despite his instructions, crossed the Rubicon, which marked the border between his province and Italy, and led his armies into Rome, essentially beginning his insurrection against Rome. For the next four years, Caesar fought a brutal civil war against his opponents, crushing them in battles while also gathering support in the Senate and being made dictator for life.

However, his triumphs aroused suspicion and contempt in many who believed that he would reestablish a monarchy. In 44 BCE, around forty senators assassinated Julius Caesar.

To this day, Caesar remains one of the most ambiguous figures in European history. Many claim that he was the hero Rome needed and that he was the right person to lead the republic out of the chaos Rome had suffered for a long time. Others believe that he was a usurper, a villain who wanted absolute power and even managed to get it for some time. Whatever the case, Julius Caesar remains one of the most fascinating men of classical antiquity, and he has been the subject of many literary and artistic works.

Despite the murder of Caesar, the civil war in Rome was by no means over. The lunge he had made toward the reestablishment of a centralized Rome had left a growing impact on Roman society and politics. Caesar's great-nephew and adopted heir, Octavian, would burst onto the political scene thanks to the loyalty of his great-uncle's armies.

Octavian would get involved in the power struggles of the late Roman Republic. He formed a triumvirate with his allies, Mark Antony and Marcus Lepidus. Octavian continued to fight the civil war in the name of Julius Caesar, avenging his death at the Battle of Philippi in 42 BCE when his armies defeated the forces of Caesar's murderers, which were led by Brutus.

The triumvirate emerged victorious and divided the Roman realm into three, with each man ruling one and even managing to expand Roman conquests at the same time. However, rising tensions within the triumvirate made cooperation no longer possible. About a decade after Philippi, the triumvirate was no more, and Octavian eventually defeated his former allies and returned to Rome, where he was greeted by his loyal legions.

The Age of the Roman Empire

Rome was still technically a republic by the time of Octavian's success against his triumvirate rivals. However, the Senate had long ceased being as influential as it had traditionally been due to the increased importance given to individual military commanders and the power their military corps gave them.

Even though Octavian marched into Rome supported by his loyal legions who regarded him as the true successor of Julius Caesar, he did not rush to declare himself the new king of Rome. Instead of showing that he had emerged victorious in the civil war and basically had all of the requirements to become the new master of Rome, Octavian took a more careful and planned-out approach. Much like his great-uncle and like the good Roman he was, Octavian hailed the republican principles upon which his society was founded, so he firmly believed that respecting these principles was what a benevolent and wise ruler would do, even if the notion of such a ruler clashed with the Roman idea of republicanism.

So, Octavian decided not to go through with radical reforms and impose his rule forcefully on the people. Instead, thanks to the power he had accrued, he found his way around the Senate and manipulated the most important political body of Rome in his favor. He kept his formal title of *imperator*—the commander of armies—while also being elected as consul year after year, something that gave him just enough leverage over the Senate to basically be the most authoritative figure in the republic. The excessive amount of wealth he had accumulated from his campaigns and the trust the army had in him made it possible for Octavian to remain, in a sense, a step above the rest of the Senate in terms of power.

Octavian's main aim, as he himself stated, was to lead Rome out of the unstable political and social state it had been in for the past few decades. He was ready to demonstrate his willingness by investing a lot of his own money into projects that would aid public life, like the construction of new roads. This approach appeared to be more and more successful as the years went by.

Everything was still nominally by the Senate, but it was Octavian who was the single most important person in all of the realm. In due time, his contributions toward stability, peace, and the reinstatement of Roman prosperity were formally noted. In 27 BCE, he was given the honorary title of Augustus, "the illustrious one," which emphasized his authority and almost sacred status. He was also given the title of princeps—the first citizen.

Octavian, who began to be referred to as Caesar Augustus, saw his power grow exponentially, although he insisted that he was not a despot or tyrant and that he was operating within the framework of the republic. That is why the form of government that operated before 14 CE is referred to as the Principate. But despite his insistence on republican principles, it was clear that he was acting outside of the republican framework. For example, Augustus chose an heir to succeed him, a deed normally frowned upon by the republican Romans.

Before his death, he chose a promising young man by the name of Tiberius, who came from a powerful aristocratic family, as his successor. Upon Augustus's death in 14 CE, Tiberius became both the princeps and the imperator, assuming the full name of Tiberius Caesar Augustus and continuing the legacy of his stepfather.

Octavian—or Caesar Augustus—was never truly an "emperor" of Rome, largely because Rome never ceased to be a republic, technically speaking. Of course, in reality, Octavian had all of the privileges, benefits, and power necessary for him to be considered the first Roman emperor, and that's why we know him as the first Roman emperor. What is important to remember is that the transition from the Roman Republic to the Roman Empire was not as clear-cut and distinguished as the transition from the Roman Kingdom to the Roman Republic. It was a gradual process that started in the 1st century BCE with the actions of Julius Caesar and which eventually led to Octavian becoming princeps and imperator and establishing a dynasty by choosing his successor. With Octavian Caesar Augustus, a new chapter began in the history of Europe: the age of the Roman Empire.

The Julio-Claudian dynasty, which was established by Augustus, would last for a relatively short time, and its emperors were by no means the best Rome would ever come to see. Tiberius, for example, who ruled until 37 CE, was not a bad administrator, but he never truly trusted the Senate. His choice of heir also turned out not to be the best decision, as Caligula, his successor, would only last for four years, during which time he engaged in lavish and unwise behavior, depleting the Roman treasury and earning himself a name as one of the worst Roman emperors. His successor, Claudius, who ruled until the year 54, was a much better politician. He managed to reform the struggling Roman economy and somewhat stabilize the situation in the empire.

After Claudius came Nero, who ruled for the next fourteen years. Nero is remembered as one of the most infamous figures in Roman history. He was known for being cruel, manipulative, and despotic. He has also been blamed for the instigation of the great fire of Rome in 64 CE. In the end, Nero would come against opposition by rebellious senators, who forced him out of Rome. The emperor committed suicide, abruptly ending the Julio-Claudian dynasty and the first succession of Roman emperors.

A brutal civil war erupted after Nero's death, which somewhat resembled the instability about a century earlier and resulted in a very chaotic situation where many people claimed to be the emperor at the same time. The civil war highlighted the importance of the army once again, as the candidate with the most military support usually found himself at the top. The Senate had little direct influence over what was happening, instead choosing to operate from behind the scenes while trying to maintain that it was still an important institution. It would appoint magistrates who, in reality, held little power.

In 69 CE, out of the chaos emerged Vespasian, a distinguished, low-born soldier who managed to maneuver his way to the top and defeat his rivals. He became the new emperor and founded the Flavian dynasty. Clearly better than his predecessors, Vespasian is responsible for reorganizing the army and reforging the emperor's relations with the Senate. His reign coincided with the overall decline of the old Roman families, something that certainly allowed him to gain the authority he needed to be in charge. Still, there were only two Flavian emperors after him: his son, Titus, who had a short but relatively prosperous two-year reign until the year 81, and Domitian, who would remain in power for fifteen years and emerge as one of the most autocratic leaders of the early Roman Empire. Due to his tendency to mess with the Senate and undermine its independence, Domitian was assassinated in 96. The Flavian dynasty ended with his death.

The Pax Romana

As we can see, the beginning stages of the Roman Empire were certainly chaotic. It was the time when the notion of what it meant to be an emperor was getting perfected, and the first few emperors experimented with this notion more than later emperors. Only a few would be fortunate to say they could stand up to the great Octavian Caesar Augustus in popularity or skill, and perhaps this was the reason behind their failure to establish themselves as beloved figures in the eyes of the Romans.

As time would come to tell, however, the standard of what it meant to be a good emperor would change in the fittingly named period of the "Five Good Emperors." This period lasted about a century, from 96 to 180. Five emperors succeeded each other and were able to turn the ship around and bring glory back to Rome.

The era of the Five Good Emperors, which included the reigns of Nerva, Trajan, Hadrian, Antoninus Pius, and Marcus Aurelius, can also be regarded as the golden age of the Roman Empire. Rome would become the largest, most powerful, and most prosperous that it had ever been, and the period of the "Roman peace"—the fabled Pax Romana—would characterize the cultural and material advancements that would culminate during the reign of the Five Good Emperors.

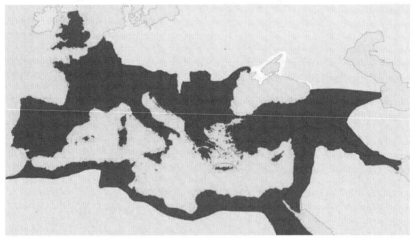

Map of the Roman Empire at its greatest extent.
https://commons.wikimedia.org/wiki/File:Roman_Empire_in_116_AD.png

Despite what its name might suggest, the Pax Romana was never truly a fully peaceful time, and historians usually date it from the reign of Augustus rather than limiting it to the reign of the Five Good Emperors. The term mostly refers to the fact that, despite the domestic instability that characterized Rome in these two centuries, no external power could challenge the dominance of Rome in Europe or the Near East.

The territorial acquisitions during this time are a testament to that fact. Octavian is responsible for consolidating the whole North African coast under the rule of Rome, whether it be in a direct way or through the empire's vassals. The conquest of Anatolia was also largely completed during this time, while the connecting lands between northern Italy and Greece, known as Dalmatia, came under Roman rule. Julius Caesar had already consolidated Rome's control of Gaul, but later expeditions conquered half of central Europe—the western part of what is now Germany. During the time of the second of the Five Good Emperors, Trajan, efforts were made to campaign into Britain and Mesopotamia. The ultimate result was that almost all of western Europe, the Balkans, Anatolia, Mesopotamia, the South Caucasus, the Levant, and North Africa were under Roman dominion. No other European empire had managed to achieve this before the Romans.

However, the true essence of the Pax Romana ran deeper than just military dominance and complete victory over the empire's foes. The Pax Romana was the age of the Romanization of conquered peoples. It was the age when the Roman culture made itself known to all of the territories Rome controlled. It was the age of economic, material, and social development, where the highs of ancient Rome, most of what we remember it for today, were created and advanced to perfection. It was the age of the imperial legacy, something we can see in what the Romans left behind in brick and stone, such as circuses, amphitheaters, libraries, temples, and public buildings. There were great feats of engineering, such as the Roman aqueducts, which provided clean water to many cities even after the collapse of the empire, and paved roads, which connected the many provinces with each other and upon which later routes would be based.

The technological innovations of the time are a great testament to the "peace" aspect of the Pax Romana. People could live comfortably with innovations like central heating, and cleanliness and orderliness were made easier with the implementation of plumbing and sanitation mechanisms.

Increased levels of migration also meant the establishment of new urban centers and the redefining of borders. During the golden age of the Roman Empire, new population centers and great cities would pop up in previously uninhabited areas in western Europe. All of them had distinct Roman (and Greek) characteristics and often included their own circuses, amphitheaters, forums, and public baths.

The city of Rome became the new center of European civilization. At its height, its population might have reached as high as one million, which was an extraordinary feat. Rome was the capital of Europe and the

Roman world and continued to act like one for many centuries, even after the collapse of the empire. Later on, its status would certainly be challenged, but the cultural, religious, and material symbols that Rome obtained during the golden age stuck.

Rome and the newly created cities were not the only ones to reach their height during the Pax Romana. Already established urban centers grew to even higher levels. Cities like Alexandria, for example, became social centers, attracting thousands of visitors and migrants who would be dazzled by the eclectic mix of cultural elements from local traditions and the Hellenistic tradition of Rome.

The intellectual heritage of the golden age of Rome is also admired today. Admittedly, Rome might have lagged behind ancient Greece when it came to philosophy, although there are iconic Roman philosophical achievements, such as Stoicism. Marcus Aurelius, one of the most celebrated Roman emperors, was a famous Stoic. Works of Roman poets and historians, like Virgil and Livy, are still widely regarded as staple reads when it comes to their respective genres.

What was more important for Rome at the time than producing iconic works of literature was the creation of able public figures who could occupy important jobs to keep things running smoothly. During the Pax Romana, Roman education allowed citizens (by citizens, we mean just men) to become skilled orators and administrators. A competent government, especially when it came to local bureaucratic branches, meant the system could persist and that law and order would be followed and respected by the people since they were confident in the officeholders.

By the time of the Five Good Emperors, most urban areas under the jurisdiction of Rome spoke Latin and Greek (although the latter was spoken to a comparably lesser extent). This would explain the prominence of these two European languages and their use in everyday affairs centuries after their inception.

Gauls, Syrians, Illyrians, Iberians, and other people groups were not Romans, Latins, or Italians, but they spoke and dressed like their conquerors. They grew increasingly proud of their Roman heritage. In 212 CE, citizenship rights would be expanded to all free male subjects of the empire, something that reflected the successful centuries of assimilation and resulted in more non-Romans occupying important jobs, even in the Senate.

To be Roman no longer meant one had to be born in Rome or in Italy. Instead, being Roman became a larger-than-life identity—an identity that shaped the Roman civilization and its successor states.

Division

The Roman peace was not destined to be eternal. Soon enough, the Roman system started to show cracks, and it became clear that temporary solutions could not make the problems disappear.

For one thing, the Roman Empire was becoming too big to govern effectively. Such a massive realm required constant attention at all times, and the Roman system was too reliant on the existence of a powerful figure who could determine the political and social direction of the empire, with local administrators dealing with local issues. But the empire was constantly expanding. More and more legions, headed by ambitious commanders who sought glory, were stationed at the empire's borders, mostly in central Europe, to fight off the barbarians. In the east, Rome was constantly struggling for dominance against the Parthian Empire.

Constant attacks from barbarians tied up more and more troops on the borders in the forests of Europe. As much as the Romans loved dominance and the assimilation of "inferior peoples" into their empire, they were hesitant to allow the Germanic tribes of central and northern Europe to settle into the territories they controlled. They were afraid that they would cause instability because they were so uncivilized.

The Germanic peoples were being pressed from the east. In the 3rd century CE, a huge wave of migration from Asia led to their displacement. The Hunnic peoples of the Asian steppes—fierce warriors and masters of the horse—were the instigators of the great migration of the 4th century. They traveled farther and farther west, decimating the people who stood in their way. By the time they had reached Europe, it was unavoidable that the barbarians, who were kept out of Roman territories by the constantly alert Roman legions, had to go somewhere. If they didn't, they would meet the wrath of the Huns.

Initially, the Rhine and the Danube served as a good boundary between the Germanic tribes and the Romans, but by the late 3rd century, the Germanic peoples were able to penetrate through the Roman defenses and settle in Roman-controlled territories. This would result in even more instability in the more remote Roman provinces, some of which would be eventually abandoned by the Romans. They would give up their territories to the barbarians in the hopes they could focus their attention somewhere else.

In the east, there had been a constant conflict between the Romans and the Parthians. This conflict had endured for over a hundred years and met with mixed success. Roman legions would sometimes manage to achieve decisive victories against the Parthian forces, but they did not amount to anything significant. The main "playground" was the Near East, especially the lands of Mesopotamia and Armenia, which changed hands many times.

The Parthian Empire would eventually be overthrown by a man named Ardashir, the ruler of the province of Fars in modern-day Iran. He took over the eastern lands and reestablished a Persian empire in the east. Believing to be the successor of Darius and Cyprus, the great Achaemenid rulers of ancient times, the Sassanid dynasty of Persia would pose a better challenge to the Roman Empire than the Parthians ever had.

Tied up on two large fronts, the Roman Empire started to show its weaknesses, which were brought on by overextension and perhaps overindulgence during the Pax Romana.

Internally, the system was beginning to fumble. In a way, a large part of the Roman economy came from victories in wars. Such dramatic territorial growth not only provided Rome with booty and loot, which was usually part of the upkeep for the troops, but also with new territories that could be used for agricultural and commercial purposes. A halt in expansion stopped this trend, meaning that soldiers were deprived of their income. And in ancient times, you never wanted to get on the bad side of the military. So, the government had to draw funds from other sources to pay for the upkeep of their legions, a task that proved to be difficult.

Additionally, the wealth disparity between the social classes of the empire had never been higher. The aristocrats kept acquiring more lands in the Roman provinces and kept increasing their personal riches, while more and more people had to immigrate from their original dwellings in search of jobs in the cities or join the armies. A couple of bad harvests, caused by unfavorable climate, created food shortages. This problem was compounded by the fact that consumption levels had grown too high since Rome had been enjoying economic prosperity.

In such a large empire, it was difficult to equally distribute resources to all of the public services that needed attention. For example, the Eastern part of the empire was richer, but the West saw a lot of trouble brewing.

Overpopulation and an increased number of slaves made things even more difficult. There were multiple slave rebellions, and the best Roman soldiers had to be called in to put a stop to their revolts.

Intrigue in the Senate never ceased. As more people obtained wealth and wanted to dabble in politics, things became even more complicated.

We could also blame the gradual decline of the Roman system on the succession of incompetent rulers who perhaps lacked the charisma and command of their more illustrious predecessors. However, the emperors who came and went in the 3rd century could do very little when it came to holding the struggling empire together. A solution had to be found somewhere. It was clear the people were powerless to change the system, as internal conflict would lead to even more chaos (as it did during the ensuing civil wars, where many people claimed to be the emperor), so a top-down approach was necessary. Rome needed reform.

Emperor Diocletian would emerge as the person who would apply a temporary bandage to the Roman problems in the late 3rd century. He managed to restore stability after his accession to the throne in 284.

Diocletian would be proclaimed emperor by his soldiers. It would take a couple of months for him to consolidate his hold over the vast empire, as his power had initially been focused in the East. By mid-285, however, he emerged as the sole ruler of the empire and got to work. His most memorable deed was the division of the Roman Empire into two. Diocletian realized the empire was too large to be governed by a single man, so soon after seizing power, he proclaimed his friend, an experienced soldier and commander who was not a noble at birth, Maximian, as his co-emperor.

Maximian was responsible for running the empire in the West, while the territories in the East would be under the rule of Diocletian himself. Nicomedia became the new seat of the Eastern emperor, located at the Bosphorus, while Maximian chose to rule from the city of Milan, although Rome still retained its status as the capital of the empire. Diocletian sought to make it easier to govern the unstable Roman Empire; he could focus on the matters of Greece, Thrace, Asia Minor, Syria, and Egypt, while Maximian would pay direct attention to the imperial provinces in the West.

Both figures assumed the title of "Augustus," which signified that they were equal in status and power. In 293, two men, Galerius and

Constantius, were granted the title of Caesar and were essentially the second-most-important people in their respective realms. Thus, the empire came to have four masters, with Diocletian and Maximian having the more important overarching positions.

The division of the empire in the Tetrarchy, as it would be referred to, was not the only contribution Diocletian made to revive the old glory of Rome. Further administrative divisions followed, with old provinces being divided into new, smaller sub-provinces, each with its own governor. On the one hand, this meant the decentralization of power, but the concept of power itself was very complex when it came to the Roman Empire at the time because different actors influenced matters in different ways (like the independent legions and commanders, not to speak of the Senate). In any case, this gradually led to the Senate losing its influence, a process that had begun long before the time of Diocletian.

Much-needed military reforms were also undertaken, resulting in the Roman army being enlarged to include about 500,000 men at arms at all times throughout the empire, thanks to the decision to bring back conscription.

Christian Rome

Aside from Diocletian's reforms, another thing for which he is remembered is his hatred and persecution of Christians. Christianity, the religion that would eventually define the history of Europe, was rather unpopular during the early days of the Roman Empire, largely due to the fact that it had not been long since its conception.

Retelling the history of Christianity is no easy task, so it would be better if we simply assess the religion's state in relation to the Roman Empire. Christianity started to develop in Palestine among the local Jewish people when the region was under Roman control. The Jews had long been a distinct people with their own unique culture and monotheistic beliefs, which were vastly different from the polytheistic, cult-oriented tradition of the Greco-Roman world. Despite their struggles, the Jewish people had managed to retain their identity under their often oppressive suzerains, eventually dispersing throughout the lands that would come to be occupied by Rome.

By the time of Augustus, Rome was already more than familiar with Judaism and the Jewish people, and the republic's policy had been to tolerate them like any other religion as long as the adherents tolerated the Roman pantheon of gods, which was seen as superior. The Romans were also aware of the Judaic concept of the Messiah, the expected king and descendant of the legendary King David, who was supposed to appear in a time of need and lead the people to glory. There was much disagreement about when exactly the Messiah would appear among the Jews and in what form he would take, which partially explains the animosity most Jews in the Holy Land had toward Jesus.

Jesus grew up in the small town of Nazareth. He preached and taught the word of God, claiming to be the son of God. The Gospels, which were written by his followers, are the accounts of his exciting life, depicting narratives that report Jesus performing miracles while also preaching the orthodox doctrines of Judaism.

Jesus would quickly gain a lot of traction in Judea, so much so that he would be condemned by the local Jewish religious leaders and be charged with blasphemy in about 33 CE. Taking him before the Roman governor of the time, Pontius Pilate, they demanded that Jesus be appropriately punished for having lied to and corrupting the people of Judea. They insisted Jesus made people believe he was the son of God while, in reality, he was nothing but a pretender. To avoid being responsible for causing further chaos, Pilate asked the public to decide the fate of Jesus, and the public decided to crucify him.

Soon afterward, the disciples of Jesus believed that he had risen from the dead, and after a short time, they claimed they saw him ascend into heaven. Of course, much like every other religion, it is difficult to know what exactly took place and whether or not the accounts given in the Gospels are actual facts. What we can say for certain is that the belief in Jesus as the Messiah never ceased.

At first, Christianity (a word that stems from the Greek name given to Jesus—Christ or "anointed one") was perceived to be a new Jewish sect, and it would not be long before it started to rise in prominence throughout the Roman lands. A council of Christians assembled in 49 CE and decided to preach the teachings of Jesus to Gentiles—the non-Jewish peoples. Christian believers soon started to go on missions.

This gradually resulted in the growth of Christianity. By the end of the 1st century, the Roman world was full of Christian congregations scattered around the many provinces. These congregations had not yet been unified under a larger "church," but they nevertheless shared a couple of things in common, like the rites of baptism (a Christian practice by which new people would be admitted to join the Christian community) and the

Eucharist (the act of feeding the believers with bread and wine to commemorate the body and blood of Christ on the eve of his arrest and crucifixion). Surprisingly enough, believers grew in numbers almost exponentially, which meant a more rigid administrative structure would be required to run the churches and congregations.

One thing that distinguished Christianity in the eyes of the Romans was the fact that many Gentiles converted. This was significant, as Christianity could no longer be conceived as just another Jewish sect; Jews themselves persecuted Christians and were hostile toward them. It was partially due to this hostile attitude that Christians were widely oppressed in the Roman Empire during the first century. They were even blamed for the great fire of Rome in 64 CE. The use of Christian believers as scapegoats became a common practice, but the public's general attitude would usually reflect the emperors' viewpoints; if the new emperor tolerated Christians, so would the public.

Two of the most well-known apostles, Saint Paul and Saint Peter, were among the many victims of this violent persecution. One particular concern many Romans had against the Christians was the fact they were increasingly unwilling to regard the Roman pantheon as sacred and get involved in Roman religious rituals. Rome regarded the "official" Roman religion and the ceremonies that came with it as a necessary part of the republican tradition and believed that it was in the best interests of the state that they be widely carried out. Since many Christians were Gentiles, it would not be fair to give them this "privilege" of disobedience since they were technically refusing to follow the Roman laws.

Nevertheless, Christianity began to grow. During the 2nd and 3rd centuries, especially in times of instability and civil war, no one had the resources to chase after Christians and spend their energy forbidding them to practice their religion. Christian theologians devised early forms of Christian doctrine in order to help give the religion more structure and make it feel more institutional. New churches were built, mostly in non-urban areas, which were financed by Christian communities. This perseverance eventually resulted in about a tenth of the empire's population being Christian by the late 3rd century, and some emperors would be tolerant toward the religion, stimulating a positive public attitude.

The 4th century would mark a pivotal period for Christianity in Rome. In the year 306, Constantine, the son of Constantius Chlorus, one of the original four rulers of the Tetrarchy, would be proclaimed emperor of the Western provinces of the Roman Empire. Constantine, who eventually came to bear the title of "the Great," would be remembered as one of the most influential emperors Rome would ever have. However, the first two decades of his reign were full of warfare and strife. Initially commanding the legions in Gaul, Iberia, and Britain, Constantine would finally emerge as the sole emperor of the Roman Empire by 324.

In 312, before he led his men into a decisive battle, Constantine made a decision that would perhaps alter the course of history forever. Having believed to have seen a vision, Constantine ordered his soldiers to put Christian symbols on their shields to honor the Christian God, saying that God would come to help them in battle. The battle was won, and Constantine, who already was quite keen on monotheism and worshiped a single sun god, became increasingly interested in Christianity. He converted to Christianity (but would not be formally baptized until on his deathbed in 337) and issued an imperial decree in 313, the Edict of Milan, which restored Christian property and worship rights that had been taken away during Diocletian's reign. It was a promising period for all of Christianity. Christians finally had the full support of the emperor, something they had never before enjoyed.

The luck of the Christians didn't stop there. In 325, Constantine attended the first Christian council at Nicaea, where bishops from all over the known world convened to discuss doctrinal matters. Aside from actually setting the doctrinal matters straight, the council would become one of the most important events in the history of Christianity. Constantine stressed the new bond between the Roman emperor and the Christian Church. This special relationship would continue to be maintained more than a thousand years after the Council of Nicaea.

Perhaps unknowingly, such open support of Christianity made the religion a new point of focus for the Roman world. It grew within the empire's borders, adapting to its customs. Christian Rome would provide the foundation for the emergence of Christian Europe, and Constantine would forever be remembered in history as the person who contributed massively to this.

The Fall of the Western Roman Empire

Soon, Constantine's reforms touched all aspects of Roman life, and they were not only focused on the cultural and religious transformation of the empire. At the entrance of the Black Sea, on the Bosphorus Strait, which was one of the most important locations as the main corridor between the East and the West, Constantine ordered the construction of a new city on the site of the already existing city of Byzantium. Constantinople, as the city would be named, was declared the new capital of the empire and would remain so for over a millennium. Constantinople succeeded Rome in becoming the largest and most prosperous city in Europe, and it became a symbol of the empire's renovation under Constantine.

Following the example of Diocletian, Constantine decided to split the empire into two in 330, a decision that would have major consequences in the future. Constantinople would emerge as the center of the Eastern Roman Empire, which was eventually known as the Byzantine Empire. Richer and less diverse, partly due to the fact that it was comprised of formerly Hellenized territories, the Eastern Roman Empire grew prosperous. The truth was that its urban areas had been highly developed during the heyday of ancient Greece and the conquests of Alexander, making its governance far easier than that of the Western Roman Empire.

The Western Roman Empire, on the other hand, was still centered around Rome, but it was clear from the very beginning that it would not be able to sustain itself for long. Most of Gaul, northern Iberia, and Britain were still largely inhabited by the Romanized barbarians. Civilization had developed less quickly in these areas than in the provinces of the Eastern Roman Empire, such as in Egypt, Greece, Anatolia, and Mesopotamia, something that contributed to the eventual decline of Rome.

Constantine's division set the two areas apart, both culturally and materially. The West would come to be increasingly dependent on the import of food from Africa and the Mediterranean to feed its population and military contingents in the less hospitable areas of northern Europe. Manpower would also decline, which meant that more and more barbarian troops had to be involved in the makeup of Roman legions. Constantinople would soon come to eclipse the might of Rome, borrowing all of the aspects that had made the latter glorious in its golden age before it was troubled by overpopulation, squalor, and corruption.

The Western Roman Empire would fall about a century after Emperor Theodosius declared Christianity the official religion of the Roman Empire in 380, completing the Christianization process of the empire. However, the collapse of the empire, as we have already discussed, was a gradual process. By the 4th century, the administrative and economic problems had become too much to deal with, and governing such a diverse and large body was proving to be more difficult. To deal with the demands of the army and the multi-layered bureaucracy of the state, Rome raised tax rates over and over again, resulting in public disorder, especially in the more remote provinces of the empire. To escape the high taxes, people often abandoned the urban areas and restarted life in the countryside, where the clutches of the bureaucrats could no longer reach them. Armies also became weaker due to the lack of funds to pay for the upkeep of the soldiers. The elite Roman legions of the past, comprised of highly trained and determined individuals, were slowly losing their quality.

An additional burden to the empire was the migratory wave in the 4th century, something we have already touched upon above. The different peoples who inhabited eastern and central Europe would be pushed more and more into the territories of the Roman Empire as the relentless Huns razed their cities and enslaved their populations. These people groups would travel to remote locations in huge numbers. For example, the Vandals, who traditionally dwelt in the northeastern part of Europe, were forced to migrate first to Gaul, then to Iberia, and finally cross to Africa. The Gothic inhabitants of the shores of the Black Sea were the group that felt the brunt of the Hunnic pressure the most, ending up moving to central Europe and Italy and disrupting the demographic makeup of these areas. They also had to flock to the territories of the Eastern Roman Empire, although Constantinople had the capacity to mobilize resources and accommodate these people groups.

In 376, the Visigoths crossed the Danube, the boundary between the barbarians and the Romans, and were allowed to settle down. But centuries of isolation and rivalry between the two meant they could not coexist together for long. Only two years after being allowed to enter the boundaries of the Eastern Roman Empire, a conflict broke out between the Visigoths and the Roman legions, resulting in the death of Emperor Valens during the Battle of Adrianople. The Western Roman Empire was horrified by the news and started to employ the barbarians as mercenary soldiers to fight off other migratory tribes.

The 5th century would spell the doom of the Western Roman Empire. The ailing empire could do little to stop the migratory waves of barbarians, whose numbers and discontent only increased. In 410, the Goths penetrated northern Italy and reached Rome, which was left defenseless, as it had been abandoned by the Senate and the emperor. The subsequent sack of Rome became the subject of Saint Augustine's *The City of God*, one of the most iconic pieces of early Christian literature. Things would get even worse, as provincial administrations would crumble in the face of hundreds of thousands of new inhabitants.

The Vandals, who had ended up in Carthage and had taken over the control of most of the western North African coast, would be responsible for yet another sack of Rome in 455. Vandal King Genseric, utilizing the political chaos of the empire and the dynastic struggle between Emperor Valentinian's successors, crossed the Mediterranean and approached the Eternal City, only to be greeted with open gates by the fearful Roman population. They just wanted to survive the wrath of the barbarians.

The year 476 is considered to be the official year of the fall of the Western Roman Empire. The structure on which the empire had depended had been crushed into pieces long before that, but 476 is a good date because it was the year when the final Roman emperor, a man who carried the names of two of the most important figures in Rome's history, Romulus Augustulus, would be deposed by Odoacer, a soldier and commander of barbarian origin who led the coup against the emperor. Romulus Augustus would be forced to abdicate, but Odoacer let him retire to an estate since he was only a teenager at the time.

Odoacer emerged as the new sole ruler of Italy, putting an end to centuries of Roman rule. However, in the east, the Roman Empire continued to exist for another thousand years. Nevertheless, the fall of the Western Roman Empire marked a pivotal moment in European and world history. A new age was to befall the continent.

Chapter 4 – The Dawn of the Middle Ages

Post-Roman Europe

The fall of the Western Roman Empire was a geopolitical event of previously unseen magnitude in Europe. For centuries, the western part of the continent had been entirely dominated by the Romans, even if local ethnic groups still dwelled in the different provinces of the empire. However, with the pressure of the great migration, new people groups who previously inhabited eastern European territories moved to the west, diffusing with the local communities and disrupting the order that had been established by Rome. The demographic changes of the continent would soon spell the doom of the empire itself, as Rome crumbled in the face of problems that arose from increasing numbers of barbarians overwhelming its legions and settling within its borders.

The collapse of the Western Roman Empire left a huge power vacuum in western Europe, and new political actors emerged. New, smaller states slowly started to form, giving the continent a new shape. It is best to first examine the state of post-Roman Europe immediately after the fall of the Western Roman Empire before we move on to discussing an influential period of European history called the Middle Ages.

By the time of the great migration and the fall of Rome, the Roman institutions had been dwindling for quite some time. Regardless, the Romanized peoples of western Europe had an established sense of what it meant to be the subject of the Roman Empire. Not only had they experienced the empire's administration and its material heritage in the form of public baths, roads, aqueducts, clothing, and other architectural and social aspects, but they had also developed a unique but uniform cultural identity. Many of them were also established Christians by the time of the migratory period. Therefore, it would be very difficult to completely eradicate the "Romanness" from these peoples, however culturally or ethnically diverse they might have been.

Thus, the new arrivals had to adopt the well-established lifestyles of the former imperial subjects, resulting in interesting developments. Additionally, the Roman Empire lived on in Constantinople. The ruler of the Eastern Roman Empire still was, at the end of antiquity, perceived by many as the most authoritative person in their lives. Of course, his control over the West was essentially nonexistent, although early Byzantine emperors would certainly try to get the former provinces under their rule many times.

The new makeup of post-Roman Europe would be determined by the existing identities of the surviving subjects of the former Roman Empire, Constantinople, and the Catholic Church, all of which would fuse with the cultures and hierarchical social structures brought by the migratory peoples.

Britain is a good example of the ethnic diffusion that took place at the time of the collapse of the Roman Empire. Three Germanic peoples migrated to Britain: the Saxons, the Angles, and the Jutes. They slowly displaced the mostly Celtic peoples who had lived on the island for centuries. The Anglo-Saxons and Jutes originally inhabited the northern part of central Europe, what is now Germany and Denmark. The ethnic diffusion and displacement that took place would eventually result in the emergence of seven Anglo-Saxon kingdoms by the 7th century. The Celtic kingdoms would be maintained mostly in Ireland, western Wales, and Scotland.

It is interesting to examine post-Roman Britain since the Romano-Britannic civilization, which had essentially been established since the 1st century CE, would almost completely be replaced by the new arrivals, to a larger extent than basically anywhere else in continental Europe. Latin was only kept as the language of learning, thanks to its importance in Christianity, and Germanic tongues became more dominant. However, much knowledge was lost after the fall of the Western Roman Empire.

Continental Europe was a different story. Roman institutions and customs continued to exist in a couple of ways, above all in the high status of the Latin language. Yes, the Germanic languages became the common tongue of the post-Roman world, but the Germanic people adopted many elements of Latin.

The political makeup of Europe was also more diverse. Gaul, for example, was slowly taken over by the Franks, who had mostly dwelt in the Lower Rhine region. One such Frankish group, headed by the Merovingian dynasty, which had originally settled in the Belgian town of Tournai, would lay the foundations for one of the most cohesive and powerful successor states to the Western Roman Empire, the state that would eventually become France. Merovingian King Clovis, who became the ruler of the West Franks in 481 and later would be elected as the ruler of the East Franks, essentially emerged as the king of northern Gaul by the turn of the 6th century. In 496, Clovis converted to Christianity through his marriage with the princess of the Burgundians, who controlled the lands southeast of modern Geneva. Clovis came in charge of the territory that connected his realms to Italy. The Frankish kingdom would prove to be one of the most important and influential in the post-Roman world.

King Clovis was a great political and military leader. After having consolidated his power in northern France and with Burgundy on his side, Clovis defended the kingdom against the Visigoths, who were a threat to him from the south. The royal marriage with the Christian Burgundians also put him on good terms with the Catholic Church, giving him the support of the bishop of Rome (later known as the pope). The church particularly liked the fact that Clovis had converted to Catholicism and not to Arianism, a form of Christianity that asserted Jesus was inferior to God, something that had been denounced as heresy at the Council of Nicaea. The "special" relationship between the Franks and the pope would persist for centuries, and the two would emerge as close allies throughout most of the kingdom's history.

Aside from that, Clovis had also given more importance to the region of Île de France, where the modern-day capital of Paris is located, though during Clovis's time, Paris was not the capital. In fact, the kingdom's structure under Clovis was nowhere near the level of ancient Rome's political organization. The hierarchical structures that would eventually lead to the development of the feudal system were still emerging, so kin relationships naturally became very important.

Future generations of Franks would regard Clovis as the father of their kingdom, especially as the kingdom would fragment from time to time into smaller entities due to succession struggles and the absence of a coherent governing mechanism that would ensure a stable hereditary rule. Nevertheless, Frankish culture and society would mix with the Latin heritage of Rome. Over time, this led to the creation of a distinct heritage of its own, like the 6th-century *History of the Franks* by Gregory, Bishop of Tours.

As for Italy itself, it would come to be under the control of the Gothic peoples, who were originally the inhabitants of the northern shores of the Black Sea. The king of the Ostrogoths, Theodoric, managed to kill Odoacer, the man who had deposed the final Roman emperor, and emerge as the de facto ruler of Italy, some of southeastern France, and a substantial chunk of territories on the eastern shore of the Adriatic Sea. In fact, in 497, he was granted the honorary title of patricius by Byzantine Emperor Anastasius, recognizing the special relationship between Constantinople and the new king of Rome.

King Theodoric maintained friendly relations with Constantinople throughout his lifetime and set up a new capital for himself in Ravenna, where most of the important politicians of imperial Rome had already moved to in the dying days of the empire. He tried his best to be a Roman and be accepted as one, but he only managed to achieve this to a certain extent. Additionally, despite his best efforts, the Ostrogothic kingdom would only last for a very short time. In the 6th century, Byzantine Emperor Justinian launched an ambitious military campaign to revive the old Roman Empire. Ultimately, he would be partially successful. The Ostrogoths were expelled from Italy. However, this resulted in the decline of the region, and the opportunity was seized by the Franks to take over some of the northern provinces of Italy.

Iberia was taken over by the Visigoths, who eventually controlled almost all of the peninsula as well as substantial territory in southern France. The Visigoths were very Romanized by the time they set up their kingdom in Spain, but factional differences and pressure from invaders would cause a lot of difficulties for them. They lost their possessions in the north to the Franks and were pressured increasingly by the Vandals from Africa.

Unlike the Ostrogoths, the Visigoths did not see the need to remain on good terms with Constantinople, operating largely independently and even successfully expelling the Byzantine invaders in 623. They would set up their capital in Toledo and convert to Catholicism in the 6th century, beginning a long tradition of Catholic dominance in Iberia. Eventually, the Kingdom of Toledo would be badly defeated by invading Arab Muslim forces, who would manage to take over most of Iberia and even push to France in the 8th century before being driven back by the Franks. This would, in turn, start a long period called the Spanish Reconquista, where the Catholic Spanish kingdoms, which had been reduced greatly in size by the Arabs, would try to take Iberia back from the Muslims.

To summarize, the chaos of western Europe after the fall of Rome would eventually start to stabilize by the 7th century. Different actors tried various ways of assimilating and adapting themselves to the lifestyles set out by the empire after its fall. Some places, like the former province of Gaul, had more luck than others, thanks to a multitude of factors. Still, the domination of the Germanic peoples meant the introduction of their customs and traditions, which created, in many cases, bad consequences for post-Roman Europe. For example, the Germanic peoples were far more aggressive; they were more willing to settle matters in ways that would be considered barbaric, at least by Roman standards. They relied heavily on kinship and more primitive societal structures compared to Rome. A good example of this was the fall of literacy rates throughout Europe, which followed deurbanization and the return to more agrarian lifestyles that would come to characterize early medieval Europe.

Strong leaders in Europe wished to be "the" successor to Rome, so they tried to uphold the strongest cultural touchstone of the empire, the Catholic Church, as much as they could to achieve this goal. However, there was only one true successor to Rome. It lay in the east, with its capital in Constantinople.

The Byzantine Civilization

It is obvious that the Eastern Roman Empire was the true successor of the ancient Roman civilization after the collapse of its counterpart, the Western Roman Empire. Over time, it would drift away from its Roman origins, especially in regard to culture, but it would manage to survive for about a millennium before it was destroyed at the hands of the Ottoman Turks in the 15th century.

By the time of the fall of Rome, the Eastern Roman Empire ruled Greece, Anatolia, Syria, and Egypt, which were some of the most prosperous and developed regions of classical antiquity. The rulers of the

Eastern Roman Empire would call themselves Romans, but they would eventually be referred to by the West as Greeks due to the obvious differences that would come to shape Rome's successor, such as a new kind of Christianity.

The Byzantine Empire—a name that derives from the old Greek colony upon which the great city of Constantinople was built—would strive to revive the old Roman Empire right away. However, it would not be until the accession of Emperor Justinian in 527 that actual efforts would be made to reach this goal.

Before Justinian, the Byzantine emperors were content to only symbolically impose their supremacy on the West and keep pseudo-imperial relations with figures like Theodoric. This symbolized the weakness and inability of Constantinople to actually reassert its dominance over Rome. Justinian would be the first emperor whose reign marked successful campaigns against the newly established Germanic kingdoms of the post-Roman world. His generals, such as Belisarius, achieved great victories against the Vandal Kingdom in North Africa and against the Ostrogoths in Italy. With these two important territories under his rule by the year 554, Justinian then launched even more far-reaching campaigns into southern Spain, utilizing the civil war within the Visigoths and managing to gain more lands in Iberia. By the end of the century, the Byzantine Empire largely controlled all of the Mediterranean, although the greater goal of restoring the Roman Empire to its largest borders was still not achieved.

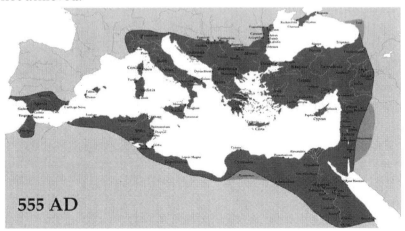

The Eastern Roman Empire in 555.
Tataryn, CC BY-SA 3.0 <https://creativecommons.org/licenses/by-sa/3.0>, via Wikimedia Commons; https://commons.wikimedia.org/wiki/File:Justinian555AD.png

Justinian also helped shape the Byzantine civilization and gave it the initial push that led to the development of its unique identity. Building on the old Roman laws, he made significant improvements toward the modernization of the legal code and created his codex after working on it for five years. Justinian's legal code would become very influential; it even replaced the Germanic legal traditions that dominated early medieval Europe. It reintroduced the notion that laws were the creation of a single ruler rather than something that were passed down in tradition, a notion that would persist in the future and be appealing to European leaders.

Justinian is also partially responsible for the development of religious differences that would cause a drift in Eastern and Western Christianity, ultimately resulting in the Great Schism in 1054 and the official separation of the Catholic Church from the Eastern Orthodox Church. Justinian had a vision to be the Christian emperor of a Christian empire and was ready to enforce the superiority of his religion, even if it meant the oppression of minorities. For instance, he took away many freedoms enjoyed by the Jews, who constituted large numbers in the empire.

The detail that caused strife between him and the Western Church was his insistence on being both the political and religious leader of his subjects, a notion that could not be accepted by the Catholic Church, which regarded the pope as the spiritual head of the material world. The Western Church differentiated itself from the state, and for many centuries, Western leaders would have to "obtain" their titles from the pope, whose power only grew as time went by, reaching its peak during the age of the Crusades. In the East, however, the emperor claimed all the power, including religious authority.

In many regards, Justinian was the first European autocrat after the fall of Rome, enjoying absolute power and acting as a special figure appointed by God. Justinian firmly believed in this notion and pushed for religious uniformity in his realm. Thus, Justinian is responsible for starting the break of Constantinople from the West. Theological and doctrinal disputes with the Western Church were common during his rule.

In short, Justinian never managed to achieve the goals he had set for himself to the fullest. He wasn't able to restore the old glory of the Roman Empire, and he did not attain the religious unity of the Eastern Church to the degree he wanted. However, his reign was vital in the course of Byzantine and European history. Justinian's era was a crucial transitional stage from the unstable times of late classical antiquity to the more stabilized period of the Early Middle Ages.

Eventually, the Byzantine civilization would cease to be the center of Europe. Plagued by domestic and foreign difficulties, it would fall in 1453. Nevertheless, the Byzantine civilization was the main successor to ancient Rome. Constantinople, one of the most prosperous cities in all of Europe and the Near East, would eventually become the center of Christianity, but challenges awaited the Byzantine Empire.

Christianity in Europe

The Early Middle Ages was a time of cultural and social development after the fall of Rome. Centuries of imperial rule in the Western Roman Empire's former territories had provided a very good framework by the time the migrating barbarians settled the lands and established new political entities. Although these people brought their unique, often distinctly pagan and unaccepted practices, one institution remained the main conservator of the "old way": the Christian Church.

As we remarked earlier, the Western Church was by no means as advanced as it is now, but that could be said about Christianity as a whole. The religion was only a couple of hundred years old by the time of the collapse of Rome, and it had only been the official religion of the empire for just over a century. Nevertheless, it had already sown itself deep into the roots of the Roman tradition, and it wanted to retain its special status even when the old imperial structure fell apart.

As barbarians came to familiarize themselves with the ruins of Rome, they also understood that the church and its officials were the most obvious remaining "Roman" aspects. Religious figures were respected in all societies. They were very educated and experienced in almost everything, including things like administration, and they possessed wealth, which further increased their social standing in the eyes of others.

Naturally, they were perceived as the remaining faces of authority in a world that had been set ablaze by recent developments. People, especially those who had previously lived in the empire before 476, looked at the church with hope. They saw it as an institution that could lead them out of the chaos of the post-Roman world, something that was quickly realized by the church itself. With new motivation and undying zeal, the Western Church sought to improve its standing within the new world order and be actively involved in its stabilization and transformation. This became especially important as the other symbol of the old order—the Eastern Roman Empire—gradually drifted apart from the West.

It is unsurprising that the bishop of Rome was seen as the most influential religious person in the West by the year 476. He presided over the most prestigious diocese, which had been believed to be formerly under Saint Peter. During the days of the empire, the bishops of Rome had been very close to the Senate and other imperial institutions, as well as to the emperor himself. When these institutions were crushed into pieces by the Germanic tribes, the church was the only reputable thing that remained in Rome. Very soon, the church, with the bishop of Rome acting as its leader, claimed that it was the main successor of the old Roman way, a statement that implied he needed to command the respect of the new peoples who settled in former Roman lands.

The bishop of Rome would come to be referred to as the pope, from *papa*, which means "father." The supreme position of the pope over the other bishops would be reinforced by Leo the Great, whose pontificate began in the year 440. An ambitious and extremely devout person, Leo assumed the title of pontifex maximus (the chief priest) and embarked on a journey to strengthen the church. The papacy, a name given to the institution of the bishop of Rome, was still part of the empire, but what Leo the Great had started would persist well into the post-Roman world.

Gregory the Great, the pope from 590 to 604, was the second pope with the title of "the great" and deservedly so. Assuming leadership of the church in an age when the early Germanic kingdoms were establishing themselves on the ruins of imperial Rome, Gregory's main aim was to make sure those tribes became Christian. Gregory oversaw the rooting out of Arianism from the newly established Germanic kingdoms in Europe. He sent Augustine, the first bishop of Canterbury, to England in 596, where he succeeded in the conversion of the region. Despite Gregory's status, he maintained friendly relations with the Byzantine emperor but did not outright submit to him as his inferior.

In short, the crucial work of some of the most important popes soon after the fall of the Western Roman Empire was vital in helping transform the religious and cultural landscape of Europe, which was increasingly populated by people with Germanic origins.

For Christianity, the period immediately after the collapse of Rome was very challenging. Leaders of the church correctly acknowledged they were under pressure from several different sides. Pagan peoples were increasingly mixing with the former Roman societies, and it was important that the church was able to reassert the status of Christianity as the continuer of Roman and civilized traditions. The political instability was of no help, as it made the process of spreading Christianity in Europe far more difficult.

The Eastern Roman Empire, on the other hand, due to these social and political circumstances, was becoming increasingly distant, both literally and symbolically, from the rest of "civilized" Europe. It became clear that Constantinople gradually lost its influence and grip over western Europe, as it was troubled by its own problems from the east and within the empire itself.

In the 7th century, with the rise of Islam, Christianity came across a new challenge. Muslim states spread very quickly from the Arabian Peninsula and took over much of the Near East and North Africa. Some of these places had been Christian for many centuries and had been led by Christian rulers. Muslim invaders launched attacks in the Mediterranean. In 652, they invaded Sicily, and in 711, they attacked the Iberian Peninsula, putting an end to Visigothic rule. The surviving Christians managed to temporarily put an end to further Arab conquests in the mid-8th century, but the Emirate of Córdoba, a Muslim state in Iberia, remained the prime target for Christian princes for centuries during the Reconquista.

Islam's sudden gain of power jeopardized the cohesiveness of Christianity, which the leaders of the church pushed for. It was clear that in order to spread the Christian religion throughout Europe, the church had to find powerful European allies.

Charlemagne

This ally came not from Constantinople but rather from the northwest of Italy. The Kingdom of the Franks, ruled by the Merovingian dynasty, had been comparably prosperous to other political entities at the time, especially in the 7th century when the Lombards were attacking Italy and the Muslims were launching invasions into Iberia. Of course, the ruling mechanisms and societal structures of the Franks were very rigid, and the Frankish king only had so much power over his large court, which was filled with powerful, wealthy nobles and aristocrats.

Nevertheless, despite this somewhat fragile system, the Franks managed to defeat the advancing Muslim Umayyads at Tours (also known as the Battle of Poitiers) in 732, forcing them to abandon their invasion of Gaul and sending them back over the Pyrenees. Charles Martel, the leader of the Frankish forces at Tours, eventually became the Franks' de facto ruler, overshadowing the Merovingians. His endeavors would also come to include territorial expansion to the east and the further defense of Frankish lands from the Muslims, something that resonated well with the church. Upon his death, Frankish nobles chose his second son, Pepin the Short, as the new king. He would be anointed by none other than Pope Stephen II, stressing the close relationship between the Frankish crown and the pope. Essentially declared as the new patrician, a title previously held by the emperor in Constantinople, King Pepin would repay the pope's gratitude with his defeat of the Lombards in 756. He also granted the city of Ravenna back to the religious head.

Pepin the Short's reign was the beginning of the alliance between the papacy and the Franks, which would last for many centuries, but Pepin's eldest son would transform the sociopolitical landscape of Europe more than any other Frankish king. Charlemagne, who came to rule the Franks in 768, was a very important figure in the history of post-Roman Europe, something to which his nickname "Charles Magnus" or "Great Charles" is a testament. Not only would Charlemagne emerge as one of the most successful conquerors of his age, but he would also take up the role of the leading Christian king and strengthen the Frankish alliance with the pope.

In 774, Charlemagne campaigned in northern Italy, defeating the Lombards and taking over much of their lands. He became their king and rescued the papacy from more chaos. In the north, his successful campaign against the Saxons led to the conversion of these pagan people, while great cities as far east as Magdeburg came to accept his suzerainty. Charlemagne's control spread even to the provinces of Bohemia, Carinthia, and Moravia, something that let him set up contact with the Eastern Roman Empire through the Danube. In the south, he helped reconquer Catalonia and installed a Christian king in Iberia to lead the effort against the Umayyad Muslims.

In short, at the height of his power, Charlemagne would come to rule a huge part of Europe, including most of modern-day France and Germany, northeastern Spain, almost all of Italy except for the realms of the papacy and Sicily, and even provinces on the eastern border of Christian Europe. He was, by all means, the most powerful man in Europe after the fall of the Western Roman Empire.

Charlemagne's conquests eventually led to an extraordinary occurrence for the time. On Christmas Day, 800, Pope Leo III proclaimed Charles as the emperor of the Romans. This was a very significant development, but it was also somewhat confusing. Were there to be two emperors now, one in Constantinople and another in the West? Also, what was Charlemagne the emperor of? He was the king of the Franks and the Lombards, and he had done great things to Christianize central Europe. But the title of emperor, which had been given to him by the pope, was a whole other level. It almost sanctified him. Granted, Charlemagne's armies had helped the pope get his realms back from the invading Lombards, but was making him the emperor of the Romans the only way the pope could repay his gratitude? Charlemagne was overwhelmingly popular with his subjects. As a descendant of the Germanic warrior-king tradition, he was perceived as being very powerful and respectful. With this new role, Charlemagne started a long process of consciously reconnecting with the Roman past.

Efficient is probably the right word to describe Charlemagne's rule. Charlemagne recognized his status and was not hesitant to internalize it in his subjects and defend it. He was the emperor and wished to remain so. He was a great influence on the Frankish church because of his already great relations with Rome. Under Charlemagne, the biggest religious institutions became just another tool for governance, but this is not to say that religious or cultural growth was in any way thwarted. Charlemagne pushed for religious reforms that emphasized the importance of the monastic lifestyle according to the teachings of Saint Benedict, laying the foundations for the strong Benedictine tradition of French Catholicism. He commissioned the copying and rewriting of the Bible, making it more accessible to different congregations throughout his empire, especially in lands where the majority of the population was still pagan. The Frankish clergy was retrained in order to spread Christianity in difficult provinces, such as in Iberia and central-eastern Europe. Aachen, his imperial seat, became a prosperous city in northern Europe, complete with great works of architecture. It was connected to the rest of the empire through a network of Roman-style roads. With Charlemagne's emphasis on learning and religion, he became increasingly associated with the image of legendary kings from the Old Testament, as he had, just like them, been appointed by none other than God's "representative" as emperor of the Romans.

Popular tradition has come to reinforce the image of Charlemagne as a benevolent Christian ruler, and when we read contemporary accounts, it is not difficult to see why. Charlemagne, an educated man who spoke both Frankish and Latin and could understand Greek, was very close to the "ideal" emperor of the old Roman times. Not only was he stoically wise, but his great physical appearance also helped him impose his authority over his subordinates. He had an ever-present sense of magnanimity and majesty around him, and it is for good reason that he has been remembered as the greatest to ever rule in the Early Middle Ages. More than anything else, Charlemagne marked a transitory stage from the unstable Europe after the collapse of Rome. He was the most evident manifestation of Europe's natural tendency, imposed as it was by the church, to conserve the great Roman past and continue the tradition in a new form. As a powerful, wise, and, above all, Christian emperor, Charlemagne was expected to be the person to lead Europe into a new era, and, to a certain degree, he was able to do so.

Charlemagne, like almost all other great rulers until relatively recently, was in large part successful thanks to his personal qualities, although the masterful administrative and bureaucratic novelties he introduced during his reign played a part. Before his death, he wished to divide his empire among his sons according to the usual Frankish way, but this did not work out since four of his five sons died before him. This meant that Louis the Pious became the sole ruler of the empire in 814, and two years later, he was anointed by the pope, continuing his father's legacy.

However, the partition of the empire would not be postponed for much longer. In 843, with the Treaty of Verdun, Louis's three sons divided Charlemagne's empire into three. Lothair, the reigning emperor, got the core Frankish lands, which contained territories sandwiched between the Rhine and Rhone rivers, including the capital of Aachen, most of the Low Countries, and Charlemagne's possessions in northern Italy. This kingdom would be named Lotharingia after its first king and would be much less ethnically diverse than the other two kingdoms. In addition to Lotharingia, there was the kingdom in the west, which included most of modern-day France and was centered around the provinces of Aquitaine, Gascony, and Septimania. Charles the Bald became its ruler. The control of the territories east of the Rhine and northeast of Italy was assumed by Louis the German.

As history would show, this partition would become very influential for the future of Europe since it essentially marked the beginning of the long process of the cultural and political division of what would later become France and Germany. Over the centuries, borders would shift countless times between these two entities before they eventually became settled.

As for the Carolingian dynasty, it would soon decline in power. Due to the partition, additional kingdoms and duchies, like Burgundy, emerged and defied the borders set forth in the treaty. It would take centuries for Charlemagne's successors to implement effective administrative systems to ensure the cohesiveness of their kingdoms and their own personal authority. Before then, local nobility and aristocracy held power in most places, making it almost impossible to replace them. Additionally, unexpected developments would also trouble the kingdoms, like the arrival of the Norsemen in the early 10th century and their settlement in modern-day Normandy. In 987, the Carolingian kings no longer controlled West Francia, giving way to the Capetian dynasty for about four hundred years. Its first king, Hugh, was elected king by the nobles.

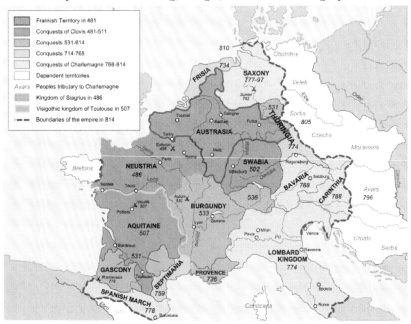

Frankish Empire from 481 to 814.
Sémhur, CC BY-SA 3.0 <https://creativecommons.org/licenses/by-sa/3.0>, via Wikimedia Commons https://en.wikipedia.org/wiki/File:Frankish_Empire_481_to_814-en.svg

The Holy Roman Empire

East Francia would come to be a particularly interesting legacy of Charlemagne. Located in the territories that had largely been left intact by the Romans during the ancient era, the political processes that began in the 10th century would eventually result in the formation of the modern country of Germany. Still, the history of East Francia is very complicated, owing, to a large degree, to the absence of much of the post-Roman heritage that existed in other parts of Charlemagne's empire, particularly in Gaul and Italy.

In 911, the last Carolingian king of East Francia would die, and Conrad of Franconia would be chosen as the new king by the kingdom's nobility. However, Conrad would be embarrassed by the Magyar peoples who lived east of his domains, as they dominated the Frankish armies and weakened East Francia.

Very soon, East Francia would come to be ruled by the Saxon emperors, a short succession of rulers who came from the province of Saxony in the north. The first of them, Henry the Fowler, would be elected in 919 by the dukes of Saxony, Swabia, Franconia, and Bavaria, and he would spearhead the kingdom's struggle against the Magyars, achieving victory. This was also the beginning of a very strong regional divide and special authority that the German regional leaders enjoyed for centuries.

Above all else, Henry the Fowler was backed by his loyal Saxons, who greatly valued the old tribal-like relationships. It was through warfare that the new king assumed and maintained power. He even managed to gain lands in Lotharingia and Denmark, making their regional rulers his tributaries.

His son, Otto I, would be elected by the princes to be the next king, partially because he was related to Henry. Coming to power in 936, he continued his father's work against the Magyars, achieving a decisive victory in 955 at the Battle of Lechfeld and taking over much of Austria. Unlike his father, however, Otto I was deeply Christian and made the church a powerful tool for himself. He set up a new archbishopric in Magdeburg, partially to help spread the religion farther east among the Slavic peoples. Later on, he invaded northern Italy, coming to aid the papacy and marrying Adelaide, a Burgundian princess with a claim on Italy. Thus, Otto assumed the Italian throne for himself. Ten years later, in 962, Otto I was officially crowned by the pope as the new emperor, marking the beginning of the Holy Roman Empire.

As it has been famously remarked, the Holy Roman Empire would neither be "holy" or "Roman" or an "empire," but these three names nevertheless contained a lot of meaning for the age. For all intents and purposes, Otto did not assume almost total control of the papacy as Charlemagne had done, nor was his realm centered around Rome. Symbolically, Otto became the new protector of the church, speaking strictly in a military role, while the governance of the church was in the papacy's hands.

Otto's realm, on the other hand, rested very much on the autonomies of local provinces and principalities, and the administration of the Holy Roman Empire (or HRE) would be heavily dependent on the cooperation of the princes who, ultimately, saw themselves as "German," whatever that meant in the 10th century. The political structure was highly volatile, but it also turned out to be effective, especially if a strong emperor like Otto was its head.

Otto's son, Otto II, was elected to be the next emperor in 973, and Otto III, Otto II's son, secured the throne in 983 despite facing internal problems. The three Ottos increasingly inched for more and more influence over the papacy in Rome, taking part in the deposition and appointment of popes to gain favors and demonstrate their status.

The Holy Roman Empire would exist until the 19th century and remains one of the most interesting political entities in European history. The HRE was a huge conglomeration of regional and smaller entities, and it sometimes consisted of hundreds of baronies, counties, and dukedoms with strong local identities.

Eventually, as we have already remarked, the unifying idea of all these different actors would be that they were German, but before then, the HRE was an ambiguous creation that hindered the development of a united German state for centuries. It was built on the cooperation of the actors of the confederation, and the emperor, although nominally the strongest person, often had little power compared to his princes.

However, from the beginning, the HRE was important because it was another manifestation of Europe's desire to connect with its classical Roman past. This time, as the name suggests, the emphasis was equally on holiness as well as Romanness, something that made the HRE very distinct.

Over the centuries, the empire would come to have complicated relations with the papacy, to say the least. Still, the Holy Roman Empire was partially responsible for ending the state of chaos that had taken central Europe by storm after the fall of the Western Roman Empire. Although it would never be as mighty and prosperous as ancient Rome, the HRE would play a huge role in the shaping of the continent, as we will discuss later.

The Norsemen

An interesting region we haven't paid much attention to so far is Scandinavia. Of course, medieval Scandinavia is most often associated with its inhabitants, the Vikings, who were master sailors, skillful craftsmen or farmers, and ruthless warriors. They are infamous for their countless raids and barbaric activities all around the northern (and later the Mediterranean) European coast.

Increasingly after the 8th century, the Scandinavians were moving out of their original homeland, possibly due to overpopulation or the harsh living conditions of Scandinavia that made sustainable farming difficult. Searching for lands to permanently settle or to raid and loot, Vikings terrorized Britain, Ireland, Germany, France, the Baltic, and even Russia. The Vikings were adamant about making contact with other peoples of Europe and were not hesitant to colonize the lands they discovered. They were the first to settle in Iceland and founded cities in Britain and Ireland, like Dublin. The Norsemen also reached Greenland and lived there for several hundred years before being likely pushed out by the local Inuit. Viking longboats sailed as far west as Newfoundland, where temporary settlements were established before 1000 CE.

The Vikings' impact on the history of northern and western European Christendom should not be understated. Appearing in England in the late 8th century, they raided the countryside and burned a monastery in Lindisfarne. Ireland came next, then the Frisian coast, and then northern France in 842. Throughout the 9th century, the Vikings managed to circumnavigate the western European coast, ending up first in Iberia and then going to Sicily and Italy, where they skirmished with Arab fleets.

The consequence of their raids in France is the most evident. Under their leader, Rollo, one Viking expedition reached as far inland as Paris, and the constant threat they posed to towns of northern France eventually forced the Frankish king to sue for peace. He agreed to grant the Vikings land in what became French Normandy. Rollo's successors were eventually integrated into the French nobility. They never completely abandoned their Scandinavian roots, but they assimilated pretty well with the newly emergent Franco-Roman culture.

The Norsemen saw similar successes after their countless raids in England. Post-Roman Britannia had already been subject to a lot of migration by the Germanic peoples, which had resulted in the relocation of the local Celtic populations to Ireland and the Scottish Highlands. The seven English kingdoms that emerged after the arrival of the new migrants are referred to as the Heptarchy. The kingdoms of Wessex, Essex, Sussex, Kent, East Anglia, Northumbria, and Mercia challenged each other for dominance for centuries, with neither one truly managing to stay on top for a long time.

In the 7th century, thanks to the efforts of the Roman Church, the English kingdoms converted to Catholicism and abandoned any inclinations they might have had toward Arianism. Yet, England would not be safe from Viking attacks, and the fragmentation of the Heptarchy and the sudden impact of the Norse raids made it very difficult to withstand the invaders. In the mid-9th century, Danish Vikings began to successfully occupy parts of central and eastern England, and for about twenty years, they were a very feared force.

After the year 871, the English started to retaliate slowly. With the accession of King Alfred to the throne of Wessex, which had been the more powerful of the Heptarchy and often had amicable relations with other Anglo-Saxon kingdoms, a united English army managed to decisively defeat the Vikings for the first time, forcing them to abandon some of their settlements and retreat. King Alfred even managed to broker a temporary peace with the Vikings in 878 and persuade the Danish leader to convert to Christianity, which had a direct consequence on the subsequent conversion of many in the Danelaw since they respected the actions of their leader. (The Danelaw was an area in England that was dominated by the Vikings in the 9th and 10th centuries.)

Slowly, the Vikings began to retreat from England as Alfred consolidated more power in the south. The Englishmen also learned how to defeat the Norsemen in open battles instead of in disorganized encounters, at which the Vikings excelled. Still, the Viking customs, traditions, and manners of speech left a lasting mark on central and eastern England.

King Alfred is largely considered to be the first English hero king, as he managed to defend the country from the invaders but also pushed England forward culturally and intellectually by moving away from the tribal Germanic origins of his people.

Soon after Alfred passed away, the Danes retaliated. In the early 11th century, Danish armies returned, overthrowing the Anglo-Saxon descendant of Alfred and establishing the prosperous North Sea Empire around 1016. Danish King Cnut was the king of Denmark, Norway, and

England until his death in 1035. Thirty years later, the final Anglo-Saxon king from the Wessex dynasty, King Edward the Confessor, would die childless, an event that triggered another wave of invasion and a struggle for succession between different actors.

Harold Godwinson, Edward's brother-in-law, was forced to confront the invading Norwegians in 1066 at the Battle of Stamford Bridge, where he achieved a decisive victory, one of the most iconic in the history of England. However, soon after, another invasion force landed in southern England. This force was led by William of Normandy, who would come to be remembered in history as William the Conqueror. Leading a huge force that was comprised of thousands of Norman, Frisian, Breton, and French warriors, William defeated Harold Godwinson and took over the throne of England. Since the Normans were originally Norsemen, it is not entirely incorrect to say that a form of Viking civilization came to rule England in 1066, a date that can be considered the beginning of a new age.

Eastern Europe

Concurrent with the Christianization of Europe, interesting developments were under way in the eastern part of the continent. The Byzantine Empire certainly had its heyday with the reign of Justinian, as the Byzantines managed to reconquer much of northern Africa and Italy, but it soon became clear that the empire was entering a period of struggle, with challenges rising on multiple fronts at once. The gains of Diocletian slipped away one by one, as Italy was taken over by the Lombards, while the rising Arab threat from the east significantly pressured Constantinople, taking over most of its possessions in Africa and the Levant.

The Muslim world was expanding rapidly, and, more often than not, that expansion came at the expense of Byzantine Christendom. The West would only come to taste defeat against the Muslims when they conquered half of Iberia and took over much of Sicily, but the Byzantines had been fighting with the Arabs early on.

No effective efforts were made to reestablish friendly relations with Rome, so the Eastern Roman Empire drifted away and gave rise to an increasingly different culture. The religious differences between Rome and Constantinople would result in the infamous Great Schism in 1054, a development we will cover later. The Great Schism led to the official separation of Western Catholicism and Eastern Orthodoxy.

In addition to these troubles, there was another frontier for the Byzantines that became more and more problematic as time went on: eastern Europe. The territories north of the Balkans were a sort of border area between the old Western and Eastern Roman provinces. In this region, a new civilization emerged as time went by, and it was plagued by constant social and demographic changes due to its proximity with the rest of "more developed" Europe and Asia through the Eurasian plain north of the Black Sea.

The people who inhabited the territory we now call "Eastern Europe" were the Slavs. The Slavs were an interesting people. They were right at the frontier of cultural and ethnic exchange from the arriving Asian tribes like the Huns and other migrating Europeans, like the Goths. They would come to outlast those who temporarily passed through their lands. The Slavs demonstrated a unique presence of mind to learn and adapt to the cultures and technologies of more advanced societies, and they even emerged as experienced warriors. This resulted in the spread of Slavic people all throughout eastern Europe, as far east as modern-day Russia, where they would kickstart a prosperous civilization by coming into contact with the Vikings, and as far west as East Francia, where they were unwelcome by the Frankish kings, who considered them uncivilized barbarians.

Bulgaria is often considered to be the first Slavic state, but technically, the Bulgars were ethnically Asian, only having adapted Slavic customs and lifestyles after settling on the Danube during the great migration. Over time, the Bulgars would fully adopt the Slavic lifestyle, launching countless raids on richer Byzantine lands to the south, where they were perceived as pagans who needed to be kept out. Centuries of struggle began between the Byzantines and the Bulgars, which persisted even after the latter converted to Christianity in the 9th century.

The conversion of Bulgar King Boris I was the first stepping stone in the history of the Christianization of eastern Europe and the beginning of a deep Christian tradition that runs in the region to this day. The Christianization of Bulgaria is also important since it resulted in the development of the first Slavic alphabet by Saint Cyril and Saint Methodius, who had been sent as Orthodox missionaries first to Bohemia and later to Bulgaria. The Glagolitic and Cyrillic alphabets, which were invented by these figures, helped rapidly spread Christianity in these pagan regions, and the gradual adoption of the alphabet by Slavs made it possible to make the Slavic culture unique. Of course, close contact with the Byzantines helped greatly as well.

But an even more impressive civilization with Slavic roots began to take shape in the 8th century farther to the east. This civilization would, after centuries of struggle, give birth to the modern nation of Russia. The origins of this civilization lay at the meeting point of the Don, Dnieper, and Volga rivers, where the dispersed Slavs were ever-so vulnerable to cultural and social pressures from not only Asia but also the Norsemen. When a raiding party of a couple of hundred Viking-style longships, with men dressed like Vikings and who fought like Vikings, landed in Constantinople from the Black Sea in 860 and attacked the city, it is unsurprising that the Byzantines were in shock. These invaders were called the Rus', and they lived in the Dnieper Valley, mostly around the city of Kiev (modern-day Kyiv).

Despite their military prowess, Kievan Rus' could hardly be called a state in the 9th century. According to legend, a Viking by the name of Rurik managed to consolidate his power in the town of Novgorod, way up in the north near the Baltic Sea. From there, Rurik's Norse descendants conquered much of the territory to the south, which was inhabited mostly by Slavs, especially those on the banks of the Dnieper.

Kievan Rus' thus came into being as a result of the mixing of the Norse and Slavic cultures. The rulers of Kievan Rus' would, for a long time, be direct descendants of Rurik and be of the Rurikid dynasty, while the people whom they ruled were mostly Slavs who adapted to the new lifestyle.

Crucially, the Rus' depended heavily on their rivers and made great use of the Vikings' naval technology to maneuver their way through the deep and wide basins in their territories. Ultimately, this made for greater north-south connectivity, which fostered trade, among other things. Kiev, which lay on the Dnieper, would become one of the most prosperous European cities outside of Christendom.

Relative economic and political stability meant cultural and literal growth. The prosperity of Kievan Rus' was recognized in the early 10th century by the Byzantines, who granted the Rus' commercial privileges, mostly to dissuade further attacks on Constantinople.

However, the political structure of Kievan Rus' was still immature, as it was shaped by heavy regional divisions. The grand prince, who was the ruler of Kiev, would impose his authority over other lesser princes and be dependent on their support in times of need. In times of peace, however, the masterful utilization of the large rivers made it possible for the Rus' to connect northern Europe with the Black Sea and, therefore, the rest of the Byzantine civilization.

However, the relations with Constantinople were always complicated. Early Rus' raiders were also called the Varangians by the Byzantines, and records survive depicting their activities as far from their original dwelling place of Scandinavia as Baghdad. For a long time, before they could be accepted as non-pagan peoples, the Varangians were regarded to be fierce warriors, not the least because they were always a thorn in the side of Constantinople. Soon enough, Constantinople began to employ Varangians in its armies as heavy infantry units, something that helped the Rus' strengthen their trade links with Constantinople.

In a couple of decades, this relationship materialized in the conversion of Queen Olga of Kiev to Christianity in 957 during her visit to Constantinople. Although her son, Sviatoslav, adhered more to pagan beliefs and was a stereotypical war-hungry Viking who cared little about Christianity, the process of Kiev's Christianization began. With the accession of Vladimir to the throne in 980, Christianity became the main religion of the Rus'. Vladimir's decision to convert might not have entirely come out of sheer belief and enthusiasm; he had provided military aid to the Byzantines and expected to marry their princess after his conversion. Nevertheless, he certainly pushed his subjects to get baptized.

In Kievan Rus' and Bulgaria, the decision to convert to Christianity was solely a political one rather than something necessary, and in both cases, the Byzantine Empire played a crucial role. The Eastern Roman Empire was far more culturally cohesive than almost any other place in western Europe. The Slavs, who lived near Constantinople, knew of the empire's prosperity and would model their states after Byzantine institutions rather than Western ones. They adopted the Orthodox faith, although the Great Schism hadn't yet officially taken place. Consequently, they drifted closer toward Constantinople than to the Frankish kingdoms of the West, which adhered to the Roman Catholic tradition.

The city of Kiev itself became iconic for its Orthodox churches, borrowing heavily from Greek architectural styles. It remained one of the richest cities in Europe for a couple of hundred years before outside factors caused its decline. Kievan Rus' was transformed into an Orthodox Christian stronghold of the East, separated from the West by the still largely pagan lands on the Baltic coast. The kingdom was always connected to Constantinople through the Black Sea. Soon enough, the center of the Rus' civilization would shift more toward the east, around the basin of the Volga River.

Chapter 5 – A Changing Europe

The Schism

The Byzantine Empire would be largely left out of the continent-wide transformation that took place after 476. In the beginning, the troubled new societies of the former Western Roman lands would look at Constantinople as continuing the old Roman traditions and the glory of the old days. Over time, however, this view would be abandoned due to, in part, the gradual separation of Constantinople from the West and the emergence of new self-sustaining societies in the West that no longer needed the "authority" of Constantinople. The social and cultural differences between the West and the East would show themselves more and more clearly as time passed and would ultimately culminate in the Great Schism in 1054.

The Byzantine Empire had been drifting away from western Europe for several centuries, and it had its own periods of stability and chaos while the West was still figuring things out. After the 7th century, it was challenged from the outside with the emergence of Islam as a new uniting ideology of the Near East and the military rise of Muslim states. But underneath this constant political and military tug of war with the Muslims, barbarians, and even Franks was a much more all-encompassing cultural tug of war between the Eastern Church and the Western Church.

We have to remember that in the early days of Christianity, the bishops of Rome, Alexandria, and Antioch were regarded to be the most prominent, heading their own churches while keeping in touch with each other to agree on different issues, be they doctrinal or organizational.

With the emergence of Constantinople as the new imperial capital and the declining power of Rome, the Byzantine bishop gained more eminence. Meanwhile, the bishoprics of Alexandria and Antioch slowly lost their importance as the Arabs took control.

The tension that existed between the bishops of Constantinople and Rome was amplified after the fall of the Western Roman Empire. The Church of Rome increasingly saw itself as the institution that was responsible for the protection and stability of its subjects after the empire's collapse since people saw it as one of the most essential Roman institutions. Thanks to the chaos that fell upon Europe after 476, the cultural and social instability that was brought by migrating barbarians into former Roman lands, and the absence of a strong spiritual rival in the West that could challenge the superiority of the Roman Church in its mission of "Romanizing" the West, the Roman Church assumed a more predominant role in society. This was not accepted by the Church of Constantinople, which had always regarded Rome as its equal. Due to the existing cultural and religious differences between the two, they slowly started to separate as time went by.

Several big differences had already existed for a couple of centuries by 1054, the year Pope Leo IX excommunicated Patriarch Michael Cerularius of Constantinople, "officially" separating the Eastern and Western Churches. The Eastern Church saw the self-declared superior status of the bishop of Rome as unacceptable and rallied around the patriarch of Constantinople to counterbalance the status of Rome. The existence of a more active theological discourse in the East, when compared to Rome's monopoly of Christianity in the West, gave birth to a lot of diverging opinions on matters of doctrine and practices. The Eastern Church, for example, was appalled at Rome's decision to assert that the Holy Spirit came from the Father and the Son instead of from the Father. Catholic priests also had a long tradition of celibacy, something the Eastern priests disagreed with. In addition, there were differences when it came to, at least at first glance, inconsequential matters, like the use of leavened bread in the Eucharist.

One of the biggest distinctions between the Western and Eastern Churches was the former's unfriendly attitude toward the use of iconography. In the Eastern Church, icons were a tool to focus people's spirituality and teaching, especially the images of Jesus, the Virgin Mary, and other saints who were considered to be important. The Orthodox Church continues to use icons today. At the height of this religious dispute, the West almost forbade their use, regarding icons as idols and a hindrance to a person's ability to worship properly. Of course, there might be more practical and political explanations for the Orthodox Church's heavy emphasis on iconography; an average medieval peasant with little to no education would be more likely to find spirituality when they saw powerful religious symbols like icons.

Thus, as the centuries passed after the fall of Rome, the Eastern Roman Empire became more estranged from the rest of Europe. Of course, the Byzantine Empire was separated from the West physically too. The overland connection between central Europe, Christian Europe, and the Byzantine Balkans was disrupted by barbarians who occupied the provinces formerly under the Roman Empire's control. North Africa was fully taken over by the Muslims. The creation of the Holy Roman Empire did not help either, and Byzantine emperors never fully acknowledged the imperial supremacy of the Latin emperors in Germany.

Of course, cultural and political exchange continued between the two, although not on the level it would have had the two parts of Europe been reunited. So, the Byzantine civilization became more and more alien to the Latins, especially as religious disputes materialized. The two sides did not make up until relatively recently, in the 20th century.

Medieval European Society

Aside from the political developments of Europe after the fall of Rome, which led to the formation of new states on the ruins of the old Roman Empire, a huge social transformation was also under way. Having emerged from the age of antiquity, Europe had to almost completely restructure its social life, and Germanic domination of the continent certainly played a role in the restructuring of the hierarchical systems that had been in place for centuries. The setbacks Europe suffered from the collapse of the Western Roman civilization were very difficult to overcome, and it would take many centuries before sustainable growth and progress could again become a European staple. We have mostly touched upon the cultural transformation of the continent after 476, mainly how the migrating peoples who settled down in former imperial territories slowly adopted Christianity. This resulted in the gradual abandonment of their old ways of life and the Romanization (which included the Christianization) of societies in France, Germany, and England. Let's turn our attention to the socioeconomic changes that took place during this era as well.

When the warring barbarians settled down, a new social order emerged, one based on the possession and access to land. Agriculture made up the largest part of the early post-Roman economy by far, and this continued to be so for more than a thousand years. The agricultural development of the less hospitable areas of northern and northwestern Europe took place during this period. These places had not experienced the thriving economic life and favorable climate that the Mediterranean offered to societies in Italy, Iberia, and Greece. Urban centers slowly depopulated, as more and more people flocked to the countryside to develop it with the use of more advanced technological tools, like new plows. Former barbarian kings, chiefs, and nobles became landowners, and their status would be determined by how much land they owned and how much their possessions produced. It was the beginning of European feudalism, which would dominate the continent until as late as the 19th century.

Wealthy landowners granted lands to poorer landowners, who were expected to provide military support in times of need. This resulted in more decentralization of the administration since Germanic kings did not have the luxury of effectively being able to govern their subjects; they were largely dependent on their cooperation, but they also had to carefully control them so that no one overtook them in wealth and status. Old loyal relationships, which had characterized barbarian societies based on blood, brotherhood, and war chiefs, began to slowly transform into more reciprocal relationships that were based on faithfulness and a sense of moral duty.

Another part of medieval European society that slowly accumulated a lot of power was the church. The Roman Church made a conscious effort early on to maintain its status quo, and the fact that it was the institution "responsible" for crowning kings helped a lot. By the year 1000, Europe was overwhelmingly Christian and devoted to the Christian cause, and the church enjoyed multiple privileges. Clergy were consistently the most educated class in European society, at least until the invention of the printing press. People believed in Christianity. It gave their lives meaning and an ideal to strive for. Thus, European rulers were quick to realize the importance of religion and began to use it as a tool for governance. They granted the church lands and helped construct monasteries to accrue favors with the clergy. The church soon came to possess quite a lot of holdings in the new European states, and the construction of monasteries in more remote areas resulted in the development of small communities around the local churches. The domains of the pope in Italy expanded as well, and the entity we now call the Papal States came into existence. The Papal States had their own army and subjects, who dwelled in the lands controlled by the pope. Soon, it became clear that for most people, the church was the second pillar of stability and power alongside their sovereign.

The foundations of the new feudal system were laid roughly until the turn of the new millennium (1000 CE), after which European society started to slowly get richer and grow. Wars persisted, and they became even more violent as technological advancements brought deadlier weapons. However, the utter chaos brought about by the fall of Rome was over by the 11th century.

We have quite a bit of statistical data from the age, mostly thanks to the censuses that were done by monarchs or the clergy. This data indicates a stable increase in the European population up until the 14th century. The numbers are all approximations, of course, but they are logical, given the economic and political state of the continent at the time. The population of western Europe was about forty million people by 476 and increased to about seventy million by 1300.

The main explanation for this increase was that more land came to be cultivated. The dense forests of central and northern Europe were slowly transformed into new agricultural possessions, resulting in the gradual transformation of the continent's physical landscape. Productivity almost doubled, and the food supply, generally speaking, increased after having suffered major setbacks that came with the collapse of Roman interconnectivity and the disruption of trade routes. More importantly, the nobles saw an increase in wealth as the system became more stable, while poor peasant workers continued to live in terrible conditions.

Beginning in about the 12th century, there was noticeable urban growth. The revival of town life coincided with the revival of trade, and this was especially true of the urban areas located on the coast or close to it. Old Roman urban centers saw considerable growth, especially in Italy, where Florence, Venice, and Genoa thrived. This was largely due to the importance and prominence of the Italian merchant class. Italians had almost total unrestricted access to the Mediterranean and could trade with Constantinople and the Muslim world. They were also ready to venture to the north and bring goods produced in Flanders and northern

Germany down to the Mediterranean.

Meanwhile, northern Europe organized its own trade league, the Hanseatic League, which ensured the flow of textiles, spices, lumber, and other goods into European markets through Russia and the Baltic corridor. These developments stimulated the growth of cities, which were rebuilt and reconstructed, thanks to the wealth that flowed into them. Roads were repaved, public areas were reestablished, and local markets attracted more inhabitants to settle close to them. Thus, the regulated development of European cities began.

To protect these centers of wealth and prosperity, defensive structures were added. Eventually, taking a walled city during a siege became very difficult. Safety meant new businesses and more dwellers, which, in turn, meant more wealth. It is not difficult to see the importance European cities had. Cultural and technological developments of the later era owe a lot to the urban revival of the early 1000s.

One crucial event that took place in medieval Europe in the 1300s was a continent-wide epidemic that decimated the European population and halted the rapid growth it was experiencing. The bubonic plague epidemic, which is referred to as the Black Death today, had drastic effects on the social changes that had been taking place.

The plague was introduced to Europe from Asia (most likely having originated in East Asian mountains). It peaked in the mid-1300s and resulted in the deaths of anywhere between seventy-five million to two hundred million people, setting back the clock for social, cultural, and economic advancements. For people living in the 21st century, when access to medical services is easier than ever before for most, it is perhaps difficult to fully grasp the scale of that catastrophe. Despite all the growth since the fall of Rome, the European economy was still quite fragile, as it was heavily dependent on agriculture and manual labor. Agricultural output was usually never enough to last for a long time if there was a bad harvest, at least for those at the bottom of the social hierarchy. Moreover, the constant plowing of land and the absence of effective fertilizers other than manure made lands less fertile, resulting in lower yields. More land was needed to expand food production, but by the 14th century, most land was already used for farming. Only a handful of regions saw irrigation development that improved farming.

Therefore, it is unsurprising that as more people contracted the plague, which spread very quickly through human contact, the whole economy started to crumble, especially in cities. Thousands of people died every day, resulting in a demographic collapse that had never before been seen. In addition to people dying from the plague, tens of thousands died of starvation. All these deaths resulted in less food output since there was nobody left to do the farming. Public disorder reached its peak. Bands of impoverished peasants sought justice and came together to take whatever they could to survive. The Black Death was a disaster that stood in the way of progress.

However, the Black Death, even though it caused a partial collapse of European society, also opened up an array of new possibilities when it slowly began to fade at the end of the 14th century. The shortage of labor shook up the landowning classes, with landowners forced to give up many of their estates simply because they could not find enough people to work them. This, in turn, resulted in the increase in prominence of other social classes, which gained more power as time went by. The best example is the merchant class. Previously, merchants had mostly been either shopkeepers or traders of luxury goods they obtained through their contacts with the East and other regions. The merchant class gained most of its power after the turbulent times of the Black Death, as the economy was forced to drift away from the countryside to the cities. The price of land, as well as the price of urban lodgings, fell dramatically, which meant those people who had their own businesses and accumulated a decent amount of money could expand their wealth more easily.

This was especially apparent in Italy, where merchants managed to obtain the most wealth and eventually emerged as rulers of different regions. The Medici family of Florence established their own dynasty and ruled one of the most prosperous Italian cities for a long time, while Venice made a lot of efforts to get rid of the old nobility in favor of new aristocrats, who were rich merchants who contributed to the development of urban life.

The rise of the merchant class meant urban development, and cities began to experience another wave of growth as trade was reestablished and the economy stabilized. Eventually, members of the merchant class became the bourgeoisie. They lived and worked in cities, enjoyed relative financial freedom, and could focus on other things than survival.

Despite this, western Europe was still feudal. In France, England, and Spain, towns and cities enjoyed less freedom than in the Low Countries, Germany, and Italy due to a more centralized political system in those places. The dominance the landowning nobility possessed was challenged by the merchants, but it never truly faded. Noble power was already well established. It had historical justification and was difficult to fully root out. But the values the nobility stood for slowly transformed, retaining its (almost obligatory) military foundations and adding the notions of loyalty and honor, which eventually gave rise to the tradition of European chivalry with an emphasis on devotion, piety, and discipline. Soon enough, there were new titles among the higher classes to distinguish themselves as dukes or barons and to indicate their status.

The concept of knighthood was also born and developed from the 11th to the 14th centuries, with the ideal of a chivalrous Christian knight becoming very prominent and remaining influential in Europe for many centuries.

All in all, a great era of European social change was under way despite some major setbacks. The Early Middle Ages is often referred to as the European Dark Ages, but that distinction is mostly based on comparing the period with the more culturally and politically prosperous period of later centuries.

The Crusades

We have already mentioned that the European identity of the Middle Ages was shaped by Christianity, but it was also shaped by the ideas of the "other," which, for western Europe, meant the Eastern Christian worlds of the Byzantine Empire and the Islamic realms that lay beyond the Mediterranean. The western European identity gradually developed in contrast to these two entities, seeing them as hostile or alien to varying degrees. It is also worth reminding ourselves of the limited knowledge the Europeans had of the physical world in which they lived. The Muslim dominions of the Near East, which had changing boundaries but largely ended in eastern Persia, were basically as much as the Europeans knew about, and even this knowledge was not extensive. These regions of the world were poorly connected, and it would take months for information to get from one place to another. Even those merchants who had the luxury of trading Far Eastern goods knew little about the lands their products came from.

By 1000 CE, Islam had emerged as a natural enemy to Christendom, both to Orthodox Byzantines and Roman Catholics alike. The increasingly militaristic Muslims dominated Christian armies for centuries after the emergence of the new religion. The Spanish Reconquista, which began soon after the Arab conquest of half of Iberia, was perhaps the first conscious struggle of Christendom against Islam. The Iberian princes' push against the Arabs, however slow it might have been in the beginning, was followed up by war-hungry and adventurous Normans, who sailed around the continent and ended up in the Mediterranean, where they challenged Muslims for the control of Sicily. The newly established Norman kingdom in Sicily was an eclectic mix of Arab, Norse, and Catholic cultures, and the pope even gave the Sicilian Normans permission to pressure Byzantine possessions in southern Italy after realizing that Catholic Normans could be an ally to the church. Western Christendom of medieval Europe had begun its long fight against its rivals.

Of course, an even better materialization of a conscious European struggle against the Islamic peoples was a series of military campaigns in Palestine known as the Crusades. This two-hundred-year period of European history would become influential, shaping the mindset of many Christian Europeans of the time. The idea of a holy Crusade, a military expedition to the Holy Land in Israel and Palestine, was born very quickly, but over the decades, it materialized into an organized endeavor that became more complex and thought out.

It all began in 1095 at the Council of Clermont, one of the biggest gatherings in European history. The council was attended by noblemen and clergy from all parts of Europe. Pope Urban II urged all Christians to fight in the name of Christ against the Muslim infidels and reclaim the holy city of Jerusalem. Of course, Jerusalem and the notion of the Holy Land had long run in the consciousness of Europeans. The assembled crowd knew very well that Jesus Christ had been born in the Holy Land. Some of the most devout Christians had gone on pilgrimages to the holy cities from time to time, but they were absurdly far away for the average European.

Despite this, Pope Urban's passionate speech convinced many important figures to start mobilizing their armies and venture out to the Holy Land. Urban made it clear in his address that the Holy Land was being ravaged by the Muslims, who denied pilgrims access to the traditionally Christian sites. He had also made it clear that those who were willing to fight in the name of Christ would attain eternal salvation and forever be remembered as heroes in their homelands, something that was more than enough for the assembled to seriously consider the idea of a Crusade and embark on the journey as soon as they could.

Of course, not everything the pope talked about was true, but little to the knowledge of others, Urban had been approached by emissaries from Byzantine Emperor Alexios I prior to the council. The emissaries brought grave news of Byzantine defeats at the hands of the Muslim Turks, who had crushed the Byzantine army at the Battle of Manzikert and had taken over much of Anatolia. Alexios wanted the West to come to Constantinople's aid and relieve the pressure. The pope saw the emergency as an opportunity to further increase his standing in the Christian world.

Thus, the First Crusade was called for at Clermont, and everyone was encouraged to try their luck. The objective was Jerusalem, and those who were willing to die in the name of Christ were promised their place in heaven. It seemed promising, but the Crusaders would come to realize what a difficult goal they had set for themselves.

The First Crusade was launched in 1096, and seven more followed throughout the years. Although the other Crusades were organized with similar goals in mind as the first one, they were directed to different locations, like Muslim Iberia and pagan eastern Europe. The First Crusade was the most experimental, but it would also prove to be one of the most successful. It was headed by several important counts, nobles, and dukes from France, Germany, Italy, and Iberia, who managed to assemble up to 100,000 men.

They got to the Levant after a long journey through the Balkans and Anatolia. By the end of 1099, they managed to defeat the Muslims and took over quite a bit of the eastern Mediterranean coast, establishing four Christian realms to retain control over the Holy Land. These realms were the Kingdom of Jerusalem, the Principality of Antioch, the County of Edessa, and the County of Tripoli. These realms came to be known as the Crusader States or the Latin Kingdoms, and for nearly two hundred years, they were the Latin Christian outposts in Palestine and other modern-day countries in the Middle East. After the infamous capture of Jerusalem in 1099, where the Christians brutally slaughtered the inhabitants of the holy city and looted their homes, the idea of the Crusade would remain in the minds of Europeans for many centuries, even after the last of the Latin Kingdoms in the Levant was destroyed in the late 1200s.

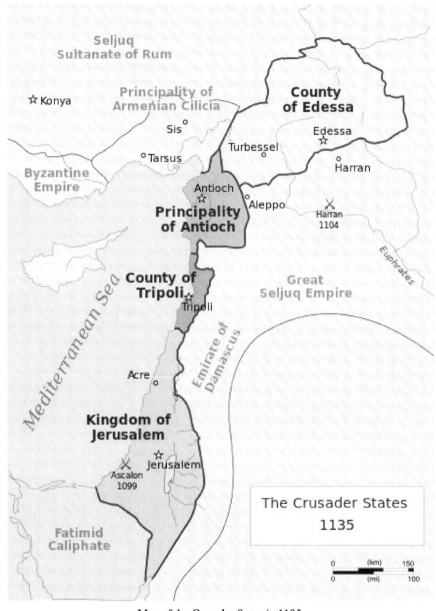

Map of the Crusader States in 1135.
Amitchell125, CC BY-SA 4.0 <https://creativecommons.org/licenses/by-sa/4.0>, via Wikimedia Commons; https://commons.wikimedia.org/wiki/File:The_Crusader_States_in_1135.svg

The success of the First Crusade set in motion a series of political developments that would come to greatly influence matters in Europe. The positive outcome of the campaign was more due to the instability of the Muslim kingdoms rather than to the military brilliance of the Europeans. When the Islamic world retaliated, it became clear that hanging onto the newly established Latin Kingdoms would be no easy task, mostly due to the lack of Christian manpower, the lust to constantly expand and take over more territories, and the political struggles between the envious Frankish nobility.

One by one, the Christian outposts of the Levant, some of them amongst the most marvelous fortifications of the known world of the time, would be lost, and subsequent campaigns to reclaim them would end in failure. In 1244, Jerusalem would be captured for good by the Muslims, and no other expedition would capture it again. In 1281, the magnificent city of Acre, the last Christian foothold in the Levant, fell.

The Crusades were ultimately an unsuccessful endeavor, largely because its whole model was deeply flawed, as it was based on unrealistic expectations and owed much to luck. The logistical challenges of organizing such long expeditions cost European leaders a lot of money for a relatively unfruitful yield. As time went by, people dared to venture out on a Crusade to find glory and attain wealth, but they saw it less as a spiritual mission. Those people who got to the Holy Land and returned home victorious were rare. Back home, they were regarded as living legends. The Latin Kingdoms themselves, which were supposed to cooperate and defend against the Muslim threat, fell out with each other, refusing to aid each other militarily. Eventually, the flow of professional soldiers to the Holy Land decreased.

The Crusades had several long-lasting social and political implications for Europe. Firstly, they reasserted the status quo of the papacy. The pope had always been a spiritual leader who dabbled in politics, but he was increasingly regarded as a powerful political figure during the Crusades and after them. It seemed as if he gave a general direction to Christendom, something that he had done before the Crusades but which materialized more clearly in the continuous urging and blessing of European leaders to fight for Christ.

In addition, the Crusades were important in reimagining and developing the European concept of knighthood. Over the course of the Crusades, knights became respected as the best warriors in Europe. An ideal knight was virtuous, brave, and, above all, Christian. The Catholic military orders helped a great deal in the development of this concept. Members of legendary organizations like the Knights Templar and the

Knights Hospitaller were some of the best and most renowned warriors in the known world. Over time, they exponentially increased their power and influence thanks to gracious donations from European lords who believed they were aiding organizations that were keeping the Holy Land safe.

The military orders would survive for centuries after the loss of the Holy Land. The Templars, who became too rich and powerful for their own good, would be brutally persecuted, first in France and then in the rest of the world. They were charged with blasphemy and satanism. Their possessions, which included numerous estates and whole castles (not to speak of the money), were seized. The Hospitallers were forced to leave the Holy Land and relocate to Cyprus and then Rhodes, where they would be a thorn in the side of the Ottomans. The Hospitallers later moved to Malta, which they built up as one of the most fortified places in Europe. They would be respected centuries after being expelled from the Holy Land and would eventually abandon their military endeavors and devote themselves to charity, returning to their origins of running a Christian hospital in Jerusalem. The Teutonic Order, the third of the "big three," would eventually find its place on the coast of the Baltic in northeastern Europe. An order of Germans, the Teutons established themselves at Marienburg and eventually came to possess their own sovereign state, fighting in the name of Catholicism against the pagans of the region.

The Fall of Constantinople

Western Christendom ultimately failed to gain anything meaningful with the Crusades. After more than two hundred years of struggle and constant expeditions to the Levant, European kingdoms realized they had largely wasted their time since no material gains had been acquired. The papacy perhaps benefitted the most, at least when it came to increasing status. The papacy cemented itself as the most respected international institution. The popes considered themselves to be the spiritual and political guides of Christian European nations, although this assertion was not fully correct. In truth, most people who answered the papal call of "Deus Vult" ("God wills it") were motivated by their own personal reasons, in addition to the belief that they were doing the right thing in the name of Christ. Nevertheless, over the next centuries, the papacy would try to impose itself on European nations to the extent that it had during the age of the Crusades. And while endless campaigning did have its costs on European economies, the Crusades eventually precipitated, perhaps unintentionally, the fall of the Byzantine Empire in 1453.

We have already mentioned the "actual" reason behind the launch of the Crusades: the Byzantines' call for help against the Turks. In fact, the Turks, who had migrated from central Asia and ran over Persia, the Caucasus, and Mesopotamia, adopting Islam in the process, had pressured the Byzantine Empire. By about 1100, the heart of Anatolia had been lost to the central Asian conquerors, who, much like their ancestors and successors, were masters of the horse but not exactly skilled in diplomacy or administration. The early Crusades certainly relieved some of the pressure on Constantinople, but the incohesive decisions of the Latins and their quarrels with each other did not produce the positive results the Byzantines had hoped for.

The Turks were not the only trouble the Byzantine Empire faced. Constantinople was challenged by a rising power in Italy: Venice. The most successful post-Roman Italian city-states became a republic that elected its ruler, the doge. Venice had a favorable defensive position and access to the sea, which led to its long and famous maritime tradition. Since the early 9th century, Venetians were under the protection of the Byzantine emperor, enjoying many privileges in the empire and even helping Constantinople fight off the Normans in southern Italy and Greece. However, the growing strength of Venice coincided with the gradual decline of Byzantine dominance in the eastern Mediterranean. The Italian city-state built a large navy and traded extensively with North Africa and Palestine, where Venetians were received better than the Byzantine merchants. By the 12th century, the Venetian Republic slowly replaced Constantinople as the most dominant power in the eastern Mediterranean and no longer acted as its vassal. It grew its holdings to include the Dalmatian and Istrian coasts and established many fortified trading outposts in southern Greece and the Aegean. Venice became increasingly independent and, noticing the declining strength of Constantinople, increasingly hostile to its former suzerains.

What broke the back of the Byzantine Empire was the Fourth Crusade (1202–1204), when the Crusading Latins set out to campaign against the Muslims in Egypt and Palestine but changed their course and attacked and sacked Constantinople. Venice had negotiated with the Crusaders prior to the expedition, agreeing that it would lend them ships to get to Jerusalem, but the leaders of the Crusade were unable to pay the price that had been agreed upon. So, Venice proposed that the Crusaders help take the rebellious Catholic city of Zara on the Adriatic coast, to which the Crusaders reluctantly agreed since they had no other choice, having come to Italy all the way from France and the Holy Roman Empire. Zara was swiftly recovered for Venice, after which the Crusaders were supposed to continue their way to Jerusalem.

However, the Crusaders met with Byzantine Prince Alexios Angelos in 1203. Alexios requested that the Crusaders make a stop in the city before reaching the Levant. He needed help in the succession dispute that had been going on in the empire. Having managed to agree with some of the Crusaders, he led them to Constantinople, which was taken relatively easily. However, not a year later, Alexios was deposed by a popular uprising, which ultimately led to the Crusaders sacking Constantinople in April 1204.

The sack of Constantinople was a harsh blow to the Byzantine Empire, which never quite managed to recover its former strength after the incident. The Crusaders, who desecrated the Hagia Sophia and stole golden monuments and statues, decided to remain in Constantinople, establishing the Latin Empire in its place, which would last until 1261 when the capital was recovered by Emperor Michael Palaeologus VIII with the help of mercenary Turks. The replacement of the Byzantine Empire with the Latin Empire was nominal since the Crusaders only temporarily controlled the capital and its surrounding areas, leading to the establishment of Byzantine successor states centered around Nicaea, Epirus, and Trebizond, as well as other regional duchies in Greece and the Balkans. Although the reestablishment of imperial power in 1261 gave the old empire some hope, it would not be long until new challengers emerged.

During the Crusades, the Turkish Sultanate of Rum, located in Asia Minor, had been a thorn in the side of the Byzantines. From the 13th century onward, the Turkish invaders had already established themselves in Anatolia and had dominated the Greeks time and time again, but they soon were unable to keep up a united state, leading to the creation of several regional Turkish powers right at the Byzantine doorstep called beyliks. Having dubbed themselves ghazis—holy warriors who fought to spread Islam to the non-religious infidel—one of the Turkish lords, Osman, would slowly start to emerge as the most powerful ghazi in the region. After consolidating his power and taking control of the lands around the Sakarya River in northwestern Anatolia, Osman founded a dynasty that would last until the 20th century. The Ottoman Empire became the largest and the most dangerous of all Anatolian beyliks, directly challenging the Byzantine presence in the region and pressuring the empire from the east while Venice was putting pressure from the west.

In the mid-14th century, the realms under Ottoman control had spread to the other side of the Bosphorus into Europe, and Ottoman ships began to control crucial maritime routes in the Dardanelles, essentially cutting off Constantinople from the rest of the Mediterranean, which was a direct hit to Constantinople's power. The Greeks could do little against the Ottomans since they were outmatched every time their armies fought. In 1389, the Ottomans managed to defeat the coalition of Bulgaria, Serbia, and Albania, establishing their suzerainty over these lands and basically sandwiching the territories under imperial control by the 1400s.

The Byzantine Empire was abandoned by the rest of Christendom. Religious, cultural, and political differences slowly led to the total isolation of Constantinople from Europe, so when Constantinople needed the West's help the most, the West wasn't willing to help. Europeans were done fighting the Crusades, having known their detrimental effects, and the Western nations were not ready to come to the aid of an Orthodox nation.

The end of the Eastern Roman Empire came in 1453. In the early 1400s, the Ottomans were forced to deal with the new Mongol threat in the East, which relieved some pressure on the Byzantines. However, the Ottomans managed to refocus their attention on the most prized city in the world: Constantinople. Having stood for about one thousand years as the most prosperous city in all of Europe, Constantinople was the final remnant of the glorious Roman Empire, and it was one of the best-defended cities. Nevertheless, Ottoman Sultan Mehmed II, one of the most brilliant military commanders the empire would ever have, was determined to take the city and finally put an end to the Byzantines. Knowing that Constantinople had been abandoned by the West and that it did not have sufficient resources to put up a good fight to defend itself, Mehmed's siege was relatively quick, thanks to his huge cannons that bombarded the city's walls for two months.

Eventually, in late May 1453, Ottoman troops stormed Constantinople, decisively defeating Emperor Constantine XI's forces and heading straight to the Hagia Sophia, which was converted into a mosque. It was meant to serve as a symbol of Muslim victory over their long-standing enemy.

Just like that, the Byzantine Empire came to an end. It managed to last about a millennium after the fall of the Western Roman Empire, but its glory was never the same as it had been in the early days of the Roman Empire.

The fall of Constantinople was historic, as it marked the heyday of a new European superpower, which had a different religion than the rest of Europe and traditions that came from Asia. The Ottoman Empire would soon come to be in possession of much of southeastern Europe, posing a direct threat to the rest of the Christian continent.

The collapse of the Byzantine Empire was the end of an era. It was the end of the High Middle Ages, which marked a paradigm shift in the history of Europe. What came next was a European period of innovation, progress, and stability, but it was also a period of war and conquest.

Chapter 6 – The Renaissance

European Kingdoms

The year 1453 is a great date to start talking about the vast social, political, and, above all, cultural changes that would take place in Europe. The period known as the Renaissance, which means "rebirth," was just as influential in the history of Europe as the early medieval era, which would come to be referred to as the Dark Ages during the Renaissance.

The Renaissance lasted from the 13th century up until the 17th century in many places, and it accelerated the processes that have produced the cultural heritage that we identify the continent with today. It also laid the foundations for a revised version of what it meant to be European, and its large-scale societal transformation left a mark on the great thinkers who would follow the early Renaissance years.

Before we dive deep into what the Renaissance actually meant for different aspects of European life, we should first talk about the political state of the continent at the time of the fall of Constantinople. By then, the map of Europe had undergone a series of changes, with several kingdoms' borders largely remaining along similar lines for centuries to come. This, in turn, influenced the later political power struggles between these states.

All in all, it was the heyday of European monarchies. European states were kingdoms or, in the case of the HRE, empires, with an all-powerful sovereign at the top of the hierarchy followed by a series of persons of varying social standings based on their birth. Having managed to settle down after a rather chaotic age, royal families, nobility, aristocracy, and other social divisions were in place and were to remain in place for many centuries. For the most part, they were left largely unchanged. Kings enjoyed great advantages, including the prestigious, almost mythical aura that surrounded them. The different administrative and legislative tasks were often handled by local institutions, assemblies, and courts in relation to the feudal social structure. Still, none quite had the power to overpower the king or queen.

Two places that embodied this state of being the best, as the nations had been unified around a central sovereign stably for centuries, were England and France, whose borders have stayed relatively similar to what they were like in the early Renaissance years. In these two kingdoms, hereditary succession and centralized power could be seen more clearly than in other places.

In France, the Capetian dynasty managed to maintain an unbroken control of the crown from the 10th to the 14th century. With Paris as its capital, the Kingdom of France was large and powerful, and the French kings were reliant on the nobles who were in charge of different provinces stretching from the English Channel in the north to the Pyrenees in the south and from the coast of the Atlantic in the west to the Rhine and Rhone rivers in the east. The French made the system work, unlike their German neighbors in the HRE, who had troubles with the imperial succession.

In England, the Normans managed to establish a rather stable monarchy after the conquest of 1066. English lords, earls, and barons assumed important roles and continued to play them for years to come. One obvious advantage England had was the fact that it was separated from the rest of the continent by a body of water, giving it much-needed security when continental Europe was torn to pieces by warfare. Crossing the English Channel to mount an invasion on England, at least after 1066, seemed less feasible, especially since the Scandinavians had given up on long-distance Viking-like raids and had settled down as Christian kings themselves. Thanks to this, English kings were able to consolidate their power over the more fragmented and less developed societies of Wales, Ireland, and Scotland, its immediate neighbors.

Interestingly enough, England and France would emerge as two of the most famous European rivals. This largely began due to English territorial claims in France, thanks to their Norman ancestors who controlled the northern province of Normandy and some western French lands. The struggle between the French and the English in the 14th century has come to be known as the Hundred Years' War, although it was a sporadic conflict between 1337 and 1453. To this day, it remains one of the most iconic wars of medieval Europe.

Throughout the course of the war, which took place almost completely on the French side of the Channel, the English came to periodically be in possession of almost all of western France. They came dangerously close to taking over Paris and the whole of France itself. Many alliances were forged throughout the war, like the one between England and Portugal and France and Scotland. The rivalry that was established between the two sides would shape the course of western European politics for a long time.

However, by 1500, England had lost all the territories it had managed to gain in France except for Calais. France slowly licked its wounds, and the monarchy reconsolidated its hold over the provinces.

The Hundred Years' War is more important for European history not because it altered the political geography of the continent but because it was, perhaps surprisingly for both nations, the first real push toward the formation of their respective national identities. This happened in France and England far earlier than in other European kingdoms, which would eventually embrace the concept of a nation-state.

By the late 15th century, great developments had taken place in Iberia, where the Reconquista was coming to a close. Iberian kingdoms had managed to almost completely push the Arabs out of the peninsula, thanks to, in part, the fervent cooperation and help they got from the Catholic military orders. The old Kingdom of Asturias, which had been established in the north as the first Christian Iberian kingdom after the Arab conquest of the peninsula, was reborn as the Kingdom of Castile and León.

In the east, the Kingdom of Aragon had united Catalonia, Zaragoza, and Valencia and had managed to pressure the Muslims out of Seville. In 1479, the crowns of Aragon and Castile were unified after the royal marriage between Ferdinand of Aragon and Isabella of Castile. The first united Spanish state was born. In the west, the Portuguese kingdom emerged, although it was tied to its Spanish neighbors while still managing to retain its independence in the most turbulent of times.

By the dawn of the 16th century, Catholic Spain and Catholic Portugal were the masters of Iberia. Forged in blood against a common enemy, the crowns of these two kingdoms would be relatively stable. The struggle against the Muslims would emphasize the role of the Catholic Church more in Spain and Portugal than in other monarchies of Europe.

Much less stability and cohesiveness were to be found in the Holy Roman Empire, where there was total political chaos. Initially, the imperial office had been closely tied to Rome, but this relationship started to disappear over time. The emperor, elected by a college of principalities, was supposedly the sovereign over hundreds of smaller states, principalities, provinces, and free cities, which included territories in modern-day Germany, Austria, Poland, Denmark, Italy, France, Switzerland, and the Low Countries. In reality, however, the emperor was much more dependent on the mercy and cooperation of his subordinates than, say, in France or England due to the many regional differences and the difficulty of effectively exercising imperial control in these regions. The emperor possessed his own lands, but those would be scattered all throughout the empire. The imperial capital shifted often. Aachen, Frankfurt, Prague, Innsbruck, Palermo, and Vienna were all seats of the Holy Roman emperor. Germany was largely left without a unifying national identity until as late as the 1800s.

Most importantly, however, in 1273, the throne of the Holy Roman Empire was assumed by the Austrian Habsburg family, which was perhaps the most famous (or infamous) family in the history of Europe. After more than a century of struggles, the Habsburgs managed to assert their power after 1438, providing emperors almost in perfect succession until the empire came to an end in 1806. Even after that, the dynastic and family ties of the Habsburgs made them kings and queens of many different European states, most importantly of the Austro-Hungarian Empire.

A rather similar situation was present in Italy, which had been affected the most by the power vacuum left after the collapse of the Roman Empire. The north was first dominated by the Holy Roman Empire, including Rome itself, while the south had been reconquered by Constantinople during the reign of Justinian. Imperial authority in the Apennine Peninsula began to slowly dwindle, and the lords of these lands eventually came to be challenged by the northern Lombards, the Arabs, and the Normans. Additionally, the pope himself was in charge of much of Italy for centuries, ruling the Papal States.

Despite this, Italy's decentralized political structure was not on the same level as the HRE, and it contained easily distinguishable states and city-states for much of the medieval era. The Republic of Venice is a good example of a strong Italian city-state that slowly expanded its power and became a dominant actor in the Mediterranean. There was also the Republic of Genoa, another city-state with a merchant tradition, the duchies of Milan and Palermo, and the republics of Florence and Pisa.

These city-states operated largely similarly to the ancient Greek city-states, controlling their surrounding territories but not much more than that. From time to time, they engaged in conflicts and alliances with each other, as well as with foreign powers that tried to impose their authority on them. Surprisingly, by the 1500s, Italy was relatively stable, with not a lot of destructive wars on the scale of, for example, the Hundred Years' War. An overarching sense of hope for the return of the glorious Roman Empire existed, but few dared to try to embark on a mission to unite the peninsula. The economic and political stability of Italy, even though it was fragmented, meant the stage was set for a wave of cultural revival that would slowly spread to the rest of Europe.

Meanwhile, a series of complex political developments influenced the state of affairs in Russia. Kievan Rus' declined in the 13th century after the brutal Mongol invasions, which eventually resulted in the destruction of Kiev in 1240. Most urban centers of the Rus' were depopulated, and the sociopolitical clock was considerably turned back. For the next couple of centuries, the Tatar Yoke, as the period of Mongol domination of Russia would come to be referred to, resulted in the gradual change in Russian society. The center of the Russian civilization shifted more to the northeast to the newly emerging Principality of Muscovy.

Russian princes, now under the suzerainty of the Mongol khans, were too disoriented and focused on squabbling with each other. They did not make any significant progress toward reunification until Muscovy was strong enough to lead the charge of expelling the Mongols in the late 14th century. Eventually, the once-great Mongol Empire became fragmented due to dynastic disputes, and Muscovy was able to consolidate enough power to become the new Kiev of Russia, although it never quite attained the prosperity the great city on the Dnieper had once had.

These developments coincided with the fall of Constantinople in 1453, and soon, the discourse of Moscow becoming the successor to the greatest European city began to be widespread. Moscow was to be the

"Third Rome" and succeed Constantinople as the center of the true Christian faith. This religious role helped the city eclipse all other Russian principalities and led to Muscovy emerging as the grand principality, becoming the seat of the future kings of Russia.

Ivan III the Great, the man who defeated the final Mongol armies, assumed the title of tsar in 1462, consciously making a connection to the tradition of Caesars, from which the title was derived. Ten years later, he married a Byzantine princess and started to copy former imperial insignia and symbols and Russianize them. He emerged as the first full-on European autocrat in the fashion of the Byzantine emperors. In 1514, with the capture of Smolensk, the boundary of Russia was basically set. The Russian Empire would come to dominate eastern Europe and a large part of Asia in the centuries to come.

Other nations slowly started to form by the year 1500, though some had more success than others. Missionary work from the West, for example, managed to successfully spread Catholic Christianity in Poland, whose first historically recorded ruler, Mieszko I, officially adopted the religion in 966. Polish inhabitants were ethnic Slavs, but their ruler's choice to convert to Catholicism distinguished them significantly from their southeastern and eastern counterparts, who chose to embrace Orthodox Christianity. Eventually, the Polish state would lay claims to Silesia, Moravia, and Cracow, challenging the Holy Roman Empire. In the east, it would take over much of the Baltic and bear the brunt of Mongol invasions.

In the 11th century, a Christian Hungary would start to take shape after the increased Christianization of the migrating Magyar peoples. Soon, Hungary would become one of the most pious Christian kingdoms, especially since it had to coexist with a constant Ottoman threat to the south and a Mongol threat to the east.

Other Balkan states were also antagonized by the growing Ottoman Empire, which would soon control all of Europe south of the Danube, including Albania, Bulgaria, and Serbia, all of which had been Christian states before being taken over by the Ottomans. In fact, the Ottoman Empire would come dangerously close to advancing deep into central and western Europe in 1529 when Sultan Suleiman the Magnificent laid siege to Vienna. However, the Habsburg army was able to push the invading Ottomans back. Nevertheless, the Ottoman Empire managed to take over much of the former Eastern Roman Empire and was surely the most powerful state in Europe by the 1500s, at least when it came to its military.

A New Age

The Renaissance era is not fully distinct from what we call the Middle Ages. It was not a full-on cultural or social break. Instead, the term Renaissance is most often used to describe the outstanding developments in science, art, and scholarship in Europe, which approximately lasted from the late 14th to the 16th century. Although no clear line can be drawn to distinguish the Renaissance from the Middle Ages, what can be noticed increasingly from the 13th to the 14th century is a series of technological and cultural changes that led to the beginning of a new age, arguably the most influential age in European history.

The Renaissance was expressed by the rise of humanism, an ideology that focused on humans, including their nature, achievements, and spirit. Humanists, who were often secular thinkers, not religious figures, wished to bridge the gap with classical antiquity. They took the image of a wise, philosophical man capable of learning, personal improvement, and mastery of nature and made it the new ideal. According to them, this kind of man had been lost after the emergence of the Christian order, which had stressed the importance of Christian absolution and forgiveness as the ideal for all. It was a daring challenge, although it did not envision a total break from Christianity. Instead, the goal of humanists was to reassert that people could break free from the limitations of what an ideal life looked like, something that Christendom had imposed upon them. Humanists wanted people to believe in their intellectual, moral, and creative abilities and to utilize them as they had done during the times of ancient Greece and Rome. They sought the revival of a virtuous, wise, noble man who was devoted to thinking, criticism, and learning. It was to be far different from the traditional scholastic philosophy of medieval Europe, which had been based on early Christian teachings and emphasized the importance of the Christian way of life.

Italy is rightfully regarded as the birthplace of the Renaissance, although the movement would spread to virtually all of Christian Europe west of Russia, where political processes prevented it from being fully embraced like other places. In the 14th century, especially after the collapse of the Byzantine Empire, many scholars, scientists, and artists began living in Italy. We have to remember that most ancient literature and wisdom gradually faded away after the fall of the Western Roman

Empire in 476, as the barbarian invasions and constant migrations led to the loss of ancient knowledge. The classics, which were available in small numbers, were only available to the literate population, which was an extreme minority. Most clergy could read, and they favored Christian dogma.

That is not to say that the medieval world did not see its fair share of important scholars. For example, Saint Augustine's philosophy was a mix of Aristotelian and Christian influences. He criticized antiquity for its lack of a plan or purpose, which had been expressed more clearly in Christianity.

Ancient classical tradition has been preserved, although not in Europe. Classical works could actually be found in the Muslim world. During the Islamic Golden Age, which lasted from the 8th to the 13th century, Muslim scholars, scientists, mathematicians, poets, and philosophers made great advances in their fields. One thing they did was preserve the Greek and Roman classical texts and translate them into Arabic. These translations were widely circulated. These classical texts were available in the Arab and Byzantine worlds for a long time, but the isolation of these civilizations from the western European civilization essentially resulted in Catholic Europe not being familiar with them.

As these civilizations came increasingly in contact with each other, especially after the fall of Constantinople when many learned Greeks emigrated westward, taking with them their prized possessions, Western Christendom came to be more and more acquainted with the cultural heritage of the ancient world. The ancient works slowly began to be rewritten and translated into Greek, Latin, Hebrew, and eventually the different languages of the European states.

The effects of this long and tiresome process were accelerated massively with the printing press. Papermaking took off after the 11th century. It had been introduced from the East, and good-quality paper was made. In the German city of Mainz, a craftsman by the name of Johannes Gutenberg put together the first printing press, which used cast metal for typefaces and oil-based ink, in about 1450. With the new printing press, copying became a far more efficient and quicker task, which boosted the production and use of books. Although the literacy rates were initially too low, which meant the commoners could not read the translated and copied texts, the Renaissance was well under way by the 1500s in the high society circles of Europe.

The elite classes of Italy spearheaded the development of the Renaissance in all forms, most clearly when it came to art. Renaissance paintings are among some of the most remarkable in the world, and for good reason. Painters developed new advanced techniques, devoted more attention to the world that surrounded them, learned human anatomy to depict the characters more accurately, and increasingly focused on mythological or biblical themes. The Renaissance brought a massive change to medieval art, which had previously been dominated by more primitive images of Christian themes.

Artists such as Leonardo da Vinci, Raphael, Sandro Botticelli, Michelangelo, Perugino, and others led the artistic movement and created some of the best works in the history of European art. These artists would be employed by the wealthy families of Italian cities, which would commission them to create paintings for private estates and public buildings.

Florence, which was ruled by the Medici family, was the cultural center of the Renaissance before the movement started to slowly take off in the north. When the movement reached its climax in the 15th and 16th centuries, Italy could boast of having some of the most unique and innovative cultural developments in Europe, which were heavily influenced by classical antiquity and the desire to learn and attain perfection.

The Reformation

The Renaissance also gave birth to one of the most vital developments in the history of Christianity: the Protestant Reformation. Accidental as it may have been, the roots of the Reformation and the criticism directed toward the Catholic Church had existed long before Martin Luther was born. In the 1500s, the church maintained its role as the most important institution in the life of Europeans, especially when it came to the lower classes. People believed greatly in the notion of life after death and wished to attain salvation. However, it was known that the religious establishment did not (or could not) serve the needs of all, being discriminatory toward some while favoring others. The need for ecclesiastic reform existed, but the Catholic Church's authority had never been challenged quite in the same way as during the Reformation.

One obvious problem was that, despite the wealth and grandeur, which was borderline extravagant nature, the church had become increasingly reliant on money. During the height of medieval Catholicism, the purchase of indulgences was a regular occurrence. Laymen who deeply believed in life after death and the authority of the clergy were encouraged to approach the church, pay a sum of money, and receive an indulgence that partially or fully forgave their sins. The church made an egregious amount of money by selling indulgences. As time passed, the practice became suspicious. Clergymen, although usually the most educated in local societies, were becoming less "professional," lazily studying the holy texts and enjoying privileged lives throughout Europe.

Martin Luther, a German Augustinian monk, formulated his *Ninety-five Theses* in protest against the church and nailed it to the door of the castle church in Wittenberg in 1517. He had personally experienced the injustices and illogicalities in the day-to-day practices of the church. In his eyes, some practices were absurd, such as the sale of indulgences, which, in his opinion, required reflection.

Luther had been a devout Catholic and an enthusiastic scholar. He had been to Rome and became a monk at the age of twenty-one. He spent a lot of his time studying the scriptures and contrasted their content with the realities of his day, coming to the conclusion that the church had diverted quite a bit from the holy writings. Luther was furious that religious figures were basically deceiving and taking advantage of commoners on a daily basis, and he wanted the system to change. The *Ninety-five Theses* he nailed on the church door was also sent to the archbishop of Mainz, who sent it to the pope in Rome.

Despite major opposition from religious and political leaders, Luther managed to spread his arguments very quickly, thanks to the printing press and the well-digestible structure of his writings. He criticized many aspects of the Catholic Church, but he most importantly argued that faith alone was enough for salvation. If a person was devout enough, they could and would attain salvation; there was no need for indulgences or even the church itself. Luther called for the decentralization of the institution and for the transition of power from the hands of the clergy to the laypeople. He wanted there to be a more direct and precise interpretation of the scriptures since he fully believed that the essence of Christianity was best encapsulated in the Bible.

Soon, Luther's arguments found widespread appeal throughout Germany. It was clear that he was making sense to the people. Other religious scholars started to formulate their own visions, and influenced clergymen began to teach according to the new doctrines that were formulated in the most recent "sects" of Christianity. Lutheranism, Calvinism, Baptism, and other movements were considered to be Protestant, and they spread around continental Europe in the 16th century onward.

That is not to say that the Catholic Church did not try to silence Luther and other Protestants. What saved Luther was the super-fragmented political structure of the Holy Roman Empire. German princes were all Catholic, but some were more sympathetic toward Lutheranism and other Protestant congregations than others due to a multitude of reasons. They converted to Protestant religions to assert their authority and stand out, as well as to overcome the tenuous authority of the church, which usually enjoyed privileges and benefits from the political leaders. Many princes supported Luther when he was summoned before the Diet of Worms in 1521, where he fervently defended his views and refused to apologize.

Even though Holy Roman Emperor Charles V declared Luther an outlaw in 1521 and Pope Leo X excommunicated him, the reformer nevertheless continued to live under the protection of the sympathetic Frederick of Saxony at the Wartburg Castle in Eisenach until his death in 1546. There, Luther continued to write and study the texts, aiming to perfect his doctrine and enlighten as many Christians as he could.

Eventually, at the Peace of Augsburg in 1555, it was officially acknowledged that German princes could choose between Catholicism and Protestantism, starting a new phase in the history of Christianity.

Protestantism came in numerous different forms, and they were all distinct when it came to questions over doctrine or the practice of religion. Some movements were more radical than others. The Swiss city of Geneva gave birth to Calvinism, which was propagated by John Calvin. Calvinism was perhaps the second most influential Protestant movement after Lutheranism.

Protestant movements slowly started to spread around Europe, but they found more success in some places than in others. France and Spain, for example, remained fervent advocates for traditional Catholicism, eventually emerging as principal allies to the pope, whereas the Netherlands and Scandinavia embraced Protestantism with open arms. In England, Henry VIII abandoned Catholicism in 1534 and proclaimed himself the head of the Church of England because he wanted to get a divorce from his wife, something that had been prohibited by Rome. The newly created Anglican Church would remain part of England for centuries to come, even if it initially faced a lot of political and social barriers.

The Protestant Reformation was deeply rooted in the humanist teachings of the Renaissance and, on the whole, embodied the best aspects of the era. It had come about after rigorous studying and had branched out, democratizing itself and the faith, as a whole, to all believers. Protestant congregations were far less strict and discriminatory and eventually came to emphasize a sense of personal struggle in addition to a sense of community. In many places, like Germany, Protestantism became associated with an early national identity, unlike Catholicism, which had been an all-encapsulating, more general religion.

Protestant teachings spread quickly, and they stimulated another wave of learning that never quite ceased. Religious texts were finally translated into local languages and made readily available to the common people, who had previously only relied on the word of the clergy to learn the Word of God. It was a great age of education and cultural advancement, although it would also lead to bloody wars and oppression.

The Age of Science and Exploration

Last but not least, one of the most important consequences of the Renaissance was advances in the natural sciences and technology, which led to a better understanding of the physical world. We have to remember that medieval Europe had limited knowledge of Earth and had not really tried to explore its boundaries beyond the Near East and Africa. Roughly speaking, for 15th-century Europe, the world was made up of three landmasses: Europe, Asia, and Africa. How far Africa or Asia stretched was still a mystery, and although some European merchants would be lucky enough to trade goods that came from the faraway lands of India and China, no effort had been made to establish reliable contact with these almost mythical places. In fact, European culture had spread all the way to western India during the conquests of Alexander. For example, in modern-day Afghanistan, Hellenistic archaeological heritage still survives, but few Europeans in the early medieval era dared to try to go further than that. An average European never even left their province during their lifetime and lived boring, dangerous, and repetitive lives. That was before the height of the Renaissance, though.

With an increased focus on learning and with scientific and technological developments being made in the 14th century onward, more people began to look beyond Europe. About a century later, in the late 15th century, Europeans were reliably crossing the Atlantic and started to colonize the Americas.

What made this possible, in addition to Europeans' curiosity, passion, and other feelings revived by Renaissance humanism, was the tough political situation. The Ottoman Empire, which had taken over the east and was knocking at the door of western Europe, had basically monopolized control of the overland trade routes that had connected Europe with India and China for centuries. In the north, the political instability and the remote and unexplored forests of Russia were far too dangerous to rely on. Thus, many Europeans started to believe they needed to find other routes to get to Asia. They needed to find a way to circumvent the trade monopoly of the Ottomans and revive Eurasian trade.

Developments in navigation and ship design made these aspirations come true. New hull and sail designs of European cog ships made it possible for experienced sailors to travel long distances and navigate severe weather conditions. When it came to navigation, the introduction of the compass made a big difference. Before the compass, which arrived in Europe in the 13th century, most likely from China, the old Viking ways of traversing the seas, which utilized the Pole Star, were the most advanced. In fact, the Vikings had managed to cross the Atlantic Ocean using this method in the heyday of their exploratory era. However, the Renaissance and the urge to learn made it possible to better understand geography and navigation. Cartography and hydrography became valuable professions, utilizing new, more advanced geometry and mathematics. Professionals would often be employed by European royal courts, as well as accompany merchant ships.

A large-scale paradigm shift was happening. Scientists like Copernicus and Galileo stunned people when they suggested the heliocentric model of the universe existed, which meant the Earth and other planets circled the sun instead of the Earth being the center of the universe, something that had been long accepted. This is not to speak of new military technology that was introduced from the East. Gunpowder was the hottest commodity for European militaries during the Renaissance, and guns and cannons would come to replace older weapons due to their effectiveness.

The prospect of new discoveries, wealth, and glory motivated many to invest in maritime exploration. Interestingly, the Europeans who made great advances in this regard in the 1400s were not the Genoese and the Venetians, two of the most well-established naval powers of Europe. Instead, they were the Portuguese and the Spanish, two stable Christian monarchies that had just managed to solidify their position in Iberia and were looking for new ways to expand and dominate. They were also the closest to the ocean and the western coast of Africa, which could provide these Christian kingdoms with the ability to orchestrate an unexpected strike at the North African Muslims.

Thus, the Portuguese went west, reaching the Canary Islands with the support of Prince Henry, who got his nickname "the Navigator" due to his investment in naval exploration. Then, they turned south, exploring the western coast of Africa, where they hoped to find gold. Portuguese explorers also took Catholic friars with them, who made sure that the "heathen" Muslims were converted. This led to the pope blessing the explorers' actions. The pope was adamant about spreading Catholicism to new territories, especially at the height of the Catholic-Orthodox Schism and the ever-present Muslim threat.

Slowly, the Portuguese continued their exploration southward, sticking to the western African coast and never truly moving deep inland. By the 1440s, they had reached the Madeira Islands and Cape Bojador, and a few years later, they reached Cape Verde. The Portuguese established themselves as west as the Azores. By the 1450s, Portugal had built its first permanent fort in Senegal, which ensured a safer connection between the homeland and the explored lands. In 1473 or 1474, they crossed the equator, and in due time, they reached the Cape of Good Hope, the southern tip of Africa, where they also established trading posts and forts. It was a magnificent achievement. To their east was the Indian Ocean, where the Arabs and Turks had traded luxury goods like spices for centuries. Finally, in 1498, Portuguese explorer Vasco da Gama managed to fully circumnavigate Africa and drop his anchor on the western coast of India. This promised a bright future for the Portuguese, who slowly started to get involved in the trade of Eastern valuables, bringing them home and supplying them to Europe.

Seeing Portugal's success, the Spanish decided to get in on the exploration game. Thanks to newly attained geographic and navigation knowledge, the Spanish Crown funded expeditions that followed the western coast of Africa. Of course, perhaps the most important Spanish expedition was that of Christopher Columbus in 1492. A passionate Genoese navigator and skilled sailor, Columbus believed that if Earth was really spherical, he could reach Asia by sailing westward. This would, in turn, open up an array of new opportunities for Europe.

To obtain the resources for his daring journey, Columbus first approached King John II of Portugal. After the Portuguese monarch rejected the idea, deeming it too impossible to be carried out, Columbus then asked the Spanish Crown. Queen Isabella of Spain commissioned Columbus the ships and gave him permission to sail under the Spanish flag. The rest was history.

After about seventy days of journeying westward with three ships, Columbus and his crew finally discovered land after an array of setbacks. However, instead of finding Asia, Columbus made landfall in The Bahamas; he had reached the Western Hemisphere, stumbling upon the Caribbean islands on his way to India. Unknowingly, he dubbed the islands he discovered the West Indies, fully believing in the fact that he had reached the coast of India. The Native American inhabitants of the islands were called Indians, a name that stuck for centuries after Columbus died. Columbus then led his crew to Cuba, briefly exploring the Caribbean basin. He left some men behind before deciding to go back to Spain. Of course, he did not know it, but he had discovered a completely new world.

Unlike the Portuguese, who had carefully inched forward year after year along the western African coast, Columbus had made a great leap all the way across the Atlantic, reaching the Americas. He could not have possibly imagined that a whole new landmass lay there and would prevent him from reaching Asia by sailing westward, although his theory, as we all know, was not incorrect. Columbus just thought the world was much smaller than it actually was.

Triumphantly returning home from his journey, Columbus requested more ships and crew. He made three more expeditions to the West Indies, gradually discovering more and more of the Caribbean and the eastern coast of the North American continent. Other Spanish expeditions also took off, reaching different islands and establishing their presence there. The Age of Exploration was under way.

The scope of this book does not allow us to cover the story of early European colonization of the Americas fully, despite its utmost importance to the history of Europe and the rest of the world. What we need to address is the fact that European colonizers slowly started to explore more and more of the New World, coming into contact with completely new and alien civilizations. The Native Americans were not similar to Asian peoples. They were primitive, at least in some regards, and the colonizers were quick to realize that.

Despite their primitiveness, the land the natives inhabited was rich with valuable resources, including gold, which became a prime target for the Europeans, who started to conquer and subjugate the natives. In the next few decades, the Aztec, Maya, and Inca civilizations in Mexico, Central America, and Peru were taken over by European settlers, who enslaved the natives and seized their riches for themselves. Great American cities like Tenochtitlan and Cuzco were occupied by the Spanish, and what is now Brazil was taken over by the Portuguese.

Soon, France, England, and the Netherlands would try their luck in colonization, leading to the establishment of new colonies in North America, Africa, India, and East Asia. By then, Portuguese explorer Ferdinand Magellan had completed his journey from Europe to India, circumnavigating the world and returning to Portugal (although Magellan himself did not fully make the trip). New geographical discoveries encouraged more Europeans to try their luck at colonization, and new lands were claimed left and right. Europe's stern military tradition and technological superiority won the Europeans countless wars over the native populations by the 1600s.

Soon, it was becoming clear that a new Eurocentric vision of the world had emerged, according to which European civilization and culture stood higher than other, more primitive cultures. Still, although "European" ideas and people were beginning to feel more and more important, there was still much to discover, explore, and think about. The Renaissance revived the cultural and material spirit of Europe. The stage was now set for bigger things to occur.

Chapter 7 – Wars, Revolutions, and Expansion

Counter-Reformation and the Habsburgs

The Protestant Reformation and the beginning of European colonization of the previously unknown world had major ripple effects on the political state of the continent from the 1500s onward. We have to remember that despite all the cultural and material merits of the Renaissance, much of Europe's social situation had stayed the same. European states were monarchies. They were often decentralized and reliant on the cooperation of the nobility. Social hierarchies were as fragmented as ever, and the Renaissance was largely unable to alter that. There were no considerable differences in the lives of peasants in the 1200s and the 1400s, for example, as long as we don't account for slight improvements in agricultural technology. Wars, intrigue, and unrest continued throughout Europe, even as the artists of the Renaissance produced some of the most amazing works in the history of art.

Thus, before we move on to the larger intellectual and cultural achievements that would enter European discourse in the later centuries, it is perhaps wise to summarize the political developments that took place when the Renaissance was still at its height.

The most obvious development was a series of religious wars caused by the new schism in Christianity. The emergence of Protestantism, with all of its different movements, caused a great deal of unrest in the previously united Catholic western Europe. This was most apparent in the Holy Roman Empire, where the decentralized political structure resulted in intermittent wars between the princes who wanted to convert to Protestantism or wished to remain Catholic. The conflict was finally resolved with the Peace of Augsburg of 1555, which can be considered the beginning of the end of united European Christendom.

The papacy vehemently tried to oppose the potential long-term outcome of Europe's religious fragmentation with the so-called Counter-Reformation. The Counter-Reformation was a movement of institutional and doctrinal reassessment and innovation within the Catholic Church aimed at solidifying the religion's foundations and clearly identifying its allies around the continent. Roman Catholicism would become more disciplined and stricter so as not to allow for another slip-up in the future like the one that had led to the Reformation. It would quickly identify and punish heresy wherever it could, eventually resulting in the establishment of the Papal Inquisition and the issue of a list of banned books in 1557.

The immediate effect of the Counter-Reformation was a renewed movement to try and pressure the Protestant European states. Still, what dominated European international relations in the 16th century was dynastic and economic struggles, although religious factors certainly played a role in the justification of conflicts and in the formation of alliances. Essentially, since the 1500s marked the break from the religious unity of European Christendom, it also marked the beginning of struggles between individual states for the sake of non-religious, national reasons, although the heyday of nationalism was still quite a long way away. During the time of French Cardinal Richelieu, whose tenure we will cover later, concepts of realpolitik and *raison d'état* began to be emphasized more, meaning that states placed more importance on rational rather than spiritual factors when it came to conflict.

In the ever-changing political landscape, which was affected by the discovery and exploitation of new lands and by the Reformation, two power axes emerged. The first of these axes was centered around the Habsburg royal family. The wealthy Austrian family had come to be the rulers of the Holy Roman Empire and would increase its influence even though the influence of the emperor started to slowly decline. The Habsburgs had come into the direct possession of several German provinces and were also the masters of the Spanish Crown. In 1519, after lobbying and negotiations, Charles I Habsburg of Spain also became Charles V Habsburg of the Holy Roman Empire. He also managed to inherit the rich provinces in the Austrian Netherlands, the modern Low

Countries of Belgium and the Netherlands, thanks to a complicated succession line. Not only that, but Charles also became the ruler of Sicily, which he had inherited from his Aragonese mother, and thanks to the voyages of conquistadors in the New World, he was the ruler of extremely rich overseas territories. His brother, Ferdinand, who would succeed him as the Holy Roman emperor, also held the lands of Bohemia and Hungary, something that strengthened the family's position even more.

The second axis of power at the time was the French monarchy. Its territories were well defined, and the expulsion of the English after the Hundred Years' War had served as a driving factor to gain more power. France was also a Catholic state, although there were some Protestant enclaves that were tolerated relatively well by the monarchy. This sense of unity gave the French an advantage against the Holy Roman Empire since they could exploit the decentralized political structure of their German neighbors and influence the divisions between the princes to their advantage.

The royal House of Valois gained power in the 14th century and would eventually be replaced by the Bourbon dynasty in 1589; however, the overall unity of France was largely retained. Still, despite the seemingly cohesive political structure of France, it was nowhere near as rich and powerful as the Habsburg realms, and the Austrian family emerged as the main rivals of France after England's defeat.

King Charles VIII of France initiated the conflict against the Habsburgs when he claimed the throne of Italy in 1494 and crossed the Alps to assert his dominance. The subsequent Italian Wars between the Valois and the Habsburg dynasties lasted until 1559 and dragged in independent Italian city-states like Venice, Milan, Genoa, Florence, and Lucca. The divisions in Italy made the region an easy target for larger powers, and constant invasions set back the process of the unification of Italy for a few more centuries.

In the end, the Italian Wars gained little for France, and for Charles V Habsburg, it was a costly distraction from the more pressing events of the Reformation, which were unfolding concurrently with the struggle. Spain retained its control over southern Italy, but it came at a high cost. As for the Italian states themselves, Venice went into a rapid period of decline, while the countryside in Florence, Milan, and Genoa was ravaged.

Most dramatically, however, the wars undermined Spain's superiority. In the first half of the 1500s, the Spanish Crown had been the most prosperous, thanks to the constant flow of resources from its American colonies. In fact, by the 1550s, Spanish conquistadors had claimed lands from the southern United States all the way to Argentina. While effective tools of governance were still being implemented, the Spanish conquest of the Americas had given the monarch an unfair advantage over other states. This advantage was utilized greatly by King Charles since he was also the ruler of the Netherlands, southern Italy, and the Holy Roman Empire.

During the Italian Wars, Charles overtaxed his American subjects and even funded campaigns in Muslim North Africa in the spirit of a true Spanish Catholic monarch, continuing, at least in his opinion, the glorious Reconquista. True, Spain might not have had the internal problems associated with the Reformation since Protestantism never quite took off there, but the depletion of its treasuries was a pressing issue. Eventually, this resulted in the decline of Spain as the most dominant European power, something that was most clearly demonstrated with the break-up of the Habsburg realms after the death of Charles in 1558. His brother, Ferdinand, inherited the Austrian and German territories and was elected as the new emperor of the Holy Roman Empire, while his son, Spanish-born Philip II, became the ruler of Spain.

The Netherlands

The decline of the Spanish monarchy and its break from the overall Austro-German axis of the Habsburgs (though King Philip II was Habsburg himself) was a very important development. It resulted in a renewed Catholic identity of the kingdom, something that was advocated by King Philip, who followed in the footsteps of his father. The ideological frontiers opened up by the Counter-Reformation, as well as the fact that during the struggle in Italy, France, a traditionally Catholic nation, had briefly allied with the Muslim Ottoman Empire for a joint offensive, resulted in Spain embracing Catholicism even more. One result of this was the mass conversion of the Native American subjects and the spread of Catholic Christianity in what we now call Latin America. Another result was the Spanish Inquisition, which officially began in Castile in 1480 and soon became a tool for the Spanish Crown to brutally deal with all non-Catholic subjects of the kingdom.

Philip's strong adherence to Catholicism eventually led to a series of conflicts that once again transformed the political landscape of Europe. Troubles began to arise in the Spanish Netherlands, which Philip had inherited from his father. The region was becoming more and more Protestant. In truth, the Netherlands had long been a problematic province to govern for the Habsburgs, but since the Netherlands was one of the most urbanized, agriculturally and commercially developed, and, therefore, wealthiest lands in all of Europe, holding onto them was a priority. Philip, the determined Catholic monarch that he was, tried to impose the decrees of the Counter-Reformation, formulated at the Council of Trent, upon these highly independent and developed territories. This, when coupled with high taxation and the efforts to strengthen the central government's control at the cost of local authorities, was not received well by the Flemish cities. The Spanish Inquisition also tried to enforce Catholicism, which was the final straw. The Flemish rallied behind William of Nassau, Prince of Orange, and rebelled against the Spanish. A long struggle ensued from the 1560s to 1648; it is sometimes referred to as the Eighty Years' War.

In the end, despite some success, the Spanish were unable to keep up a prolonged military campaign in the north, and the Flemish opposition entrenched itself around the city of Antwerp, pushing back the Spanish armies to the southern countryside. The division between the still Spanish-controlled Netherlands and the rebels resulted in the establishment of the modern-day borders between Belgium and the Netherlands, which were called the United Provinces back then. Even England, which had been inactive at first, joined the Dutch. The Spanish Armada set to mount a naval invasion of Britain would be destroyed by a storm, further undermining Spanish power.

After a long stalemate, during which neither side made advances, the Peace of Münster was agreed upon between the Spanish Crown and the States General from the Seven United Provinces of the Netherlands. The new United Provinces was to be the first major republic in Europe after Venice. In due time, thanks to its cultural and economic prosperity, the Netherlands would emerge as one of the strongest naval powers in Europe, establishing colonies around the world and maintaining a strong maritime tradition. The new state was to be based on the principles of personal and provincial freedom, religious tolerance, and anti-Spanish sentiments.

The Thirty Years' War

With the decline of Spain, instability brought by the Reformation and Counter-Reformation, the emergence of new regional powers in the form of Sweden and Poland, and the ambitious intrigues of the Habsburg and the French Crowns, Europe in the 17th century would first experience what can truly be called an all-European war. The Thirty Years' War, as it would come to be known, was more of a conglomeration of several conflicts instead of one war. It would last from 1616 to 1648. The Thirty Years' War would come to redefine the political and cultural borders of Europe and introduce new power dynamics that would largely remain in place until the rise of Napoleon at the beginning of the 19th century.

It is believed that the Thirty Years' War began in 1618 before the imperial election in the Holy Roman Empire. Protestant Bohemia and its Austrian allies rebelled against future Emperor Ferdinand II, who had tried to impose Roman Catholicism upon them, essentially disregarding the terms of the Peace of Augsburg of 1555. Despite Ferdinand's success in silencing the Bohemian rebels, the conflict expanded beyond the HRE, and new actors began to get involved, justifying their entry by citing ideological factors and allegiances, although they, for the most part, joined to gain more political power.

For example, due to the chaotic political structure of the HRE, the rulers of Sweden and Denmark, who held territories that were part of the empire, quickly became involved, entering an anti-imperial alliance to undermine the emperor's power and expand their holdings. By the late 1620s, the Habsburg monarchy had been opposed by anti-Catholic and anti-imperial coalitions, including several German principalities, Sweden, and even the United Provinces of the Netherlands. Meanwhile, Catholic Spain under Philip III emerged as a natural ally to Emperor Ferdinand, the king's brother-in-law, mostly because it had already been engaged in a conflict against the Dutch. Just like that, the Eighty Years' War, which eventually resulted in Dutch independence, got tangled up in the much larger Thirty Years' War between Catholic and Protestant alliances.

Also important was the concurrent struggle between the Habsburgs and the French. The French noticed how disunited the German princes had become and sought to exploit the opportunity despite the fact that France was a Catholic monarchy. The Catholic French, under the leadership of Cardinal Richelieu, one of the most accomplished political figures in the history of Europe, had the help of Lutheran Sweden and the Calvinist Netherlands. They supported the anti-Catholic and anti-imperialist German princes' struggles against the emperor.

Richelieu, a clergyman, former foreign secretary, and eventually the chief minister of France, had climbed the ranks of power during the reign of the second Bourbon monarch of France, Louis XIII, who was only nine years old when his father, Henry IV, passed away, leaving him in charge of the country. Richelieu wanted to centralize the power of the monarchy and make France less dependent on its traditionally strong nobility. Despite his Catholic background, he was more than willing to pursue anti-Catholic policies to assert the interests of the sovereign state of France, which, in his opinion, stood higher than the Catholic state of France.

After joining the war against the Habsburgs after the Peace of Prague of 1635, according to which many German princes agreed to a ceasefire and pretty fair terms, France overwhelmed Emperor Ferdinand III and his allies, resulting in the Peace of Westphalia of 1648, which ended the Thirty Years' War.

In the end, the Peace of Westphalia turned the European cultural and power dynamics upside down. Firstly, it reconfirmed the religious plurality of the Holy Roman Empire, which had been asserted in 1555, and even extended the privileges previously given to Lutheran and Calvinist princes. The HRE, on the whole, was transformed. The Austrian Habsburgs, who continued to be emperors, now directly controlled the eastern part of the empire, including Austria, Bohemia, Silesia, Carinthia, Styria, and Tyrol. The Spanish Habsburgs, on the other hand, retained control of the Lower Netherlands (which would eventually become Belgium). Sweden also claimed some northern German provinces and even got a vote in the Imperial Diet. It was the most dominant power in the Baltic. With the decline of Spain and the Habsburgs, France started to become the most dominant power in western Europe, thanks largely to the domestic reforms of Cardinal Richelieu.

In many regards, the Thirty Years' War can be considered the final major war that happened because of the developments made during the Renaissance. It was also the first major all-out European war. More destruction was yet to come, though.

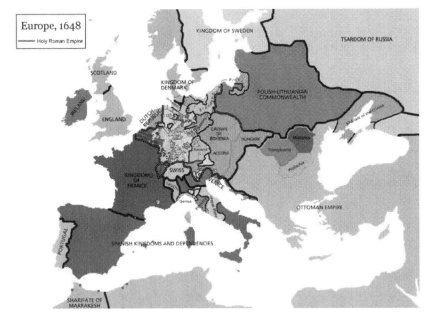

Europe after the Peace of Westphalia.
This file is licensed under the Creative Commons Attribution-Share Alike 3.0 Unported license.
Image can be found at https://commons.wikimedia.org/wiki/File:Europe_map_1648.PNG

England and the Enlightenment

While the events of the Thirty Years' War were occurring, major developments were unfolding in England. After abandoning Catholicism for the Anglican Church, England became one of the most powerful Protestant states in Europe, despite the fact that it took about three monarchs for Anglicanism to finally find a permanent place as England's official religion. Queen Elizabeth I, one of the most successful and popular rulers in English history, spearheaded English ascendancy to greatness after her coronation in 1558. Loved by the masses, she embodied the concept of a powerful monarch and managed to strengthen England politically, especially during times of war with Spain.

However, as great as Elizabeth I was, she had no heirs. James, Elizabeth's relative, would become the first king of England and Scotland. He came from the House of Stuart.

James was a very ambitious man. By the time he had become king of England, he had ruled Scotland for more than twenty years, making him a very experienced ruler. During his reign, England would start to increasingly get involved in colonization and exploration. The first Protestant missionaries would land in New England in North America, establishing a small community that would ultimately turn into the Thirteen Colonies. James made peace with Spain to stop the financial bleeding that had been brought about by the war, and he was reluctant to get involved in European affairs unless absolutely necessary, starting a long tradition of isolation. He was also the first to refer to himself as the king of Great Britain since he ruled both Scotland and England. Despite this, the Stuart line of English kings would become infamous for their differences with Parliament.

By the early 17th century, when the conflicts between the English monarchs and Parliament started to arise on a regular basis, Parliament had already been an old institution, though it did not have the power it enjoys today. Parliament became the main legislative body of the country besides the king's court and evolved after its humble beginnings during the reign of Edward I in the 1200s. English monarchs basically realized that some regional representation of distinguished persons was essential to govern the country effectively, though they never fully relied on Parliament or its laws. The king could, for example, pass his own laws whenever he pleased, though this was rather rare, or he could just dissolve Parliament.

The English Parliament had two chambers, the upper House of Lords and the lower House of Commons, and with the increased emphasis on education and professionalism that had been brought about by the Renaissance, Parliament started to be more actively involved in the domestic affairs of England. The English public also liked to vote in parliamentary elections, although only certain men over a certain income threshold could do so. In short, England was nothing like the constitutional monarchy it is today, nor did it adhere to the principles of democracy and republicanism like ancient Greece or Rome. However, in the age of absolutism, which we will discuss in detail later, it was a relatively unique monarchy.

The 1600s would come to be a decisive era for England and its parliamentary tradition, as Parliament would oppose the monarch in the English Civil War. By the time James's son, Charles I, became king in 1625, the crisis in England started to become more apparent, fueled by economic, religious, and social problems. Charles, much like many of his European contemporaries, was a firm believer in the absolute, God-given authority of kings, the "divine right of kings," so he pressured the English Parliament, which had taken important roles in administration and governance. Charles's decision to defend the United Provinces from

Spain was unpopular with Parliament, which had to account for the military expenses by overtaxing the subjects of the kingdom. The result was that Charles dissolved Parliament in 1629, not recalling it for another eleven years.

His decision in 1639 to support the introduction of the *Book of Common Prayer* in Scotland imposed the English style of worship in non-Anglican Scotland. Of course, this was met with a lot of opposition from the Scots, resulting in a rebellion known as the First Bishops' War. Charles was forced to briefly recall Parliament (known as the Short Parliament) to raise more taxes, but the ensuing conflict with Scotland ended with a Scottish victory after they took Newcastle in 1640. Charles had to recall Parliament again to fill his treasury.

The newly assembled Parliament did not dissolve for twenty years and worked vehemently to make sure that Charles's unruliness never repeated itself. It started to pass laws that reduced the powers of the king, imprisoned royal supporters, and challenged Charles's self-perceived absolute authority. When another rebellion erupted in Scotland, Parliament granted its support to the Scots, beginning the civil war between the English Royalists and Parliamentarians (also known as Roundheads).

By 1645, the Parliamentarians had gained enough support and momentum to defeat the king's armies at the decisive Battle of Naseby. In 1646, Charles was defeated, although for the next two years, great unrest occurred in England, which Charles could have reasserted his power over had he been smart. As the victorious Parliamentarians disagreed about the reforms that should be passed, Charles and his supporters rose up, only to be soon defeated. Charles was imprisoned once again and was charged with tyranny and treason in 1649. Parliament found him guilty, and Charles was beheaded.

Parliamentarian and soldier Oliver Cromwell became the leading political figure during the short interregnum period that followed. He led the army to silence rebellions that popped up throughout Britain and Ireland, defeating the Scots as well as the Irish. The republic was dubbed the "Commonwealth," but as much as Parliament tried to introduce ambitious constitutional reforms and shake up the English administrative bodies, it soon became clear England was not ready to go fully independent without a leader like Cromwell.

Despite the fact that order was restored after a decade of instability, the monarchy made a comeback in 1660 after the death of Cromwell. Parliament agreed to bring back the king, who was Charles's son, Charles II, who promised to adhere to Parliamentarian principles and tolerate religious freedom in his domains. Struggles between the king and Parliament would continue, but the future hegemon of the world was on its way to balancing an absolute ruler with a nationally representative legislative body, unlike many of its contemporary European neighbors.

The English Civil War was one of the first conscious struggles against the monarch's absolute authority and can also be considered one of the earliest products of the intellectual movement that started to take Europe by storm during the 17th and 18th centuries. This movement was known as the Enlightenment. Although historians usually pinpoint England's Glorious Revolution of 1688 as the first manifestation of the Enlightenment, when the overtly Catholic King James II was deposed in favor of Protestant William III of Orange, who was invited by prominent Englishmen to restore order, the developments of the English Civil War were certainly a prelude to it.

The Enlightenment was a byproduct of the increased zeal for learning, empiricism, and explanation brought about by the Renaissance, as well as the emergence of absolutist monarchs in Europe who tried to centralize all the power in their respective states for themselves. The experimental science of Galileo, Copernicus, Newton, and Descartes, the bravery of the Spanish and Portuguese explorers, and Martin Luther's and other reformers' struggle for religious reform showed that humanism, which had been rooted in the classical tradition and emphasized humans as being creative beings that deserved certain rights, had been correct. Reason, logic, and thought were the new ideals to be upheld. Scientific breakthroughs emphasized this very well by asserting that it was possible to find the truth by following a certain methodology, and intellectuals started to apply reasoning and experimentation to important philosophical matters.

The result was the movement we now refer to as the Enlightenment, which originated in Britain and spread to France before eventually sweeping through the whole continent. Prominent thinkers like John Locke, Thomas Hobbes, and Jean-Jacques Rousseau started to write about the existence of a social contract, an imaginary agreement between members of society about the organization of society, which had led the human race out of the anarchic and chaotic times when everyone strove for their own survival and did not cooperate. While social contract theorists might have disagreed on what was the best form of governance and societal organization, they did try to break out of the traditional way of thinking, namely the assertion that monarchs had the God-given right to rule and that their subjects should respect that at all costs.

Enlightenment thinkers started to point out that how the state should be organized was up to the people since the state was supposed to serve the interests of the people. The monarch or any other person or body responsible for governing should be held accountable for whether or not their rule served the interests of the people, even if they claimed to have the God-given right to rule.

The Enlightenment slowly emerged as a challenge to authoritarian rulers, and the events of the English Civil War and the Glorious Revolution were the first to make that clear. In England, "the people" (although it was still to be figured out who exactly they were) had not hesitated to criticize and, if needed, get rid of the monarch altogether, stressing the need for more representation and a higher form of society. Of course, the age of democracy was still a long way away, but the ascendancy of liberal and nationalist values, which would develop throughout the 19ᵗʰ century, would transform the political landscape of Europe and, later, the whole world.

European Absolutism

The newly formulated political philosophy of the Enlightenment essentially advocated for a complete paradigm shift. The notion of a social contract and of a state belonging to the will of the people were still alien concepts for late 17ᵗʰ to early 18ᵗʰ century Europeans. The only republics that had existed in Europe had been the Italian city-states, but they were oligarchies controlled by powerful, wealthy families. The United Provinces of the Netherlands had a similar structure. The Holy Roman Empire, although technically a monarchy, did elect its emperor, but only the most powerful princes were represented at the elections. Plus, the Habsburgs kept being the emperor for centuries, utilizing their influence in imperial elections. In England, even though Parliament had already been a well-respected body, it would only slowly start to accrue more power in the late 1660s, eventually resulting in the constitutional monarchy that still exists in the United Kingdom today.

Something more common was strong monarchies, with the king (rarely a queen) at the top of the hierarchy followed by persons distinguished by birth and religious clergy. As much as the Renaissance had amplified the standing of merchants, bankers, lawyers, and other professionals, the overwhelming majority of European societies were still reminiscent of the Christian, feudal, agrarian, hierarchical system that had dominated the medieval era.

Although the Spanish Empire in the 1500s, with all its colonial and European endeavors, can be considered one example of an absolutist state, France would see this kind of extremely authoritarian political system come to full fruition. In 1643, Louis XIV became king of France, rejoicing over the spoils of the Thirty Years' War and managing to assume almost total power over the judicial, economic, cultural, and legislative matters of the country. He continued, almost perfectly, the process of political centralization in France that had been started by Richelieu. Louis understood that he ruled a deeply hierarchical society, with the nobility and the clergy at the top and lowborn peasants at the bottom. Thus, he focused his attention on making sure that none of the higher classes questioned his absolute authority, granting loyal servants and allies of the Crown many privileges while still keeping them at arm's length. He was a strong defender of the Catholic Church, as he realized its potential use in governance and how it could further strengthen his position. He asserted the Catholic Church's dominance over the Protestant minorities of his kingdom called the Huguenots.

Louis had the strongest European military, which had just been victorious in an all-continental war and had humiliated its enemies. No European power dared to invade French lands, and they all respected and feared France's involvement in international affairs. Overseas, France was getting more active in colonization, with a particular focus on North America. The state's military and political strength worked greatly in Louis's favor. Although France's growing strength would be checked by an alliance made of the Dutch, English, and the Habsburgs during the Nine Years' War, the Peace of Ryswick of 1697 did not significantly weaken Louis's position.

What was even more important, at least for Louis himself and the rest of the European monarchs, was the symbolic and aesthetic aspect of absolutism, which Louis managed to perfect as well. Since he was the most important, honorable, wisest, and pious person in France, he managed to create the image of what an ideal monarch should look like, constructing luxurious palaces like Versailles, glamorizing himself and the royal family to the fullest extent, asserting the French culture and its values the most civilized and advanced, and enjoying an overly lavish lifestyle. By all means, Louis XIV was the center of France, and he led the country for more than seventy years. Controlling the political and religious affairs of his state and backed by a strong military and cultural achievements, Louis's reign was the embodiment of what absolute power looked like.

Many tried to grasp absolute authority to the extent that had been managed by Louis XIV. The Habsburgs constructed lavish palaces, but they never managed to reach the same kind of political stability as Louis. The Spanish monarchy, on the other hand, continued to decline. It increasingly became reliant financially on its colonies and struggled to assert its power. After the War of the Spanish Succession, the throne of Spain was occupied by a Bourbon, and the Spanish Netherlands was gone once and for all. Italy was as fragmented as ever, but the once-great city-states were no match for the militaries of the larger empires that surrounded them. The Kingdom of Sweden was a powerful monarchy in the north; it increasingly became involved in continental affairs, although its gains in the Baltic would constantly be challenged. Poland (officially known as the Polish-Lithuanian Commonwealth in 1569) occupied a large territory. Poland and other eastern European Christian kingdoms like Hungary were constantly challenged by the Ottomans and never reached the development levels of western European states in the 1700s. England, the United Provinces, and land-locked Portugal were focused mostly on their non-European territories, rarely and hesitantly getting involved in mainstream costly European affairs.

Interestingly, one place where absolutism manifested itself very clearly was Russia. The cultural and social changes brought about by the Renaissance never managed to reach Russia in the 15th and 16th centuries, and it was not until the accession of Tsar Peter Romanov in 1682 that other European nations started to take Russia seriously.

We have already mentioned that the Russian princes, after struggling for over two centuries under their Mongol conquerors, finally rallied behind Muscovy, beginning a new chapter in Russian history in the late 15th century. For the next two hundred years, the last members of the Rurikid dynasty, descendants of the legendary Norseman Rurik, the founder of Kievan Rus', managed to consolidate their power, some with more success than others. Despite this, the harsh geographic location of the new Russian civilization, now centered around the city of Moscow far more to the north and far more to the east than the previous center of

Kiev, made it difficult for Russia to get involved in European affairs until the latter part of the 17th century. To the east and south, the Tatar descendants of the Mongols were still a threat, but they were gradually defeated, stretching Russian claims as far east as the Ural Mountains and even beyond that. Ukraine belonged to the Cossacks, who had shaky relations with the Russian princes. To the west, with the increased power of Sweden and during the heyday of the Polish-Lithuanian Commonwealth, the Europeans were putting more and more pressure on Russia. The basin of the Black Sea and the Caucasus, the other regions for potential Russian expansion, were dominated by the Ottomans, Tatars, and Persians.

Slowly but surely, however, Russia became more and more involved in the affairs of the West, especially since it was in constant struggles over its western provinces with the Polish and the Swedish. Although a Slavic state, it had no ethnic or racial unity, but a unifying identity for the state had always been the Orthodox Church, whose importance. Moscow, as the new Orthodox (and, in the eyes of the Russians, true Christian) center of the world, grew, and the developments in the Russian Church in the 17th century and the instability that followed increased the standing of the tsar. Russian monarchs started to gain more power and influence, and a new chapter of Russian history began with the Romanov dynasty. Tsar Peter Romanov the Great, as he would come to be referred to, was perhaps the most influential figure in the history of early modern Russia. His efforts were directed toward creating a conscious break from the ambiguous Russian past and a backward, corrupt society and instead embracing progressive European principles. Reforms introduced by Peter the Great touched every aspect of Russian life.

Peter managed to centralize power in Russia to such an extent that it could certainly be comparable to the height of Louis XIV's reign. He abolished the old-fashioned local councils and installed new loyal governors in the most remote provinces to ensure a steady and reliable flow of taxes and to maintain order. He pushed for urbanization and industrialization, beginning to exploit the rich natural resources of the vast Russian lands. Peter founded new colleges and modernized the military. His love for shipbuilding and his personal experiences after his travels to the Netherlands and England were crucial in increasing Russian naval power. He encouraged learning and the abandonment of old, useless traditions. He also forced the Russian bourgeoisie to dress, speak, and behave like Europeans.

Peter managed to crush his enemies, claiming more lands in Asia, establishing relations with Persia and China, and defeating the Swedish in the Great Northern War. He seized the coasts of the Baltic and established a foothold in Finland. His crown jewel, the cherry on top, was the construction of a new capital called Saint Petersburg, located on the coast of the Baltic and modeled after the greatest European cities. Saint Petersburg would soon become the new center of Russian civilization, hosting its biggest and only port that did not freeze in the winter.

During Peter's reign, Russian society began to wake up from a deep slumber after centuries of domestic strife and instability brought about by Eastern and Western conquerors. Russia started to identify more with Europe, but it would still take about one hundred years before it would start to truly integrate itself with European society. Peter was a true autocrat, assuming the title of emperor in 1721 and greatly contributing to the radical development of his empire. The administrative, social, military, and economic reforms of his reign put Russia on the map for many Europeans. For the Russians, Peter would begin a long and, in many instances, gruesome tradition of absolutist monarchs and their tendency to try and assume centralization on his scale.

Russia became a European state where European absolutism thrived on a similar level as France. Eventually, both regimes would meet similar ends.

The French Revolution

With the rise of absolutism and the gradual stabilization of European political order after the turbulent times caused by the Reformation, the 18th century did not see many conflicts that considerably changed the political landscape of the continent. Italy was still not unified and faced increasing pressure from Habsburg Austria, which was emerging to be its own powerful state outside of the boundaries of the Holy Roman Empire. In northern Germany, a new influential actor was emerging in the form of Brandenburg-Prussia, with Berlin as its capital. Russia was expanding, gradually pushing the Ottomans and Persians out of the Caucasus and stretching its possessions deep into central Asia. The Ottoman Empire, on the whole, was a dying state, having to yield more and more of its European territories to Balkan nations due to increasing pressures from Safavid Persia. France, Britain, Spain, Portugal, and the Netherlands were mostly focused on their overseas territories, vying for more lands, trade routes, and resources.

The overall social trend of the continent was the decline of the feudal system and a sharp rise in the influence of the bourgeoisie, an elite class of wealthy commoners who wanted to gain more political power. This, in turn, caused mass wealth discrepancy and an increasingly inegalitarian society, which led to a decline in living standards.

Nowhere was this trend more apparent than in France. After the heyday of Louis XIV, French society became less hospitable for the poorer classes, especially the peasants, who were constantly lorded over by the newly emergent bourgeoisie. The peasants and poorer citizens bore the tax burden, especially after France's expensive involvement in colonial affairs and its struggle to finance overseas endeavors. French colonies, while providing resources for back home, were overshadowed by the more prosperous holdings of the British and the Dutch, who controlled most trade routes and had emerged as natural rivals to France.

To weaken the impact of its chief rival, Great Britain, France decided to support the Thirteen Colonies during the American Revolution, granting arms, money, and equipment to the American rebels, who, in the end, managed to break free from the British in 1776, establishing the United States of America. Still, despite the fact that the American Revolution had been a success and Britain's position had been weakened, France faced a deadly economic crisis and inflation, the brunt of which was borne by the poorer classes who could not deal with the rising prices and shortage of goods. In the 1780s, this was followed by a food shortage caused by a series of bad harvests. By the late 1780s, France, the most populous and most unequal country in Europe, had found itself in a terrible situation.

The turmoil of the 1700s would finally reach its peak in 1789 with one of the most influential developments in European history: the French Revolution. The economic, social, and political troubles had become too much. Additionally, the Enlightenment and what the movement advocated played a role. France had been the place where critical remarks toward the Ancien Régime had been widespread. People like Rousseau, Voltaire, Montesquieu, and others advocated for change and for the general public to be more involved in the process of governance. The success of the American Revolution was another factor. In the Thirteen Colonies, British subjects protested against the overly high taxes made by their overseas suzerains, especially since they had no representation in the British Parliament and, therefore, no possibility to change things. After years of war, the colonists emerged victorious over the British. They elected their own leader and made their government as representative as they could.

In France, the poor classes had no representation and were constantly overlooked in the decision-making process. They felt alienated from the bourgeoisie and even more from the monarchy. The absurd lifestyle that was enjoyed by the royal circle was shameful and outright offensive to the peasants, who could not even get by reliably day to day. The famous anecdote that was first written by Rousseau in his *Confessions*, which was published in 1782, describes the social situation of France the best: When a "great princess" was told that the peasants had no bread, she replied, "Then let them eat brioches." The bourgeoisie's complete disconnection from the heavy burdens of everyday life is captured brilliantly here, and it is not surprising that this anecdote was eventually attributed to Queen Marie Antoinette, wife of Louis XVI, to convey her indifference to the struggles of the poor.

The French Revolution began when the Estates-General was assembled for the first time in over 170 years for reelections and discussion of financial reform. The financial reform, which had been passed by King Louis XVI's ministers about a year earlier, had been a failure, causing mass discontent among the public, so the Estates-General convened to solve the issue.

However, the assembled were soon confronted with one problem. The Estates-General, which held its elections in the spring of 1789, had been the most representative body of the French monarchy, consisting of three "estates" or groups of peoples: the clergy (the First Estate), the nobility (the Second Estate), and the peasants (the Third Estate). Out of these three, the peasants had the most representation, a whopping six hundred members, while the nobility and the clergy were represented by three hundred members each. Despite this, there was a fundamental problem. If the Estates-General voted by head (meaning each person gets one vote), the peasants, theoretically, would never be outvoted. If it voted by estate (meaning that each estate gets one vote each), the peasants, who were more numerous, would be outvoted by the nobility and the clergy. The system was flawed since the nobility and the clergy almost always supported each other and overshadowed the voice of the peasants, who found it practically impossible to carry out their desired agenda.

Thus, the Third Estate was outraged after a month of debates that yielded no results, so its members finally decided to declare themselves the National Assembly. They threatened to proceed without the consideration of the other two estates. The members locked themselves in the tennis court of the king in Versailles and, surrounded by royal troops, swore an oath in June that they would not disperse until France had a new constitution, one that granted them more rights and pushed for more equality and representation.

Meanwhile, due to the heavy burden of the financial crisis, people protested all over the country, putting pressure on King Louis XVI, who was not exactly the best or most decisive politician. Slowly, the upset masses took over the streets and overcame the police. Moreover, members from the First and Second Estates joined the National Assembly, which would change its name and become the National Constituent Assembly.

On July 14th, 1789, crowds in Paris stormed the Bastille prison, a symbol of royal privilege and tyranny, and the peasants revolted in the provinces. It was a protest of an unseen scale. In August, the National Constituent Assembly abolished the feudal regime and the tithe tax. Later that month, they issued the Declaration of the Rights of Man and of the Citizen, a historic document modeled after the American Declaration of Independence and Enlightenment political theory. The document asserted liberal principles, freedom, and equality.

The king had to yield as his own soldiers were starting to turn against him. By October, when the revolutionaries escorted the royal family from Versailles to Paris, Louis basically held no executive power. His supporters were disorganized, and the drive of the revolutionaries was overwhelming. The French Revolution was well under way.

The first months under the National Constituent Assembly's leadership proved to be pretty effective, as the representative government sought to address economic and administrative problems to maintain its legitimacy and lead the country out of the crisis. It fully abolished feudalism and granted the right to vote to over half the country's male citizens, something that was very progressive by 18th-century standards. To address the huge public debt, the assembly made the decision to nationalize and sell the properties of the French Catholic Church, which angered the Catholic clergy and the papacy. This policy resulted in a huge redistribution of wealth and property, and the debt was gradually paid off.

The new regime also introduced a new administrative divide of France's territories, splitting it up into more administrative units that allowed for more effective governance. The judicial system was made more independent, with judges being locally elected. Principles of freedom and equality were promoted, and over time, they became embedded in the French national consciousness. The new constitution also sought to create a constitutional monarchy, with legislative and executive powers shared by the monarch and the elected judicial body, but Louis XVI, instead of cooperating, tried to flee the country, influenced by the high society members of the bourgeoisie who hoped to restore the pre-revolutionary status quo and increase their political standing. However, the king and his family were caught before they could escape the country.

The initial stage of the French Revolution had ripple effects all throughout Europe. The revolutionaries believed they fought for universal principles and declared that it was every person's right to rebel against their authoritarian monarchs. The French radicals hoped that the revolution would spread in volatile regions of Europe with a similar sociopolitical climate. The European monarchs, though, were not too keen on the disturbance that had been caused by France. Holy Roman Emperor Leopold's and Prussian King Frederick William II's courts were flooded with French bourgeois and aristocratic émigrés, who urged them to take action to preserve France's monarchy. In fact, Leopold's sister, Queen Marie Antoinette, had written to her brother to invade France and rescue the monarchy, believing that he would suffer the same fate as her if he allowed the revolution to mature.

In light of these developments and the existing rivalry between the nations, France declared war on Austria on April 20th, 1792. Both the king and the revolutionaries supported the decision: the revolutionaries wanted the revolution to triumph in other parts of Europe, and the king hoped that his position would be strengthened after a quick victory.

The French Army invaded the Austrian Netherlands, but the revolution had caused disorganization and a lack of discipline in the French Army, which suffered defeats early on. To make things worse, Prussia joined Austria in an alliance against France, and the alliance pushed the French soldiers back, crossing the border and advancing to Paris. Surprisingly, this boosted the revolutionaries' drive, and they rallied together to defend against the invaders.

Blaming the royal family for the instability, revolutionaries stormed the Tuileries Palace in the summer of 1792 and captured the royal family.

They also attacked members of the Parisian aristocracy. The increased drive strengthened the army, as more and more revolutionaries enlisted, which resulted in France's decisive victory against the Prussians at the Battle of Valmy on September 20th, 1792. The French Army followed up with a counter-offensive against the Austrians, occupying northwestern Italy and even pushing deep into Germany and reaching Frankfurt.

If that was not enough, to boost the spirit of the revolutionaries even further, a new assembly, the National Convention, abolished the monarchy on September 21st and proclaimed a republic. Then, to make things even more intense, the National Convention put the king on trial. Led by Maximillian Robespierre, the Montagnard faction of the National Convention, which was more radical and anti-royal and advocated for more egalitarianism among the classes, overruled the Girondin faction, which was mostly comprised of moderate bourgeois members. Louis XVI was charged with treason and was condemned to death. He was executed on January 21st, 1793. His wife, Queen Marie Antoinette, suffered the same fate nine months later.

The execution of Louis XVI was a shocking development for European monarchs. If the king had been sentenced to death in France, then their own positions were not safe. Early in 1773, Great Britain, Prussia, and Austria formed a coalition of European monarchies and convinced Spain, Portugal, and the Italian states to join in the war against France. The pressure of the new coalition pushed France back, but it also strengthened the revolutionary cause just as it had a year earlier.

In the National Convention, the Montagnard faction took complete power. They introduced the Law of the General Maximum, which placed regulations on pricing, new taxes for the richer classes, the further redistribution of wealth, and the confiscation of non-radical bourgeois properties. Although this radical move led to opposition in various forms throughout France, Robespierre and his henchmen imposed the so-called Reign of Terror on everyone against the revolution, leading to the arrest of hundreds of thousands of people and the execution of tens of thousands. France was basically transformed into a police state. Public gallows and guillotines were stationed all around Paris. The Montagnards also introduced conscription and urged more people to join the army, resulting in over one million active soldiers.

The Reign of Terror would last for just under a year, ending in July of 1794, when the tides of war were already being swung back into France's favor. Crucially, the triumph of the French forces at the Battle of Fleurs in June 1794 rendered the radical changes useless. Nevertheless, it was difficult for Robespierre and the radical members of the National Convention to give up power. They were increasingly accused of having gained too much power for themselves, and they were eventually persecuted and condemned, with most of them being sentenced to death by the end of July.

Although the monarchists and the conservatives tried to regain power in the provinces and revert the changes made by the revolution, they were beaten back by an aspiring general named Napoleon Bonaparte. Soon, the French Revolution and the history of Europe would enter a new age.

Napoleon

A new constitution was drawn soon after the French victory at Fleurs, which provided new institutions for governance in the absence of a monarchy. In November 1795, the National Convention approved the reorganization of the government into the Directory, which was led by five executive figures (called the Directors). They would be supported by two legislative bodies: the lower Council of Five Hundred and the upper Council of Ancients. This essentially transformed France into a bourgeois republic, and it seemed like a sustainable model of government. However, the four-year tenure of the Directory would be troubled by internal and external instability. Still, by 1795, the French Army had managed to occupy Belgium and the Rhineland, forcing Prussia, the United Provinces, Tuscany, and Spain to leave the conflict.

Around the same time, a young soldier from Corsica by the name of Napoleon Bonaparte would rise through the ranks of the French Army. An educated and passionate military officer who adhered to the principles of republicanism, Napoleon distinguished himself while leading the French forces for the National Convention and suppressing rebellions and counterrevolutions around the country. He was a dedicated Jacobin, supporting more radical egalitarianism and believing that France was able to be a republic. His distinguishments earned him the job as the commander of the Army of the Interior—a very prestigious post—and soon, he was appointed the commander of the Army of Italy.

After achieving a series of victories in northern Italy, Napoleon defeated the Sardinian and Austrian armies. He marched to Vienna and forced Austria to agree to an armistice in 1797. The Austrians gave up their claims on Holland and recognized the independence of northern

Italy, which was reorganized as a republic by Napoleon. By the end of the year, only Great Britain remained at war with France, which had, against all odds, managed to defeat every major European power on different fronts while struggling to maintain stability at home.

However, it would not be long before the violently and radically established Directory would meet its end. The royalists fled the country but sought to restore the monarchy and take back power from abroad. Domestically, the radical and quick changes had greatly altered the political situation of the country, and long-term stability for the lower classes had not been achieved. The new regime had introduced countless measures to combat wealth inequality but to no avail.

In the end, the French Revolution would shoot itself in the leg: the power it had entrusted to the military to pacify and divert the citizens' attention away from the troubles at home came to bite the Directory in the back. Two years after Napoleon's magnificent Italian campaign and a year after he had led his soldiers to the faraway lands of Egypt to weaken British influence and threaten British India, Napoleon returned to Paris. There, he found a volatile situation. More and more Jacobins were urging for the radical suppression of the monarchists, including even Director Emmanuel Sieyes, who proposed the idea of a coup d'état to Napoleon. The young general, having gained the loyalty of his forces, agreed to save the republic and conclude the revolution. In November 1799, Napoleon and his forces dispersed the legislative councils, stormed government buildings, and made the directors resign. A new system was set up. France was now to be a consulate ruled by three consuls, with Napoleon becoming the First Consul.

The next decade and a half after the establishment of the French Consulate would be some of the most action-packed in European history and would lead to the full-scale transformation of the continent's social and political landscape. The rise of Napoleon was a new stage of the French Revolution. However, although the First Consul claimed that he adhered to the principles of republicanism, the reality was very different. In fact, in due time, Napoleon basically brought the monarchy back in a renewed form. He first declared himself to be First Consul for Life and, in 1804, proclaimed France to be an empire, with himself as the emperor.

This was a startling development, although for the five years before the "official" proclamation of the empire, Napoleon had largely acted as an absolutist ruler anyway. He brought back the Reign of Terror, as he arrested and executed people as he pleased. He limited freedom of speech and the press and ruled with an iron fist while he led the French Army to victory throughout the continent. Nevertheless, he justified his proclamation of the empire with a popular plebiscite, which did, in fact, vote for him.

Napoleon, who is remembered as one of history's greatest military minds, led France into war once again against the whole of Europe, and he seemed to be winning it for the first ten years. In 1803, Britain, Russia, Sweden, Naples, and Sicily came together in a coalition to stop Napoleon. Even though the British navy managed to defeat a joint Franco-Spanish fleet at the crucial Battle of Trafalgar to dissuade the invasion of Britain in 1805, the French Army ravaged continental Europe, running over the opposition wherever they encountered it. Ultimately, seven coalitions would be created to resist Napoleon's advances, with some achieving more success than others, but almost all of them were comprised of the same states, including Great Britain, Napoleon's chief enemy and one he never quite managed to defeat, as well as Austria and Prussia, both powerful nations in their own regards but which were always outmaneuvered by the French. There was also Russia, which was a new challenger on the scene. Russia sent forces that were no match for Napoleon's professional army corps.

The efforts of the coalition were of no use in the beginning. Spain was a puppet state of Napoleon's, and France directly controlled the Rhineland, the United Provinces, and much of Italy, giving Napoleon much-needed resources to keep up the war effort.

The French forces marched to the east, gaining decisive victories at Austerlitz, Jena, and Friedland, before forcing the coalition to agree to the temporary Peace of Tilsit in 1807. The peace added new French client states to the map and essentially gave Napoleon control of western Europe. Napoleon also invaded Portugal, the last remaining ally of Great Britain on the continent, and took Lisbon in 1807. However, his decision to depose the Spanish royal family and install his brother as the new king of Spain produced instability in Iberia, leading to about seven years of guerrilla warfare, which tied down the French troops.

The fifth coalition was defeated in 1809, just two years after Tilsit, and the newly struck peace agreement reconfirmed Napoleon's possession of half of Europe. The western German principalities were reorganized into the Confederation of the Rhine, the Polish territories east of Berlin were made into the Grand Duchy of Warsaw, while Switzerland, the Kingdom of Italy (in the northern part of the region), and the Kingdom of Naples to the south all became client states of France. Napoleon had managed to conquer essentially as much of Europe as Charlemagne. But he still wanted more. After the defeat of the fifth coalition, Napoleon set up the Continental System to try to impede the European nations from trading with Britain in order to weaken France's main rival and prepare for another invasion.

Map of the French Empire's greatest extent.
Alexander Altenhof, CC BY-SA 3.0 <https://creativecommons.org/licenses/by-sa/3.0>, via Wikimedia Commons; https://commons.wikimedia.org/wiki/File:Europe_1812_map_en.png

However, Napoleon soon had to change his plans as Russia was constantly violating the Continental System, resulting in his fatal mistake: the invasion of Russia in 1812. Although he assembled the greatest army he ever fielded, counting about 600,000 men in total, with the majority of the regiments coming from the occupied territories, Napoleon's hasty tactics did not work in the vast lands of Russia. The Russians correctly recognized they were no match for the professional French forces and retreated farther and farther east, depriving Napoleon of supplies and stretching the time before winter completely destroyed the French. Napoleon even managed to take Moscow but was forced to begrudgingly abandon the invasion in December 1812 when he noticed that about 90 percent of his troops had either died or deserted due to the harsh conditions.

As he was retreating, a new coalition made up of Austria, Prussia, Russia, and Sweden assembled and defeated Napoleon at the Battle of Leipzig in October 1813. Then, they continued their march to the west, chasing Napoleon to Paris as the British-supported Spanish guerilla fighters pressured the French from the south.

Napoleon was forced to abdicate in April 1814. He was exiled to the island of Elba, and the Bourbon monarchy was reinstituted in France for a short time. However, Napoleon managed to escape captivity in February 1815 and was reinstated as emperor thanks to help from his loyal supporters. It seemed as if the glory days of his early conquests might return. However, his second tenure would only last one hundred days, as he would be decisively defeated at the Battle of Waterloo in June 1815, resulting in yet another exile, this time to the remote island of St. Helena, where he would spend the rest of his days.

Chapter 8 – The Long Nineteenth Century

Post-Napoleonic Europe

The Napoleonic Wars transformed the sociopolitical landscape of Europe. France would never be the same again after Napoleon's final defeat in 1815. Under Napoleon, the principles of the French Revolution and the novelties brought by it became institutionalized in the French national consciousness. The new administrative divide, the legal code, social and political institutions, and society's adherence to values like personal liberty and the freedom of speech all became very important to French society. As it has been remarked, Napoleon was a revolutionary despot. He deeply believed in the French Revolution but assumed total power due to his personal ambition and narcissistic tendencies. Although his campaigns had brought destruction and bloodshed to the continent, they also produced an array of side effects that would echo very loudly throughout the 19th century.

The most immediate consequence of the Napoleonic Wars was the creation of a new European political order, something that was determined in what was essentially the first modern all-European conference. The Vienna Congress would convene to discuss peace terms and the state of European affairs after Napoleon's defeat. All the major powers were represented. Tsar Alexander I of Russia personally attended, Prince Klemens von Metternich represented Austria, King Frederick Wilhelm III and Prince Karl von Hardenberg of Prussia were there, and Viscount Castlereagh was the representative of Great Britain. Other European states were also present.

After nine long months of negotiations, the Vienna Congress redrew the map of Europe. Almost all of France's gains after the French Revolution were nullified and the French borders were restored to how they had been in 1789. France's neighbors were strengthened to dissuade another outbreak of French aggression. The United Provinces got hold of Belgium, while Prussia got new territories in the Rhineland.

In place of the Holy Roman Empire, which had basically been destroyed by Napoleon after his conquests in 1806, the German territories were redistributed, and the independence of hundreds of small principalities was abolished. The old territories were reorganized in the new German Confederation, which contained up to forty states instead of over three hundred, with Austria as its chief actor. Prussia, Baden, Hanover, and Bavaria were to be the four biggest German states after that.

Britain gained valuable overseas territories, including Sri Lanka and the Cape of Good Hope. A new Kingdom of Poland was also created, although it was subject to Russian influence.

More importantly, the Vienna Congress led to the reorganization of Europe into conservative states in order to avoid the volatile political processes that had been caused by the ideas of the French Revolution. It was an attempt to maintain peace between monarchies now that order had been restored, and it largely worked for over fifty years since no major European conflict broke out during that time.

But as much as the leaders at the Vienna Congress hoped to maintain eternal stability, Napoleon had managed to spread the principles of the French Revolution throughout the continent and even the world. Post-Napoleonic Europe would eventually give rise to nationalism, which would take the continent by storm. Napoleon's legacy was the awakening of patriotic feelings among the different peoples of Europe, people who had previously struggled to find meaning and common identity, like in Germany and Italy. The Declaration of the Rights of Man and of the Citizen would be reinterpreted by different societies again and again, and Europe would experience a new revolutionary age.

Not all European revolutions in the first half of the 19th century were successful. Nevertheless, one common thing that united all of them was their objection to the conservative remnants of the old regimes. They wanted more liberalization. Nationalism also played a big role. For centuries, people had accepted the fact that the sovereign was all-powerful and possessed the God-given right to rule, but the French Revolution altered that conception. Similar developments had also resulted in the English Civil War and eventually in the establishment of a constitutional monarchy in Great Britain, but it was Napoleon's zeal to spread the principles of the French Revolution that truly made Europeans rise up throughout the 19th century.

In the beginning, nationalist uprisings of Christian nations in the Ottoman-controlled Balkans resulted in the independence of Serbia and Greece by the mid-1830s. The Ottoman Empire had long controlled the Christian-occupied Balkan lands, and these nations had tried time and time again to assert their independence, although they never had the drive to achieve their goals before the rise of nationalism. This further weakened the already ailing Ottoman Empire, soon to be called the "sick man of Europe," which was one of the states where Western Enlightenment ideas never quite managed to penetrate. The Ottomans had to give in, especially as other big European nations provided their support to the revolutionaries, hoping to see the Muslim empire weakened even more.

Things were different in other parts of Europe during the so-called revolutionary wave of the 1830s. Greece, which managed to gain its independence in 1832, was a rare example of a successful revolution. Belgium would also be recognized as independent from the Netherlands in 1831. In France, the situation was different. After King Charles X's conservative decrees, which limited the freedom of the press and decreased the influence of legislative bodies that had been set up during the French Revolution, radical liberals revolted, forcing him to abdicate. Nevertheless, the bourgeoisie was not keen on establishing a republic and fully giving in to the radicals' demands, so they brought in a new replacement for the king: Louis-Philippe, Duke of Orleans, a relative of the Bourbons who also personally participated in the French Revolution in his youth. The July Revolution, as the instance became known, restored the constitutional monarchy in France, which became just a tad bit more liberal than it had been before. Elsewhere, however, revolutions were swiftly dealt with by conservative monarchs. In Italy, Poland, and Germany, liberals hoped for a general wave of social change and concessions from their sovereigns, but they did not achieve much.

Another wave of European revolutions would follow. Known as the "Springtime of Nations," the revolutions of 1848 also had mixed results for the revolutionaries. Throughout the continent, liberal nationalist forces rose up, especially in multiethnic and diverse places like the Austrian Empire, Germany, and Italy. The general aim of the revolutionaries appeared to have been the establishment of nation-states. For example, Hungarian, Czech, and Austrian nationalists rose up with the hopes of ending the conservative rule of the Austrian Empire, which limited the sovereignty of these different peoples within its borders.

Overall, the revolutionaries demanded more freedoms, representation, and participation in governmental processes, and the rising instability and food shortages caused by recent bad harvests fueled the movements. The revolutions achieved some long-lasting results. Serfdom was abolished in Austria, Denmark was no longer an absolute monarchy, constitutional monarchies were established in Sardinia and Prussia, and France extended suffrage to all male subjects. However, the Springtime of Nations did not lead to the transformation of the existing order on a grand scale. Many movements were brutally suppressed by conservative rulers, who lent each other their support, fearing that the end for one meant the end for the other. Tens of thousands died, and even more were arrested or exiled, but social changes were becoming more and more apparent. Soon, the revolutions of 1848 would give way to unifying movements in Germany and Italy, forever changing the course of European history.

The Unification of Italy and Germany

As one of the last indirect consequences of the French Revolution, the unification of Italy and Germany in the mid-19th century can be considered one of the most influential developments in the history of modern Europe. Germany and Italy had effectively been disunited ever since the fall of the Roman Empire, and they never managed to achieve the stability, cohesiveness, or political centralization that had been made possible in France, England, or Spain. The absurdly complicated nature of the Holy Roman Empire, a series of complex feudal successions, interests of external factors, and lack of domestic will to unite had prevented German and Italian unification until the 19th century. Nevertheless, the people who lived in these areas considered themselves to have been German and Italian due to the cultural and material heritage they shared with each other. There was no doubt that a person from Venice shared more similarities with a person from Sicily than he did with somebody from Vienna. However, political developments throughout the Middle Ages and the Renaissance prevented these two nations from clearly asserting their sovereignty and forming their own nation-states. Everything would change after the French Revolution.

Due to the liberal thoughts of the Enlightenment, the surge of nationalism that took Europe by storm after the French Revolution, and the conquests of Napoleon, which transformed the continent, both Italy and Germany were suddenly put on a course toward national unification and sovereignty after centuries of division. The Vienna Congress imposed an uncomfortable political order on these two nations. In place of the Holy Roman Empire, smaller German states were reorganized into the German Confederation, which lacked unity and cohesiveness. The Kingdom of Prussia in the north was now the most powerful German state, and it had the ambition to expand even more and assert its dominance in the region. A large part of Germany was also controlled by Habsburg Austria, which, despite its origins, can be said to have been culturally close to the rest of Germany. Austria was a multinational and multiethnic empire containing Hungarian, Polish, Czech, Serb, and Italian populations. Austria also directly controlled a large part of northern Italy, influencing the smaller kingdoms that occupied it. The Habsburg Empire, although overstretched, was ready to give everything to maintain the status quo and preserve the old order in the lands it controlled since it had just been humbled by Napoleon's campaigns and was adamant about not slipping up again.

Meanwhile, liberal and nationalist movements became more prominent in Germany and Italy after the Vienna Congress. The secret society of the Carbonari in Italy, for example, headed by Italian Republican Giuseppe Mazzini, advocated for the unification of smaller Italian states into one republic to avoid the instability and chaos that had dominated the peninsula for such a long time. In Germany, it was obvious that if national unity were to be achieved, it would either have to include either Prussia or Austria since both saw themselves as chief influences and did not wish to give up their leverage over the less powerful German Confederation.

However, the revolutionary movements after the Napoleonic Wars had mostly ended in disappointment for the liberals in the two nations. Despite managing to temporarily achieve some concessions from the conservative regimes, their reaction was always much stronger and stricter, resulting in the suppression of many movements. In addition to Prussia and Austria, France also closely monitored the nationalist developments in Germany and Italy, knowing that the emergence of a strong state on its borders could become a potential threat.

We cannot cover the history of the unification of Italy and Germany in great detail here, although it is a very important subject, but we shall go over the key developments that influenced them and eventually resulted in the emergence of two of the most powerful nations that are still going strong today. In Italy, the process of national unification would be headed by the Kingdom of Sardinia-Piedmont, which controlled the island of Sardinia and the northwestern territories of the region by the time of unification. After the Napoleonic Wars, it slowly emerged as one of the more powerful Italian states, along with the Kingdom of the Two Sicilies, which controlled the southern part of the peninsula and the island of Sicily. Austria, as we have already mentioned, was the chief actor in the northeastern part of the region, with the Papal States controlling much of central Italy, including Rome.

In 1848, the anti-Austrian and nationalist uprisings in Italy gave Sardinia-Piedmont a false sense of potential success and declared war on Austria. However, the Habsburgs were able to quell the revolts and even managed to defeat the Sardinians by August. Then, in November, a popular uprising in Rome led by Giuseppe Mazzini and another radical nationalist, Giuseppe Garibaldi (who had been forced into exile in South America for over a decade, where he also participated in revolutionary activities), managed to seize control of the city and its surroundings, forcing Pope Pius IX to flee the city. The revolutionaries proclaimed a short-lived Roman Republic and intended to fight for further unification of the Italian states, but papal authority was eventually restored by a French expedition in July 1849.

Despite these initial setbacks, Sardinia would be able to turn things around for the better in a couple of years after Camillo Benso di Cavour, a moderate conservative, entered the cabinet of king's ministers in 1850. His laissez-faire economic policies managed to reduce Sardinia's public wealth and improve the financial situation of the country. Much more importantly, under his leadership, Sardinia improved its international reputation, joining the Crimean War in 1855 on the side of the French and the British. The army Cavour sent to Crimea was successful, earning him a spot at the table in Paris as one of the victors.

The newly achieved international standing turned out to be crucial. Cavour asserted that as long as the Austrian Empire was involved in Italian affairs, the unification of the Italian peoples would be impossible, stimulating a huge anti-Austrian wave in the public. This eventually led to a new secret alliance between France and Sardinia. Cavour, determined to expel the Austrians and achieve unification, allied with the French, promising to grant them territories in Savoy and Nice in return for their military assistance. Having obtained French support by 1859, Sardinian King Victor Emmanuel II made a patriotic speech in which he urged all of Italy to rise up against Austria, leading to another war. This time, with the help of the French, Austrian forces were defeated in Lombardy, and the peace agreement that followed in November saw Austria cede control of the province to Sardinia-Piedmont.

Crucially, at around the same time, a thousand Carbonari revolutionaries under Giuseppe Garibaldi invaded Sicily and conquered the island in less than three months. In May 1860, Garibaldi declared that he ruled Sicily in the name of Victor Emmanuel II and crossed to the mainland, eventually deposing the Sicilian king in Naples. With the success of the Republicans and the recent diplomatic and political victories of Sardinia in the north, Parma, Modena, Romagna, Tuscany, Naples, Sicily, Umbria, and Papal Marches all held plebiscites and overwhelmingly voted for the annexation to Sardinia. By the end of 1860, almost all of peninsular Italy, with the exclusion of Rome (which was still under papal control) and Venetia (which was under the control of Austria) had been unified. In March 1861, in Turin, the Kingdom of Italy was officially proclaimed, with Victor Emmanuel II as its king. It was to be another constitutional monarchy.

Meanwhile, similar developments were starting to take shape in Germany. After the Vienna Congress, the establishment of the Zollverein—a customs union under Prussian leadership—saw many German states from the German Confederation drift toward Berlin. The question of Grossdeutsch (Germany including Austria's German possessions) or Kleindeutsch (Germany without the Habsburgs) was becoming more and more prominent, especially after the revolutionary wave of 1848 and the setbacks of the Austrian army in Italy had raised questions about the Habsburgs' might.

Throughout the 1850s, the German states closely monitored the nationalist developments in Italy. Prussia had tried to seize the initiative but was forced to back down after Austria, backed by Russia, threatened war. In 1862, however, with the rise of Otto von Bismarck as the prime minister of Prussia, the process of German unification would accelerate. Bismarck, although a conservative himself who was not too keen on the establishment of a republican regime in a united Germany, had a very strong character and aptness to adapt to international political situations. Bismarck understood the volatile position of Austria after its setbacks in Italy and knew that France was interested in German unification. Meanwhile, Russia had ceased to play an important role in European affairs after its defeat in the Crimean War in 1856, and a newly unified Italy was very hostile toward the Habsburgs. Ideally, Bismarck could assert the dominance of Prussia in Germany, unite the members of the German Confederation in the Kleindeutsch without Austria, and establish a constitutional monarchy that would please a large number of German liberals.

In the end, Bismarck would be able to do just that, though it took many years of political maneuvers and bloody conflicts. In 1865, Prussia and Austria were drawn into a conflict over the duchies of Schleswig-Holstein in the north, two German territories that were ruled by the Kingdom of Denmark. Two years earlier, German nationalists had risen up against the Danish king, and the German-Danish War of 1864 had resulted in a landslide victory for the German Confederation, which supported the nationalists in Schleswig-Holstein and was led by Prussia, with its reorganized military under Bismarck. Austria and Prussia could not settle on what to do with the duchies after Denmark's defeat, leading to a complete deterioration of relations between the two powers. Crucially, Bismarck managed to ally with Italy before further escalation, promising to grant the newly established Italian Kingdom the province of Venetia in exchange for its military support against the Austrians if war broke out. Meanwhile, Vienna convinced France to stay neutral and rallied most states of the German Confederation behind itself, as they saw Austria as the guarantor of their sovereignty against the increasing ambition of Berlin.

What followed was a brief but decisive war in Germany known as the Seven Weeks' War, which ended in August 1866. Perhaps surprisingly for everyone at the time, the Austrian forces were defeated by the Prussians, who appeared to have been much more disciplined, organized, and better equipped. Led by Helmuth von Moltke, they overwhelmed the demoralized Austrians and achieved a decisive victory at the Battle of Sadowa. The Treaty of Prague essentially took Austria out of the German question and granted Venetia to Italy. The northern German territories were moreover reorganized into a new North German Confederation, with Prussia as its leader and the Prussian king as its president. Those German states that chose to remain independent in the southern part of the former German Confederation were allowed to join the Zollverein.

In the next five years, the unification process of both Germany and Italy would be completed. Bismarck knew the German states that had chosen to become independent would not drift toward Austria again, but he needed some trigger to convince them to join the federation and form a united German nation. In the end, this turned out to be another war, this time against France, in which the independent German states came together to defeat a common external enemy.

The Franco-Prussian War broke out over the question of the succession of the Spanish throne, as Prussian King Wilhelm's relative, Prince Leopold, was a candidate to become the new Spanish king. A Hohenzollern family member at the head of another neighboring nation alarmed France greatly; it had not expected Prussia to emerge unscathed from the war with Austria, and the newly united North German Federation had upset the balance of power in Europe. France hoped to retaliate by asserting its dominance in the Rhineland, possibly by gaining new territories, and was quick to declare war on Prussia soon after Bismarck's manipulations of the Spanish succession.

Bismarck had hoped for something like this all along and easily convinced the rest of the German states to come together against the French, who were, to the surprise of many, swiftly defeated by Prussian-led German armies. French Emperor Napoleon III was forced to abdicate, and the German forces managed to penetrate France as deep as Paris, besieging the city while the new republican government pleaded for peace.

The result was magnificent for Germany. France ceded Alsace-Lorraine to Germany, and the southern German states officially agreed to join Prussia and form a unified German Empire, with Kaiser Wilhelm as the emperor. Proclaimed at Versailles in January 1871 while Paris was still being bombarded, the new unified German state would soon come to dominate continental Europe, exploiting weakened Austria and France and challenging Great Britain, which had quietly emerged to become a global hegemon.

As for Italy, the Franco-Prussian War freed up Rome and its surroundings, which had been occupied by French soldiers ever since they had restored the authority of the pope. In 1870, Italian forces entered and seized Rome after fighting papal forces, but Pope Pius IX refused to recognize his defeat, retreating to the Vatican, where he declared himself to be a prisoner. Instead of resolving the matter violently, the Italians allowed the pope to remain isolated in his palace, a situation that would last until 1929. Meanwhile, they claimed Rome as the new capital of their kingdom. The unification of Italy and Germany was thus complete.

Map of Europe after Italian and German unification.
Alexander Altenhof, CC BY-SA 4.0 <https://creativecommons.org/licenses/by-sa/4.0>, via Wikimedia Commons; https://commons.wikimedia.org/wiki/File:Europe_1871_map_en.png

The Industrial Revolution and Pax Britannica

At around the same time, Europe was undergoing another revolution, but this was not political. The Industrial Revolution had far-reaching material and sociopolitical implications. Ever since the 18th century, steady technological innovations in the fields of agriculture, production, transportation, infrastructure, and the transfer of information revolutionized the world. Gradually, European economies would be modernized, and previously agrarian peasants and artisans would migrate to factories, working machines and producing equipment that transformed societies.

The invention and the refining of the steam engine opened up an array of new opportunities for Europeans. The new engine could transform steam into energy very efficiently for the time, but it needed iron and coal to function.

The results were staggering. Throughout the 19th century, the Industrial Revolution led to previously unseen levels of urbanization, the emergence of new social and economic classes, the establishment of capital as the chief source of wealth, the fostering of international trade, and the appearance of a new cultural and social order that visually and immaterially changed the look of Europe and the rest of the world.

Not all of Europe would be lucky enough to experience the Industrial Revolution from the get-go, however. By the mid-19th century, only Great Britain could have been considered a relatively mature industrial economy, but the rest of the continent would soon start to wake up and try to catch up. The reasons for the prominence of early British industrialism are multifold. The main reason was the fact that technological inventions first appeared in Britain in the second half of the 18th century. More and more British farmers, textile workers, and miners noticed that the new inventions could do twice their labor in half the time and were increasingly investing in the machines. This was followed by a protectionist trade policy and the British government's insistence that Britain should not give up the advantages it had accrued so far to its continental rivals by exporting machinery and new techniques.

The relative political stability in Britain was another factor. While Europe was busy fighting wars and suppressing revolutions, the social and political situation was far more stable in Britain. In fact, social strife would become one of the consequences of the Industrial Revolution, as more and more workers flocked to the factories, causing rapid urbanization and sometimes overpopulation of cities. In the cities, people experienced bad working and living conditions.

Despite these difficulties, the industrialization of British society was faster than anywhere else for more than fifty years, resulting in a rather radical physical transformation of Britain. Not only did Britain have the most comprehensive railway network in all of Europe (something that would eventually become a staple of industrial societies), but more and more industrial cities with black, smokey skies, courtesy of hundreds of factories that burned coal at all times, began to appear.

Industrialization, coupled with the general increase in living standards and urbanization, led to stable population growth throughout Europe. France, being the largest country at the beginning of the century, was no longer the most populous, as it was overshadowed by the newly united German state and even more by the growing Russian Empire, which gained new territories in the east. More people meant the opportunity to field larger armies, so the continent witnessed increased militarization during the 19th century. War was one of the aspects of life that was industrialized and made more modern, as more nations devoted vast resources to military research and the production of arms on a large scale, in addition to the adoption of new tactics. Eventually, by the end of the century, this would lead to an all-out arms race between the two main superpowers of Europe, Great Britain and Germany.

Nevertheless, for most of the long 19th century, as the period from the French Revolution all the way to the breakout of World War I is sometimes referred to, there was one state that managed to emerge on top of the new world order and maintained its position. This was Great Britain. The period of social, military, and economic stability it underwent resulted in it establishing itself as a global hegemon. The era of British hegemony came to be known as Pax Britannica ("the British Peace").

There were some obvious markers of the British Peace. We have already mentioned that the isolation enjoyed by Great Britain gave it political leverage over the rest of the continent, which was often engulfed in wars. Britain had been the only place Napoleon never managed to invade, and the main reason behind that was the fact Britain is an island. Over time, the British Royal Navy would become the most superior in the world, and the British domination of the seas would guarantee the nation's economic and military stability. Britain's isolation gave it the opportunity to monitor the political activities of the European nations and act as an international mediator.

Before the end of the century, no European nation managed to achieve levels of development similar to Britain, which became the main actor in global trade thanks to its extensive colonial network. By the 1880s, British colonies in Canada, Australia, India, Indochina, and the Middle East provided the mainland with an egregious amount of raw materials, which could then be transformed into luxury goods and everyday products. In addition, Britain controlled valuable points in key trade corridors, like the Strait of Gibraltar, the island of Malta, and the newly constructed Suez Canal, which was completed in 1869 and significantly cut the time for the maritime transport of goods from the Indian Ocean to the Mediterranean Sea. After the Berlin Conference of 1884/85, Britain would gain a large share of the African continent, something we will discuss later.

All in all, the Pax Britannica gave the nation socioeconomic and political stability, unlike other European nations at the time. However, other states would soon be inclined to catch up.

The Bismarckian System and European Imperialism

A very complex international order emerged in the 19th century, especially after the unification of Italy and Germany, which ended about a thousand years of instability and chaos that had been caused by the nature of the Holy Roman Empire and the power vacuum in the region. Germany assumed the mantle of the next strongest nation after Great Britain, owing largely to the policies of its chancellor and the main architect of the unified German state, Otto von Bismarck. After his victory against the French in 1871 and the proclamation of the German Empire, Bismarck believed the only way to maintain and further German dominance in continental Europe was by isolating France.

In 1873, his diplomatic maneuvers led to the formation of the League of Three Emperors with Austria and Russia, as these nations had clear memories of what France had been capable of doing. Although this league was vulnerable mainly due to Austria and Russia falling out over the Eastern Question, which concerned the organization and future alignment of the Balkan nations as they slowly became independent of the feeble Ottoman Empire, the alliance nevertheless achieved the goal of isolating France or at least temporarily preventing France from enjoying as much freedom and power as it would have liked. In 1879, Bismarck reconfirmed the Austro-German alliance with a new treaty, and in 1882, Italy struck a defensive alliance with both nations, chiefly against potential aggression from France.

Meanwhile, Germany was leading continental Europe in modernization. A united German state led to what Cardinal Richelieu had feared centuries earlier; it had become too powerful, too economically independent, and too militarily capable for others to check it. The small German principalities that had been scattered around the region could no longer be exploited.

After unification, Germany was quickly industrialized and urbanized, with a clear class divide between the aristocratic, middle, and lower classes. Its military had also proven itself to have been very capable, having defeated both Austria and France in quick succession. The wealth-voting system guaranteed the rich aristocracy had control of the economic and political processes of the state. The rich aristocrats were Bismarck's main allies throughout his tenure as chancellor.

The state of Germany was radically different from the situation in Russia and Austria, whose main problems were their multiethnicity and economic backwardness, which had ripple effects when it came to their international standing, military, and social stability. The Austrian Empire was the most prominent example of a state where the rise of nationalism proved to be a big problem. In 1870, the Austrian Empire contained several different nationalities, including millions of Germans, Poles, Romanians, Ruthenians, Slovaks, Croats, Serbs, Czechs, and Italians, all of whom had distinct ethnonational identities but were under the suzerainty of the Habsburgs, who were from Austria. This resulted in perpetual instability within the empire and in the eventual equality of the Hungarians, who achieved recognition as being part of a dual monarchy in 1867 after a series of independence struggles, military crackdowns, and suppression.

After 1867, Austria was transformed into a dual monarchy, now to be called the Austro-Hungarian Empire, although there were no real constitutional or political changes that gave Hungarians more recognition or a sense of independence other than their name being included in the title of the monarch, who was Franz Joseph Habsburg. The Habsburgs would never quite manage to deal with the multiethnic nature of their empire, largely because they tried too hard to maintain the conservative status quo. This, in turn, led to relative backwardness in economic and military matters when compared to Germany, France, and Great Britain.

Austria-Hungary also saw itself as the natural leader of any new Balkan nations that might gain independence from the neighboring Ottoman Empire, another ailing state that was nowhere near as powerful as it had been five hundred years earlier. Ottoman control of their Balkan and predominantly Christian subjects gradually faded away, resulting in ambiguous relationships with many of them. Conservative Ottoman rulers and strong Islamic clergy kept the empire from modernizing and embracing the nationalist, industrialist, and liberal principles of the Enlightenment. External threats like Persia, Russia, and even Great

Britain, which had colonial interests in Ottoman-controlled territories, further weakened Istanbul. The "sick man of Europe" was struggling to keep up with the changes in Europe, even more so than Austria, which was at least considered to have been a "European necessity," according to Bismarck.

Crucially, Russia had an interest in the Balkans, as it saw itself as the noble protector of the large number of Orthodox Slavs in the region. In fact, Russia shared many similarities with Austria-Hungary, especially when it came to its reluctance to allow liberal or nationalist movements to flourish. The conservative, autocratic tsars of Russia did everything to maintain their absolute power, although they realized the merits of industrialism. Throughout the 19th century, Russian tsars were in a constant tug of war with domestic forces that advocated for reform and liberalization. Russian rulers did not wish to pursue industrialization since it would amplify the voices of these groups and lead to the emergence of a new social order that might reduce the power of the monarchy. Russia was also the most populous state in Europe at the time, thanks to its rapid expansion in Asia, and it was perhaps the richest when it came to possessing natural resources. Still, it could not manage to accumulate a significant advantage over its European neighbors. When it was tested militarily at the end of the century and the beginning of the 1900s, it became clear that it could not keep up.

Thus, the decade or so after the unification of Germany and Italy saw the state of affairs slow down just a little bit. Bismarck's insistence on keeping peace in Europe by engineering a complex set of alliances chiefly directed toward isolating France was working, and to a large extent, all nations were pursuing their own interests. Austria-Hungary and Russia closely monitored the developments in the Balkans. They were reluctant to go to war with each other, so they refrained from getting actively involved, preferring to focus on strengthening the conservative institutions in their nations. Great Britain enjoyed an isolation policy and was the hegemon of the world, while the once-great powers of Spain, the Netherlands, Portugal, and Sweden were slowly declining in importance with the emergence of the new world order. In France, the phase of constant instability, wars, revolutions, and social strife had faded, and its defeat against Germany in 1871 served as a cold shower to the French nation, which pursued industrialization.

Germany, on the other hand, was on the rise, having gained an economic advantage over its continental neighbors. Kaiser Wilhelm II assumed the throne in 1890 and dismissed Bismarck, who had already done so much for the prosperity of the German state. His replacement, however, was Baron von Holstein, who diverted Germany from the Eurocentric political path the country had chosen under the leadership of Bismarck in order to challenge Great Britain's position as the most powerful nation in the world.

Believing that stable peace had already been achieved in Europe and that Germany had the capability of transforming its industrial prosperity into world domination, Holstein pushed for the policy of *Weltpolitik*, which sought to transform Germany into a dominant world power like Britain. Many things preceded this. Most importantly, there had been a renewed interest in colonialism, which manifested itself during the Berlin Conference of 1884/85. Having stabilized after a long period of conflicts and instability, European nations began to increasingly pursue colonial activities and became involved on a larger scale in Asia. The rich Chinese and Japanese markets were up for grabs, even if these two Asian states were extremely isolationist and showed no interest in trading with Europeans. Europe's technological superiority allowed European nations to slowly assert their dominance over the new colonies, something that was especially prevalent in the Indian subcontinent, which was subject to British control. With new weapons, more advanced tactics, influential methods of communication like the telegraph, and efficient ways of travel, thanks to the steam engine, fewer Europeans were needed to establish and maintain effective control of less developed native societies, as the case had been in India.

This trend, coupled with the perception that the era of expansion in Europe had practically faded, led to a revived interest in colonization. The Berlin Conference sought to stabilize overseas relations between European colonial nations. Its main aim was to carve up Africa among the Europeans, who had already made quite a bit of progress in the colonization of the continent, in order to avoid conflicts and regulate areas of interest. The result was the Scramble for Africa, after which the European nations asserted their dominance in different African regions, leading to the almost complete colonization of the continent and the heyday of European imperialism. France, Great Britain, Germany, Belgium, Italy, Spain, and Portugal all got substantial chunks of the African continent for themselves. Europe was stronger than Africa, where history had not led to the same technological or industrial processes as it had in Europe. This notion was, rather incorrectly, supported in the eyes of European colonizers by Darwin's revolutionary idea of natural selection and survival of the fittest, which quickly became popular in intellectual circles after initially being published in the 1850s.

An unwanted consequence was the emergence of the notion of social Darwinism and the misunderstood application of the principles of the survival of the fittest to the societies of the world. Social Darwinism asserted that some ethnicities and nationalities were naturally more advanced and developed than others and, thus, had the right to assert their dominance over inferior ones. It was the resurgence of an inherently racist and xenophobic view of the world, which led to brutal imperialist practices in African and Asian colonies. This brutality was justified by the idea that Europeans were naturally socially, technologically, culturally, and morally superior to the people they colonized. The rhetoric of bringing the Enlightenment to backward colonial societies became more and more prominent and only reinforced imperialism.

Germany's focus outside of Europe and the increasing colonization that followed the 1880s would lead to the completion of European alliance systems. Holstein's preferred change in the direction of German national policy and his backing of Austria when it came to matters in the Balkans resulted in a new Franco-Russian alliance, which was signed in 1894. France was more than happy to find a friend in Europe and happily financed industrial projects in Russia in hopes that Saint Petersburg would support Paris if a war broke out against Germany.

Moreover, international developments like the Meiji Restoration in Japan, which saw the complete transformation and modernization of a previously isolationist Japanese society and its emergence as a new regional power in Asia, as well as Germany's insistence in trying to catch up with Britain, eventually resulted in Britain's decision to end its long period of "splendid isolation" and get more actively involved in the political developments of Europe. Germany was militarizing at a quicker pace, investing in the development of a strong enough navy to challenge the supremacy of the British Royal Navy. The United States was also becoming a factor, defeating the Spanish and completing the construction of the Panama Canal, which could affect the existing trade routes and hurt Britain's economy. Thus, Great Britain sought to balance itself against the rising threats, chiefly against Germany. Its 1901 treaty with the US was a statement of the friendship between the two nations, while the Entente Cordiale alliance with France in 1904 ended centuries of Anglo-Franco rivalry and cleared up the colonial disputes between the two countries.

France was more than happy to ally with Britain to counterbalance against Germany.

Three years later, during the Anglo-Russian Convention of 1907, Britain improved relations with Russia, settling matters regarding the two powers' positions in Afghanistan and Persia. This eventually led to the formation of a new British-French-Russian axis in opposition to the Triple Alliance of Germany, Austria-Hungary, and Italy. By the early 20th century, these two camps had increasingly become prevalent. They supported each other in international disputes that chiefly concerned the state of affairs in their colonies while continuing to industrialize and modernize to overshadow their rivals.

In 1914, the international diplomatic processes that began due to Bismarck's insistence on achieving European peace, coupled with more and more militarization and competitive industrialization, would lead to the deadliest conflict in the history of Europe and the beginning of a new era.

Chapter 9 – The Making of Modern Europe

The Road to World War I

In hindsight, it may be easy to say that Europe in the 20th century was prone to an all-out destructive war. The peace that had been maintained after German and Italian unification was carefully constructed, built on the preservation of order and the pursuit of national interests. Europe did not want peace for the sake of peace. European nations wanted to increase their political standing in the new international order and to dominate their neighbors. An industrialized and militarized society would guarantee that they would not lose a war, or at least so they thought. In reality, multiple things could have triggered a new war, like colonial conflict or revolutionary activities. In the end, a conflict would arise from the most volatile European region of the time, the Balkans, where nationalism was gaining more traction.

As the Ottoman Empire slowly lost its grip on the Balkan nations, more independent nation-states formed in the region. By 1907, the Ottomans were almost out of Europe, only controlling Macedonia. Greece, Montenegro, Serbia, and Bulgaria were all independent. Bosnia and Herzegovina, on the other hand, while nominally under the suzerainty of the Ottomans, were administered by the Austro-Hungarian Empire, which sought to exploit the weakness of the newly created small Balkan nation-states and gain more ground in the region. With the Austrian annexation of Bosnia and Herzegovina in 1908, Serbian aspirations were further reduced. Tensions were particularly high between the Austro-Hungarian Empire and Serbia since millions of ethnic Serbians lived in the empire, and recent political developments in Belgrade led to a radically anti-Austrian government coming into power. Serbia also enjoyed the privilege of having its independence guaranteed by Russia, its Orthodox Christian big brother, and Saint Petersburg had high stakes in the Balkans, where it sought to increase its influence at the cost of the Habsburgs.

Troubles would begin when Italy, which had interests in Ottoman-controlled Libya, declared war on the Ottoman Empire in 1911 and invaded Africa. Suddenly, the Balkan nations realized they would not have a better time to strike against the Ottomans to completely end their dominance in the region. The Ottoman forces were tied up fighting Italians, and domestic developments in Istanbul had led to the establishment of a liberal government, which was very weak. Thanks to Russian assistance, in October 1912, the alliance of Serbia, Bulgaria, Montenegro, and Greece declared war on the Ottoman Empire. The alliance would achieve a quick victory in May 1913, and the result would be the complete expulsion of the Ottomans from the Balkans. Albania was granted independence, and Ottoman-controlled Macedonia was partitioned between the winners.

A month later, however, the Balkan alliance would fall apart over territorial disputes in newly won Macedonia, leading to the Second Balkan War, which saw Bulgaria fight against Greece, Serbia, and Romania. Bulgaria was defeated, and the main consequence was additional territories for Serbia.

Now having emerged victorious from two short wars, Serbian nationalism was at an all-time high, especially after the creation of the Narodna Odbrana (National Defense) organization, which sought to pursue anti-Austrian activities. Soon, much of Serbian nationalism turned violent. The Black Hand society was a byproduct of the National Defense and called for violent measures, including bombings and assassinations of Austrian politicians and statesmen.

What transpired next forever changed history. Serbian nationalists planned and carried out the assassination of Austrian Archduke Franz Ferdinand, who was visiting the Bosnian capital of Sarajevo, on June 28th, 1914. While touring the streets in an open car, the initial attempt to blow up Franz Ferdinand, one of the Austrian figures who advocated for federalism to deal with the multiethnic problems that had arisen in the empire, failed, and the suspects were arrested. However, after an unlucky wrong turn that the driver took, nineteen-year-old Gavrilo Princip, one of the assassins who had fled the previous scene, managed to fire his revolver and kill both Ferdinand and his wife.

The diplomatic maneuvering that followed the assassination of Franz Ferdinand is often referred to as the July Crisis. Throughout the month, European powers tried to find adequate reactions to the political crisis that had been created. Initially, some viewed the matter to only be a local issue; however, the developments that would unfold would eventually trigger the alliance systems and lead to the outbreak of World War I.

At first, Austria was hesitant to pursue military action against Serbia, realizing that a radical terrorist action was technically not the Serbian government's responsibility. Vienna preferred to wait and inquire, knowing that Russia could come to the Serbians' defense. Still, inaction meant a diplomatic defeat for Vienna, so the decision was made to present a list of demands to Belgrade, the refusal of which would give the Austrians enough justification to declare war. On July 23rd, Austria's ultimatum to Serbia included demands that, in the eyes of Belgrade, was an infringement of Serbian national sovereignty. Russia also backed Belgrade's position.

Even more crucial was the reaction in Berlin, which quickly reaffirmed Vienna had Germany's full support. Germany's position toward Austria was the infamous "blank cheque," meaning that Germany was ready to support any action Austria decided to take. This decision was made in light of recent domestic developments. The costly arms race with Britain and rapid industrialization had led to turbulent social processes and a financial burden on German citizens. The German Social Democrats gained more power in the Reichstag and advocated for the middle and working classes, disrupting the balance of power since control had previously been in the hands of German aristocrats. Thus, for the staff of Kaiser Wilhelm II, which had never quite managed to achieve the prestige of Bismarck and his cabinet, war was a potential option to further Germany's standing in the eyes of the public. Kaiser Wilhelm II himself was not too keen on war himself. However, Germany was confident in its military, especially since the French-funded military reforms in Russia had not yet been completed. In the event of war with Russia, the German high command believed that the German forces could easily defeat the Russians, even if France, Russia's primary ally, intervened.

Thus, on July 25th, when Belgrade only partially acquiesced to Vienna's demands, Austrian Emperor Franz Joseph was convinced by his general staff and German allies to declare war two days later. Russia declared partial mobilization against Austria. While the German ambassador to Russia tried to convince Tsar Nicholas II that Austria did not intend to annex its Serbian ally, it was too late. A day later, Nicholas II announced the full mobilization of all Russian forces on the country's western border, meaning that Russia was getting ready for war with Austria-Hungary and Germany. To the surprise of Germany, France was ready to support Russia, as the French prime minister's diplomatic mission had coincided with the assassination of Franz Ferdinand. When the diplomatic mission returned to Paris in late July, public sentiment was also militaristic.

The German high command was extremely confident in earning a victory and felt there was a chance to assert Germany's continental might once and for all. So, the German high command put in motion its Schlieffen Plan, which was designed to wage a successful two-front war against Russia and France based on quick and decisive offensives and envelopments. On August 1st, Germany declared war on Russia, and on August 3rd, it declared war on France. Germany also demanded the safe passage of its forces through Belgium in order to put the Schlieffen Plan into motion, but when Belgium refused, Germany declared war on Belgium.

Italy, seeing that the Austrians and Germans were waging an offensive war instead of being attacked first, decided to opt for neutrality so that it did not break the terms of its defensive Triple Alliance. Finally, it was Britain's turn to act. The war was a breaking point for the British Parliament. The Balkans were of no interest to the British, and due to domestic instability in Ireland, it was not the best time to end the isolationist policy and join a continental war. However, after the German troops forcefully made their way into Belgium, Britain realized that yielding to German pressure might be fatal for its aspirations for global hegemony. London thus demanded Berlin stop all military action in Belgium, and when that demand was quickly refused, Britain decided to declare war on Germany, joining World War I on the side of the Entente on August 4th, 1914.

The Outbreak of the Great War

It is impossible to fully cover the in-depth history of World War I, a conflict that was at the time often referred to as the "war to end all wars."

WWI was a conflict of a previously unseen scale, spilling over from Europe and affecting the rest of the world directly and indirectly. No one suspected in the beginning that the war would last for four years. This was mainly because decades of relative peace and the quick militarization of Europe had given virtually all European nations a sense that their tactics and military strategy were superior and that all of them would be able to achieve quick victories over their enemies. This false sense, however, was shattered only a couple of months into the war. The belligerents acknowledged that due to such radical advances in weaponry, the whole art of war had completely transformed. New guns, artillery, and mechanized pieces had rendered much of the old military knowledge useless, and trench warfare quickly became a staple of World War I.

Front lines would sometimes stretch for hundreds of kilometers at a time, with both armies digging themselves in the trenches a couple of kilometers apart from each other. The dangerous "no man's land" was spread between them. Trenches gave modern armies safety and defended them from direct gunfire, but crossing no man's land was a nearly impossible job, as the advancing infantry would have to get through vicious fire from machine guns and cross rows of barbed wire.

After the initial stage of the war had resulted in a stalemate on the Western Front (where most of the fighting took place in Belgium and France) and, though to a lesser degree, on the Eastern Front (on the Austro-German-Russian border), advances were mostly made after long artillery bombardments or thanks to occasional flanking maneuvers that would soften up the morale of the troops and allow the enemy to break through.

By the end of 1914, after about six months of fighting, several things had become apparent. The initial stage of the war had been a disappointment for the Central Powers (Germany, Austria-Hungary, and eventually the Ottoman Empire). Germany encountered stiff resistance from the French, Belgian, and British forces on the Western Front, and the attempt of both sides to outflank each other resulted in the infamous "Race to the Sea." By late October, the front stretched from Switzerland, which had remained neutral in the war, all the way north to the English Channel, with Germany having achieved an initial breakthrough but having been thwarted over the course of autumn.

The Western Front would be in a stalemate for the next two years despite countless efforts from both sides to achieve an advantage. The stalemate allowed the German high command to transfer many of its freed-up forces to the Eastern Front, where the situation was much more volatile. To everyone's surprise, the Austrian forces were tied up by the Serbians in their offensive, so Germany had to come to aid its ally to help finish off the conquest.

German military might would become especially prevalent in the fight against Russia, which, in the initial stages of the war, was holding off on its own against the Central Powers. This was mostly due to the fact that the fighting was mostly taking place in Russian-held Poland and Ukraine, whereas the heart of the Russian state around Moscow was not threatened. Despite this, German forces were far superior to anything Russia could provide. Troubled with low morale, supply issues, a lack of discipline, and inferior equipment, it was only a matter of time before Russia would be broken.

A more troubling development for Russia and the Entente was the Ottoman Empire's decision to enter the war on the side of the Central Powers. Enver Pasha, the leader of the Young Turk government, had admired German military prowess from the very beginning and negotiated the Ottoman Empire's entry into the war in return for future territorial concessions in the Balkans and the Caucasus, two regions the Ottomans contended with the Russians. In October 1914, the Ottoman Black Sea fleet sank two Russian ships and bombarded valuable coastal cities in Ukraine while Ottoman forces prepared for an offensive in the Caucasus. Russia was forced to declare war and was now effectively isolated from its allies.

The entry of the Ottomans opened up new prospects for the Entente, which had struggled to break through on the Western Front. The continuous attempts to break the stalemate led to the loss of hundreds of thousands of British and French troops by 1915, so a new plan was devised to organize a maritime invasion of the Ottoman lands and break through to Vienna and eventually to Berlin from the Balkans. What followed was the infamous Gallipoli Campaign, which saw thousands of allied forces from France, Britain, and their colonies attempt an amphibious assault of the Gallipoli Peninsula in the Dardanelles. Over 300,000 Ottoman troops and 250,000 Entente forces died in the span of about a year before the British were forced to call off the assault, having gained no valuable progress by January 1916.

Other nations got involved, too, most importantly Italy. With the ambition to be a great power, everyone recognized from the beginning that Italy could not remain neutral in the war. Both the Entente and the Central Powers sent emissaries to Rome to request Italian support. In the end, Italy chose to join the Entente, having been promised territorial concessions in the Balkans at the expense of Austria and lands in Africa. In May 1915, Italy declared war on Austria-Hungary, but no advances would be achieved on the southern front either. For what it was worth, the Central Powers were lucky to find out about the Italian forces' relative incompetence, as the Italians tried unsuccessfully time and time again to cross the Isonzo River in the north and penetrate the Austrian heartland.

The Central Powers were joined by Bulgaria in September 1915. Bulgaria was promised parts of Macedonia and revenge on Romania, which was considering entering the war on the side of the Entente. Romania joined the Entente in August 1916, motivated by the recent surprising successes of the Russians on the Eastern Front and hoping to receive Transylvania.

Romania's entry marked the end of the first half of the war. No significant advantage had been achieved by either side, but the Great War had already resulted in millions of casualties. Great battles were fought between the Germans and the allies at Verdun and at the Somme, while the Russian forces in the east managed to recover some of the ground that was lost to the Germans after Tsar Nicholas II personally assumed control of his forces in a desperate attempt to turn the tide of the war.

In December of 1916, the Russians would be exhausted from their counter-offensive, as German and Austrian reinforcements arrived from the other fronts thanks to the stalemate. Moreover, Romania, the latest ally of the Entente, had overestimated the strength of the Russians. After declaring war on Austria, Romania tried to break through, but a united Bulgarian-German-Ottoman counterattack led to the complete defeat of the Romanian forces. The Central Powers seized Bucharest in early December, allowing them to gain a new border with Russia, which meant they could potentially flank the advancing Russian forces from the southeast. This was a huge opportunity and would eventually result in further losses for the Russians.

On the other hand, Germany had suffered defeats overseas, as British and French colonies launched their own offensives against German overseas possessions. Japan, an ally of Britain since 1902, also decided to join the war, being more than happy to help the British expel the Germans out of Chinese ports and East Asia.

The Collapse of the Old Order and the Defeat of Germany

After a series of offensives on all fronts, which yielded only insignificant results for both sides, more pressure was exerted on belligerent powers domestically. The powers had opted to declare a state of total war, meaning they put everything on the line as they desperately tried to achieve victory. It was a make-or-break situation for all of Europe. The war had caused an economic crisis, and social movements for peace took European nations by storm. All of this was brushed aside by the high commands, who were adamant about emerging victorious at all costs.

New, more destructive weapons were invented. World War I was the first war that saw the widespread use of chemical weapons. Mustard gas and tear gas were utilized to break the morale of the entrenched enemy, but countermeasures would soon be adopted. Eventually, chemical warfare would become internationally banned due to its deadly consequences.

Germany also increasingly relied on its navy, especially its growing submarine force, which was a thorn in the side of the British Royal Navy. Soon after the adoption of total war, the German high command declared that it would not hesitate in sinking any enemy ships, be it civilian or military. This, when coupled with the instability at home, caused great challenges to the Entente as well as the Central Powers.

One place where this demonstrated itself the most was Russia, which could not withstand the pressures of 1917. The myth of the great Russian army had been debunked early into the war, and the country had already struggled socially and economically under the tsar's conservative regime. After more than a million casualties on the Eastern Front, Russia had not managed to gain any advantage over the enemy, and the defeat of Romania provided the Central Powers with a new prospect to weaken the Russians from the south. The Russian population experienced a massive food shortage, and the lower classes were affected the most. Tsar Nicholas II tried to avoid dealing with the internal instability by going to the front himself.

This all set the stage for the Russian Revolution in early 1917, which eventually ended with the abdication of the tsar and the establishment of a socialist regime in Russia. During the February Revolution, hundreds of thousands of people protested in Saint Petersburg, and the police were not able to contain the discontent of the masses. The leading protesters, together with members of the Russian Parliament, proclaimed a provisional government, leading to the tsar's decision to abdicate.

The power vacuum that was created in the country eventually led to the October Revolution, which saw the overthrow of the provisional government and the radical socialist Bolshevik Party, led by Vladimir Lenin, come to power. Lenin, a veteran activist and a passionate adherent to Karl Marx's theories regarding the revolution of the proletariat against the corrupt bourgeoisie, had actually been exiled previously from Russia. However, after the chaos of the February Revolution, he was smuggled from Switzerland back to Saint Petersburg with the help of the German high command. After Lenin seized power in the coup d'état in October, he proceeded to declare the Great War was not a war between nations but one between classes. Realizing that he could not gain more power in Russia without peace, he negotiated a separate armistice in late 1917 with the Central Powers.

Thus, the fighting on the Eastern Front ceased. According to the terms of the Treaty of Brest-Litovsk, Russia ceded control of a huge portion of its western territories, which was, incidentally, the richest when it came to industrial production. Lenin's regime rejected any requests from the Entente to rejoin the war, and Lenin tried to consolidate full control of Russia as internal fighting tore the country apart during the events of the Russian Civil War, which would last for the next few years. Eventually, the communist revolution in Russia would be successful and lead to the creation of the Soviet Union.

With Russia out of the war, the Central Powers could now use their freed-up contingents on the Eastern Front and swing the tide of the war in their favor. However, new developments occurred that upset their plan. What really swung the tide of the war was the entry of the United States on the side of the Entente, not as a direct ally but as an "associated power." The US had long pursued a policy of isolation and did not wish to interfere in European affairs, though the nation had gradually increased its political, military, and economic power throughout the 19th century. America was an industrial powerhouse with a large population and a distinct identity. European nations had chosen to ignore its rise to power (perhaps unknowingly) due to the country's decision to remain isolated from the developments in the Eastern Hemisphere. Even when World War I broke out, America remained isolationist, thanks to the efforts of President Woodrow Wilson, who advocated for peace and conflict resolution from the very beginning. Even so, the country underwent dramatic economic growth thanks to increased requests from the Entente for supplies, munitions, and materials.

US public opinion began to swing in favor of entering the war after Germany adopted a policy of total war. German U-boats sank a civilian ship called the *Lusitania* in May 1915, killing more than a hundred US citizens (though the ship did carry munitions to Great Britain). President Woodrow Wilson tried to calm the enraged public and sent a delegation to Europe for peace overtures, which was unsuccessful. Over time, as German attacks on ships with Americans on board continued, the US started to become more affiliated with the Entente, even breaking off diplomatic relations with Germany after successful British propaganda that depicted English-speaking Brits and Americans as brotherly people.

The final straw, however, would come in March 1917 when British intelligence intercepted the infamous Zimmerman Telegram, which was intended to reach the Mexican government. The telegram urged Mexico to declare war on the US in order to stop it from supplying the Entente. The message promised Mexico territorial gains in the southern United States if the Central Powers won. British intelligence urgently communicated the contents of the telegram to Washington, and Mexico denied any conspiracy with the Germans to avoid being dragged into the conflict. In early April 1917, the United States of America declared war on Germany and joined World War I on the side of the Allies.

The entry of the US was able to provide much-needed morale and material support to the deadlocked Western Front, while much of the German divisions were still stuck on the Eastern Front, fighting against nationalist contingents that had risen up after Russia had relinquished claims on its Polish, Ukrainian, and Baltic territories. Domestic problems also caused the complete financial collapse of Germany, and German allies were unable to provide any support since they were struggling themselves. After having overworked and overtaxed its population, with millions dead on the front lines, and having only defeated Russia, the German high command was in tatters. More and more people advocated for peace in large German cities, while the Kaiser and the aristocratic elite desperately tried to leverage the situation any way they could. Suffering from the lack of morale and supplies, German divisions tried to break the deadlock on the Western Front by putting more pressure on the Entente, but their offensives were rebuffed in early 1918.

By the summer, Austria-Hungary and the Ottoman Empire were in shambles. With the entry of Greece on the side of the Entente, British and French expeditionary forces successfully launched offensives in the Balkans, pressuring the Central Powers and decisively defeating Bulgarian contingents. Austria-Hungary collapsed from the inside; Czechs, Croats, Bosnians, Serbs, and Poles started to declare independence and rose up against the Habsburgs. Italy also managed to break through after fighting eleven battles at the Isonzo. With the Entente on the counter-offensive on the Western Front and with the Ottomans, Bulgarians, and Austro-Hungarians all succumbing to the pressure, Germany finally gave in and signed an armistice on November 11th, 1918.

World War I was finally over, though the consequences that awaited Europe would bring even more destruction and carnage.

Shaping Post-war Europe

Since the scale of World War I had previously been unseen, with many different belligerents and conflicting interests, many nations started agreeing upon the terms of the peace before the war even ended. The Treaty of Versailles would become the most comprehensive document regarding the settlement of matters after the Great War.

After the unconditional surrender of Germany and the other Central Powers, the largest and most important international conference since the Vienna Congress would take place in Paris at the Palace of Versailles, where delegations from all over the world assembled to discuss the new world that was to emerge after the war. Great Britain, the US, France, Italy, and Japan, as the principal victors of the war, held the most influence, and they would lead the conference starting in late 1918.

After rigorous negotiations, the completion of ceasefire agreements, and new important developments, such as the revolution in the Ottoman Empire and the emergence of the democratic nation-state of Turkey with Mustafa Kemal Ataturk as its leader, the results of the Paris Peace Conference were game-changing.

Europe changed completely. Multiple new democratic nation-states were created in place of the old Austro-Hungarian, German, Russian, and Ottoman empires. With the Habsburgs out of power, Austria-Hungary was finally split up. Czechoslovakia, Poland, Austria, and Hungary were all created, and Romania was enlarged at the expense of old Habsburg and Bulgarian lands. A completely new state called Yugoslavia was also born; it was a confederation of Serbian, Croatian, Slovene, and Bosnian lands, with the Serbian king as its leader. The independence of Estonia, Lithuania, Latvia, Belarus, Ukraine, Georgia, Azerbaijan, and Armenia was also recognized, and the territories that were attributed to them largely resemble the territories these countries occupy today. The Ottoman Empire was reduced to a Turkish nation-state in Anatolia, while its lands in the Levant were split between the French and British.

The Treaty of Versailles was also a direct attempt (and a successful one) at radically weakening Germany's power. The Weimar Republic took the place of the old Reich, and France regained control of the Alsace-Lorraine province that it had lost in 1871. The Rhineland, the most economically advanced German region, was to be demilitarized, and the German Army was to be reduced to a mere shadow of its former self. The Entente had seen what a strong and unified Germany could do, and they wished to avoid that at any cost, hence their decision to fully blame the outbreak of the war on the Germans, even though the reality had been much different.

Even more importantly, Germany had to pay absurd war reparations to the victorious nations, something that would result in the total collapse of the German economy and antagonistic feelings toward the allied nations. The Treaty of Versailles was deliberately punitive, unlike treaties that settled other matters like the break-up of Austria-Hungary or the reorganization of colonies. Few predicted back then that it would have devastating results in the future.

The League of Nations was another creation of the Paris Peace Conference. Thanks to the insistence of President Woodrow Wilson, it was to be the first international institution with the aim of being an arbiter to avoid another conflict and ensure the sovereignty of its members. Out of the forty-two original members, twenty-six were non-European. However, the League of Nations would ultimately be a futile attempt to create a truly effective international organization. The lack of bonding agreements, institutions, and mechanisms and the fact that it had been created so quickly eventually resulted in the League of Nations not being effective enough at preventing outbreaks of war and violence.

Still, the Paris Peace Conference shook up the state of the world and upset the balance of power in Europe. The United States was finally regarded as a worthy superpower and enjoyed a new dominant position. Before 1914, Europe's economic and political systems, though largely built on distrust and self-interest, had been extremely effective, having provided massive industrial and societal growth to the nations that had embraced it, like Britain and Germany. After the war, these systems were completely turned upside down. Everyone was in debt, and the old economic order would not be restored.

The dominance of the US was fragile, which is reflected in the fact that the economic boom the country experienced during the "Roaring Twenties" was largely caused by the loans it had given to struggling European economies. The US also chose not to join the League of Nations, a rather illogical development that further undermined its newly supposed dominance over the rest of the world.

Despite Wilson's and the rest of the victors' best efforts to reshape the world into a more stable one built on the principle of democratic liberal nationalism, the unplanned consequences of the Paris Peace Conference would soon come to bite the world in the back.

The Rise of the Third Reich

A complete economic collapse shocked the world soon after the end of the war. Although European production, inflation, and overall economic output slowly stabilized by 1929, a worldwide economic crisis would follow. This was because the foundations of post-war economies were very fragile. The US had become the largest exporter of capital and valuable resources, such as coal and iron, and lent millions of dollars to struggling nations, which, in turn, depended on the American economy. The post-war boom that the US stock market experienced would culminate in 1929, and the collection of American loans, coupled with psychological factors and hysteria that caused a drop in demand, caused the US stock market to crash, leading to the virtual breakdown of American businesses and American foreign investments.

The Great Depression, which would roughly last for the next ten years, caused a massive financial crisis around the world, with mass unemployment, a lack of production, and the devaluation of world currencies. The economic gains that had occurred due to the Industrial Revolution, including new professions and jobs, higher standards of living, and urbanization, were all set back, especially in more developed societies.

The mass economic crisis had immense sociopolitical consequences. Above all, those who suffered the most from the crumbling economy came to increasingly believe that the attempt at forging a liberal democratic world order had been a total failure. The failure of capitalism around the world further improved the standing of economically left-leaning parties, such as those who adhered to Marxist principles. In Russia, the Bolsheviks managed to consolidate their power, defeating the opposition in the Russian Civil War and advocating for a worldwide communist revolution. The creation of the USSR (Union of the Soviet Socialist Republics) was the manifestation of the imposition Russian Bolsheviks placed on their neighboring states, which saw class, rather than nationality, as the main differentiator between the people. For the architects of the USSR—Vladimir Lenin, Leonid Trotsky, and Joseph Stalin—a worldwide rise in socialism was an inevitable phenomenon. While socialist movements did not gain much prominence in the 1930s in western Europe except for some exceptions, in Asia, communism was the main drive behind the revolution that resulted in the Chinese Civil War and the emergence of the second-most prominent communist state in world history.

The rise of fascism also took place, first in Italy and then later in Germany. Despite being victorious in the war, Italy did not quite manage to fully achieve its ambitions, and Italian lifestyles were greatly affected by the war. Moreover, the rising prominence of socialism in the country further disappointed many Italians, who believed that Marxists were unproductive and unfit to rule. Italian society had always been conservative due to the importance of the Roman Catholic Church, and nationalism had played a big role in the country's unification in the 19th century.

The impotence of liberalism and an increasingly anti-socialist sentiment gave birth to the fascist movement, a word that originates from the Italian word *fascio* or "bundle." Soon after the end of the war, under the leadership of Benito Mussolini (who incidentally was an ex-socialist), the fascist movement began to take off. The movement was reinforced by many disheartened young nationalists who were ready to take power away from the socialists by any means necessary, including violence. Elections and other democratic processes were not acceptable to the young fascists, who would band into gang-like groups and harass socialist politicians and union meetings. They basically institutionalized violence in many parts of the country. In 1921, they formed the National Fascist Party, and a year later, they managed to achieve significant results in elections.

Eventually, the political situation in Italy became highly unstable, and at the king's insistence, the fascists formed a coalition government led by Mussolini. In the next four years, the party, which had terrorism at its roots and denounced liberalism and socialism alike, managed to slowly consolidate its grip over Italy. In 1926, elections were suspended, which, unsurprisingly, was not opposed by the public. Italian fascism was built on the rhetoric of hate, passion, and energy. In reality, though, the movement lacked ideological roots that could make its "revolution" more tangible. In hindsight, it was a desperate, ambiguous movement that could in no way prove to be self-sustaining, and Mussolini himself, though successfully managing to reinforce his image as an all-powerful dictator, was a poor totalitarian ruler.

Throughout the rest of the 1920s, Italian fascists did not manage to achieve any significant, measurable victories, politically or economically, though they did manage to antagonize and capture the anger of much of the troubled public. The failure of fascist policies and Mussolini's rule was brushed aside as radical Italian nationalism exploited many Italians who had grown distrustful of the existing system. More importantly, it would have radical implications for Italy's northern neighbor, Germany, where a similar sociopolitical and economic climate resulted in a complete revamp of the government.

The fascist movement found refuge in Germany, which underwent a radical transformation during the 1930s from a defeated nation that had suffered the most after the Great War to the most powerful state in all of Europe with ambitions to conquer the world.

Post-war Germany suffered inexplicably, much more than Italy had. Many of the measures in the treaty had been directed toward making sure that the German state could never again manage to gain power similar to what it had had in 1914, and the economic depression of the late 1920s crushed whatever public morale the German nation had managed to accumulate since its defeat. The Weimar Republic, much like its Italian neighbor, had been unsuccessful in achieving prosperity. Its failures had also made an ideological interpretation of post-war and even pre-war events possible—something that was exploited very well by a new ruler named Adolf Hitler, who would come to power in 1933.

A radical nationalist and anti-Semitist, Hitler had been involved, though rather unsuccessfully, in German politics during the 1920s. However, things started to go in his favor after the popularity of the Nationalist Socialist German Workers' Party, also known as the Nazi Party, managed to make him the chancellor of Germany in 1933.

Much like Mussolini, Hitler was a passionate agitator and an enthusiastic speaker, but unlike Mussolini, his messages were much simpler to understand. Hitler had a strong character and was not afraid to identify scapegoats who were responsible for Germany's social and economic ruin and the humiliation the nation had suffered during and after the war. He antagonized the masses against German Marxists, who, according to him, worked with German Jews to undermine the nation. In his eyes, they were threats from within that prevented the country from regaining its dominant status.

Of course, revanchism was something that gained him a lot of popularity among the troubled masses, who blamed their troubles on international actors. Interestingly, Hitler also sought a complete reinterpretation of German cultural and social life by "purifying" it, which meant excluding all ethnically non-Aryan peoples to form a truly cohesive, unique, and pure German state for the "ethnically superior" Germans.

Coupled with his talent for making powerful speeches and an amazing propaganda machine, complete with influential visual elements like new symbolism and the masterful usage of new technologies like the radio to bend the people's ears toward his cause, Hitler was able to skyrocket to popularity. The Nazi Party enjoyed this popularity largely because it gave new meaning to the struggling German population.

After becoming the chancellor, Hitler slowly penetrated through every national institution on his way toward gaining absolute power. Democratic processes ceased completely, but the people did not have a strong reaction to that. International reaction to his meteoric rise to power was ambiguous, as European leaders did not exactly know how to react, especially early on. Some even believed that Hitler was just another nationalist leader like Mussolini or Ataturk, hoping to revive the spirit of the German nation. No one was willing to admit that he would take measures to undermine the Treaty of Versailles's terms. It was also apparent that no one was willing to take a stand against Germany, at least until it was too late.

One thing that Hitler's rise to power showed was that the international order the victorious nations of the Great War had strived to establish was very immature. The German question (how Germany should repay for the damages caused by WWI) had been an important one, and everyone knew that, but nobody was willing to answer it. The United States, the chief engineer of the state of the post-war world, was undergoing a radical economic collapse and blamed the hardships of the Great Depression on the Europeans. US public opinion had shifted, once again, toward isolationism after the decision to get involved in European affairs had apparently misfired. It was also rather impossible for France and Great Britain to contain Germany; they had failed to do so even when they had Russia on their side in 1914. With such a fundamentally new society in the form of the Soviet Union, which was antagonistic from the very beginning toward western Europe and the liberal capitalistic status quo, western Europe had lost an ally. The French knew of their military inferiority in comparison to the Germans and opted to mostly focus on a defensive strategy, while the British were overstretched. They could not police continental Europe, where they historically had little stake and their vast colonies at the time.

The rise of fascism in Italy isolated the country from its former western European allies. Mussolini's decision to invade Ethiopia and reassert his dream of creating an Italian overseas empire in 1935 was left unchecked by both France and Great Britain, though it clearly violated the Covenant of the League of Nations. As a result, not only did Ethiopia lose its independence for several years, but Hitler, who was already well on his way toward gaining absolute power, saw that the post-war order was fragile.

A year later, when a civil war broke out in Spain between leftists and conservatives, Hitler and Mussolini became each other's allies, though the latter previously had a dubious view of the former's actions. Both Germany and Italy sent military divisions to support Nationalist General Francisco Franco against left-wing socialists, who were, in turn, granted support by the communist Soviet Union.

This resulted in the formation of three ideological and political camps before World War II broke out in 1939: the democratic camp, led by France and Britain (and, to some extent, the US), which struggled to maintain its unity against these new challengers; the increasingly aggressive fascist camp of Hitler's Germany and Mussolini's Italy (and partially Franco's Spain, where the situation never became quite the same as it had in the other two countries); and the communist camp, with the Soviet Union as its leader, which insisted on a communist revolution and the complete overturning of the capitalist world order.

When Italy violated the agreements of the League of Nations, Hitler took that as a sign to also start breaking the terms of the peace that had undermined the German society. In 1935, he announced the beginning of German rearmament, something that directly broke the Treaty of Versailles. Soon, German troops entered the demilitarized zone of the Rhineland, where the previously stationed French and British troops had been removed in 1930. No attempt was made by either to punish Germany. What were Britain and France going to do, go to war again after their own states had been wrecked by the most devastating conflict in history?

The Führer's decisiveness was endorsed by the public and would lead to Germany seizing Austria in 1938. The Anschluss, as it was called, was supposed to be seen as the destined reunification of the German and Austrian peoples, who shared the same language and culture. A similar justification was made when Germany seized the Czech part of Czechoslovakia soon after the Anschluss, which was the real manifestation of Hitler's and Germany's long-lost dream of unifying Greater Germany. Britain again backed down in March 1939 as Hitler expanded outside of the virtual bounds of Greater Germany, taking the Slovak part of the former Czechoslovakian state.

However, Prime Minister Neville Chamberlain drew the line there, knowing of Hitler's ambition to take the Polish corridor between East Prussia (a chunk of German territory in the east) and the mainland, which also contained the old German city of Danzig. Chamberlain offered a guarantee to other eastern European countries in case of German aggression. To everyone's surprise, Hitler proceeded to declare war on Poland in September 1939, having obtained support from his supposed chief enemy, the USSR.

Stalin, who believed that he needed more time to complete the industrialization and transformation of the backward Russian society into a global threat, reluctantly and secretly agreed to partition Poland between the Soviet Union and Germany. He signed a non-aggression pact with Hitler in the summer of 1939. As a long-term plan, he perhaps knew that Moscow and Berlin were mortal enemies, something that was largely caused by the anti-socialist propaganda on which fascist ideology stood. Diplomacy between authoritarian leaders is flexible and often seems confusing to the outside observer. For the fascists, the Soviet communists were among their main enemies and vice versa, but they did not hesitate before agreeing to partition Poland. The fate of the world was to change forever based on this decision.

The Second World War

On September 1st, 1939, Hitler's Third Reich declared war on Poland. Two days later, France and Great Britain declared war on Germany, although perhaps from the very beginning, it was clear they could not decisively act in time to save the Polish from the German offensive. About a month later, Soviet and Nazi soldiers divided the country once more. Unlike in 1914, when Germany had declared war on its European neighbors because it had felt threatened, the French and the British now had the onus on them to act. However, public opinion in both countries was not supportive of another war.

The German Wehrmacht (the unified armed forces of the Nazis) was too difficult to defeat early on, and the Allies' decision to weaken the Germans economically by blockading the seas would be answered by Hitler with an invasion of Denmark and Norway in April 1940. German forces achieved decisive victories there, taking control of the rich supplies of both countries and following it up with a brilliant offensive on the Western Front. Reminiscent of the Schlieffen Plan, German forces went around French defenses at the border and, advancing through the Low Countries, attacked throughout the Ardennes, catching the French completely off-guard.

The Germans reached Paris by summer. On June 22nd, the French government signed an armistice, relinquishing its claims to the northern part of the country to Germany and relocating to the town of Vichy in central France. It also broke off relations with the British after the latter reluctantly sank French boats during their expeditionary forces' retreat from the continent in order not to allow Germany to take hold of them. Britain was left without an ally.

Britain faced a German attack almost immediately after, but under relenting pressure, the British were able to rally behind Winston Churchill, who had become prime minister after his successful tenure as admiral during the Great War. Churchill managed to gain the support of the British public and emerged as the type of leader his country needed. Giving powerful motivational speeches almost daily and reaching the homes of every Brit through the radio, Churchill was able to revive a feeble national sentiment in the hearts of the British citizens.

The Royal Air Force was able to repel German air attacks, which still devastated southern parts of the country, and the Royal Navy dissuaded the Germans from attempting to invade. By December 1940, Hitler had been unable to break the British despite throwing everything at them, so he decided to turn his attention elsewhere.

The infamous Operation Barbarossa, named after the former Crusading Holy Roman emperor, Frederick Barbarossa, envisioned a blitzkrieg through the vast eastern European lands controlled by the Soviet Union and the quick overthrow of the Soviet government. Hitler's plans were ambitious, but while he had been busy running over France and trying to break Britain, Stalin had managed to quickly expand his territories by defeating Finland and annexing the Baltic countries. Hitler, seeing Russian expansion, wished to quickly put an end to it, but there was another, even more vital factor that convinced him to attack his fellow dictator in the east.

Deeming the Germans ethnically superior, Hitler had always personally hated the Slavs and had persecuted them inside Germany. He believed he was supposed to crusade in the name of the truly superior Western civilization and impose it upon the communist Slavs controlled by Stalin. Italy also officially joined Germany by declaring war on France and Britain in June 1940 and launched offensives in the Balkans, trying to defeat Greece. This provided Hitler with an ally that, in his opinion, could provide him with enough support to defeat Stalin.

After the Axis (as the alliance came to be called) forces invaded Yugoslavia and Greece in the spring of 1941 and took over much of southeastern Europe, Hitler declared war on the Soviet Union in late June and launched Operation Barbarossa. Stalin, though not completely caught off guard by the declaration of war, ordered a mass retreat of his troops, which were being overwhelmed by the much better-quality German forces. By late 1941, the Germans had come dangerously close to capturing Moscow, but suffering from overextension and the harsh conditions of the Russian winter, they were stopped by a Soviet counter-offensive.

Despite pushing the Soviet forces out of much of eastern Europe, Stalin did not break under pressure. He knew that he was now Churchill's main ally, but he also hoped for help from somewhere else.

When Hitler declared war, it was largely known that the US, headed by President Franklin Roosevelt, was basically an undeclared enemy of Germany, though the president had stated he would support Britain to the fullest extent while remaining neutral. The Land-Lease Act of March

1941 allowed the Allies to receive aid without payment, and with the Atlantic Charter, the two leaders of the free world (Churchill and Roosevelt) had basically declared Germany their common enemy.

However, the United States would not enter the war on the side of the Allies until December 1941 after a Japanese air attack on the American naval base of Pearl Harbor basically left Roosevelt no other choice. The Japanese Empire was an ultra-nationalist and militaristic state in East Asia and sought to replace the hegemony of the Western powers in the region by expansion. Japan hoped that by declaring war on the US, it would be able to quickly seize key Allied points. Japan was also assured by Hitler that Germany would also declare war.

Hitler kept his promise, declaring war just four days later on December 11th, but the whole operation turned out to be a fatal decision. Hitler hoped that the Japanese would be able to tie up the Americans in the East, reducing their assistance to Britain and the USSR in the West, allowing him to knock them out of the war. However, this did not happen. Instead of only focusing on the Pacific theater and defending Allied territories in Asia, where the US was heavily supported by British colonies, Washington, DC, never abandoned its British allies in Europe. America even increased its aid in early 1942.

Meanwhile, Japan's alliance with Germany and Italy amounted to little in practice, as Japan was isolated from its European allies and left to deal with the Americans alone. Unlike World War I, Roosevelt, the man who was lauded as saving America from the Great Depression, enjoyed much more united public support and was confident in his ability to change the course of the war in favor of democracy—a true American principle.

The entry of Japan and the US into the war was what really made the conflict a world war, although fighting had taken place outside of Europe, mainly in Africa and the Middle East, even before they joined. Britain sheltered the exiled governments from the democratic European countries that had fallen to Germany, including a delegation from France headed by Charles de Gaulle. Although de Gaulle was not a member of the "official" government of Vichy France, he was perceived as the leader of Free France. Only Portugal, Spain, Switzerland, Turkey, and Sweden remained neutral in Europe.

War ravaged throughout North Africa and the Levant, where the Allies fought against Italian and German troops for Libya, Egypt, Syria, and Iraq. Iran was invaded by British and Soviet forces in 1941, as the

British suspected the Iranian government of colluding with the Germans. The Allies managed to seize Iran's valuable oil reserves, which were of great help to the war effort. Fighting was done against Japan in Indochina, Malaysia, and the Philippines. Only a minority of countries were left outside of the conflict.

The entry of the United States began to swing the tide of war back in favor of Britain and the Soviet Union. The German forces had been unable to achieve significant breakthroughs on land after 1941. Important victories were achieved by the Americans during the battle for Midway Island in 1942, where they turned back a large Japanese force and seized strategic initiatives in the Pacific theater. In Africa, thanks to cooperation from British colonial forces, Ethiopia was liberated from the Italians, and soon, the Axis powers were defeated in the battle for North Africa, something that made the invasion of Italy from the south possible.

The Soviet forces, on the other hand, managed to emerge victorious in some of the bloodiest battles in the heart of Russia. The Soviets held Stalingrad on the Volga, suffering more than a million casualties but inflicting almost as many on the enemy after a battle that lasted for five months. The bloody siege of Saint Petersburg (Leningrad) lasted for two years and four months. Germany was finally forced to break it off in January 1944 after the Soviets had defended the city with their teeth.

In the Battle of the Atlantic, British and American naval forces managed to emerge victorious over the deadly German U-boats, although hundreds of German submarines sank millions of tons of shipments destined to reach Britain. All of these setbacks demoralized the Axis, and the increased enthusiasm of the Allies swung the tide in their favor.

Hitler was on the retreat by 1944, and his allies were of no help. Romania and Hungary had also joined the war on the side of the Axis, but they contributed little to the overall war effort. The incompetence of the Italian forces resembled the Austrian forces during World War I, as they were unable to achieve anything significant without German support. Mussolini's regime collapsed after an amphibious invasion of Sicily by the Allied forces in July 1943, and the new government signed an armistice with the Allies. Hitler sent German forces to northern Italy and helped Mussolini regain power, establishing a puppet state called the Italian Social Republic. However, the Allies soon broke through, and Mussolini was captured and hanged by an angry street mob in 1945.

As the Germans had been fighting to defend its south, the Soviets were on a counter-offensive in the east. In June 1944, after months of preparations, the Allies managed to land in Normandy after having organized the greatest amphibious expedition in history. After fierce fighting, the D-Day operation was successful, and the Allies were able to establish a beachhead in northern France.

A year later, British and American forces pushed in from the west while Stalin's armies reached Berlin. Hitler's control of continental Europe was virtually nonexistent by the spring of 1945. The continent had been reduced to ashes when Hitler committed suicide in late April 1945 in Berlin. On May 8th, 1945, Germany surrendered.

The war in East Asia took a bit longer. Japan only surrendered unconditionally after the United States dropped two nuclear bombs on the cities of Hiroshima and Nagasaki in late August, unleashing destructive power of an unseen scale. World War II was finally over in September 1945, six years after the German declaration of war on Poland. With the world in ruins, pressure was now on the Allies to try and rebuild once again.

Europe Divided

As the Allies advanced through German-occupied territories, they encountered hundreds of prison camps designed to accommodate political prisoners and slave laborers with the primary aim of systematically and comprehensively wiping out the Jewish population of Europe. This was a shocking discovery. Though Hitler's anti-Semitism was well known, the world was oblivious to the existence of such a deadly machine, which had operated largely under the radar and resulted in the extermination of six to seven million Jews by 1945.

The unveiling of the darkest chapter of European history came gradually as the Allied troops liberated the concentration camps, which had been created to "re-educate" the "inferior" non-Aryan peoples but which actually served to brutally torture and murder those Hitler despised the most. Systematic, cruel, and irrational murder of this scale had previously been unseen, but what was more impressive was the highly organized administrative and bureaucratic structure that had been put in place to carry out the Holocaust, which is perhaps the greatest tragedy in European history and a dark spot that will forever remain in world history.

The Nazis committed atrocities that they justified through obscure reasoning. Today, the crimes of the Nazi regime are still imprinted in the German national consciousness.

This development reconfirmed Churchill's conviction that if the Allies had lost the war, the whole world would have been overcome by Hitler's evil. The situation was now more challenging. European civilization had sinned beyond belief, so it had to be completely rebuilt, socially and psychologically, in addition to politically and economically.

The victorious powers had to confront this reality. The future of Europe was already largely decided in February 1945 at the Yalta Conference, when Churchill, Roosevelt, and Stalin met to negotiate, confident in their victory in the war. The main thing upon which they agreed was the division of Europe into two camps. Stalin wanted eastern Europe, where communist regimes would be established. He believed that he deserved it; the Soviet Union had suffered more than twenty million military and civilian casualties, far more than the combined number of the victorious nations. For the most part, he got what he wanted. After 1945, Poland, Czechoslovakia, Hungary, Romania, and Bulgaria all became communist. There was also the pressing German question. Stalin wanted a piece of that as well, especially since the Soviet forces had taken Berlin. Germany was thus divided into Soviet, American, British, and French-controlled zones. Essentially, Germany had a communist East and a democratic West. Berlin was also divided into the Allied-controlled western zone and the Soviet-controlled eastern zone.

Stalin was satisfied. The war had made possible what the communists had hoped for since the Russian Revolution. Half of Europe was now effectively under the political umbrella of the Soviet Union, and in due time, the Chinese communists would manage to triumph in their long civil war.

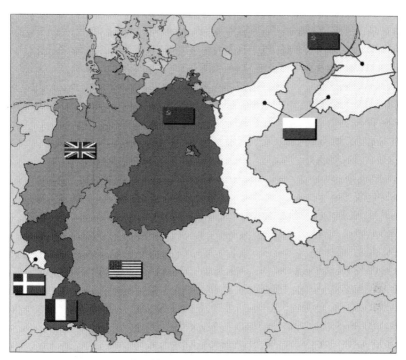

Division of Germany in 1945.

The overall political outcome of World War II was the emergence of the Soviet Union as a dominant force in European and world politics. The status quo that had been maintained throughout the 19th century and up until 1914 and later, with the exclusion of the Soviets from European affairs until 1939, was no more. Great Britain, the only western European nation that had managed to hold its own against the Nazis, was a shadow of its former self. Yes, Churchill had rallied the British population, and the British fought bravely during the war, but it was the Americans who kept Britain afloat until 1945. The United States was the new international arbiter of the world, not Britain. Britain tried to retain its position as the global hegemon, but it could no longer truly stand up to the military and economic might of the Soviet Union or the United States. The era of the pound sterling was coming to an end, replaced by the era of the US dollar. Britain's colonial empire was still there, though more and more countries soon realized that the British were unable to defend them. As a result, Britain's colonial enterprise started to dwindle.

A similar fate was to befall France, which, unlike Britain, had been humiliated during the war but was reinstated to its former self after the

Allied victory, thanks to the efforts of Charles de Gaulle. Nevertheless, it could not escape the fact that post-war Europe was no longer as influential as it had once been. Europe was largely out of contention for dominance in the balance of power. Now, international politics was to be dominated by the United States and the Soviet Union. The Cold War between the two camps would last for the rest of the 20th century.

Changes to the Eastern Bloc.

A new international organization was also set up. Dubbed the United Nations, or the UN for short, its aim was to provide a rational, widely agreed-upon way of managing international affairs, much like the old yet ineffective League of Nations. This time, however, there were major changes in the organization's structure and the countries' commitment to maintaining the mutually agreed-upon principles. The most apparent change was that both the United States and the Soviet Union became members of the UN from day one, along with forty-nine other members. The members could debate and vote equally on matters in the General Assembly, but there was also a much more prestigious Security Council, which contained five permanent and six rotating members. Alongside the US and the USSR, France, Great Britain, and China formed the permanent members of the Security Council. Each permanent member had (and still has) veto power in order to make the procedures more balanced.

The whole purpose of the UN was not to allow international conflict to break out on a scale similar to 1914 or 1939, and it intended to provide a platform for all nations to specify their interests and diplomatically resolve their disputes. Since its founding, the organization has grown to include up to two hundred members, and it remains the most prestigious and all-encompassing organization to date. It is headquartered in New York.

The main weakness of the UN, to this day, is the absence of an enforcing mechanism and the fact that it is predicated upon mutual cooperation between states. Still, the essence of the UN persists rather healthily, and even if it has been unable to stop bilateral conflicts, it is thanks to the UN's leadership and its imposition of the principles of the new world order that Europe has never again seen a war like World War II.

The United States emerged as the natural leader of the free, democratic world. Americans never wanted further territorial expansion, let alone another war, though they did come to realize early on that they were in an ideological war, fighting against the Soviet communists who had already imposed themselves in much of eastern Europe. Therefore, the United States offered post-war Europe help in the form of the Marshall Plan. The US sent economic aid to help Europe reconstruct itself after a devastating war and make sure that democratic processes would not be undermined by the rising Soviet influence in the east. When the Marshall Plan was announced, both French and Italian parliaments had communist parties in it, and Britain was also starting to put more trust in the leftist Labour Party, but there was no real tangible threat of communism spreading. The Marshall Plan was the first step in ensuring that remained the case. The flow of US capital into western Europe was crucial in accelerating post-war economic recovery in the UK, France, and West Germany, whose Allied-occupied zones would soon unify into one sovereign state.

Moscow, on the other hand, pressured the eastern European communist governments to refuse American aid, something that hindered economic growth in the region and allowed the Soviet Union to have direct influence over its allies in eastern Europe.

This struggle between the United States and the Soviet Union to achieve ideological, economic, and military dominance over the other would continue well beyond European borders and came to be known as the Cold War. The two greatest powers of the world tried to influence political processes around the globe, even participating in and funding parties in countries like Korea, Afghanistan, and Vietnam. The fact that both powers had nuclear missiles made it so that neither side ever directly warred with the other. Nevertheless, the Cold War would come to dominate the political processes in Europe for the rest of the 20th century, and no new major wars would break out that would paralyze the continent as it had in the past.

Constructing a United Europe

By the end of World War II, six European nations were still empires, with colonies overseas in Africa, the Americas, Asia, and Oceania. Great Britain, France, Belgium, Portugal, the Netherlands, and Spain would soon come to realize that it was more and more difficult to hold onto their old overseas possessions, at least without altering their approach. Western Europe, weakened by war and aided by the US, was no longer able to play a dominant role around the world as it had during the heyday of imperialism and industrialization. Having direct control over the colonies came at a great expense.

British citizens, for example, though always maintaining their sense of pride, which was a remnant of old British successes in world politics, slowly came to shift their attitude regarding the colonies and the British Empire. Though many did not want to give up the territorial gains they had made, especially those that had guaranteed the economic and political development of the country over the past centuries, they, in many regards, had to. After the war, a gradual process of decolonization began. Europeans slowly retreated from places like India, Indochina, Malaysia, and Africa, where they had asserted their dominance over the local peoples for a very long time, often with the use of force. If the Europeans, led by the Americans, wanted to reconstruct the world and base it on liberal democratic principles, decolonization was necessary. They had failed to do it in 1918, and their inability to maintain peace had led to the deaths of hundreds of thousands of people who were in no way ever connected to continental Europe. These people all had their own sense of nationality and sovereignty.

The imperialist model was flawed for the 20th century, and Europeans slowly started to abandon it, though they never fully gave up their standing. The British Commonwealth, however symbolic it may be, still persists to this day, and some overseas territories are still administered directly by European governments.

Decolonization was the first step in realizing that the new world order could not be based on intra-European competition and that Europe could only reemerge from the ashes through cooperation. For the first time, European nations started working toward a long-lasting peace, respecting each other's territorial, cultural, and material sovereignty and interests. After the war, a new Europe would be constructed based on democracy and socioeconomic integration. At first, this might have been to balance against the existing communist threat in the east, but over time, European integration would purify itself, emerging as the best model of international cooperation in the world to this day.

While the Soviet Union was economically and socio-politically dominating eastern Europe, western European nations were getting to work. The European Coal and Steel Community (ECSC), formally established in 1951, was one of the first conscious steps at fostering interdependence between the nations of the founding members, which were France, West Germany, Italy, Belgium, the Netherlands, and Luxembourg. The ECSC, engineered by French Foreign Minister Robert Schuman, created a common market with decreased regulations for the two primary resources needed to maintain a war effort: coal and steel. The High Authority was created to enforce the agreement between the nations and consisted of members of parliaments from the member countries.

The project was overwhelmingly successful, and it opened up a way for further integration between the countries. If a common market could exist for these goods, then why can't it exist for others? The western European nations thought that deeper integration made sense. Separately, these countries could not stand up to the might of the US or the USSR, so the only way for them to find their place in the shifting balance of power was through economic and political cooperation.

The European Coal and Steel Community would provide the blueprint for the creation of the European Economic Community (EEC) in 1957. Member states agreed to create a common market not only for goods but also for capital, services, and labor, which provided new opportunities. As the endeavor was very successful, European economic and socio-political integration would soon grow to include more western European countries. New members would be admitted to the European Community, as the international organization headquartered in Brussels came to be called. The year 1973 saw the United Kingdom, Ireland, and Denmark join. Greece joined four years later. Portugal and Spain joined in 1986.

Member countries all had different histories and cultures, but they had similar goals and aspirations. For the first time in history, European nations were determined to work together toward mutually beneficial outcomes.

As more and more European supranational structures were created, it made more sense to merge them together. The result was the European Union, which today contains twenty-seven member countries and about 6 percent of the world population. Today, it is the most prosperous model of political and economic integration between countries. Most of its members use the same currency and coordinate their national and supranational policies.

Map of the European Union.
https://commons.wikimedia.org/wiki/File:European_Union_map.svg

While western European nations enjoyed financial assistance from the United States and the umbrella of military security that the new alliance of the North Atlantic Treaty Organization (NATO) provided, eastern Europe had to live through a much more troubled 20th century after World War II. Communist governments, even after the death of Stalin in 1953, continued to be heavily influenced by Moscow, and due to the Soviet Union's insistence on specific economic and social policies, these nations were unable to develop on a level similar to their western European neighbors. This is not to say that people in these countries were unaware of the relatively more prosperous lives western Europeans enjoyed. In communist East Germany (the German Democratic Republic, or GDR), many people fled their homes and migrated to the democratic Federal Republic of Germany in the west. This was a problem for the communist government and even more for Moscow. Communist life was by no means as stable and free as government propaganda made it out to be. Propaganda from the West was, though exaggerated at times, largely true. People in democratic, capitalistic societies enjoyed virtually unrestricted access to goods and services, owned private property, and were, on average, increasing their personal wealth, while eastern Europeans struggled.

When East Berliners woke up on August 13th, 1961, having already lived separated lives from their Western co-citizens, they saw that the GDR government had commenced the building of a wall to separate the two sides of the city and prevent the East Berliners from going to the West. This was a shocking development, and the GDR, with the backing of Moscow, supported brutally enforcing the new laws. If one wanted to cross on either side, they had to undergo thorough checks, and guards, who would be stationed along the wall, were permitted to shoot anyone who disobeyed.

For about the next three decades, the Berlin Wall stood as the main symbol between the West and the East. It was the physical manifestation of Stalin's "Iron Curtain," as the communist takeover of the eastern part of the continent had been dubbed by Winston Churchill immediately after the war. Churchill had been one of the first to realize the alliance between the West and the Soviets was only useful during the course of the war when a much worse enemy had to be defeated. And the two camps, as time showed, could not properly coexist with each other.

The Cold War, while never resulting in an all-out conflict between the US (and the rest of the democratic world) and the USSR, made this clear. And the fact that the communist perception of the world had been built upon a total ideological lie also started to become apparent. After the death of Stalin in 1953, the new First Secretary of the Central Committee of the Communist Party of the Soviet Union, Nikita Khrushchev, slowly started the process of "de-Stalinization," which ended the reign of terror. The Soviet Union was already showing more cracks by then but managed to hide them since Stalin had centralized all means of power in his hands.

The existing system in the USSR, while having managed to create a state that was on par with the US, was not far off from the absolutely horrific system that had existed in Nazi Germany, especially during the long tenure of Joseph Stalin. Forced labor camps existed in the Soviet Union, much like they had done under Hitler, and millions of people were victims. The West was, again, seemingly oblivious to this. The Soviet secret police made sure to enforce strict censorship and loyalty to the regime on all subjects of the state, resulting in the formation of a brutal system that unlawfully persecuted millions. The USSR indoctrinated and brainwashed its citizens on a previously unseen level, but a system that is built completely on lies and fear is doomed to fail eventually.

Other communist nations, especially in Europe, came to realize this. Their governments, though having imposed themselves and their seemingly egalitarian policies on the people, had nothing to show in reality. While western Europe was rebuilt and reorganized into a much more prosperous political and economic union of free countries and people, eastern Europe struggled. Many demonstrations and uprisings took place in the biggest cities of eastern European communist countries, and while most of them were violently suppressed, the communist governments increasingly had to give in; perhaps they knew that what the people were truly fighting for was stronger than whatever they had given them. The direct influence of Moscow also dwindled over the years, as economic growth stagnated due to more share of the funds being devoted to the arms race with the United States instead of being invested in local economies. Events like the Prague Spring in 1968 resulted in the gradual rights of free speech and travel, as well as, to a lesser extent, the decentralization of the economy, which had spillover effects on other communist regimes outside of Czechoslovakia.

In the 1980s, under unrelenting pressure from the recent Western economic success and in an increasingly hostile political climate, Mikhail Gorbachev proclaimed the policies of perestroika and glasnost, designed to slowly integrate the isolated Soviet market into the global economy and liberalize the political landscape. The implications were massive, but some were unintended.

In 1989, after decades of dominance, communist governments throughout eastern Europe started to give in to the protesters' demands. The Berlin Wall came down on November 9th, 1989; after nearly three decades of total isolation, the two parts of the city reunited once again. The fall of the Berlin Wall symbolically represented the end of the Cold War. The democratic Western world had finally triumphed against the communists.

Two years later, the Communist Party of the Soviet Union would collapse, and the fifteen republics would finally become independent, among them the European nations of Russia, Estonia, Latvia, Lithuania,

Ukraine, Belarus, Moldova, Georgia, Azerbaijan, and Armenia. The fate of Europe had changed radically once again. In time, the new republics would be integrated into the European family.

Conclusion

With the dissolution of the Soviet Union, a new chapter of European history began. In addition to the republics formerly part of the USSR, new ones emerged in the Balkans, as Yugoslavia would crumble in time, facing much of the same issues that other communist nations had faced in Europe. The break-up of Yugoslavia into Serbia, Croatia, Bosnia and Herzegovina, Slovenia, Macedonia, and Montenegro would be much bloodier than the break-up of the Soviet Union, leading to one of the first truly devastating wars in continental Europe since World War II.

The Yugoslav and Soviet successor states would be integrated into the larger European family on different levels, but few would be able to fully escape the instability stemming from the overthrow of the communist regimes. Ethnic wars and civil wars dominated not only the Balkans but also the Caucasus, where the situation was just as volatile. Recently, with the full-scale Russian invasion of Ukraine, the balance of power and the status quo maintained after the 1990s has been radically shaken up, leading to the development of more turbulent events. A lot happened after the 1990s in Europe, perhaps too much to try and summarize here. Still, there is surely more to come.

European history is, to a large degree, the history of civilization as we know it. It is full of wars, intrigue, conspiracy, and bloodshed, but it is also equally full of peace, prosperity, innovation, and progress. Many things contributed to the development of European history, but what centuries of power struggles led to is ultimately a region of stability. After the Second World War, Europe gradually stabilized, almost fully escaping its violent roots; perhaps it is impossible to fully do so. Nevertheless, Europe became associated with progress and strength. It is home to some of the most advanced democratic regimes, valuing freedom, individuality, and love. As we saw, the core European values have changed time and time again, adjusting to the rise and fall of different cultures and empires and subject to the preferences of dominant arriving or departing peoples.

We cannot overstate the influence Europe and its history have had on the rest of the world. In the 21st century, humanity lives in a Eurocentric world. Nobody can say for sure what caused this to happen or why some developments transpired in Europe and not in other places that ultimately resulted in this relatively small place having such a large impact on the rest of the globe. Still, for some reason, those European values that started to appear after the end of the Middle Ages have emerged as the most acceptable throughout the world.

Despite turbulent periods, Europeans always bounced back, emerging stronger than they were before and, in the process, leaving a rich cultural heritage that dazzles curious minds to this day. European history is much more than the history of a continent, as Europe is much more than a continent. It is, for all intents and purposes, an idea in itself—an idea of progress, human dignity, equality, and freedom.

Part 2: The Renaissance

An Enthralling Guide to a Period of
Rebirth in Arts, Science and Culture

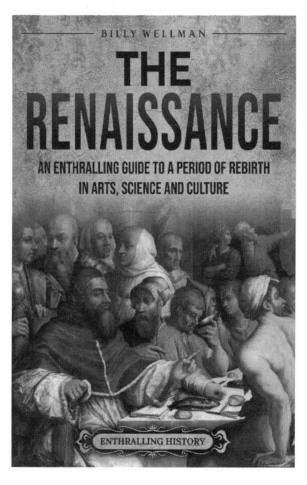

Introduction

Today, most curious people know of the Renaissance, at least through the amazing artistic works of Leonardo da Vinci and Michelangelo. Perhaps this is to be expected, as the paintings, sculptures, and architecture of the Renaissance never fail to dazzle viewers lucky enough to experience them in person. Indeed, visual art is one of the most iconic parts of the period in Medieval Europe we now refer to as the Renaissance, but there is so much more to unpack within the movement that one might even get overwhelmed. The Renaissance is comprised of various aspects, all carefully correlated with each other, that together produced one of the most prosperous, intellectually profound, and aesthetically pleasing periods in the history of Europe. This book aims to cover this period by unpacking every detail that made it what it is today and by analyzing the causes and consequences of the Renaissance.

The Renaissance, or "rebirth," is a fitting name since it entailed a complete re-imagination of European civilization, an awakening from a deep slumber of ideological, technological, and moral stagnation and uncertainty. A full rebirth of what "Europe" stood for did take place, though perhaps unknowingly for many people. Though the Renaissance today is seen as the continent's strive towards progress, it manifested itself most clearly in the upper echelons of European society, while the lives of the poorest were hardly, if at all, affected. Still, after the chaos that beset Europe after the collapse of the Western Roman Empire—the main pillar of civilization and stability of the continent for hundreds of years—it is the Renaissance that is credited with recovering European civilization and setting it back on the right track from the depths of the Dark Ages that immediately followed the fall of Rome. Renaissance thinkers bridged their time with the long-lost or forgotten knowledge of the ancient world, the ancient Greeks and Romans, that was full of glory and stability and displayed man as the center of the world. What made the Renaissance so special was that it recognized this, skipping the ideological vacuum that had emerged in the post-Roman world caused by the migration of new peoples, the destruction of old power structures, and the establishment of Christianity as the new moral center of the world.

Ultimately, this rebirth was concerned with more than European values and putting man back on center stage. It was also an age of unparalleled scientific progress, accelerated by the diffusion of knowledge from the East and the constant desire to learn more and grow one's horizons. New discoveries and theories shocked the state of the world and people's understanding of it. The theories of Copernicus, a Polish astronomer and mathematician, challenged the geocentric model of the Earth accepted for ages, which saw the Earth as the center of the universe. Instead, Copernicus mathematically proved that it was, in fact, the Earth and the planets that moved around the Sun—something that was, at first, vehemently condemned by those to whom it posed the most danger—the leaders of the Catholic Church. In the 16th century, Italian scientist Galileo Galilei contributed much to our understanding of the natural world, laying the foundations for what would eventually become the revered scientific method, perfecting the telescope, and finding more evidence for the heliocentric world. These and many other scientific and mathematical novelties accelerated the Renaissance and gave it new meaning. Man was placed at the center of attention and made curious and capable of overcoming difficulties, whether through his virtues or science and learning.

This book seeks to tell the history of the Renaissance—arguably one of the most influential periods in world history—that transformed European material and immaterial life, opening new avenues of thought, ideology, and exploration. The first chapter of the book will serve as an introduction, summarizing the state of pre-Renaissance Europe to provide a better context for the developments that increasingly took place after the late 13th century. Then, the middle of the book will cover different major developments of the Renaissance, whether political, social, or economic, that shaped the continent. We will look at some of the biggest Renaissance names, like the infamous Medici family of Florence, great artists like Raphael and Botticelli, thinkers like Erasmus and Luther, scientists like Galileo, and many others who influenced the movement and helped it become what it is remembered as now. By looking at some of the most important breakthroughs in thought and technology, we will contrast Renaissance Europe with Europe of the Middle Ages. Finally, the book will conclude by assessing the bigger impact of the Renaissance on the continent's history and the socio-political dynamics that would unfold after the late 16th century.

Chapter 1 – Pre-Renaissance Europe

The Fall of Rome

Ancient Rome deservedly occupies a place among the most important civilizations in history. From 8th century B.C. to the 5th century A.D., the history of what we refer to as ancient Rome is full of exciting developments that still exert their influence today—for example, by the sheer scale of the material cultural heritage that exists in the ruins of once-great Rome. Transitioning from a kingdom to a republic to an empire, the state that grew out of the Italian Peninsula at its height incorporated all of Western Europe, North Africa, England, much of the Balkans and Anatolia, and the Levant. Rome was the greatest empire in the known world by a huge margin, excelling not only in warfare but also in statecraft—creating one of the most iconic forms of government to this day, built on the principles of republicanism. To put things into perspective, while the Romans exercised control over territories hundreds of miles away from the great city of Rome through a network of carefully-designed bureaucracy, northern, central, and eastern Europe were still tribal and sometimes nomadic. These peoples, referred to as barbarians by the Romans, were scattered around the dense forests of the European continent. They constantly struggled against the Roman legions, who sought to take over their lands and bring "civilization" and the Pax Romana—the Roman Peace—to them.

By the final days of the Roman Empire, the notion of Pax Romana had become internalized into the consciousness of the empire's subjects. Roman society was very hierarchical and clearly stratified, and most people living in the empire were not considered Roman citizens until very late. Still, Rome had a sense of grandeur and might it still exerts today to some extent. Though constantly involved in economic, military, and political troubles, the empire symbolized stability, victory, and peace. Due to its adherence to republicanism and civil law, the Roman Empire inspired many people, including commoners, who at least could compare their lives to the lives of barbarian "savages." Roman citizens were part of a huge, interconnected world and cherished this fact, though most were less privileged than others. During the heyday of the Roman Empire, it seemed like the empire would last forever, constantly expanding and civilizing the rest of the known world.

However, all empires eventually fall, and Rome is perhaps the clearest example. Over time, the sheer size of the empire became practically unmanageable. We must remember that Romans administered very remote provinces in an age when the most effective method of communication was sending messengers on horseback from one place to another. This could sometimes take weeks or even months and was associated with a myriad of problems, even if the Romans managed to build a cohesive network of roads to connect their domains. Eventually, it became clear that Britannia or Syria, for example, could not be simply governed from Rome. So, the administrative system of the empire became more and more decentralized, giving more and more power to locally-appointed governors. Constant clashes with barbarians or upset local populations increased interdependence between the governors and the Roman legions, undoubtedly the most professional and strongest in the world at the time. This meant that power became fragmented, and the Roman Senate—the republican governmental body of the empire—could no longer effectively exercise its direct influence. This is, eventually, how Rome went from an empire to a republic. The rise of powerful individuals, often commanders with many loyal legions, could hardly be contested. A system built on deliberation, public discourse, and the prevention of dictatorships collapsed. The Senate still held some legislative power, but the real power lay in the hands of the emperors.

When the emperors were wise and capable of governance, Rome experienced few problems. In fact, the reign of the "five good emperors" from the end of the 1st century to the late 2nd century is considered one of the most prosperous times of ancient Roman civilization. However, if the individual emperors could not cut it and were unsuited to rule—perhaps too distracted or simply drunk—holding such a massive empire together was practically impossible. This resulted in many civil wars in which different commanders fought each other for power and influence in the state, while the Senate always plotted from behind the scenes to install whomever it saw most fit to rule. To fix the problem, the empire was divided in the 4th century into the Western and Eastern Roman Empires. Eastern Rome, with its new capital at Constantinople, was richer and more prosperous than its Western counterpart. Though governed by the Romans, the Eastern Roman Empire was essentially based on the social and cultural heritage of ancient Greece, the old Hellenistic world that included the Balkans, Anatolia, Syria, Palestine, and Egypt. It was distinct from the Latin Western Roman Empire (culturally, above all) and had fewer political struggles.

The Western Roman Empire, on the other hand, was a dying state from the day it was formally separated from the East. Victim to constant civil wars, barbarian invasions, and economic troubles, it lacked effective administration to keep it together. The situation got worse in the 5th century, when the great migration of people from the east altered the demographic state of Europe, forcing many barbarians, who had previously lived at the peripheries of the empire, to flock into its borders. Hundreds of thousands of people migrated from the east to the west, and Roman legions could not stop them from entering the borders of Rome. They settled in Germany, France, northern Italy, Iberia, and Britain, and their migration was not exactly peaceful. Vandals, Goths, and Anglo-Saxons overwhelmed Roman armies, while the Asian Huns, ferocious warriors on horseback who had caused the great migration of European people, decimated the Roman countryside, and pillaged the land.

The result was the fall of the Western Roman Empire in 476 A.D., when the last Roman Emperor, Romulus Augustus, was overthrown by the Germanic king of the barbarians, Odoacer, who declared himself the ruler of Italy. The rest of the empire, already quite decentralized, was quickly seized by different barbarian forces. Visigoths (Western Goths) established their own kingdom in Iberia and the southern part of the old Roman province of Gaul. Vandals, whose atrocities during the sack of Rome in 455 gave the word "vandalism" its meaning, occupied much of the North African coast. Northern Gaul and most of modern-day Germany were divided by the Franks, Saxons, Alamanni, Frisians, and

Thuringians, while the British Isles were invaded by the Angles, Saxons, and Jutes. While the Eastern Roman Empire would continue to exist for another thousand years, these peoples took over the ruins of the old Western Roman Empire and founded their own kingdoms (though, in the beginning, their hold over the territories was just as superficial and lacked political structures). The fall of Rome in 476 ushered in a new period we now call the Middle Ages—about a millennium of chaos and uncertainty in which Western Europe tried to stabilize and find its identity, which was lost with the collapse of the Western Roman Empire.

Post-Roman Europe

Post-Roman Europe was drastically different. The power vacuum created by the collapse of the Western Roman Empire needed to be filled, but the barbarians who had just arrived and set up kingdoms in old Roman territories were by no means advanced societies. They objectively lacked the level of sophistication the ancient Roman and Greek civilizations were known for. Though they had complex belief systems, their organization was largely tribal, and their hierarchy depended on relationships between war chiefs and their subjects. Many barbarians marveled at the heritage the Romans had left (as in the British Isles), attributing them to the works of mythical creatures like giants, as they were unaware of the Roman civilization and its merits. The overwhelming majority of society was illiterate, with no real incentive to study and learn. Admittedly, barbarians knew how to fight, but they did not exactly know what to do when they were not fighting. Confusion and uncertainty beset the European continent. We must remember that many commoners who inhabited different provinces in Gaul, Iberia, or Italy had experienced both Roman and barbarian rule but did not know with whom their allegiance lay. Were they to look at Rome, now under Odoacer and his successors—before they were eventually replaced by other warring barbarian dynasties—or were they to look at the newly emergent "kings" of their territories?

Immediately after the fall of Rome, as the political organization of the continent was still adjusting, two centers of influence emerged. At first glance, they seemed to emerge as potential successors of the stability previously provided by the Roman Empire. One, obviously, was the Eastern Roman Empire, also known as the Byzantine Empire—a name that stems from the great city of Byzantium (Constantinople), which claimed to be the true successor of the Roman traditions and way of life. Constantinople had long eclipsed Rome as the greatest city in Europe and was reaching its prime around the time Rome was being sacked by the Vandals. Combining Roman governance and administration with its Hellenistic traditions and heritage, the Eastern Roman Empire was the largest and the richest power in Europe. Its inhabitants had also been affected much less by the great migration than the rest of Europe. It was a thriving society, much more stable and peaceful than whatever the rest of the post-Roman world could offer, though it did have its own problems. In the beginning, the Byzantine Empire seemed interested in emerging as the new pillar of stability, and barbarian kings sometimes declared their allegiance to the emperor in Constantinople. Emperor Justinian, for example, one of the most successful Byzantine emperors, managed to reconquer a significant part of the old Western Roman Empire, with his legions taking over much of Italy, North Africa, and Iberia in the 6th century. Constantinople seemed ready to offer "mandates" to new kings in return for their cooperation or allegiance to help legitimize them in the eyes of the population.

However, as time passed, it became clear that Byzantium could not provide a suitable alternative for the rest of post-Roman Europe. The main problem was that it was too far away from the new barbarian kingdoms, many of which were simply uninterested in basing the source of their power in such a far-away realm. Yes, perhaps in the eyes of the population, formal or informal connection with Constantinople meant something, but it yielded no practical results toward the consolidation of power and establishment of new dynasties. New kingdoms could not be dependent on some artificial relationship with Constantinople. This was even more apparent once the Eastern Roman Empire became culturally distinct from the West. Latin was replaced with Greek, and old Roman deities and symbolism were gradually left out in favor of Hellenism. Constantinople looked increasingly to the east instead of the west, especially as Justinian's gains were slowly lost. Grabbing onto the barbarian West was simply unnecessary when the empire had many of its own problems.

The second alternative, the one that eventually triumphed over the option of Byzantium, was none other than the Roman Catholic Church. Christianity had become the official religion of the Roman Empire in 313 with the Edict of Milan, and though it had made quite a bit of progress in supplanting different religions in Roman territories to emerge as the sole most dominant one, the fall of Rome in 476. hindered that process. Still, by the time new barbarian kingdoms were establishing themselves in place of the old Roman domains, the Catholic Church, headquartered in Rome, also vied for influence, seeking to Christianize the new barbarian kings and complete the process of making Europe fully Christian.

A complicated dynamic soon emerged. As the new kings sought to absorb old Roman structures and Romanize themselves to appear more glorious or prosperous to their subjects and gain more legitimacy, they stumbled upon Christianity, which, for them, symbolized the might of the old Roman Empire. This was especially so because Byzantium was also Christian, and the East-West Schism had still not officially occurred. The bishopric of Rome, the most prestigious alongside the bishoprics of Constantinople, Jerusalem, Antioch, and Alexandria, thus started to form informal alliances with the new barbarian rulers, who increasingly became Christian. Since their societies were heavily dependent on the actions of their ruler, owing to the old tribal chief loyalty, they followed the lead of their kings and adopted Christianity. In that way, they could get another Christian "mandate" to legitimize themselves. If the bishop of Rome recognized their kingship and accepted them as Christian kings, then surely they were worthy of being the successors of the great Roman Empire, though what that meant was still unclear.

The role of Christianity in Europe was amplified with the emergence of a new, soon-to-be rival religion in the Arab world known as Islam. Spreading like wildfire, Islam took the Middle East and North Africa by storm, as devoted Arab warriors went on jihads to spread the religion throughout the world, creating significant problems for Byzantium. By the 8th century, they had taken over much of the Levant, Persia, Egypt, and Carthage, destroying the kingdom of the Vandals and expanding into Iberia, whose recently Christianized Visigoth kings were almost fully wiped out. Eventually, Muslim incursions were ended by the Franks at the Battle of Poitiers in 732, commanded by Charles Martel, but most of Iberia would remain Muslim for many centuries to come.

The emergence of Islam and its rapid expansion was a unifying factor for the Christian Church in Rome and the new barbarian kingdoms of Europe, who embraced Christianity and gained the favor of the bishop of Rome—the pope. Most importantly, Charlemagne the Great, king of the Franks and the man who would conquer half of Europe in the late 8th century, received special papal approval. Forcing the Germanic tribes to convert to Christianity after decades of waging war and extending the borders of his realms to include most of modern-day France, the western half of Germany, and northern Italy, Charlemagne was a devout Christian and often generous to the pope. Eventually, in the year 800, Pope Leo III crowned him the Holy Roman Emperor at St. Peter's Cathedral in Rome, essentially making him the new suzerain of Europe on par with the emperor in the East.

Charlemagne's triumphs and his successful Carolingian dynasty asserted the dominance of the Roman Catholic Church as the undisputed central institution of post-Roman Europe by the year 1000. As time passed, new kingdoms and principalities emerged from the chaos of the post-Roman world, synthesizing new values of Catholic Christianity with the feudal system. Christianity overwhelmingly dominated the cultures of new state-like formations, with the pope as the most respected authority. The system that eventually emerged from the Early Middle Ages sought to stabilize the problems that had arisen after the fall of the Roman Empire.

Dark Ages

The Early Middle Ages is, largely speaking, the stereotypical "medieval" period depicted in today's culture and embedded in the consciousness of many people. It was a time when the sharp hierarchical divisions of Europe were still being institutionalized, those that would remain unchanged for hundreds of years. All the power was concentrated either in feudal lords, barons, dukes, and kings or in Catholic religious authorities, who held much influence over the political figures. The overwhelming majority of the population lived in terrible daily conditions, dependent on good harvests and the will of their suzerains. Constant wars and raids often decimated the countryside. And though the overall political structure of the western half of the continent was slowly stabilizing, most people's everyday lives were by no means peaceful. Literacy rates were horrendously low, with only the clergy and the members of the highest class being educated. Cities and towns were small, centered mostly around marketplaces.

In addition to generally uninteresting, repetitive, and harsh living conditions, the Early Middle Ages can also be characterized by a cultural and ideological uniformity, the likes of which was perhaps never again present in Europe. After the fall of the Roman Empire, especially after the year 1000, Christianity stood proudly at the center of everything European. This was largely because the Church viewed itself as the unifying force of Europe—something that was true to an extent. This, in turn, resulted in the clergy emerging as among the most universally respected and authoritative figures to the members of the high and low classes of society. Devotion to a truly Christian way of life was considered the most noble and virtuous thing a person could practice since attaining salvation was supposed to be the objective of every Christian. People would go to great lengths for this—going on distant pilgrimages and donating to the Church were among the best and most common things done by the people who could afford them. The role of the Church and Christianity was reconfirmed with the era of the Crusades—the 200-year struggle of European Christendom to conquer the Holy Land of Jerusalem and its surrounding areas from its Muslim rulers. In the eight main campaigns that began in 1095, tens of thousands of Christians died fighting in the name of Christ. But Christendom could not achieve any long-lasting victories in the Levant, forced to eventually abandon its gains.

Still, the Crusades reconfirmed papal authority and became a very prestigious endeavor during the 12th and 13th centuries. It was implied that devoted rulers would campaign to the Holy Land if Rome called a crusade, and success in the campaigns was associated with great honor and dignity. The Crusades also helped to fully separate the Western Catholic Church of Rome from the Eastern Orthodox Church, with its head being the patriarch of Constantinople. The differences that stemmed from the cultural variation between the West and the Byzantine Empire eventually escalated further and further, resulting in issues between the two camps regarding the interpretation of Christian doctrines and scriptures. In the 11th century, the patriarch of Constantinople was excommunicated from the Church by the pope, and the Eastern Church officially separated from the Western Church. In 1204, during the infamous Fourth Crusade, a group of European Crusaders changed their course and unexpectedly sacked Constantinople, though they had been headed to the Holy Land. This put an irreparable strain on the relations of the Eastern and Western Church.

An important development right before the beginning of the Renaissance was the almost doubling of Europe's population between the years 1000 and 1300, peaking at about seventy-five million people. Europe's rapid population growth owed itself to the relative stabilization of affairs after the chaos of the collapse of the Roman Empire. However, by the mid-14th century, at least a third of the European population died due to the Black Death epidemic, setting back progress considerably. Spreading from Asia, the bubonic plague ravaged Europe, with its victims dying either shortly after contracting the disease or after suffering long and gruesome deaths. Urban areas experienced rapid depopulation, and the labor shortage caused by the epidemic triggered even further damage. Population levels would not be the same until about 1550.

The bubonic plague exposed Europe to its main problem—the continent was perpetually vulnerable to large-scale disease outbreaks, unable to combat them due to a lack of medicine. The poor folk particularly suffered from the diseases, vehemently praying to God they could avoid the misfortune, but to no avail. The plague set back Europe's development for who knows how many years. Life expectancy declined considerably. About a fifth of all newborns would die before they could live for even one year.

This, combined with constant wars between states and the ideological and cultural standstill of Middle Ages Europe, resulted in this period being deemed the "Dark Ages." However, this term was not applied to the period until much later, when the succeeding periods resulted in progress, learning, and relative prosperity compared to the misery of the Dark Ages. In fact, it is quite surprising that, not even two hundred years after it had been decimated by the plague, Europe would be a completely new place. Instead of empty, rat-infested, dirty, and muddy streets of European towns, clean, paved roads would emerge, often full of people. The development of new professions would encourage the re-growth of urban areas. High society would thrive as the rediscoveries of ancient texts would awaken a long-lost European culture, one that had remained unknown for about a thousand years. Scientific and technological progress would greatly improve the quality of all aspects of life and lead to a new drive to learn, explore the world, and grow as human beings. In short, after centuries of stagnation and idleness, Europe was primed for a rebirth.

Chapter 2 – The Birth of Rebirth

Entering the Renaissance

As mentioned, European towns and cities grew rapidly in size and population during the 12th and 13th centuries. This was largely due to the level of sovereignty these cities experienced compared to France or England. Due to the complex nature of the Holy Roman Empire (composed of hundreds of individual free cities), for example, baronies, provinces, and other administrative groups were very decentralized, though formally ruled by an emperor. This meant that individual entities had more freedom and were constantly competing with one another. This was especially true for ones in Germany, the Low Countries, and Northern Italy.

In the Low Countries, cities benefitted from being close to a coast at the crossroads of northern trade routes. Due to the lack of centralized Italian states, many different city-states had also popped up in Italy, much as in ancient Greece. These city-states, while all "Italian," were ruled by different rulers and constantly competing with each other. Urban growth was most prevalent in these areas because of this. Since these cities were not supported from outside—as, say, smaller towns in France or England would have been tied economically or administratively to the rest of the king's realms—many different institutions and services, such as hospitals, universities, or guilds, were concentrated together.

Urban growth and the decentralized city-state structures of Europe can certainly be considered a prerequisite of the Renaissance. In Northern Italy, where the most marvelous achievements of the Renaissance took place and from where the movement originated, for example, there were about twenty city-states by the 14th century.

We must remember that the movement or period we now call the Renaissance was not separate, broken off from the Middle Ages from the beginning. Rather, the developments took place gradually and simultaneously from about 1350 to 1530, centered in Italy and then spreading to the rest of the continent. The Renaissance was a combination of artistic, intellectual, scientific, socio-political, and technological progress that transformed how Europeans viewed life and affected the continent and the world for generations to come. Urban growth and the increased interconnectedness of different regions of the continent by the 14th century was a huge benefactor to kick-starting the process.

The Italian Peninsula, situated conveniently at a crossroads between the rest of Europe and the eastern world across the Mediterranean, was a perfect place for the cultural and material exchange about to take place. Thanks to the expansion of trade and commerce in the 12th century, several Italian city-states became very prosperous and could hold their own against bigger empires. Venice and Genoa, for example, were powerful trading empires, basing their power on their maritime capabilities. The pope controlled Rome and its surrounding areas, and the Kingdom of Naples held the south, while Florence and Milan were among the most influential city-states in Northern Italy. Social divisions did exist, but despite their diverse lifestyles, they were all interconnected. These urban relationships had only existed on this scale during the height of the Roman Empire, when city councils, courts, and public gathering areas were greatly organized and looked after. Moreover, Italy was where Roman heritage was most visible—in the most literal sense of the world— something that made the inhabitants of the city-states proud.

One way the Italians consciously reconnected with their Roman ancestors was through the political organization of their city-states. From about the 13th century, most Italian city-states were republics ruled by popular assemblies. The size and nature of the assemblies varied, but they were very similar to ancient Roman rule since they were usually comprised of wealthy male elites. Participation in public life was regarded as an honor, so there were clear distinctions between who was fit to rule and who wasn't (though that did not mean social mobility was impossible). Wealthy merchants, for example, were as influential as the nobility, though they may not have held as much land. The bulk of the urban population was made up of local artisans and shopkeepers specializing in this or that industry and contributing their lot to the thriving scene of the city. This kind of social division also reflected the ancient Roman patrician-plebeian divide.

Still, political life was just as dynamic. Powerful families of the Italian city-states often had conflicting interests, vying for power from different sources and competing to emerge dominant. Some city-states would descend into outright hereditary rule because of this. For example, the Visconti family had become the most powerful in Milan, thanks to its huge textile manufacturing business, but would be overthrown in the year 1447 by the Sforza family, which imposed its own despotic rule on the city for years. The infamous Medici family, on the other hand, managed to become hereditary rulers of Florence, building up their fortune by monopolizing the banking industry. By contrast, the Republic of Venice was about as republican as it could get. Its ruler—the doge—was elected by a popular assembly, the Senate, and held executive powers that would be balanced by the Great Council and the Senate. This system of checks and balances, while not exactly resulting in the representative democracy that is the most common form of governance today, was nevertheless a rarity in the medieval world. It stemmed partly from the cultural and intellectual novelties and rediscoveries we will cover later. In part, it represented those rediscoveries and novelties by replicating the type of polity preferred by the ancient Romans.

The New Cultural Center of Europe

It is not surprising that Florence is considered the cradle of the Italian Renaissance, from which all other developments of the movement occurred in later stages. It is the city most associated with the Renaissance even to this day, and several factors contributed to its emergence as the new cultural center of Western Europe. The city-state underwent tremendous economic and cultural growth from the 13th to the 16th centuries, and all of the factors played complementary roles in Florence's meteoric rise.

Located in the northern part of the Italian Peninsula in the province of Tuscany, Florence was a modest city on the Arno River after the collapse of the Roman Empire. It experienced similar levels of instability as other places in that part of the world for the first 500 years or so after the fall of Rome. Still, its convenient location and smart governance eventually combined to make it one of the most prosperous cities in Europe. Ruled by wealthy merchants, known as the *grandi*, Florence accrued considerable wealth that its rulers poured into the city's development. The *grandi* commissioned artisans, architects, and craftsmen to upgrade their own estates, which were close to the city or inside its walls, and so contributed to making Florence look good, as well. Government officials were elected from several merchant guilds, so the power stayed in that class. It was a typical oligarchy, where the means of power was in the hands of a few rich individuals. These, in combination with lawyers and city militia, enforced the laws and conducted foreign affairs. Popular councils also convened to discuss civic matters, again building on the traditions embedded in the consciousness of many from ancient Roman times.

In the 14th century, hardships fell on Florence and the rest of the continent due to the spread of the Black Death. The city's lower classes revolted in the Ciompi uprising, pressuring the elites and demanding more economic and social equality. This led to a rather turbulent period in the history of Florence that would partially end about 1434 when Cosimo de' Medici and his family emerged at the top of Florentine politics. One of the richest families in Italy by that point, drawing its wealth from overseeing one of the most efficient banking systems, the Medici gained the loyalty of the city's militia and overthrew the other rulers. This move was partially motivated by the family's will to expand its influence and wealth, and both goals were successfully reached. Then, through the manipulation of the electoral system in place, Cosimo de' Medici took control of the most important offices of the government and emerged as essentially the sole ruler of the prosperous city-state.

The tenure of the Medici further accelerated Florence's rise to power. In 1406, the city-state conquered the neighboring city-state of Pisa, extending its control and territories and possessing another rather rich city. The Medici capitalized on this gain—control of Pisa gave them direct access to the sea, through which they grew their wealth. Textile manufacturing and commerce thrived in the city, and knowing that the Medici were to be their patrons, more and more people flowed in. By the mid-15th century, the city had become one of the most urbanized areas in Europe. High levels of urbanization had ripple effects in other aspects of life—most prominently on literacy rates. Numerous new schools and universities were constructed, creating a more competent workforce that boosted the income of the city and the development of very well-cultured, tasteful, and proud citizens. In other words, all the pre-requisites for the great cultural advancements that were to come (and were already slowly taking off by the time the Medici gained power) were in place: the city was thriving economically, thanks to the wise rule of its new leaders, and its society was stable and dynamic.

Rediscovery of the Ancient Past

As Florence and the rest of Northern Italy emerged as the new economic and social center of Western Europe, the situation was ripe for a massive cultural breakthrough, which manifested when the Italians started to place more and more emphasis on the rediscovery and celebration of classical texts. This process also started around the 14th century, and by the time the Medici took over Florence, it was at its peak.

One of the most influential of those who jump-started the cultural achievements of the Renaissance is Francisco Petrarca, better known as Petrarch. A poet and scholar of Tuscan descent, Petrarch received his education in the southern French town of Avignon during the first half of the 14th century. During this time, conflicts and rivalries in the papacy and the influence of the French kings had resulted in the turbulent "Avignon Papacy" period, when two rival popes simultaneously claimed to be the head of the Catholic Church. One of them had a court in Avignon, which meant that the French town had a concentration of well-educated clergymen and lawyers. Petrarch was thus lucky to end up in Avignon, where he became a master of the ancient Latin language and started copying ancient works from manuscripts available in the papal court there. At this time, essentially the only people who had access to these texts were the clergy, but few were as enthusiastic about uncovering more of them as Petrarch. His passion for learning eventually led to the recovery of the great Roman writer Cicero's *Letters to Athens* from the cathedral of Verona, further motivating the Tuscan youngster to continue searching for ancient manuscripts. He traveled throughout Europe and found more and more such texts, which had been stored deep within the libraries and crypts of the old Christian cathedrals. Ultimately, Petrarch became one of the most prominent scholars of 14th-century Europe, accruing great knowledge of ancient literature and spreading his passion to many others, like Giovani Boccaccio, who also started to collect classical literature.

Petrarch, Boccaccio, and other collectors and scholars of the classical texts found something new, something compelling, about these texts. Unlike the scholastic tradition of the medieval world, which focused primarily on the study of law, medicine, and theology through the application of reason to philosophical and theological questions, these texts shifted attention to the study of liberal arts that were perceived to be of great importance during antiquity. Logic, grammar, music, astronomy, geometry, arithmetic, rhetoric, and metaphysics were all subjects adhered to by ancient Romans. Together, they made up the *humanitas* (humanities)—a category that emphasized wisdom and virtue, the exploration of which gave more intellectual freedom and satisfaction to the individual. Thus, those who studied the humanities were dubbed humanists, and the movement they began was known as humanism.

A crucial development in the mid-15th century in the East accelerated the development of humanism and the spread of a passion for learning. In 1453, the Ottoman Turks laid siege and captured the great city of Constantinople. The Byzantine Empire, which had survived for about a thousand years after the fall of Rome, was destroyed. Muslim Turks had pressured the Byzantines for many decades, and the territories of the once-great Eastern Roman Empire were slowly taken over. The fall of Constantinople and the preceding events that led to it resulted in the migration of Byzantine Greek scholars to the West, and most of them ended up in Italy. They brought with them even more classical texts and culture of ancient Greece, which had been relatively well-preserved but unavailable to the rest of Europe due to the socio-political and cultural division between the Byzantines and the West. Ideas brought by Byzantium were translated from ancient Greek into Latin and other modern languages and diffused greatly with the existing learning tradition that had begun in the early 14th century. Most importantly, the rediscovery of classical Greek philosophy, mythology, and history was vital to the development of the humanist movement and eventually emerged as one of the staples of the Renaissance.

Therefore, as more and more of the classical past was uncovered in the 14th–15th centuries, the medieval way of thought that had remained stagnant for several hundred years began to evolve. Humanism viewed the classical past as the most glorious era in history and celebrated the intellectual achievements and moral virtues of ancient Romans and Greeks. They believed that the medieval scholastic tradition had focused on trivial things while ignoring something far more important—the nature of man. This central aspect of humanist thought was greatly influenced by Greek philosophers like Aristotle and Plato, who had posed questions regarding morality, virtues, and truth and wanted to learn more about these phenomena outside the traditional lens of understanding. Withdrawing into philosophy and just speculation was not enough for the humanists. They needed to posit the ideals of man so that everyone could attain them. Early Renaissance thought bridged the gap to classical antiquity, which had put humans, with all their best and worst qualities, at the center of their universe and sought to revive this understanding and institutionalize it in the minds of medieval people.

Chapter 3 – The Essence of the Renaissance

Drive to Synthesize

The main outcome of the rediscovery of and better familiarization with classical antiquity was the drive to understand more by synthesizing classicism and Christianity. Old texts emphasized the ability of humans to basically achieve anything they wanted. Petrarch was one of the first to reassert that. He believed in the innate ability of humanity to be wise and make conscious, rational decisions, and this did not exactly mean the abandonment of the Christian way of life. Humanist thought was unique because it sought to combine the main morality of Christianity with the best version of man that was to be found in classical antiquity.

For example, one area where this manifested perfectly was the re-adoption of a certain outlook on life strongly celebrated in ancient Rome and Greece: individual involvement in public affairs. Ancient Romans and Greeks hailed the principles of republicanism and democracy. They believed that a truly wise and kind man must get involved in the most pressing issues of his city or state. If one could in any way contribute to bettering public life, be it through teaching, taking up arms, or voting, it was almost expected. For the ancient thinkers, a strong state was complementary to the formation of a thriving, self-sustaining, virtuous society, and vice-versa. The branch of humanism that re-emphasized this is often referred to as civic humanism. Civic humanists believed ancient Greek and Roman societies were so prosperous because people understood how important it was to be involved in public affairs for the greater good. Those who failed to do so were undeserving of being considered "good."

Early Renaissance retained its close ties with Christianity. This was not unexpected since, by that time, the Christian way of life had become a normality for Europe. Instead, it synthesized the best of classicism and Christianity, and the way it did this was marvelous. The most prominent example is Dante's *Divine Comedy*, written in 1321. In his masterpiece, Dante voyages through Hell, Purgatory, and Heaven (all of which were part of Christian doctrine and depicted so). There, Dante encounters historical and mythological beings, some awaiting their entry to Heaven and some suffering terribly for their sins. Among those suffering are people from contemporary Italy known to be corrupt, fraudulent, or evil. Dante thus employed civic humanism in this way, too—he painted the failure to participate in public processes for the greater good and deliberate malicious actions as among the worst sins through a Christian lens. This was a rather creative example of how classical tradition was combined with the Christian outlook on life. *Divine Comedy* remains one of the best works of literature to this day.

Another way the synthesis of Christian and classical understandings of life was achieved was by reinterpreting classical antiquity through a Christian lens. The work of classical poets, such as Virgil—a central character in Dante's *Divine Comedy* whose epic *Aeneid* sought to personify the ideals of a virtuous Roman citizen—were reinterpreted. The main character of the epic, Aeneas, was depicted by humanists as allegorically undergoing a Christian struggle to find salvation and purity of soul through his journey of seeking duty for the great Roman Empire, as mentioned in the original epic. This was a way of appropriating the classical ideology and outlook on life in contemporary settings. Humanists claimed that classical tradition was not incompatible with what Christianity stood for and sought to amplify the relationship between the two.

In fact, not only did the Renaissance not abandon Christianity for antiquity, it was likely the period when Europe embraced the religion the most. Hundreds of new cathedrals and churches were constructed in Italy and throughout the continent, which had distinctive Renaissance architectural styles and were decorated with works of Renaissance artists. Religious education also took off, and more and more people started to indulge themselves in the study of Christian scriptures and doctrines. This resulted in the further institutionalization of Catholicism in the lives of every European. Additionally, with more time devoted to the study of doctrine and the essence of the religion, the late Renaissance gave birth to one of the most influential religious diversities to emerge from Christianity: the Protestant Reformation. Later, we will cover how Protestantism was born in 16th-century Germany and built on the humanist ideas proposed in the early Renaissance to transform the lives of millions of Christians forever.

The Individual Back in Center

A fundamental break of the Renaissance from the way of thought of the early Middle Ages was putting humans back at the center of attention. During the Renaissance, men and women were reasonable beings, capable of attaining wisdom, morality, and virtue by themselves without the guidance of the Christian Church that had been imposed on Europeans increasingly after the fall of Rome. Just as in classical antiquity, individuals could be great and heroic. They could venture out to the unknown with the desire to learn more about the world and themselves and emerge successful in their endeavors. They were no longer to be considered eternally stained by original sin. Rather, they could and would prosper in a world full of possibilities if they tried hard enough and put their all into it. Independence and autonomy of choice were emphasized by humanism and considered to be the greatest qualities humans possessed. The emphasis on individualism also resulted, in a way, in the development of the autobiography as a common genre of literature. More and more people undertook writing diaries, for example, which only further boosted the desire to learn.

The definition of what it meant to be civilized was also expanded. At first, the Italian high society began to dress better and cleaner and behave more proudly. Good manners and general conduct were appreciated, and more and more writers emphasized this. Castiglione, for example, stressed the need to institutionalize higher conduct. People should understand why they were behaving the way they were and then effortlessly act that way, with their behavior becoming an essential, natural part of them, like breathing. This was largely based on breakthroughs in humanist thought of what it meant to be virtuous, polite, and wise, and more attention was devoted to stoic manners. People started to speculate what it meant to be an "ideal man," once again combining what they had rediscovered in classical tradition with what their Christian life had taught them. Knowing how to read and write in several languages, familiarity with public etiquette that was becoming increasingly dynamic, being capable of painting, singing, playing musical instruments, or being good at physical activities generally came to be valued more. Education and a will to learn and explore were also vital for the idealistic vision of the "Renaissance man," even if they were rather unattainable for most people, who had no means to pursue so many passions at once.

On the other hand, the Renaissance's claim of having rediscovered the essence of humanity meant little progress regarding the status of women, who continued to live under the same social restrictions as before. This was partly because women were still considered the sinful descendants of biblical Eve. For this reason, they were associated mostly with negative emotions and attributes such as deceit, chaos, and jealousy. They were often depicted this way in Renaissance art (something we will touch on later). In families, boys were almost always favored over girls, who were either quickly married off or sent to convents, where at least they could get some education. Women were regarded as less competent in almost all activities, a conception that would persist for many more centuries.

Chapter 4 – Italian Renaissance Art

Proto-Renaissance

Renaissance art is what the period is perhaps most remembered for. In Italy, Leonardo da Vinci, Raphael, Michelangelo, Titian, Sandro Botticelli, Donatello, and others pioneered breakthroughs in painting and sculpture; German and Dutch artists such as Albrecht Durer, Jan Van Eyck, and Rogier van der Weyden further explored the artistic horizons. Like every other aspect of the period, Renaissance art manifested the new way of thought introduced with the onset of humanism and the rediscovery of classical traditions. Evolving from religious scenery and themes, which dominated painting before the Renaissance, Renaissance paintings also placed humans at the center of attention, outlining their physicality and seeking to explore their inner emotions. Renaissance painters depicted everything from ancient mythology to historical events, biblical pieces, and everyday life. Through the development of new painting techniques and a more complete understanding of the human body, Renaissance painters produced some of the most memorable pieces of art to this day. Similar things can be said about sculpture and architecture, which improved massively, borrowing heavily from ancient times.

Before we examine the essence of Renaissance art and how it developed over a century and a half, it is first better to look at how what came directly before the Renaissance revolutionized the human understanding of art. By the 13th century, as already mentioned, religious themes dominated painting. In Italy, artists often based their works on Byzantine (Greek) iconography, developing the Italo-Byzantine style. Painted on small, portable canvases and utilizing the tempera medium derived from mixing water-soluble pigments with egg yolk (whose main advantage was that it dried fast), these paintings all looked rather similar. For example, although commissioned by different churches or cathedrals, depictions of the Madonna and Child were usually done on a golden background, and the details of the characters inside the paintings were often fixed or hardly modified. Taking center stage, the Virgin would hold Jesus in one position, with her head tilted the same way, wearing similar clothes and with similar, subtle facial expressions. This was the universally accepted way to depict the Madonna and Child, and the pioneers of medieval art, such as the Florentine Cimabue and Sienese Duccio, always painted them this way.

By the end of the 13th century, a new painter burst onto the artistic scene of Northern Italy, one who is often considered the influence from which other Renaissance artists borrowed significantly. Giotto di Bondone, better known as simply Giotto, was an apprentice of Cimabue who made one of the first breakthroughs in medieval Italo-Byzantine painting. His style was distinct from his predecessors in that he depicted more dynamic scenes and made the figures of the characters fully three-dimensional. Giotto was one of the first whose paintings told some sort of a story and had characters dynamically interacting with one another. His style was an evolution of the iconographic style of the Byzantine school, with his characters having distinct characteristics in different paintings and frescoes he completed. *The Lamentation* is probably the most celebrated of Giotto's works. Biblical characters lamenting Christ and the angels depicted above all have distinctive facial features and emotions. They are in motion and are fully interacting with each other. This was vastly different from the works of his predecessors, who essentially repeated the attributes of their characters and depicted them as ascetic, detached beings.

Giotto, Lamentation (The Mourning of Christ)

Early Renaissance Art

Historians consider the year 1425 as the end of the Proto-Renaissance period and the beginning of the Early Renaissance, which was once again mostly concentrated in Florence and immediately surrounding areas. By this time, Giotto had already become a renowned artist in Northern Italy, and his contemporaries were starting to emulate his style, which was unknowingly revolutionizing art as they knew it. They stuck to depicting biblical scenes, of course, and were mainly employed by different churches to complete their interior design with frescoes. For example, *Annunciation of the Shepherds* stands out in the Florentine Church of Santa Croce. Painted by Taddeo Gaddi, the figures inside the fresco are all clearly in motion and interacting with one another. They have distinct three-dimensional shapes, much like those in Giotto's work. What's special about *Annunciation* is the color contrast, as the bright upper half of the fresco greatly contrasts with the darker lower half, making it one of the earliest works that utilized shading in such detail.

Unfortunately, the misfortunes brought by the Black Death in the latter half of the 14th century halted the developments of the Renaissance a bit, or at least postponed them to the beginning of the 15th century. Around the same time, the public perception of artists began to change. Before, they were mostly considered craftsmen—people one could simply hire to do the job one wanted, just as one could have hired an artisan or a potter for their services. But a change of attitude towards art coincided with the breakthroughs of humanism and the gradual rediscovery of ancient works, which emphasized the beauty of the soul and celebrated human ability, viewing art as something prestigious, not just another profession. Artists no longer regarded painting or sculpting as something they did because they needed the money to survive.

Leonardo da Vinci, perhaps the man who most represents the spirit of the Renaissance, considered his work a manifestation of "higher art," not a mere profession or craft. Humanist ideology, which emphasized learning and the pursuit of greatness and perfection, played a big role in developing such an understanding. Artists started to believe that they should constantly improve their work, even if it took years. Motivated to perfectly capture the essence of this or that biblical, mythological, or historical event, they thus started to increasingly journey beyond the bounds of traditional art styles, focusing on trying to make the viewer understand the severity and seriousness of the situations depicted in their paintings. Soon, a byproduct of this was that paintings started to feel more real and natural as characters became more dynamic and started to resemble real human beings with real feelings.

The Neoplatonist understanding of life, rediscovered with humanism and developed as a rather prominent outlook, also contributed to this conception of art. Neoplatonism suggested that ideas such as goodness or beauty existed outside the realm perceivable to humans in everyday life. It emphasized the need to perfect oneself to attain the closest possible version of these ideals. This conception was increasingly shared by Renaissance artists as the movement matured. Throughout the development of Renaissance art, one can observe how, from monotonous paintings that depict characters that are identical in their forms and manners, paintings began to become more diversified. This evolution can be observed in the works of one the first truly Renaissance artists—Massaccio—whose fresco, *The Tribute Money,* is still in the Brancacci Chapel of the Basilica de Santa Maria del Carmine in Florence. The fresco depicts a biblical scene in which Jesus instructs Peter to find a coin in a fish's mouth to pay the temple tax. Jesus is pictured with his disciples and one tax collector in the center. The fresco can be further divided into two additional parts to the left and right sides. On the left, we can see Peter by the water, searching for the coin, while on the right, he can be observed already paying the tax collector.

The Tribute Money *by Masaccio*
https://commons.wikimedia.org/wiki/File:Masaccio7.jpg

This is a bit strange at first—how exactly does the fresco attempt to tell the whole biblical scene at once, and why is Peter depicted three times at three different points inside the fresco? This is exactly what is revolutionary with Masaccio's work. This was a fresco unlike anything of its time, combining three different parts of the biblical scene with a trick. In the fresco, Christ is what's known as the vanishing point, a point inside the painting toward which eyes are drawn first. The clever use of single-point perspective and color contrast amplifies the visual effect of the fresco. Additional scenes are only then noticed, creating a cohesive picture. Overall, the painting is dynamic, achieved partly by using new techniques. On the other hand, the new objective to depict beauty realistically—something emphasized greatly by humanism—is also present, making the fresco a stylistically distinct piece of work.

Crucially, the early 15th century also saw a massive increase in artists' guilds. New, aspiring artists would enroll in these organizations as apprentices of more senior painters and sculptors and undergo formal training. As time passed, the status of these guilds increased, and the quality of their painting rose, as well. By the mid-15th century, prestigious guilds competed, and guilds of different cities developed their own distinctive styles, or schools, of painting. Eventually, the Venetian school, for example, which included distinguished Renaissance painters such as

Titian, Giorgione, Veronese, and Tintoretto, emphasized the subtlety of colors and their effortless diffusion with each other over the use of clear lines to differentiate between the subjects of the paintings. Successful "graduates" of artists' guilds were recognized by contemporaries and employed for the rest of their lives, hired by private citizens who wished to decorate their estates and enrich their collections or different churches.

In Italy, the development of a tradition of patronage of the arts was just as important as the development of new techniques and styles in the arts for the flourishing of the Renaissance. For example, wealthy families, some of old patrician descent and some having obtained their riches thanks to the recent economic growth, would cordially invite distinguished painters to their rich villas and commission them with work. This was also beneficial for painters, who could work for their patrons without restrictions or distractions and deliver the best quality work they could—which went in tandem with their new humanist outlook on life.

Humanist scholars were also fortunate enough to receive patronage from the wealthy as their or their children's educators. Having obtained general knowledge of the humanities and natural sciences, they made great tutors. They were good secretaries and advisors, paying close attention to improving the behavior of their patrons, developing the official conduct inside their courts, and taking charge of correspondence with other individuals of status. This was largely because the renewed interest in an active life also included paying attention to things that might have seemed trivial to Europe of the Middle Ages. How one was involved in public affairs was just as important as *what* was done, and the whole procedure should exert wisdom and a sense of familiarization with the new norms. Wealthy families should not behave well just because they were wealthy. Rather, they should institutionalize good conduct and manners, making them a part of everyday life—an endeavor in which the tutors came in extremely handy.

The Medici were among the most prominent patrons of the arts. Thanks to their excessive wealth, they often commissioned architects to design their estates, for example. In turn, such close contact with the vanguard of cultural development elevated the status of the Medici and made them far more prestigious than they already were. Cosimo de' Medici, for example, the man responsible for growing the influence of his family, was a passionate collector of ancient manuscripts and devoted time from his busy schedule to learning. The Medici financed the often-ambitious projects envisioned by Renaissance artists, who needed a lot of materials and time to complete their work. Knowing they were set in all other ways, artists thus put their hearts and souls into pursuing their passion and producing the best they could. Michelangelo, for example, was one of the most prominent of those who benefitted from the goodwill of the Medici, even getting to design the Medici tomb in the Basilica of Saint Lawrence in Florence. The humanist education of the patrons also resulted in them often specifying what they wanted the artists to do—which scenes or characters to depict and how. Personal portraits or everyday themes were also common. The artist and the commissioner agreed on the price, first based on the order size, for example, and later on an assessment of the artist's skill.

An interesting practice that became common when artist-patron relations changed for the better, for example, was including the patron inside the painting as one of the characters. Like most other things in Renaissance art, this was much different from what came before. Masaccio's *The Adoration of the Magi,* one of the most celebrated works of the early Renaissance painted in 1426, features the portraits of the notary who commissioned the painting and his son. In this way, artists often paid homage to those who "looked after" them, growing the bonds between them and their patrons even more and developing a more cohesive, friendly, and dynamic culture where cooperation was just as valued as skill.

Interestingly, however, it is not a painting that is considered the earliest Renaissance work in Florence. It is, rather, a church door for the Florence Baptistery, designed by Lorenzo Ghiberti for a competition held to specifically select the best design in 1401. Based on the biblical theme of the Sacrifice of Isaac, Ghiberti's work features a small relief sculpture on the surface of the door, depicting the scene. Its style is reminiscent of the other paintings we mentioned earlier. Characters are dynamic and alive, with distinct characteristics, and all come together to create a scene. The work is heavily influenced by classical art, as, for example, Isaac is depicted as a masculine man with a great physique—a prominent characteristic of ancient Greek and Roman art pieces since a healthy body was believed to have a healthy soul. The Florence Baptistery features sets of doors designed by artists other than Ghiberti, who took twenty-seven years to complete his work after winning the competition.

The Sacrifice of Isaac

In short, the first half of the 15th century was crucial for developing the artistic culture in Northern Italy. Thanks to stylistic and technological breakthroughs in painting and sculpture and the strong patronage of the arts by the wealthy families of Florence, Venice, Milan, and other cities, early 15th-century artists were essentially the vanguard of the great things that would come after them. Thanks to the development of new techniques that uniquely captured and utilized light, paid more attention to shadows and perspective, and depicted characters as dynamic beings with emotions and distinct physical attributes that interacted with each other, art became very different from what it had been for the previous few hundred years. Artists like Masaccio and Masolino became great inspirations for the gigantic figures of the High Renaissance—the period that came after the first half of the 15th century.

High Renaissance

In arts, the period known as the High Renaissance started at the end of the 15th century, around 1490. Lasting until about 1530 in Italy, this era's works are perhaps the most recognizable of all art. Of course, as in most events throughout history, the break from the Early Renaissance did not happen at once, so no point can be identified as the beginning of the High Renaissance. What contributed to the development of the style of the period was the shift of the patronage role from the wealthy to the Catholic Church. Indeed, by the end of the century, Italy was struck with a subtle economic recession, the effects of which would only magnify as years passed. This was because of the complex political climate that existed in the region. When the city-states were at the height of their political and economic power, bigger nations became increasingly interested in gobbling them up. France and the Holy Roman Empire showed increasing interest in expanding their territories and influencing the prosperous city-states of Northern Italy like Florence, Genoa, and Milan. Spain, on the other hand, mostly focused its attention on the southern part of the peninsula. These external factors further contributed to the escalation of already-turbulent relations the highest classes of these cities had with each other, resulting in increased struggles for power and influence. This turmoil had a ripple effect on Renaissance art, which until then comfortably enjoyed the patronage of the wealthy families of Northern Europe.

Luckily, however, artists of that time found refuge in another equally (or arguably even more) reputable patron—the Church. Of course, patrician families still employed various artists to work on their estates, but the upper hand was assumed by the papacy, which had grown its power and influence exponentially. Indeed, as already mentioned, with the importance of Catholicism growing throughout Europe amid the political troubles in the East and in Iberia, the Church had become one of the main arbiters of affairs in Europe. The papacy had also accrued enough means to start rebuilding the ruined territories of central Italy it controlled, including the once-great city of Rome, which had been reduced to a shadow of its former self due to constant invasions throughout the Middle Ages. In the 1470s, excavation projects had uncovered much of ancient Rome, parts of the city that had been completely forgotten. This was partly due to the renewed interest in classical antiquity, which owed a lot to the development of humanist thought. The wealth of the Church was also constantly increasing, as opposed to private families, who were dependent on the existing social dynamics.

Thus, the time was right for the Church to once again take the lead in financing and looking after the artists. By this time, however, art had moved on from the relatively universal and monotonous Italo-Byzantine style and had become far more expressive than ever. The development of new techniques and the increasing interest in more realistic and creative depictions was an opportunity for the Church. The Church claimed it was the most influential and oldest institution in Europe, embodying stability, peace, and the spirit of human life through its God-given mandate. Visual aesthetics were important in reinforcing this image, and employing some of the brightest artistic minds to design the interiors and exteriors of churches, religious courts, and papal palaces was a great way to achieve this.

Art of the High Renaissance was greatly influenced by this sense of aggrandizement under the papacy's influence. Therefore, it is no surprise that art became far larger than before. High Renaissance artists painted on huge canvases, and their paintings would often be the only thing hanging up on the huge halls of papal residences. This is not to speak of the frescoes and sculptures from this period, which would often take multiple years to complete. The content of the art and the style also became quite complex, as if evolving from the works of the Early Renaissance period. The High Renaissance realized the increasing diversion of artists from the depiction of rational order to grand, ambitious scenery aimed at obtaining a powerful reaction from the audience. Canvases were filled with complicated scenes that were aesthetically pleasing due to the impressive way the characters were depicted. Michelangelo's work in the Vatican's Sistine Chapel is one example. Michelangelo glorified the physical and emotional attributes of his biblical, mythological, and historical characters, sometimes to the point that the many details in the frescoes overwhelm the viewers. Paying great attention to detail and the perfection of techniques, High Renaissance art can indeed be considered the magnum opus of Renaissance art or art in general. The distinct style to which it gave birth is called Mannerism (Grand Manner), capturing the essence of art from this period. The heightened scale, dramatic, exaggerated imagery, complexity, and attention to detail are all attributes of Mannerism that dominated the High Renaissance.

During the High Renaissance, some of the most iconic names in the history of art emerged. Leonardo da Vinci, Raphael, and Michelangelo are often considered the "big three" in this period of rebirth, though artists like Titian, Giorgione, and Bellini are also among some of the most memorable names from this period. In this chapter, we will look at these artists and examine what makes them so special in the context of the Renaissance and art in general.

Leonardo da Vinci - The Renaissance Man

If one person will forever be associated with the Renaissance and everything it stood for, it is certainly Leonardo da Vinci. Da Vinci was born in 1452 in Florence, and his father was a distinguished notary in the city. Through him, young Leonardo ended up in the workshop of Andre del Verrocchio, where he greatly developed his artistic capabilities in painting and sculpture. Having a creative mind from a young age, da Vinci was interested in studying more about the world around him. His personal notebooks from his formative years depict many sketches of different things, such as military weapons or mechanisms of various uses. In the 1470s, Leonardo was accepted into Florence's guild of artists, but it was around 1482 that he truly began his successful career. In early 1482, at the invitation of Duke Ludovico Sforza of Milan, the 30-year-old Leonardo decided to pursue his career prospects in Milan, being employed in the duke's court. It is unknown exactly what attracted the artist to Sforza's court, especially since he had just landed some of the biggest commissions of his early career as a member of the Florentine guild. However, he abandoned the projects he had started to work on in his native city and remained in Milan for the next seventeen years before eventually returning to Florence in the year 1500.

Even though da Vinci is often remembered first and foremost as a painter, his body of work is relatively small, and only seventeen of his paintings survive. What characterizes his style the most are two aspects. The first is his ability to capture human emotion. Art experts often praise Leonardo for expressing a wide range of emotions with the faces of his characters. His *Mona Lisa*, of course, is a prime example of this. Completed during the final years of his life, the *Mona Lisa* revolutionized how portraits were to be painted. The half-body of the only character of the painting—arguably the wife of Florentine merchant Francesco del

Giocondo—is the main focus. She is sitting down with a deep, subtle, infamous smile, in great harmony with her ambiguous background of nature. The two parts of the painting effortlessly fuse with each other, perhaps symbolizing the overall link of human beauty and nature and the fact that the two coexist and should coexist at all times. Effortless fusion and transition between objects of interest are achieved thanks to a technique that Leonardo pioneered himself—sfumato or "shadow." This is the second most prominent characteristic of Leonardo's paintings. The subtle brush strokes produce an effect of the manipulation of shade and color, thus leading to a seamless transition from light to dark colors without using sharp lines to contrast objects from one another. Sfumato is what makes Leonardo's paintings truly unique. The tones it generates help the viewer seamlessly move their eyes from one point of the painting to another and amplify the mysteriousness and the range of emotions captured on the faces of da Vinci's paintings, as in the *Mona Lisa.*

The Mona Lisa by Leonardo da Vinci
https://commons.wikimedia.org/wiki/File:Mona_Lisa,_by_Leonardo_da_Vinci,_from_C2RMF_re touched.jpg

Another of Leonardo's iconic paintings is the *Last Supper.* Painted in the mid-1490s in Milan's Santa Maria delle Grazie, it depicts the exact moment in the Bible when Jesus tells his apostles that one of them will betray him. Shocked by this news, the apostles are depicted to be agitated, discussing among themselves with great animation. Jesus sits in the center, in splendid isolation from the rest of the chaos. The only other character in the painting that is depicted as calm as Jesus is Judas, who, sitting to the right of Jesus and wearing green, realizes his mistake and has a deep look on his face, contemplating his decision to betray Jesus. The composition narrates the biblical scene, greatly capturing the confusion and chaos that emerges at the Last Supper after Jesus reveals that he knows of his betrayal. All the characters have distinguishable expressions and seamlessly interact with each other, creating a great scene overall that flows smoothly. Unfortunately, partly due to Leonardo's indecisiveness regarding what technique to use to paint the fresco, the painting deteriorated by the mid-16th century and was not restored until after World War II. Still, Leonardo's *Last Supper* became a footprint for all future depictions of this scene and is still celebrated today for its innovativeness and ability to narrate the story.

The Last Supper by Leonardo da Vinci
https://commons.wikimedia.org/wiki/File:%C3%9Altima_Cena_-_Da_Vinci_5.jpg

As much as he was a painter, however, Leonardo was also a scientist, biologist, anatomist, botanist, architect, sculptor, physicist, and engineer. Due to his undying curiosity, he personally researched all these fields, mastering his understanding of natural and physical sciences only to use this knowledge in his artistic career. Leonardo deeply believed that first-hand experience and knowledge of the human body, for example, was conducive to good painting. He also believed it was a good painter's obligation to make their characters as realistic as possible by employing the knowledge of anatomy. This was a very humanist conception of human ability—Leonardo thought that humans could perfect their work by putting in enough effort to study the subjects they wished to paint, the trajectory of light and shadows, and the nature of perspective. In his notebooks, which he carried with him all the time, he made annotations in pencil, observing the objects around him and pondering how they operated in real life to best capture them in painting or sculpture. In addition to including well-known concepts, Leonardo also explained relatively new ideas about spatial organization in paintings through lighting and shadows and concepts such as lateral recession, all of which would be expanded by his successors. One thing about his notetaking that is rather unusual and further emphasizes his genius is his ability to mirror-write. Since he was left-handed and extremely talented, mirror writing probably came naturally to him, and his sketches and notes can only be deciphered if one reads them with a mirror.

There are hints in Leonardo's writings that he was probably compiling his knowledge to produce a comprehensive, proto-scientific study of painting. By combining his vast theoretical framework with practical applications of the knowledge he had gathered, his book or treatise could have been directed toward aspiring artists as a potential guide to painting. In it, various techniques and their applications would be explained, and his main idea would be to promote the *saper vedere*—the art of knowing how to see. He deemed this very important, especially for anyone who claimed to be an artist. From his notebooks, we can see that Leonardo considered painting and sculpture not just another profession but a higher form of work, a humanitarian subject or a science of its own. In the long term, his emphasis on implementing empirical evidence and experimentation may have influenced the development of the scientific method, which transformed the way scientific studies are conducted in all fields.

Leonardo da Vinci is also the man who almost single-handedly accelerated the study of anatomy. Again, anatomy and the understanding of the human body was something he hoped to use in his artistic work, in his pursuit of perfecting his style and technique. Probably interested in the subject from his days with his teacher, Verrocchio, he invested more time into his research once he moved to Milan. Working with several prominent hospitals of the time, Leonardo was permitted to dissect human bodies to better comprehend their fundamental structure. Primarily, he was concerned with studying parts closely linked with motion, such as the skeletal structure and muscles. Mechanical activity was of great interest because he would most often be painting it, and the knowledge seemed most useful to him. We can see his deep understanding of the human physique from his sketches, which are dotted with graphic depictions of the body in different positions, both static and in motion. Though he was technically not a professional doctor or anatomist, he nevertheless helped advance the contemporary understanding of the subject and demonstrated his skill in art. His *Vitruvian Man*, which also takes its place as one of the most instantly recognizable paintings, is a great demonstration of the knowledge he gathered of the human body and the application of geometrical principles to it—another field he greatly loved. The perfection of the *Vitruvian Man* reflects the existing humanist outlook on life: the human body with all its perfections and imperfections could be considered a microcosm, a symbol for the greater universe. Understanding it was just the first step in understanding the much larger world.

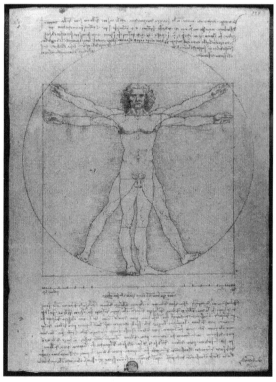

Vitruvian Man by Leonardo da Vinci
https://en.wikipedia.org/wiki/File:Da_Vinci_Vitruve_Luc_Viatour.jpg

Last but not least, Leonardo can be considered a brilliant engineer and an architect. Having a creative eye and a deep understanding of key mathematical, physics, and geometric principles, it is unsurprising that Leonardo's notebooks are full of interesting designs, ranging from military to civilian technology, public and private buildings, and plans for whole towns. Through diagrams and patterns, he identified different machines and the mechanics behind them, such as transmission gears or hydraulic presses. Leonardo helped his cities greatly with his practical knowledge, helping design canals, fortifications, streets, and overall urban planning. He also developed the first prototypes of the modern tank and flying machines, rather carefully outlining the physics behind them but ultimately lacking a power source to generate enough for his works to come to fruition.

All in all, Leonardo da Vinci, with his undying will for self-improvement and exploration of the world, and his application of the knowledge gathered from empirical experience to the arts to perfect his work, is the person who most embodies the spirit of the Renaissance. A man of many talents and interests, he not only revolutionized painting and produced the most iconic artistic works to this day but also significantly expanded knowledge in most fields of science. Leonardo refreshed the Renaissance with his ambitious projects and big ideas. He was already considered among the most accomplished people in Italy when he passed away in 1519.

Michelangelo and the Grandeur of the Renaissance

After Leonardo da Vinci, the artist who comes to the minds of many who explore the Renaissance is Michelangelo di Lodovico Buonarroti Simoni, better known by his first name. A younger contemporary of Leonardo, Michelangelo was born in 1475 to an aristocratic family in Florence and became one of the most renowned artists in history throughout his almost 90 years of life. Much like Leonardo, he did not only limit himself to painting and pursued sculpture and architecture very enthusiastically. In fact, despite his monumental achievements in these three fields, he considered himself primarily a sculptor, as he never abandoned the practice throughout his career, focusing on painting and architectural design only in certain periods of his life. Considered the most talented artist of his time, Michelangelo is an example of a Renaissance artist who became extremely popular during his lifetime, with his biography published by his contemporary, Giorgio Vasari, in 1550. To this day, he remains one of the most influential artists ever, the author of some of the most iconic works that still inspire and amaze millions today and embody the essence of the High Renaissance the most clearly.

Much like Leonardo, Michelangelo also started out as an apprentice of an accomplished painter, Domenico Ghirlandaio, during his teens. He was quickly recognized by Lorenzo de Medici, through whom he became more acquainted with classical antiquity—one of his main sources of inspiration throughout his career. It was through Medici and the sculptors associated with the ruler of Florence that he got into sculpting. However, he preferred to work in marble rather than bronze, which was more common in his day. This was undoubtedly due to the influence of classical antiquity on the young artist. By the end of the 15th century, due to the decline that had beset Florence and the Medici family, Michelangelo moved to Bologna and then to Rome, completing the first of his major projects—the tomb of St. Dominic. The influences and the developing style of Michelangelo can clearly be seen in the design and the grandness of the tomb, which would become definitive features of most of the artist's work. The statue of *Bacchus*, completed in 1497, is the earliest surviving large statue by Michelangelo. Forging the ancient Greek god of wine from one large life-sized marble block, Michelangelo created a statue that effectively captures the essence of Bacchus as he is depicted in Greek mythology. He is a youthful, lively god who cares a lot about entertainment and drinking, but his deep, focused gaze on the winecup he is holding hints at the fact that he has become a victim of his own self. *Bacchus* is one of the first examples of Michelangelo's work where his deep technical understanding of marble sculpting, human physique, and emotion combined with his knowledge of the ancient world.

Bacchus by Michelangelo
https://commons.wikimedia.org/wiki/File:Michelangelo_Bacchus.jpg

This work served as a great introduction to Michelangelo's career. Two years later, he completed his *Pieta*, which has become an iconic work of the artist. Commissioned by a French cardinal, *Pieta* portrays the Virgin holding Jesus after the Crucifixion. Lamenting her son on her knees, the relationship between the two bodies is seamless, giving it a pyramid structure. Mary is depicted as a younger version of herself as described in the Bible and looks down on Jesus, whose lifeless, skinny body is resting on her overwhelmingly large gown. Michelangelo again sculpted both figures from one marble block, which was very difficult. *Pieta* is hailed as one of the finest works of the Renaissance, as it captures the contrast between life and death, man and woman, horizontal and vertical, while at the same time marvelously outlining the physical and emotional attributes of the characters.

The Pieta by Michelangelo

After *Pieta* came perhaps the most renowned work of Michelangelo—an expression that is up to interpretation since all his works are so renowned. *David*, which was commissioned to the artist in 1501, was unveiled at the central square in front of the Palazzo della Signoria in Florence in 1504. Coming in at 5.17 meters (17 feet) tall, *David* can be considered Michelangelo's first true homage to classical antiquity, reflected in giving the statue such a large size, characteristic of classical sculptures. To this day, *David* is considered among the best examples of what the Renaissance (and the humanist movement, in general) stood for—the excellence and perfection of the human body and, thus, according to the contemporary perception, of the human soul. With *David*, Michelangelo demonstrated that his understanding of the human body had only increased after his debut. Initially, since the authorities of the Florence Cathedral had commissioned the artist to complete the statue, they had considered placing it on the cathedral's rooftop. As Michelangelo neared completion, however, it became apparent that the statue was too big to be lifted to the top, and instead, a council convened to decide where it would be put. Many artists and city authorities were present, including Leonardo da Vinci and Sandro Botticelli.

David by Michelangelo
Michelangelo, CC BY-SA 4.0 <https://creativecommons.org/licenses/by-sa/4.0>, via Wikimedia Commons; https://commons.wikimedia.org/wiki/File:Michelangelo%27s_David_-_right_view_2.jpg

David and other works from the early 1500s, including the statue *Madonna of Bruges* and the painting *The Holy Family*, contributed greatly to the development of Mannerism and its establishment as a central style of the High Renaissance. In all these works, Michelangelo's creativity and skill can be recognized, as well as his influences—the greatest of which is da Vinci, who had returned to Florence in 1500 and become acquainted with the 25-year-old Michelangelo.

After completing *David*, Michelangelo skyrocketed in popularity and began working on several ambitious projects in Florence. But he never managed to finish any of them. This was because he was approached by Pope Julius II, who invited the artist to Rome to work on a tomb that would consist of up to forty large statues. Due to political complications in the region, however, which included the turbulent relations between Italian states, this project never began. Michelangelo left Rome for a time, only to return in 1508 to start working on his undisputed magnum opus in painting—the ceiling of the Sistine Chapel. The Sistine Chapel was an integral part of the Vatican Palace, where many ceremonies were conducted. But its main part had already been completely designed, so Michelangelo was to paint a relatively less important room. The initial plan envisioned by the pope and his associates was to devote each of the twelve segments of the ceiling to a depiction of each of the Twelve Apostles. However, after Michelangelo agreed to start working, he applied his own vision to the plan—leading to the creation of one of the most legendary works to this day.

Michelangelo did not completely abandon the pope's vision, though he moved it to the sides of the ceiling. Instead of depicting the apostles, he painted seven prophets and five female sybils from classical mythology on the sides, devoting the central part of the ceiling to the nine scenes of his choosing from Genesis. Three stories were about the creation of the world, three about Adam and Eve, and three about Noah. The corners were filled with other biblical figures from the forty generations before Christ. This colossal work took nearly five years to complete, and Michelangelo worked on it alone, which amplified the difficulty of the job even more.

Michelangelo's idea behind the narrative structure of the ceiling was drastically different from the pope's idea, which saw the ceiling as a potential bridge between the scenes of the Old and New Testaments that were depicted on the walls of the Chapel. The apostles were exactly thought to represent this link in the best way. Michelangelo, however, did not focus on depicting virtuous, devoted apostles to emphasize the biblical sense of goodness they represented. Instead, humanity's disgrace can be identified as the overarching theme of the ceiling. Contrary to what one might initially think, this is a humanist conception at its heart. Renaissance humanism was not only about depicting man with all his inherently good qualities; it was also about identifying the bad qualities of humanity and, in this way, underlining the innate ability of humans to improve and overcome them. This was Michelangelo's vision. Through his characters and scenes, he wished to portray some of the worst things in the Bible, signifying the flaws of humanity and that it could only be saved by Jesus. Even though the physiques of his characters are all reminiscent of the maximum amount of perfection possible, as was the convention in the Renaissance and in antiquity, Michelangelo did not necessarily make his characters noble, virtuous, or stoic. Instead, the faces of characters in individual paintings are full of mystery and sadness. This is the case, for example, with Adam, in the arguably most famous piece from the ceiling—*The Creation of Adam*. The physiques are near perfection, but the emotion is almost always negative and full of grief. Uncertainty is a central theme and gives the whole composition a unique style. Michelangelo's stylistic decisions for his work in the Sistine Chapel were instrumental in the full-fledged development of Mannerism.

An image of the ceiling of the Sistine Chapel

Antoine Taveneaux, CC BY-SA 3.0 <https://creativecommons.org/licenses/by-sa/3.0>, via Wikimedia Commons;
https://commons.wikimedia.org/wiki/File:Sistine_Chapel_ceiling_02_(brightened).jpg

After completing the ceiling of the Sistine Chapel, Michelangelo's career only accelerated further, though that is not to say there were no speed bumps on the road. For example, having finally obtained funding from Pope Julius II to work on the tomb, originally commissioned by the pope in 1505, Michelangelo was soon left disappointed as funding for the project disappeared with the pope's death in 1513. His best work from this project that survived is *Moses,* clearly a Mannerist sculpture with an exaggerated physique and facial expressions. Michelangelo's deep understanding of human anatomy also shows in this work. Later, until the mid-1530s, Michelangelo would be employed by Pope Leo X—the son of Lorenzo de' Medici (a fact that signifies the influence of the Medici and the political turbulence of Renaissance Italy)—and his successor, Pope Clement VII. Mostly spending time in Florence, Michelangelo devoted much of his time to working on the design of the Medici tomb and chapel. He also created most of his architectural designs during this time, once again expressing the best of his unique, Mannerist style and demonstrating his knowledge of military technology when he helped with the fortifications of Florence.

In 1534, Michelangelo returned to Rome at the request of Pope Paul III and would also return to fresco painting after about twenty-five years since the completion of the ceiling of the Sistine Chapel. This time, he was to paint the Chapel's end wall. The topic was the Last Judgment. Perhaps the very last of his greatest works, *The Last Judgement* is painted in a style completely different from the ceiling. By the time of its painting, Michelangelo had fully embraced Mannerism, which can clearly be seen from the excessive quality and quantity of figures, all with exaggerated physiques, depicted in the fresco. Pictured in the center of the giant fresco is Christ, raising his right arm as if to save all who are depicted on his right and lowering his left arm to damn all those on his left. Combining a multitude of biblical characters while fusing in mythical (or pagan) elements like Charon in the bottom right, who is ferrying the damned souls to Hell, *The Last Judgment* might at first be overwhelming to the viewer. There is so much going on that, at first, it seems as if the fresco lacks structure. But as the eye explores the genius of Michelangelo, the dynamism and multiple narratives of the fresco are instantly outlined. The over-exposed physiques of its characters fuse in seamlessly with the relatively simpler colors than those used on the ceiling of the Chapel. Even more impressive, Michelangelo was sixty years old when he painted the fresco.

The Last Judgment by Michelangelo

In his final years, Michelangelo almost completely focused on architecture, designing such important parts of the city of Rome as the dome of St. Peter's Basilica and portions of the Capitol Square. Though he would not live long enough to see his ambitious, grandiose projects fully completed, his plans would be gradually fulfilled after his death and still dazzle viewers. Made illustrious during his lifetime, Michelangelo is rightfully considered one of the greatest artists of all time due to the sheer magnitude of his work and the influence of his style that would last for generations. His compositions are some of the most unique in the world and perfectly capture the spirit of the Renaissance. Grand and sophisticated, Michelangelo remains the ultimate star artist of the Renaissance.

Raphael and the Flexibility of Renaissance Art

The artist considered the third "giant" of the High Renaissance is Raphaello Santi, better known as Raphael. Born in 1483 in the Duchy of Urbino, Raphael was the youngest contemporary of the three but had a much shorter career due to his early death in 1520. He became interested in art through his father, a relatively unsuccessful painter who knew many artists in the city. Raphael eventually went to the city of Perugia to study painting. Although the art scene in Urbino and Perugia was not as developed as in other larger Italian cities like Florence or Rome, young Raphael would be very much influenced by his idols from these cities, discovering their work at a young age. Still, by 1500, his apprenticeship in Perugia had ended, and he had made quite a name for his talent and enthusiasm for painting. Around the same time, he became acquainted with an already-established Renaissance artist, Pietro Perugino, who gave a lot of advice to Raphael when it came to perfecting his painting techniques and later became a big source of inspiration for him.

Raphael completed his *Marriage of the Virgin* in 1504 for the church of San Francesco in the province of Perugia. Painting in oil on a round-headed panel, Raphael seemed to be greatly influenced by the work of his superior, whose *Marriage of the Virgin* is very similar. Following the same stylistic and narrative choices as Perugino, Raphael's painting nevertheless appears more advanced in almost every way, especially in the characters' facial expressions. The temple in the background indicates that, by this time, Raphael had already mastered the manipulation of perspective, something that gave his painting a much more dynamic and completed feeling. The relationship between the architecture in the background and the characters in the foreground is also reminiscent of Perugino's style. This would be an aspect Raphael would only further advance in his later paintings.

Marriage of the Virgin *by Raphael*

Marriage of the Virgin by Pietro Perugino

https://commons.wikimedia.org/wiki/File:Pietro_Perugino_cat66.jpg

Another iconic painting of Raphael from this time is his *Vision of the Knight*, completed around the same time as *Marriage*. A perfect example of the importance of symmetry in painting, the painting is split in the middle by a narrow tree. The sleeping knight lying in the center is thought to be ancient Roman general Scipio, who, according to Cicero's accounts, had to choose between Virtue and Pleasure, represented by the two women on either side. Virtue, on the left side, is much more stern and robust, holding a sword and a book. The background on her side is more rocky and hard, emphasizing the difficulty Scipio would encounter in pursuing this quality. On the other hand, Pleasure is depicted with more liberty, wearing a looser robe, her hair visible, and holding a flower. In a way, the two ladies are not depicted in a contest with one another since the symbolic objects that they are holding can be attained in synthesis. The sword signifies knighthood and honor, the book stands for knowledge and wisdom, and a flower represents love—all qualities necessary for an ideal person, consistent with the humanist vision. With great use of various shades of blue, mastery of perspective as seen from the seamless fusion of the background with the characters in the front, a symmetry that is obtained by splitting the painting in two, and the narrative and symbolic background the painting represents, *Vision of the Knight* is one of the most perfect examples of Renaissance art and signifies the genius Raphael had managed to achieve in his early years.

Raphael's Vision of a Knight

Already considered one of the brightest of his generation, Raphael also completed *St. Michael* and *Three Graces* during his time in Perugia, but it soon became clear that he was ready to expand his horizons. The move to Florence served this purpose. Drawn to the center of Italian art thanks to his admiration for Leonardo and Michelangelo, he explored new technical and narrative styles pioneered by these become visible in Raphael's works almost instantly after his decision to move to Florence. A series of Madonnas he completed throughout the late first decade of the 1500s are a testament to this. Painting the Virgin became a staple of Raphael synonymous with his style and personality, and the pure and uncomplicated way he depicted the Madonna marveled his contemporaries. Managing to capture her innocence as described in the Bible, Raphael's Madonna was also intimate and virtuous, a fundamental aspect of Renaissance painting. His colors became darker and his shading more profound owing to the influence of Leonardo. In his *Deposition of Christ*, completed in 1507, Raphael shows his deep understanding of the human body and paints a dynamic picture full of story and character. The *Deposition* perfectly captures the essence of the biblical scene, combining the grievous expressions on the faces of the lamenters and the lifeless expression of Christ, creating a complicated and dynamic scene full of chaos.

Deposition of Christ *by Raphael*
https://commons.wikimedia.org/wiki/File:Raffaello,_pala_baglioni,_deposizione.jpg

In 1508, Raphael was brought to Rome by Julius II, and the last twelve years of his career were when he truly reached his peak. Architect Donato Bramante suggested Raphael (still a relatively young artist at that time) to the pope, who, as mentioned, had ambitious plans for the decoration of the Vatican and the improvement of the public spaces in Rome. He commissioned Rafael to start painting the walls of the papal apartments, known as the Stanza.

Raphael's work in the Stanza della Segnatura is considered his magnum opus. The four walls of the chamber all have frescoes by Raphael. His *Disputation of the Sacrament* is an amazing piece of work that depicts Christ and other biblical and historical figures disputing Christian doctrine. It is Raphael's attempt at representing individuals who had been most important in developing the Christian religion as it was and is meant to symbolize the triumph and superiority of the Catholic Church. Christ is, of course, at the center, flanked on either side by the Virgin Mary and John the Baptist and other important biblical characters like the apostles, King David, Moses, John the Evangelist, and Abraham. A multitude of historical characters are also pictured below Christ. They are some of the most vital theologians from the history of Christianity, such as St. Augustine and Ambrose, several popes (including Pope Julius II), Jerome, and St. Thomas Aquinas. The painting also includes depictions of Savonarola, a Florentine friar and revolutionary who was the theocratic ruler of Florence for a short time, Dante (for his contributions to the fusion of Christianity and classicism), and Aristotle—one of the biggest inspirations of medieval scholarship. Finally, to pay homage to his mentor, Raphael also included Bramante, making for an eclectic mix of individuals. He believed they were most crucial—not only for the development of human thought and understanding of Christian doctrine but also for the thriving of the Church and religion as a whole. This latter understanding of the Church's position was characteristic of High Renaissance when it became the main patron of arts in Italy.

Disputation of the Sacrament *by Raphael*

Raphael's *School of Athens,* on the opposite wall of the *Disputation,* is commonly considered his magnum opus. A homage to classical scholarship and his contemporaries, the fresco is a celebration of philosophy and knowledge unlike any other. The center of the fresco is occupied by Plato and Aristotle, the central figures for Raphael in the development of philosophic thought, each representing their own ideological bases. To the left, Plato is depicted as an older man pointing to the sky, hinting at his understanding of the world of ideas, holding his *Timaeus.* Aristotle, depicted as a younger but still a mature person, is gesturing downwards—emphasizing his main perception of particulars and holding his *Nicomachean Ethics.* The two central figures of the fresco are surrounded by other important members who have contributed to the development and perfection of secular knowledge, including Anaximander, Diogenes, Socrates, Parmenides, Zeno, Epicurus, Pythagoras, and Archimedes. The fresco also includes depictions of people such as Alexander the Great, Ptolemy, and Zoroaster, as well as a personal portrait of Raphael, who is looking directly at the viewer from the bottom right corner. The man writing in the middle is also supposedly Michelangelo, depicted by Raphael as Heraclitus. Greek mathematician Euclid, who is bent over and measuring on the right, is supposed to be Bramante. A perfect culmination of the High Renaissance, *The School of*

Athens is a beautiful fresco that points to Raphael's fascination with the individuals depicted in it. Combining this sense of admiration with a masterful expression of perspective and lighting, *The School of Athens* remains perhaps the most celebrated of Raphael's works.

School of Athens *by Raphael*

Commissioned by the pope, Raphael was also instructed to paint the Stanza di Eliodoro, and the artist's work there is a step forward in his ability to express narrative and technique. The contents of the frescoes in this Stanza are far more straightforward than those depicted in the other, lacking the allegorical and symbolic meanings of *The School of Athens* and *Disputation* but nevertheless excelling in form and storytelling. *The Mass at Bolsena, Liberation of St. Peter, Expulsion of Heliodorus,* and *Meeting of Leo the Great and Attila* all display Raphael's mastery of color and shading techniques, owing to the influences of Michelangelo and Leonardo. The manipulation of light and the transition from darker to lighter parts in these frescoes are excellently accomplished, and the fusion of multiple sources of light only amplifies their effects on the viewer. In addition, paintings the artist completed around the same time as his work in the Stanzas, such as *Triumph of Galatea,* demonstrate Raphael's understanding of the human body and may even be considered early

Mannerism. Still, the characters in these works are shown to be glorious and epic, with an emphasis on clearly showing their perfect physical attributes. At the same time, Raphael also painted some of the most subtle and gentle works in his career, reminiscent of his early work. For example, in his hailed *Sistine Madonna*, completed in 1513, Raphael recaptures the serenity and innocence that characterized his early career. However, this depiction of Madonna is far richer in color and more interesting in narrative than his previous work. It seems as if *Sistine Madonna* is a culmination of the artist's exploration of the theme, as his other depictions of Madonna from this period, such as *Alba Madonna* (1508) and *Madonna di Foligno* (1510), serve as preludes to this work.

Sistine Madonna, *Raphael*

https://commons.wikimedia.org/wiki/File:RAFAEL_-_Madonna_Sixtina_(Gem%C3%A4ldegalerie_Alter_Meister,_Dresden,_1513-14._%C3%93leo_sobre_lienzo._265_x_196_cm).jpg

What can be observed from Raphael's move to Rome is the fact that he often worked on multiple projects at once. Despite his relatively short lifespan, he managed to leave behind a substantial body of work that is celebrated to this day. In fact, in the last decade of his life, he became so popular thanks to papal patronage and his excellence that he emerged as a prominent portrait painter in the city. His portrait of *Baldassare Castiglione*, completed in 1516, is a great example of the flexibility of Raphael's artistic ability. He could paint grand, majestic biblical or mythological scenes full of complex characters that synthesized to form a complicated narrative. In addition, he could also capture sophistication, purity, and innocence all at once in his characters, evidenced in his various paintings of Madonna and the portraits he completed in his later career. In fact, Raphael's amazing ability to switch effortlessly between such drastic styles of painting can be observed in the final years of his life with his last work, *Transfiguration*, which was commissioned by Cardinal Giulio de' Medici (soon to be Pope Clement VII) in 1517. Having a pyramid structure, *Transfiguration* combines shade manipulation and color contrast, emphasizing the main idea of the narrative depicted in the painting. The painting has been interpreted as Raphael's first real Mannerist work, and some art historians even consider the style to be more reminiscent of the Baroque period, which would come a couple of hundred years after the Renaissance.

Transfiguration, *Raphael*
https://commons.wikimedia.org/wiki/File:Transfiguration_Raphael.jpg

All in all, Raphael is rightfully considered among the three biggest names of Italian High Renaissance art alongside Leonardo da Vinci and Michelangelo. His supreme ability to combine the serenity and grandeur of his characters with a creative way of conveying narrative and symbolism in his paintings rightfully makes him one of the most brilliant minds of the time. Hailed during his lifetime as an extremely talented and tasteful individual, Raphael enjoyed papal patronage in Rome and even participated in overseeing larger architectural projects undertaken by Leo X. His untimely death from a fever at the age of thirty-seven came as a tragedy to the contemporary Italian society that was familiar with his genius. Raphael's funeral mass was organized in the Vatican, and the great artist was buried in the Pantheon of Rome, a gesture of the eternal city eternalizing one of its most accomplished individuals.

Chapter 5 – Renaissance Science and Technology

Shifting Paradigms

The Scientific Revolution was an equally impactful part of the Renaissance as the cultural advancements that took place in Europe increasingly after the 14th century. Of course, it is important to remember that all the things we have mentioned and are about to cover were taking place around the same time. The developments in science and technology resulted from the birth of humanist thought and a renewed will to explore, which began in Italy and then spread further to the rest of Europe. As previously emphasized, the biggest change that gradually took place in the minds of the most educated members of the otherwise uneducated European population was a fundamental paradigm shift. With a new desire to better understand nature and become its master—a humanist conception at its core—Renaissance scientists managed to make revolutionary findings. Together, they contributed to changing the existing Christian understanding of how the world worked and started the long process of a paradigm shift in the medieval era, which would reach its peak with the Age of Enlightenment a few centuries after the height of the Renaissance.

Interestingly, with the rediscovery of ancient texts, people also regained access to a lot of previous scientific knowledge in different fields, such as astronomy. Ancient Greeks and Roman scientists had speculated about the design of the world and had used several different means to obtain the knowledge they believed would confirm their findings. The scientific method, though partially present in ancient Greece in the works of Aristotle, for example, was still underdeveloped. By the 11th century, it had been advanced mostly in the Arabic world, during the Islamic Golden Age, where science and mathematics were much more developed than in Europe. In the Muslim world, experimentation had slowly begun to be understood as a reliable method of testing theories and obtaining knowledge. Arab mathematicians, physicists, and physicians, such as Ibn al-Haytham (Alhazen) and Ibn Sina (Avicenna), developed the scientific method from its applications in classical antiquity. Crucially, this happened because they had access to classical literature and translated it into Arabic. Alhazen and Avicenna knew of Aristotle, Epicurus, Democritus, and other ancient Greek philosophers and theorists and built upon their knowledge.

With the rediscovery of ancient knowledge and the gradual diffusion of knowledge from the East to Europe, the scientists of the 12th and 13th centuries started to get acquainted with all these conceptions. The scientific method (the version applied at the time) was gaining more and more traction. Unfortunately, just like everything else at the time, the Black Death stopped much of this move forward when it wiped out millions of people in Europe, literate and illiterate. Still, with the Renaissance, increasing interest was shown in obtaining knowledge, and several contemporary developments accelerated the spread and the desire to obtain knowledge.

The Printing Press

A monumental technological breakthrough in the mid-15th century changed the way Europeans accessed and perceived knowledge: the development of the printing press by a German goldsmith, Johannes Gutenberg. By the time Gutenberg completed his version of the printing press around 1440, the Early Renaissance and the socioeconomic progress it brought had made it almost necessary for information to be produced and transferred more quickly than before. Scholarship had developed considerably with the rediscovery of classical literature and the new writings of medieval scholars motivated to contribute to the existing body of knowledge with their own discoveries. Translation and copying, however, took time and were mainly done by the clergy in the monasteries and cathedrals. But demand and interest were very high among the public, especially those in the higher classes with more means of acquiring knowledge.

In the 15th century, however, several other important developments inspired Gutenberg to create his printing machine. First was the introduction of Chinese-type paper to Europe from the East through the Arabic world. The Arabs had close trade contact with the distant Chinese civilization and had learned the craft of papermaking from them before the Renaissance flourished in Europe. In Europe, several different presses had existed from ancient times, mostly used for making wine or manufacturing cloth. Gutenberg aimed to fuse the two together, creating perhaps the most revolutionary piece of technology in Europe since the wheel.

The design was relatively simple. Gutenberg's printing press began with creating metal pieces for each character, punctuation mark, or symbol. These pieces were made using typecasting, a method where molten metal was poured into molds with the reverse image of each character. Once the metal type pieces were ready, they were arranged correctly on a composing stick. The compositor, the main person behind the process, assembled the type in a mirrored manner, reading the text backward. To apply ink, the typeset text was carefully transferred from the composing stick to the form, a large frame placed on the flat bed of the press. The ink, which was oil-based and sticky (and also developed by Gutenberg), was applied to the raised surfaces of the metal type using inkballs or ink rollers. Next, a sheet of slightly damp paper was positioned over the inked type by hand or using a wooden frame called a tympan. This ensured that the ink would transfer well onto the paper. To initiate the printing process, the compositor pushed a lever connected to a screw-operated platen. The platen exerted significant force when pressed down, creating an impression by making contact with the inked type and transferring the ink onto the paper. After the impression was made, the platen was raised, and the printed sheet was removed. This process was repeated for each sheet, allowing for the production of multiple copies of the same text.

The first book ever printed was the Bible, known as the Gutenberg Bible, and only a handful of copies of the very first edition survives today, all of which are believed to be extremely valuable. A direct consequence of Gutenberg's invention was the printing revolution—the exponential spread of printing throughout Europe that contributed greatly to the circulation of knowledge and different ideas, only accelerating the process started by the Renaissance. Not only that, but the printing press led to the creation of thousands of different jobs as more cities adopted the press in pursuit of utilizing it to its full benefit. By the end of the 15th century, up to 300 cities in Western Europe had a printing press. Germany, Low Countries, and Northern Italy especially benefitted due to their decentralized but highly urban political structures. This resulted in a drastic increase in book production and, consequently, increased literacy rates throughout Europe, which had circular, complementary effects. According to some estimates, by 1500, Europe had about two hundred million copies of different books. The printing revolution also gave way to the subsequent scientific revolution, which would take Europe by storm in the next century-and-a-half and produce some of the most marvelous findings in the Renaissance.

The Scientific Renaissance

The Scientific Renaissance applies to a period from the mid-15th century to the mid-17th century. At this time, most advances in astronomy, anatomy, mathematics, physics, medicine, and other natural sciences took place in Europe, ultimately ushering in an even more sophisticated and advanced Age of Enlightenment, as mentioned. The Scientific Renaissance was a gradual process. Its prelude was the rediscovery of ancient texts, which caused a renewed, increased interest in these fields. As more scholars started to flesh out their theories regarding the different aspects of science, the invention of the printing press would help greatly in the diffusion of knowledge among them and the public. The result was a new spirit of the scientific community and the "formal" establishment of such a community in the first place.

The Scientific Renaissance included multiple paradigm shifts. One already mentioned was the development of the scientific method and a more coherent theory of reliably obtaining knowledge. The conceptions of Copernicus, Galileo, Kepler, Harvey, and later Newton, for example, resulted in a gradual move away from the traditional, medieval way of understanding the world, the most obvious characteristic of which was placing the Earth in the center of the universe. Contrary to popular perception, however, what took place was not a "scientific revolution"—a term that has been applied to describe scientific progress and discoveries from the late 16th to the 18th centuries. We must understand that change took place step by step. As ancient knowledge was being rediscovered, the theories being developed by Renaissance scientists and scholars were initially only known to a handful of people. Crucially, the Polish astronomer and mathematician Nicolaus Copernicus first proposed the revolutionary heliocentric model of the solar system, challenging the prevailing perception of the Earth. His seminal work, recorded in *De Revolutionibus Orbium Coelestium* (On the Rotation of the Celestial Spheres), laid the foundation for a new and deeper understanding of the universe and revolutionized scientific thinking.

Though Copernicus was challenged by the religious authorities, who correctly perceived the proposed model of the Earth as dangerous to their power, the works of other scientists, like Galileo, reconfirmed the concepts of the Polish astronomer. Galileo Galilei is another monumental figure of the Renaissance. An Italian scientist of the 16th–17th centuries, Galileo made outstanding contributions to the fields of physics and astronomy, as well as to the development of scientific instruments. Most notably, he improved the telescope to make new observations, such as discovering Jupiter's moons and observing the phases of Venus. Galileo's work further substantiated the heliocentric theory and cast doubt on the prevailing Aristotelian cosmology. German astronomer Johannes Kepler, who formulated his three laws of planetary motion, also expanded on Galileo's work. These laws provided a mathematical explanation for the motion of the planets around the Sun and further strengthened our scientific understanding of celestial mechanics. Still, the Catholic Church was also discontented with Galileo and denounced his science as heresy.

In addition, we have already mentioned the breakthroughs in the field of anatomy by Leonardo da Vinci, who was partly motivated to depict the human physique as perfectly as he could in his artistic works. However, medicine and anatomy also advanced greatly during the Renaissance in Northern Europe. Flemish physician Andreas Vesalius, for example, revolutionized the study of anatomy with his influential set of books *De Humani Corporis Fabrica Libri Septim*, emphasizing the importance of direct observation and careful dissection, correcting longstanding anatomical misconceptions and making great strides in our understanding of the human body.

Overall, the history of Renaissance science marked a significant shift from reliance on ancient authority to direct observation, experimentation, and mathematical reasoning. This paradigm shift laid the foundation for the scientific revolution that unfolded over the following centuries, ushering in a new era of scientific inquiry and discovery. The Renaissance catalyzed the development of modern scientific methods and knowledge, enabling humanity to broaden its understanding of the natural world and embark on an extraordinary journey of exploration and innovation. More fundamentally, it also weakened the Catholic Church's authority since it was becoming apparent that the Church could not effectively combat the claims of new science with its old, strict, and doctrine-based views. This was especially prevalent as more and more people became literate and had new means of obtaining books. The decline of the Church's influence was accelerated by another greatly important development of the Renaissance in the 16th century—namely, the Protestant Revolution.

Chapter 6 – The Northern Renaissance

Contextualizing the Northern Renaissance

We must remember that the Renaissance was not confined to Italy. Instead, as time passed, it slowly spread from the peninsula north of the Alps. Some main themes that characterized the movement in Italy were replicated and advanced in the Holy Roman Empire, France, Netherlands, England, and even Poland. The Northern Renaissance built on the intellectual, artistic, and socioeconomic developments of the Italian Renaissance, producing a comparably rich heritage that would influence history for centuries to come.

The context of the Northern Renaissance was highly similar to that of the Italian Renaissance. After the population decline and other associated harms caused by the Black Death, the situation slowly normalized again in Europe. This meant a new wave of migration to the urban areas and, consequently, the development of a more interconnected and prosperous society. One result was the centralization of most political entities north of the Alps. For example, full-fledged kingdoms with more clearly defined borders and structures started to emerge from the chaotic remnants of the Middle Ages in France and England. In the Holy Roman Empire, the political structure was still very much decentralized. However, the growing influence of the Austrian Habsburg dynasty was beginning to show. In fact, by the 16th century, the Habsburgs directly controlled many of the German lands in Central Europe and were kings of Spain and suzerains of the Dutch city-states. International borders had started to loosely resemble their modern versions, though constant wars ensured that the influence between international actors was heavily contested. Higher levels of urbanization and increased trade in Northern Europe challenged the trading monopoly of the Italian states in the Mediterranean. Because a new centralized Russian state had also started to take shape, the goods from Asia could reach the northern markets through Russia much more easily, not only through the south.

In turn, the growth of cities resulted in a growing demand for new services and goods, further accelerating economic growth. In turn, economic prosperity was the prerequisite for fostering the cultural and intellectual needs of the people, which were also aided by existing trends in Italy. More universities were founded and matured in the 15th and 16th centuries, becoming centers of idea exchange. Ancient texts that had fascinated Italians, Greeks, and Arabs for centuries (increasing numbers of which were slowly being uncovered in the 14th and 15th centuries) were scattered around in the cathedrals north of the Alps—the main repository of knowledge in this region, as well. Still, these developments came about half a century or so later than they had in Italy. A growing network of scholars, merchants, and artists contributed to the diffusion of these ideas, eventually resulting in the development of Northern Humanism, which owed a lot to Italian humanist thought but also had its own distinct character. Finally, Gutenberg's printing press greatly accelerated knowledge exchange in the rest of Europe, producing a thriving culture that certainly rivaled Italian Renaissance.

Perhaps the most influential figure who contributed the most to the development of Northern humanist thought was Erasmus of Rotterdam. Born in Rotterdam, Holland, in the late 1460s, Erasmus became a prominent humanist, theologian, and scholar, and his ideas and achievements laid the foundation for important advances in a wide variety of fields. Erasmus' role in the revival of classical scholarship in Northern Europe was immense. Erasmus' most notable early work, *Adagia,* published in 1500, is a collection of proverbs and sayings from Greek and Latin sources. This work proved Erasmus' erudition and encouraged the adoption of classical wisdom in contemporary society, as it was perceived to be timeless knowledge that anyone could use in any situation. As a prominent scholar and advocate of what humanism stood for, Erasmus believed in the transformative power of education and defended it. He emphasized the importance of classical language, literature, and critical thinking in curriculum. Erasmus earned a reputation as a prolific author of textbooks and educational treatises, such as *De Copia* (1512), which taught his students the art of rhetoric and effective communication. His ideas influenced educational institutions throughout Europe and laid the foundations for modern educational practice.

Though Erasmus was a devout Catholic, he also advocated for a return to the original teachings of Christianity, believing in the importance of personal piety and true Christianity. His most famous work, *In Praise of Folly* (1509), satirically criticized corruption and excesses within the Catholic Church. He was one of the main Renaissance scholars to deeply study the Bible to better understand Christian doctrine. More importantly, in 1516, he concentrated his findings and interpretations of the Scriptures into a new, translated edition of the New Testament known as the *Novum Instrumentum*. By providing original texts, Erasmus hoped to promote a more informed and critical understanding of Christian doctrine. For him, the essence of Christianity was not in blindly following the directions of the Church or its authorities when it came to prayer, for example. Instead, he stressed the need to apply critical reasoning to doctrine, in line with the rest of the Renaissance movement. With the Church's monopoly over the dissemination of religious knowledge, common people could not truly interpret the meaning of Christianity for themselves, Erasmus believed. He thought that intellectual dialogue and understanding between different religious and cultural groups was essential to the progress of society, emphasizing peace, harmony, and tolerance. Eventually, Erasmus' emphasis on personal faith and biblical scholarship laid the foundation for the later Protestant Reformation, which would directly affect the lives of millions of Europeans.

The Reformation

Though it is often regarded as its own phenomenon, the Protestant Reformation can certainly be regarded as one of the most fundamental developments of the Late Renaissance period, directly influenced by the intellectual and social dynamics of the early stages of the movement. A revolution in the 16th-century Catholic world that eventually resulted in the creation of a new branch of Christianity distinct from both Catholicism and Eastern Orthodoxy, the Reformation had far-reaching implications. Protestantism (represented by a mix of denominations) is still the fastest-growing Christian movement in the world.

German theologian Martin Luther is often considered the main man behind the Protestant Reformation. However, it is important to understand that the movement took shape gradually and had different centers and leaders in Western Europe. In the Swiss city of Geneva, for example, John Calvin led the Protestant movement against the Catholic Church and is also considered an instrumental figure of the Reformation. This chapter will briefly cover the history of the Reformation in the context of the Renaissance and how exactly this development was caused by the intellectual and cultural drive for rebirth that was characteristic of the period.

When looking at the Reformation through the lens of the Renaissance, two things must be acknowledged. The first is the influence of Erasmus' writings and his study of Christian texts on the leaders of the Reformation (which we will get to later when we discuss what motivated Luther, Calvin, and others to go against the authority of the Catholic Church). The second is the state of Catholicism in the 16th century, which is directly connected to the developments in the Early and High Renaissance periods. As already mentioned, the influence of the Catholic Church as the most important institution of Europe grew with the Renaissance movement. The regional churches of different European kingdoms were very powerful but still subject to the authority of the papacy, which controlled a lot of land and resources in Central Italy. The structure of the Church was very centralized and hierarchical, with clear distinctions between the different ranks of the clergy and their roles. The papacy was also heavily involved in the political matters of the world at the time, viewing itself as a sort of international arbiter. Indeed, when rulers were endorsed by the Church and had the religious authorities on their side, their power was much more apparent and present. This was because the meaning of life for an average low-class medieval or Renaissance person was set by the principles of religion. To the laypeople, the Church was their main spiritual guide, and understandably so. Most people were illiterate and uneducated, content with following the rules the Church authorities set out for them. Living by the rules and standards of the Church was comfortable, even if problems existed in the fundamental nature of the Church and its roles—something that would be outlined by Luther and other leaders of the Protestant movement.

With the development of humanist thought that emphasized critical thinking and increased the spirit of inquiry, scholars started to identify aspects of the Catholic Church they found problematic. At its core, the overarching idea the leaders of the Reformation had was a gradual move away from the strictly hierarchical nature of the Church and a return to the doctrinal basis—something that had been outlined by Erasmus of Rotterdam and others.

Among the important criticisms that would be stressed later was the intrinsic corruption in the Church. The sale of indulgences was one of the problems. In the medieval era, one could approach a priest and ask for forgiveness for sins, paying them a certain amount of money for the sins to be absolved. Indulgence could also be directed at releasing the individual from the judgment of purgatory—a state of suffering after death where the souls of sinners would answer for their sins, according to Catholic teaching. The Catholic Church supposedly obtained a large portion of its income this way. When the profit from selling indulgences combined with instances of nepotism, the illegitimacy and incompetence of the clergy, whose interpretation and teaching of doctrine was dubious, and the special privileges churchmen all over Europe enjoyed, a sense of protest was born among those who recognized the nature of the problems.

Moreover, by the 1500s, as we have seen from the lavish and ambitious projects undertaken by the popes, the wealth of the Church had skyrocketed. More money meant more influence on political affairs, which, in turn, meant more ways of getting more money. Overall, according to the protesters, it was a fundamentally flawed system that had gone corrupt and diverted from its roots. The Catholic Church needed some changes.

Although efforts had been made centuries before the Renaissance to implement changes in the Church, October 31, 1517, is usually considered the "beginning" of the Protestant Reformation. It is a significant date because it was when Martin Luther—a religious scholar and professor—nailed his Ninety-Five Theses on the door of Castle Church in Wittenberg, Germany. In the Theses, Luther outlined the main problems with the present state of the Church. He attacked the religious authorities for permitting such a flawed system to persist for centuries and exploit the lives of ordinary people. He also proposed changes that could save the state of the Church, emphasizing salvation by faith alone (*sola fide*) and the authority of Scripture (*sola scriptura*). Clearly influenced by Erasmus, Luther's main idea was that the true meaning of Christianity was in the Holy Scriptures and that the way it was taught in contemporary churches was fundamentally different from how it was intended to be taught in the ancient texts. Luther's ideas spread quickly throughout the main urban centers of Germany (Holy Roman Empire) thanks to their effective reproduction by the printing press. The reaction from Church authorities came quickly—they denounced him as a heretic and even excommunicated Luther in 1521. However, reform also seemed attractive to many individuals, including political and religious figures, who began implementing them in their local congregations. In this matter, the decentralized political structure of the Holy Roman Empire came in handy. Since local princes held the most authority in their chiefdoms, principalities, city-states, or baronies, they could implement the changes however they wanted and escape imperial or papal authority. Frederick III the Wise, the Elector of Saxony, was a political leader who protected Luther from the papal authorities by hiding him in the Wartburg Castle, where the theologian continued to immerse himself in religious research in late 1521. Over the next few years, Luther worked on his translation of the Bible into German to make it more accessible to the masses. His version was published and reprinted all throughout the German-speaking world. Over time, more and more parts of Europe embraced various forms of Protestantism thanks to the rapid dissemination of ideas that many found attractive and relevant.

Other important reformers include John Calvin, a Frenchman who had fled his country of origin for Switzerland, where religious freedoms were much more respected than in France. In Geneva, he became further acquainted with Luther's ideas and agreed with many of them, eventually developing his own version, known as Calvinism. Over time, Calvinism would become the main Protestant movement in most of Switzerland, the Netherlands, Scotland, and parts of France, centered on its understanding of the doctrine of predestination. Huldrych Zwingli would lead the Protestant movement in Zürich, which eventually merged with Calvin's denomination in the mid-16th century. Together, these versions of Protestant thought emphasized moral discipline and hard work and would emerge as a main foundation for the development of capitalism, as it would be later outlined by sociologist Max Webber. More radical versions of Protestantism, such as Anabaptism, also developed and were adopted to varying degrees in different parts of Europe. The key difference with Anabaptists was that they rejected the conventional practice of infant baptism, believing it was not mentioned in the original Scripture. As time passed, more individual theologians and scholars would propose subtle changes to previously-accepted forms of

Protestantism, leading to the creation of more denominations and what scholars have deemed the "democratization" of religion. Based on the main idea of interpreting the essence of the Holy Scriptures as best as possible without the restrictions and proposed interpretations of the Catholic Church, Protestantism flourished in most of Germany, the Netherlands, Scotland, and Scandinavia. The Catholic Church's influence, on the other hand, was mostly maintained in Italy, where its presence was the strongest, as well as in France and Spain.

The social and political implications of the Reformation would be apparent centuries after the end of the Renaissance. First, it triggered many religious wars on the European continent, with coalitions of Catholics and Protestants going toe-to-toe to impose their beliefs on the other. The Thirty Years' War, for example, is one such conflict, greatly altering the power dynamics among the European powers in the 1600s and contributing to the spread or containment of Protestantism around Europe. Protestantism also became a main factor in England's subsequent political turmoil, leading to King Henry VIII's decision to abandon Catholicism and instead "found" his own version of Protestantism, known as Anglicanism. Secondly, it led to the conflicts of the English civil war, which would cement Anglicanism as the official religion of the state, combining the role of the head of state and church, which is still a central aspect of the British monarchy today. More fundamentally, Protestantism led to the emergence of diverse religious beliefs and practices within Europe and the rise of religious toleration in some areas. Previous church structures and hierarchies would be fully modified to make room for new religious dynamics. All in all, the Reformation would embody the spirit of the Renaissance that stressed an individual interpretation of Scripture and the importance of education, contributing to increased literacy rates and the establishment of schools and universities.

Northern Renaissance Art

The Reformation is just one of the developments that can be considered part of the Northern Renaissance, though its peak took place late in the period and essentially bridged the Late Renaissance with the early stages of the Enlightenment. The Northern Renaissance was full of many cultural achievements just as celebrated as those of the Italian Renaissance. Again, the extensive interconnected nature of Europe in the 15th century contributed greatly to the flourishing of cultural exchange between Italy and Northern Europe. Non-Italian humanist thought and the rediscovery of ancient knowledge also made it so that some of the artistic developments of the Northern Renaissance took place at almost the same time as in Italy.

Hieronymus Bosch, Pieter Bruegel, Jan van Eyck, Albrecht Dürer, Rogier van der Weyden, and Jean Fouquet are among the most recognized names of the Northern Renaissance. The styles they developed sometimes reflected and tried to copy the developments in Italian art and sometimes responded to them. Perhaps the main difference between the two styles is that Northern Renaissance painting did not focus as heavily on religious or mythological themes as Italian Renaissance painting, though both were present during the early stages. Instead, scenes of everyday life were often depicted in Northern Renaissance art. These works, known as "genre scenes" or "genre art," offered a glimpse into the lives of ordinary people, including home environments, landscapes, markets, and interpersonal interactions.

The Northern Renaissance genre scene was distinguished by its naturalistic approach and attention to detail. Artists tried to accurately portray their subjects and capture the nuances of human gestures, expressions, and interactions. They paid special attention to the details of clothing, furniture, household items, and the architectural elements of the spaces depicted. By carefully rendering these elements, the artist created a sense of authenticity and allowed the viewer to connect with the scene on a personal and relatable level. In contrast, Italian Renaissance painting was much grander and more ambitious, often depicting narrative scenery that was difficult to comprehend if the context or title of the work was not known. Instead of showing excerpts from the Bible, ancient mythology, or history or presenting viewers with overwhelming imagery that made a great impression at first glance, northern painters often depicted people of different social classes performing their respective activities, a much subtler approach to conveying the story inside the paintings. They showed the lives of farmers, artisans, merchants, and aristocrats, reflecting the diverse social structure of Flemish, Dutch, and German societies at the time. Scenes of rural life depicted peasants working in the fields, herding cattle, and participating in seasonal events. Street vendors, markets, taverns, and workshops are featured in urban genre scenes, depicting the bustling energy and exuberance of city life. All in all, these subjects were much more relatable for the average viewer.

Narrative storytelling also played an important role in genre scenes in the Northern Renaissance. Artists used these scenes to convey moral messages, fables, or humorous anecdotes. The characters' actions and interactions within the composition were carefully crafted to tell a specific story or capture a moment in the human experience. These stories often reflect the values, customs, and social conditions of the time, providing viewers with insight into the moral, social, and cultural context. A notable example is the work of Pieter Bruegel the Elder. His paintings, such as *Peasant's Wedding* and *Hunters in the Snow*, depict detailed and expansive scenes of peasants engaged in various activities throughout the seasons. Bruegel's work visually documents everyday life and communicates deeper social, cultural, and moral issues. His scenes served as observational representations of reality and vehicles for artistic expression and social criticism. They provided insight into the human experience, capturing the joys, struggles, and oddities of everyday life. By portraying the everyday and familiar, they resonated with viewers and inspired them to reflect on their lives and the world around them.

As we mentioned, to convey this style, great attention to realistically depicting the characters and objects in the paintings was extremely important. So, Northern Renaissance art laid important foundations for the subsequent realism movement in later centuries. Northern Renaissance artists wanted to bring the human being to life, emphasizing anatomical accuracy and natural proportions. They paid close attention to the details of facial features and accurately recorded individual features and expressions. Using light and shadow helped create depth and three-dimensionality and added realism to the characters. Obviously, Italian art was a great influence. The garments and textiles depicted in Northern Renaissance art are meticulously crafted and demonstrate the artists' technical excellence. Fabrics are carefully rendered to reveal intricate patterns, folds, and textures. This attention to detail extended to the depiction of jewelry, accessories, and other decorative elements.

In addition to the human figure, Northern Renaissance artists focused on capturing the natural world with precision and detail. Landscape painting emerged as a major genre, and artists painted landscapes realistically. They paid particular attention to the depiction of vegetation, trees, bodies of water, and atmospheric effects. These landscapes were often sprinkled with symbolic and narrative elements that added layers of meaning to the natural landscape. On the other hand, in the works of some of the most distinguished Italian painters, the focus is rarely directed toward nature; the emphasis is on the paintings' characters. Backgrounds of paintings from the Italian Renaissance are often simple and rarely heavily detailed in contrast to the Northern Renaissance style. This attention to detail also led to the flourishing of still-life painting. Everyday objects such as flowers, fruits, food, and daily necessities were meticulously cared for, and attention was paid to texture, color, and lighting to enhance the sense of realism. The desire for realism and naturalism in Northern Renaissance art went hand-in-hand with the scientific and intellectual developments of the time. Notable artists associated with Northern Renaissance realism and naturalism include Jan van Eyck, Albrecht Dürer, and Hieronymus Bosch.

In turn, a growing interest in individualism, human psychology, and the expression of social status and identity was expressed in the development of portraiture as a prominent genre of the Northern Renaissance. Artists such as Hans Holbein the Younger and Jan van Eyck used meticulous techniques to capture the physical features of a seated person with astonishing accuracy. They emphasized facial features, hair, clothing, and accessories and executed them meticulously. Through their technical skill, they wanted to capture even the tiniest nuances and imperfections, creating a faithful representation of the sitters, combining the realistic aspects with great technique and even scattering symbolic representations of ideas in the paintings. Northern Renaissance portraits were often commissioned by wealthy commoners, clerics, or aristocrats who wanted to assert their social status and transmit a particular image to posterity. They were prominently displayed in private homes, guild halls, or public places and served as visual proof of a model's wealth, influence, and achievements. These portraits also strengthened family ties, social networks, and dynastic legacies. In Italy, however, portrait painting did not flourish to the same level as in the Northern Renaissance.

Thus, rooted in Northern humanism and important regional socio-cultural developments such as the Reformation, the Northern Renaissance developed its own identity independently from the Italian Renaissance. The socio-cultural factors that had resulted in the active patronage of Italian artists were largely absent from the North, most apparent in the Church's authority, which would slowly diminish as the Reformation gained more traction. While Italian artists had the resources to work for years on grand and ambitious projects commissioned by the papacy, this was largely untrue for the Northern painters. In the North, art was commissioned by members of different social classes, making the product more diverse but simple and relatable. This, in turn, meant that the profession of an artist also developed differently than in Italy, emerging as more of a traditional job that made money for the artist instead of a career only fit for the extremely talented minority. This was apparent not only stylistically but also in the dispersion of Northern Renaissance artists in many different places instead of being concentrated in only a handful of cities, as in Italy. Overall, the Northern Renaissance produced some of the most memorable works of art of its time that clearly reflected the socio-cultural and economic factors present in Northern and Central Europe.

English Renaissance

The Renaissance reached England a bit later than the rest of continental Western Europe and stayed there later, until the early 17th century. Still, English social developments that precipitated the move from the medieval way of life and thought to the Renaissance greatly resembled those in Italy and Northern Europe. Thus, to conclude the history of artistic and cultural achievements the Renaissance entailed, it is only fitting to look at how the movement flourished in England. As mentioned earlier, England would be among the states in Europe whose political structure would become centralized and more fixed during the Renaissance period, as opposed to Italy, which was still fragmented by the end of the 16th century. The Reformation is usually considered the main reason behind the political centralization and the newly-assumed role of the monarchy in England. With the adoption of Anglicanism—a religious and political tool crafted by Henry VIII to escape the papacy's influence—the monarchy's position was stronger than ever. From the mid-16th to the early 17th centuries, the strength of the Crown allowed the cultural movement in England to prosper, but differently from Italy, Germany, and the Netherlands. The English Renaissance is now mostly remembered not for its visual arts but for its literature and drama.

The emergence of literature as the central aspect of the cultural heritage of the Renaissance in England was due to a widely-accepted notion that God's greatest gift to humanity was the tongue. Figures like Roger Ascham, a writer and the tutor to young Princess Elizabeth I, defended this idea and urged the masses to educate themselves to read and write properly. It came in handy that by the 1500s, the printing press had already found its place in the biggest cities and universities throughout England, making the spread of literary texts much easier. Moreover, with the new translations of the Bible from Latin or Greek into vernacular English, more and more people were interested in buying books—a direct effect of the Reformation. Thus, literature would flourish during the English Renaissance, shifting from medieval traditions to a more humanistic approach to literature in which more fiction books were being written. Owing to the rediscovery of ancient Roman and Greek texts, many of which were legendary plays by authors like Sophocles or Aristophanes, playwriting also emerged as a great part of this revival.

At the forefront of English Renaissance literature is none other than William Shakespeare, considered the greatest playwright of all time. Shakespeare's plays are a testament to his mastery of language, depth of characterization, and exploration of universal themes. His works, such as *Romeo and Juliet*, *Hamlet*, and *Macbeth*, continue to be performed and studied around the world. The appeal of Shakespeare comes from the fact that his plays are entertaining. Following the humanist tradition, his work demonstrates deep insights into human nature, love, power, and the complexity of human existence. Characters are fully fleshed out, with distinct personal qualities, engaging in interesting dialogues with each other that prove Shakespeare's abilities as a great playwright.

Another influential figure in Renaissance theater was Christopher Marlowe. Marlowe's work challenged the conventions of the time, bringing a darker and bolder style to the stage. His most famous play, *Doctor Faustus*, dealt with ambition, temptation, and the consequences of morally questionable decisions. Marlowe's plays are known for their intensity, poetic expression, and complex character exploration.

In addition to drama, poetry played an important role in Renaissance literature. Edmund Spencer's epic poem *The Fairy Queen* is considered a monumental work of the period. Celebrating the virtues of chivalry, love, and honor, it weaves together a complex narrative that blends allegory, myth, and history. Spencer's poetry became the defining work of English literature, testifying to his mastery of language and poetic imagery.

The rediscovery of ancient drama and the creation of new works by local artists inspired the establishment of theater culture in England more than in any other European country. Public theaters such as The Globe became centers of artistic expression, attracting people from all walks of life, including the aristocracy and the emerging middle class, and reflected the changing social and political conditions. Theater stages served as platforms for exploring complex issues and ideas, often challenging traditional beliefs and values. A wide variety of genres were popular, including tragedy, comedy, history, and romance.

The development of theater culture only increased the popularity of contemporary writers and playwrights. Shakespeare's works, for example, crossed borders and appealed to a wide range of audiences; they were even translated into different languages in the 1700s. Exploring themes of love, power, politics, and humanity with unprecedented depth and complexity, his plays were staged in open-air theaters where audiences could witness the spectacle of live performances, experience shared emotions, and gain collective catharsis.

English Renaissance theater culture was not confined to London but spread across the country. A company of actors toured different cities, bringing the magic of the stage to different communities. The spread of theater made it possible for people of diverse backgrounds to engage in the arts, contributing to the democratization of culture. The rise of English Renaissance theater also brought about the formation of theater groups and the emergence of famous actors. These actors have become cultural icons who embody the characters and emotions portrayed on stage. Theater was so popular that it became an integral part of the social fabric of the time, attracting audiences from all walks of life.

In conclusion, the renewed interest in classical learning and an appreciation for human potential were central humanist themes the English Renaissance shared with the movement in other places throughout Europe. However, the Renaissance in England can still be considered vastly different from the Northern and Italian Renaissances. The Italian Renaissance focused on art, architecture, and sculpture. The masterpieces discussed earlier exemplify the artistic achievements of the era. In contrast, the English Renaissance prioritized literature and drama, with playwrights and poets becoming cultural icons of the time instead of sculptors or painters. Moreover, the Renaissance styles of Italy and Northern Europe represented more secular worldviews, fascinated by the beauty and harmony of the physical world. Beginning with the depiction of religious themes, the movement matured to the expression of realism in everyday life or the glorification of human ideals in Mannerist paintings. In contrast, the English Renaissance retained strong ties to religious themes and moral considerations, as seen in the moral dilemmas explored in the works of John Donne and Shakespeare's plays.

Another important difference is the socio-political context in which these Renaissance periods occurred. The Italian Renaissance was supported by wealthy patrons such as the Medici family and later the Church, who support artists and scholars financially and intellectually.

The Northern Renaissance owes its flourishing to the patronage of members of different social classes. In contrast, the English Renaissance featured the emergence of a middle-class audience that actively participated in theatrical culture, transforming theater into a more inclusive and accessible form of entertainment. Yet it would not have been as impressive without the support of the Crown, which contributed many resources to developing the cultural heritage so celebrated today.

Chapter 7 – The End of the Renaissance

Colonization

The history of the end of the Renaissance is complicated. This is mostly because we cannot definitively identify a single point when the Renaissance was no more. If nothing else, the whole history of the movement demonstrates that the Renaissance was not something with a definite starting and ending point: the social, political, economic, and cultural developments that took place from the late 14th to the 16th centuries were all deeply fused with each other. In addition, though we will later examine the end of the Renaissance in terms of the ceasing of artistic and intellectual progress, it can be argued that the Late Renaissance directly gave way to the Age of Enlightenment. Indeed, the advancements in political, economic, and scientific thought characteristic of Europe (especially of France, Britain, and Germany of the 17th-18th centuries) can be seen as direct consequences of the renewed will to learn and explore the world, which began with the Renaissance. Still, when we speak of the decline of the Renaissance, we usually mean the economic and political downfall of the Italian Peninsula in the 1500s—the place most associated with the Renaissance. Thus, now we will examine what caused the troubles and instability in Italy (and, to a lesser extent, the rest of Western Europe) that contributed to the traditional concept of the decline of the Renaissance by the end of the 1500s.

The beginning of the age of colonization can certainly be considered one of the factors that indirectly affected the decline of Italy as the cultural and economic center of Europe. Interestingly, the drive to colonize partially resulted from the development of Renaissance thought. We have mentioned that humanism stressed the importance of self-realization and humans' innate ability to master nature, which resulted in scientific and technological progress. One such technological development that revolutionized the way things were perceived at the time was the perfection of the design of caravels—smaller-sized, fast, and highly maneuverable sailing ships that allowed sailors to explore new maritime frontiers. Meanwhile, in the mid-15th century, due to the expansion of the Ottoman Empire and its blockade of Eastern trade by control of the southern Mediterranean, Europe needed to rediscover new trade routes. The Italian city-states of Genoa and Venice had monopolized the influx of trading goods from Asia in the Mediterranean, giving them an unfair advantage over merchants from France, England, or Iberia. Northern trade routes were also less developed at this time, as political troubles in Russia had destabilized the region and disallowed the establishment of reliable trade routes to Europe through Russia.

Thus, as a new way to circumvent the barrier of the Ottoman Empire was needed, the brightest and most creative minds of Western Europe started to look to the West instead of the East. Portugal and Spain would lead Europe in the endeavor to discover new trade routes to Asia. In the late 1400s, these powers gradually started to sail their way down the West African coast, discovering less civilized peoples and establishing trading outposts. A growing sense emerged that there was much to be explored to the south and especially to the west. In 1492, the infamous voyage of Christopher Columbus aimed to prove exactly that. Columbus, an experienced sailor and curious explorer from Genoa, believed that the rich Asian continent could be reached by sea if one traveled far enough to the west since it lay in the east. Technically, Columbus was correct—he had correctly identified the spherical shape of the Earth. However, due to the limited knowledge of geography outside of Europe at the time, he underestimated the size of the Earth. He had no idea that a huge landmass—which we now call the Americas—existed between Europe and Asia. Still, Columbus put his ideas into practice, obtaining funding and resources for an expedition from the Spanish Crown in 1492. But, as everyone knows, he did not reach India as he had imagined he would. Instead, Columbus landed on the Caribbean islands in October 1492, incorrectly identifying it as India and incorrectly dubbing the local American population Indians.

Thus began the age of colonization, which would transform the fate of European civilization forever. Establishing a reliable way from Spain to America, Columbus organized four expeditions, exploring the Caribbean basin and the eastern coast of Central America. Nobody had known that a landmass existed there, even though Europeans had, in fact, reached the place centuries before Columbus. Viking explorers led by Leif Eriksson had ventured all the way to Newfoundland around 1021. Unable to establish a foothold so far away from their home, they had abandoned their settlement. Knowledge of this legendary achievement had, of course, been lost in medieval Europe, so Columbus' discovery was a huge deal. Eventually, though Columbus firmly thought he had found a western route to India, Europeans realized that a whole new continent had been accidentally discovered and proceeded to explore it. What they found in the first decades of the 1520s were full-fledged civilizations in Central, North, and South America. The Europeans were able to easily overpower them with technological superiority. The Aztec, Maya, and Inca civilizations were tragically wiped out throughout the next few decades. The Europeans brought many communicative diseases for which the Native Americans had not developed immunity due to millennia of isolation.

Taking over the territories of the Native Americans, which were rich in natural resources and full of exotic foods, reliable trade routes were slowly established by Portugal and Spain—the two earliest and most successful players in colonization. These powers sent more and more exploratory missions to America to claim the lands in the name of their sovereigns and establish permanent settlements with permanent links to the European continent.

However, the influx of gold, silver, tobacco, and other extremely valuable trading goods into Europe by the mid-16th century came as a direct hit to the economies of the Italian city-states, which had never engaged in colonization mainly due to the lack of resources available to the centralized monarchies of Iberia and later France, England, and even the Netherlands. Economic decline was accelerated by the discovery of maritime trade routes to India by Portuguese explorer Vasco da Gama, which only increased the economic influence of Portugal in the Atlantic and Indian oceans. Soon, the once-great Italian city-states of Genoa, Venice, and Florence were greatly challenged by the new players in international trade, and their excessive wealth gradually declined.

Trade patterns and economic focus would thus shift away from Italy, meaning that the old patrons of the Italian Renaissance culture no longer had means of financing the projects of Italian artists. Meanwhile, the Church's role as a patron also diminished with the Reformation. As the papacy invested more funds in fighting the spread of Protestantism, fewer resources were given to artists to continue creating the magnificent works characteristic of the High Renaissance, for example. Less demand resulted in less overall quality, and the subsequent drain of artistic and intellectual talent accelerated the decline of the Renaissance in Italy—at least compared to its previously amazing cultural output.

Political Factors

Finally, a series of troubles caused by political instability slowly had a snowball effect on the cultural output characteristic of the High Renaissance. We remarked in the beginning that, though they enjoyed a period of prosperity, Italian city-states were weak relative to the larger kingdoms beyond the Alps. The Ottomans also increasingly pressed in from the East, having finally defeated the Byzantines in 1453, and would reach the peak of their power in the next century or so. The Peace of Lodi, signed in 1454 by Venice, Florence, and Milan, was an agreement to come together if any of them were attacked by the Turks or the French—the two powers perceived to be the biggest threat to the Italians' sovereign interests. The treaty was upheld for the next four decades or so, and political turmoil was avoided in Northern Italy. However, it would not be long before their inner quarrels would render the whole system useless and lead to a period of political decline.

By the end of the century, however, Italy became a battleground for perhaps two of the strongest Catholic factions in Europe—France and the Holy Roman Empire. Following the absorption of the kingdom of Burgundy (which was primarily French) into the Holy Roman Empire, relations between the Habsburgs and the French kings started to deteriorate. To retaliate for losing his influence on Burgundy, King Charles VIII of France launched an invasion into Italy and press the claim he had on the throne of Naples. Aided by the Sforza family of Milan, which had had strenuous relations with the southern Italian state for a long time, Charles invaded Italy in 1494 with about 30,000 men. Naples, on the other hand, allied with the Papal States and Florence, both of which had the common interest of keeping the French out of the peninsula. For Florence, the domination of the French would mean the end of economic freedom and prosperity. Pope Alexander VI, however, a member of the infamous Borgia family, knew very well of the troublesome past of the papacy under the influence of the French kings during the 1300s and the dubious situation the so-called "Avignon papacy" period had caused for the Catholic world.

However, the Italian coalition was not nearly strong enough to stop Charles, whose army included professional mercenary infantry from Switzerland, considered among the best in Europe, and Scottish longbowmen. He defeated what the Italians had to offer relatively quickly. Seeing their armies defeated, the Medici offered the French control of Pisa in exchange for keeping them out of Florence. This act was perceived as treacherous by the Florentine republicans, who had long protested the despotic rule of the Medici. They thus overthrew the ruling family after about sixty years of rule and established the Great Council as the new main legislative body of the city—the same one that commissioned *David* to Michelangelo. King Charles would continue his devastating march south but was eventually repulsed from the Italian Peninsula by the Holy Roman Emperor and King Ferdinand of the Crown of Aragon—soon to be the king of Spain.

In the late 1490s, the political instability in Florence would become unfathomable as Savonarola—the chaotic and ambitious friar we mentioned briefly—took control of the city, resulting in his ex-communication by the pope. For a brief time, Savonarola's influence reduced Florence to an ambiguous theocratic republic—or the closest thing to it—before the revolutionary was denounced and murdered by the Florentine citizens in 1498. Just one year later, the French returned to Italy, this time under King Louis XII, whose main aim was to capture Milan. He was aided in this endeavor by the papacy. What complicated the situation even more was the passing of Pope Alexander VI in 1503. The Borgia family lost control of the papacy, and the new pope, Julius II, was not so keen on keeping the alliance with France. The Frenchmen were defeated by the Spaniards once again, with the Spanish Crown, then controlled by the Habsburgs, claiming the throne of Naples for good. The year 1512 then saw the Medici rise to power in Florence once again with the help of the Spanish, and the French were driven out of Milan. In 1515, France recaptured Milan, but Charles I Habsburg of Spain (who was also Charles V of the Holy Roman Empire) would finally defeat the French in Italy in the 1520s.

The long wars weakened the Italian city-states beyond the possibility of recovery. Only Venice resisted German or French domination, but it was also slowly losing its former might due to the influx of goods from the New World into the markets of Europe. More fundamentally, the Italian nobility, largely replaced by the wealthy merchant class since the turn of the 14th century, started to regain their former power, returning to prominence in some cities. Even when the Medici again regained control of Florence in 1530, the art that was being produced no longer reflected the glory and optimism that had characterized the High Renaissance in the city. Many people recognized the drawbacks of the lack of a centralized political structure in Italy, which had become a battleground of foreign armies. Niccolò Machiavelli had laid this out the best in his 1513 work *The Prince*, which recognized the need for a strong ruler to rally the quarreling city-states to unite Italy and reach the old glory of Rome. A Renaissance work at its core, *The Prince* is Machiavelli's reflection on the political history of Italy and his lamentation of it, as well as his proposal for what it could have been. He posited his principles based on ancient writers such as Cicero and used historical examples to support his arguments.

Still, despite the public perception of the political situation, Italy suffered even more humiliation in the 1520s, as already mentioned. As a final nail to the coffin, Charles V's armies sacked Rome in 1527, at a time when the Catholic Church had already suffered immensely due to the turbulent processes begun with the Reformation. By then, the impulse of the Renaissance, born (or reborn) in the Italian Peninsula, was well on its way north, beyond the Alps. Though the movement had effectively ended in Italy, with only Venice, the city of Titian and Giorgione, maintaining its status as the center of artistic life, the Renaissance was alive for another century in the rest of Europe, producing a cultural heritage that has become invaluable today.

Conclusion

The Renaissance remains among the most influential periods in European history. With it came a great series of changes that altered the fundamental way life was perceived in Western Europe. Through an intellectual, artistic, and cultural rebirth, it ushered Europe out of the shadows of the Middle Ages and into an age of innovation, exploration, and enlightenment. It was a time of great curiosity and thirst for knowledge. The rediscovery of classical literature and advances in humanist philosophy ignited a passion for learning and set off a wave of scientific, artistic, and literary achievements that have transformed society. Leonardo da Vinci, Michelangelo, Galileo Galilei, Shakespeare, and other great men of their time revolutionized their fields and left an indelible mark on the world. Renaissance art captured the essence and undying spirit of human existence and embodied the ideals of the time. This ambition was expressed in sculpture, painting, architecture, and literature. Building on the brilliant heritage of classical antiquity, the quality of the culture during the Renaissance is often regarded as the pinnacle of European civilization.

The Renaissance also reassessed society and its values. Humanism emphasized personal worth, worldly knowledge, and human achievability. This era drove advances in anatomy, astronomy, and mathematics that questioned long-held beliefs and paved the way for a more rational, empirical worldview. The printing press invented by Johannes Gutenberg enabled the mass dissemination of this knowledge, leading to the democratization of information and the birth of the modern publishing industry. Spreading across Europe, stimulating cultural exchange and encouraging new ideas, the Renaissance should not only be considered an Italian movement. Its legacy continues to this day, and its influences can be seen in the principles of democracy, human rights, and the pursuit of knowledge that underpin the modern world. The Renaissance represents a period of transition and renewal in which the seeds of modernity were sown and continue to thrive.

For these reasons, when we look back on the Renaissance, we will always remember what it stood for—the indomitable human spirit always striving for perfection and improvement, the desire for mastery and a better understanding of nature, and the transformative impact of art and culture. The Renaissance continues to be a testament to humanity's ability to shape its destiny and create a brighter future through breakthroughs in thought and the undying curiosity that emerges from it.

Part 3: The Enlightenment

An Enthralling Guide to a Period of Scientific, Political, and Philosophical Discourse in European History

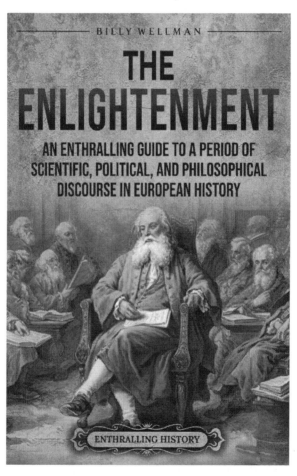

Introduction

This book will take you on a journey to a time that changed the world's political, social, and cultural fabric. The Enlightenment started at the end of the 17th century and lasted until the beginning of the 19th century. There was a significant shift in thinking, as prominent intellectuals and philosophers began to challenge traditional sources of authority and knowledge. They embraced reason, science, and progress, paving the way for a new era of freedom and democracy.

The Enlightenment, which primarily took shape in Europe, was a pivotal moment in the history of ideas. It was a time of monumental intellectual upheaval based on the belief in human reason, a desire for progress, and a need for social, political, and economic reforms. The impact of Enlightenment ideas is significant and long-lasting, as they shaped our understanding of democracy, individualism, equality, and human rights.

This book will delve into several aspects of this period and learn about its central themes and ideas. We will also look at its key figures and institutions and their impact on today's world.

We aim to provide an overview of this critical period of history while explaining its relevance to contemporary issues and debates. What sets this volume apart from others is its construction of the Enlightenment. Rather than treating the period as a massive unified movement, we'll focus on the diversity of views and conflicts that characterized it.

Our goal is to bring you knowledge and provide vivid descriptions of the people, places, and events that shaped this fascinating era. You'll meet the greatest thinkers and visionaries of the age, from Voltaire and Rousseau to Locke and Hume. You'll witness the birth of democracy and the fight for human rights and see how the Enlightenment paved the way for the world we know today.

We will attempt to break down barriers and make knowledge accessible to people from all walks of life. The ideas and events of this period are too important to be confined to the ivory towers of academia. Everyone should have the opportunity to explore and understand the Enlightenment.

To achieve this, we've taken great care to present history in a clear and accessible manner, using simple language and providing examples that are easy to follow and understand. We have avoided engaging in esoteric debates and using technical jargon, focusing instead on the major themes, ideas, and events that defined the era. History books can often be dull and difficult to read, so we have worked hard to make this book interesting and entertaining, with plenty of real-life stories and anecdotes that bring the history of the Enlightenment to life.

We believe that history is not just a recitation of dry facts and figures but a rich tapestry of stories and experiences that can captivate and inspire us all. Whether you are a student of history or simply curious about the origins of modernity, this book will provide a roadmap for a better understanding of the Enlightenment era.

We invite you to join us on this fascinating journey of discovery and to experience the power and drama of the Enlightenment era.

Enjoy.

Chapter 1 – Before the Enlightenment

As the sun set over the grand old buildings and monuments of Paris, the city's finest minds gathered in a dimly lit salon, their voices hushed as they discussed the latest ideas racing across Europe. With its heady mix of reason, science, and philosophy, the Enlightenment swept through the salons and coffeehouses of Europe like wildfire, igniting a passion for knowledge and freedom in the hearts of all who dared to dream of a better world.

From Voltaire's biting satire to Rousseau's passionate pleas for justice, from Newton's laws of motion to Descartes's cogito, ergo sum ("I think, therefore I am"), the Enlightenment opened minds and challenged established ideas in ways never before seen. And as the people of Paris spilled out into the streets, eager to seize the day and embrace the future, a sense of excitement and possibility hung in the air like a beacon in the darkness, signaling all who dared to follow.

The Enlightenment was an intellectual and cultural movement in the 17th and 18th centuries characterized by a focus on reason, individualism, and skepticism toward traditional authority. But before the Enlightenment, Europe experienced several incredible events and cultural movements that shaped how society was organized and operated.

The Middle Ages

The Middle Ages lasted from the 5th to the 15th century and was a time of great upheaval and change. These were not happy times, as the masses typically suffered during this period. It was a time of feudalism, where kings and lords held power over their vassals. The majority of people lived in rural areas. Wars and diseases affected their lives, making them miserable.

The Middles Ages is typically seen as starting in 476 CE when the Western Roman Empire fell to the Germanic leader Odoacer, who staged a revolt and deposed Emperor Romulus Augustulus. Europe went into a period of chaos.

Barbarian hordes swept across the continent, destroying everything in their path. The once-great city of Rome was destroyed, and the people of Europe were left without anyone to defend them from these invaders.

But from the ashes of the old world rose a new one. The Carolingian dynasty, led by the great emperor Charlemagne, emerged in the 8th century. He built an empire that spanned the length and breadth of Western Europe and began to re-establish order in the region.

But this did not last long. Eventually, Europe became one large religious state. Although there were many kingdoms in Europe, they had one thing in common; they were all Catholic. The spiritual hierarchy and the secular rulers had to find a way to share the power, each wanting more.

The Catholic Church played a key role, as it was the supreme authority. The pope was (and still is) the head of the Catholic Church, and he could make life very difficult for the rulers who wanted to go against him. Some kings tried to restrict church activities, and the church, in turn, attempted to control the affairs of the state, even going as far as to excommunicate those who disagreed.

For the most part, though, people clung to their faith. Priests toiled to preserve the knowledge of the ancients. The cathedrals of Europe rose, reaching toward the heavens. The church was a powerful force that provided stability and the foundation for social cohesion.

As you can see, the Middle Ages presents a confusing and often contradictory picture of a society attempting to structure itself politically on a spiritual basis. And this was a time of contradictions and extremes, a time of incredible beauty and terrible brutality. But through it all, the people of Europe endured, clinging to hope and faith for a better tomorrow.

The Renaissance

The Renaissance emerged in the 14th century and lasted until the 17th century. It was a period of cultural and artistic rebirth marked by a renewed interest in classical learning, literature, and the arts. Historians have identified several causes for the emergence of the Renaissance following the Middle Ages, such as increased interaction between different cultures, the rediscovery of ancient Greek and Roman texts, humanism, and various artistic and technological innovations.

Humanism emphasizes the value of human life and achievements. It is an approach to a life based on reason and common humanity, recognizing that moral values are founded in human nature and experience alone.

Italy, the birthplace of the Renaissance, celebrated the power and potential of the individual to achieve greatness. Scholars and artists rediscovered the ancient wisdom of Greece and Rome and infused it with their passion and vision. Painters like Leonardo da Vinci, Michelangelo, and Raphael created works of breathtaking beauty and splendor, capturing the human form and spirit with a vividness and intensity never before seen.

Meanwhile, scientists like Galileo, Copernicus, and Newton challenged the church's traditional beliefs. They opened up new vistas of understanding the universe and our place in it. These scientists changed our understanding of astronomy, mathematics, and physics. They laid the framework for the Scientific Revolution, which would transform the world forever.

But the Renaissance was not just a time of intellectual and artistic achievements. A great upheaval was also taking place in the social and political circles. The old feudal system was winding down with the rise of the middle class, the development of new forms of government, and the growth of the banking sectors.

And in the end, the Renaissance left a profound legacy that continues to shape our world today. It gave birth to the idea of individualism and the belief that we have the power to shape our destiny and achieve greatness. It fostered a spirit of innovation, inquiry, and creativity that has driven human progress ever since. And it provided a model of beauty, wisdom, and harmony that has inspired generations of artists, scientists, and thinkers to reach for the stars and achieve the impossible.

The Reformation

The Reformation took place in the 16th century. This religious movement challenged the authority of the Catholic Church, leading to the formation of Protestantism. It was a time of religious and social upheaval, as people questioned the power of the Catholic Church and sought new ways to connect with God.

At the heart of the Reformation was a burning sense of moral outrage and spiritual longing. Many people felt the Catholic Church had become a bloated, corrupt institution that cared more about power and wealth than the spiritual well-being of its followers. They saw the Vatican's opulence and the clergy's decadence as a betrayal of the faith of the early Christians.

As a result, a group of bold and visionary reformers emerged. These thinkers were determined to restore what they believed were the actual teachings of Christ and create a more authentic form of Christianity. The fiery and charismatic Martin Luther led the charge.

In 1517, Martin Luther published a document called Disputation on the Power of Indulgences, better known as the Ninety-five Theses. This document outlined ninety-five issues about the Catholic Church's teachings.

We won't cover all ninety-five theses, but one of the most critical issues, at least in Luther's view, was the Catholic Church's role as an intermediary between the people and God. The Catholic Church allowed people to purchase indulgences to forgive their sins and reduce their time in purgatory. Luther argued against this practice, believing instead that salvation was a gift God gave to those with faith.

He also believed that believers should be less dependent on the Catholic Church and its pope and priests for spiritual guidance. People should have an independent relationship with God, take personal responsibility for their faith, and refer to the Bible for spiritual guidance.

This Reformation quickly spread throughout Europe, sparking a wave of religious and political conflicts. The movement formed a new sect of Christianity called Protestantism. This name refers collectively to the many religious groups that separated from the Roman Catholic Church due to differences in practices and beliefs.

The Scientific Revolution

The Reformation brought about a change in religious thought, and the Scientific Revolution brought about a change in how people acquired knowledge. People's thinking about the natural world changed dramatically between the 16th and 17th centuries. It was characterized by a shift away from traditional beliefs and toward the use of reason and observation.

Francis Bacon

One of the key figures of the Scientific Revolution was Francis Bacon, an English philosopher, statesman, and scientist who lived from 1561 to 1626. Few individuals can compare intellectually to this great man.

Bacon's dedication to the pursuit of knowledge was legendary. He believed science should be based on empirical evidence and that experiments and observations should be used to test theories. His approach to science was revolutionary. He emphasized collecting data and conducting experiments to verify or disprove scientific hypotheses.

Galileo Galilei

Another important figure of the Scientific Revolution was Galileo Galilei. He was a brilliant Italian astronomer, physicist, and mathematician who dared to challenge the prevailing beliefs of his time. His scientific contributions are still relevant today, even after more than four hundred years.

For instance, his work on mechanics laid the foundations for the modern study of physics, including the principle of inertia. He improved the telescope's design and made groundbreaking observations of the moon, the phases of Venus, and the moons of Jupiter, providing evidence for the heliocentric model of the solar system proposed by Copernicus. Heliocentrism claims that the sun is the center of the universe.

However, Galileo's support for this revolutionary idea directly conflicted with the powerful Catholic Church, which held that the Earth was the center of the universe. Galileo refused to back down and continued to pursue his scientific investigations. After the publication of the Dialogue Concerning the Two Chief World System in 1632, Galileo was ordered to appear before an inquisition in Rome. He was charged with heresy for his belief that the sun was at the center of the universe.

To avoid being killed, Galileo agreed not to spread that teaching anymore. As he was being taken away, he allegedly mumbled, "Eppur si muove (And yet it moves)." Galileo spent the rest of his life under house arrest.

Isaac Newton

Isaac Newton was born in England in 1643. Newton was a prodigious child who would become one of history's most brilliant scientific minds. His contributions to science were nothing short of awe-inspiring.

He is best known for his theory of universal gravitation and made an incredible contribution by formulating calculus, a new branch of mathematics. He also made significant advancements in mechanics, optics, and chemical research.

Newton became a dominant scientific force in Britain following the publication of his book Principia in 1687. The three laws of motion and the principle of universal gravitation he proposed helped explain why the planets orbit around the sun and why objects fall to the ground. His groundbreaking body of work, known as Newtonian Mechanics, is still taught in schools today. The publication of this work is typically used as the end date for the Scientific Revolution. The lines between the Scientific Revolution and the Enlightenment blur a little. We chose not to cage individuals like Newton and Descartes to only one movement, as their ideas inspired thinkers during both.

Newton's ideas and discoveries laid the foundations for some of the most important scientific and technological discoveries to come. He was a trailblazer and visionary thinker who challenged the prevailing beliefs of his time to explore the unknown with fearless curiosity.

René Descartes

René Descartes was a French philosopher and mathematician. He believed in the power of reason and thought that knowledge could only be gained through careful reasoning and skepticism.

Descartes believed in a radical approach to knowledge that rejected the authority of tradition and emphasized the importance of individual reasoning and experimentation. He is famous for his statement, "Cogito, ergo sum" ("I think, therefore I am"), which encapsulates his belief that our ability to reason is the foundation of all knowledge. Descartes was also a mathematician and is considered "the father of analytical geometry. He will be mentioned again because his philosophical ideas greatly impacted Enlightenment thinkers.

Political and Social Thinkers

Political and social thinkers also contributed to the rise of Enlightenment ideals. John Locke and Jean-Jacques Rousseau were just two figures who put forward the importance of individual freedom and social and political reforms. Their ideas challenged traditional forms of government and social organizations. They helped pave the way for new political and social systems based on reason, justice, and human rights. We will examine these thinkers more closely in another chapter. Still, they are important to mention here since they significantly impacted the rise and spread of the Enlightenment.

Growth of Trade and Commerce

The growth of commerce and trade played a role in the Enlightenment. As Europe became more interconnected through trade and business, people were exposed to new ideas and perspectives from different cultures. This exposure to new ways of thinking helped fuel the Enlightenment's emphasis on reason and progress.

The Printing Press Was the Key to the Enlightenment

The printing press was the most important invention in spreading the ideas of the Enlightenment. Although the printing press had been around for centuries in China, the new, improved printing press developed by Johannes Gutenberg in the mid-15th century helped to disseminate ideas and information more widely and rapidly than ever before. Before the printing press, books were primarily produced by hand, which made them expensive and difficult to produce in large quantities. As a result, access to advanced knowledge was mostly limited to a small group of elites, such as wealthy aristocrats, religious leaders, and scholars.

Gutenberg's improved printing press made it possible to mass-produce books and other printed materials at a much lower cost and with greater speed than before, allowing them to reach a much broader audience. Before the invention of printing, the number of books in Europe could be counted in thousands. By 1500, after only fifty years of the creation of the improved printing press, more than nine million books had been published. Since books became cheaper and more readily available, the middle class could access them, which led to an exponential increase in literacy rates.

The first books created on Gutenberg's printing press were religious texts, such as the Gutenberg Bible, printed in Mainz, Germany, in the 1450s. After the success of the Gutenberg Bible, other religious texts were printed using the new technology. The first books published in English were also religious texts, such as other Bibles, hymns, and psalms.

The famous astronomer Johannes Kepler wrote some of the first science books printed on the printing press. In 1609, Kepler published Astronomia Nova (New Astronomy), which outlined his three major laws of planetary motion:

(1) The planets move in elliptical orbits with the sun at one focus.

(2) The time necessary to traverse any arc of a planetary orbit is proportional to the area of the sector between the central body and that arc.

(3) An exact relationship exists between the squares of the planets' periodic times and the cubes of their mean distances from the sun.

This text was followed by Harmonices Mundi (The Harmony of the World) in 1619, which explores the mathematical relationships between planetary motion and music.

Another notable scientific work was Nicolaus Copernicus's De revolutionibus orbium coelestium (On the Revolutions of the Celestial Spheres), published in 1543. This work proposed the heliocentric model of the solar system, with the sun at the center and the planets orbiting around it.

Galileo Galilei's Sidereus Nuncius (Starry Messenger), published in 1610, described his observations of the moons of Jupiter, and William Harvey's De motu cordis (On the Motion of the Heart), published in 1628, described his discovery of the circulation of blood in the human body.

The printing press played a crucial role in unlocking the Enlightenment. First, it made it possible for Enlightenment thinkers to publish and spread their ideas more widely, allowing them to reach a larger audience. It also facilitated the creation of a public sphere where people could freely exchange ideas and opinions, leading to new forms of political and cultural discourse. Finally, it helped to break down the traditional barriers to knowledge, making information more widely available to people from all walks of life.

The Major Ideas of the Enlightenment

These ideas and values helped to pave the way for the Enlightenment by providing a framework for new ways of thinking and understanding the world.

Let's lay out the most important ideas of the Enlightenment. The reason was perhaps the most prevalent and influential Enlightenment idea. Enlightenment thinkers believed people could understand and improve the world through reason and scientific inquiry. These thinkers rejected superstition, dogma, and traditional authority, instead emphasizing critical thinking and rationality. They sought to create a more just and equal society and advocated for democracy, freedom of speech, and religious tolerance.

Individualism was another feature of the Enlightenment. Enlightenment thinkers rejected the traditional authority of the Church and the Divine Right of kings, instead championing the rights of the individual. They believed that all people were equal and everyone had the right to pursue their interests and goals. Individualism helped to create a more liberal and democratic society. Different thinkers had different views on who was equal. For instance, Rousseau did not believe women were equal to men, while Locke believed women could rationalize just like men.

Enlightenment thinkers valued the scientific method and believed knowledge could be gained through observation and experimentation. They thought science was the key to understanding the natural world and solving many problems plaguing society. This emphasis on science led to discoveries and advancements, helping shape their understanding of the world.

Did People Easily Embrace the Enlightenment?

The popularity of the Enlightenment varied depending on the time and place. The Enlightenment was a widely influential movement in Europe that significantly impacted society, politics, and culture. Enlightenment ideas and values spread through various channels, including academic institutions, literary works, and salons where intellectuals gathered to exchange ideas.

A painting of a salon. The men have gathered to listen to Voltaire's latest work.
https://en.wikipedia.org/wiki/File:Salon_de_Madame_Geoffrin.jpg

However, not everyone embraced the Enlightenment. Many conservative forces, such as the church and the monarchy, saw the beliefs of many Enlightenment thinkers threatening their power. They sought to suppress its ideas through censorship and persecution of intellectuals.

There were also significant regional differences in the popularity and impact of the Enlightenment, with some countries and regions, such as France and Germany, seeing a powerful influence.

The understanding of the Enlightenment varied widely among different segments of society. While Enlightenment ideas significantly impacted intellectual and cultural elites, not everyone could fully grasp the complex philosophical and scientific concepts associated with the movement.

Despite these challenges, the ideas of the Enlightenment had a significant impact on Western culture and society, particularly in science, politics, and philosophy. The Enlightenment promoted using reason and empirical evidence to understand the world, pursue additional knowledge and education, and value individual liberty and democratic governance.

The End of an Era: Looking Forward to the Enlightenment

For all its darkness and uncertainty, the pre-Enlightenment era was a time of great creativity, innovation, and boundless imagination. From the towering spires of Gothic cathedrals to the delicate brushstrokes of

Renaissance masterpieces, from the haunting melodies of troubadours to the intricate tapestries of courtly love, the pre-Enlightenment era was a rich mosaic of human achievements and a testament to the power of the human spirit to overcome the greatest of obstacles.

And so, as the last embers of the fire died away and as the night settled in around them, the people of the pre-Enlightenment world could rest easy in the knowledge that their legacy would endure, that their dreams would live on, and that the future would be brighter than they could have ever imagined.

Chapter 2 – Monumental Rise of Enlightened Philosophy

In the heart of London, a man walked briskly over the cobblestone street, his eyes fixed on the horizon. His name was Francis Bacon, and he was on a mission.

Bacon had spent his life searching for a new way of understanding the world based on logic and observation rather than superstition and tradition. And now, as he watched the sun rise over the rooftops, he knew he was making a difference. For Bacon and many other philosophers of his day, the dawn of the Enlightenment was at hand, and nothing would be the same again.

Philosophy is a discipline that has been central to human thought for thousands of years. It involves the critical study of fundamental questions of morality and life. Why are we here? What is our purpose? Philosophical insights provide a framework for critical inquiry, moral and political reasoning, and a deeper understanding of the human experience. Philosophy also plays a vital role in shaping our values and beliefs.

Francis Bacon's Empiricism

Francis Bacon, who lived from 1561 to 1626, was an English philosopher and scientist who developed a philosophical concept called empiricism, which proposed knowledge comes from sensory experiences. In other words, we can only understand the world through our senses.

Empiricism was a departure from the traditional approach to knowledge, which relied on intuition or revelation. Bacon argued that knowledge gained through observation and experimentation was more reliable than knowledge gained through abstract reasoning. Empiricism is grounded in concrete evidence and could be tested and verified through further observations and experiments. Experimentation aims to apply theories to real-world observations, record the findings as empirical data, and present them to people.

Bacon argued that everything you know and believe comes from what you can physically experience. For example, if you know that concrete is hard, it is only because you fell on a concrete floor and realized this. If you know that your father is kind, it is because he has done kind things in the past. You only know what you have experienced; anything you have not personally experienced is mere conjecture and not to be trusted.

Bacon's empiricism had a significant impact on the development of science. His emphasis on experimentation laid the foundation for the scientific method, which involves making observations, formulating hypotheses, conducting experiments to test those hypotheses, and analyzing the results. This approach to learning was seen as a powerful tool for challenging traditional ideas and superstitions and for promoting a more rational and evidence-based worldview.

Descartes's Rationalist Beliefs

One of the most famous images of Descartes.
https://en.wikipedia.org/wiki/File:Frans_Hals_-_Portret_van_Ren%C3%A9_Descartes.jpg

René Descartes lived from 1596 to 1650 and was a French philosopher, scientist, and mathematician. In 1622, Descartes moved to Paris. He was a lively fellow and enjoyed life in Paris, where he gambled, rode horses, and fenced. He attended court, concerts, and plays regularly to amuse himself.

As a philosopher, his beliefs were centered around the idea that reason and logic were the primary sources of knowledge. He believed that by using our innate capacity for reason, we could arrive at certain knowledge that was beyond doubt. Descartes argued that sensory experiences, while important, were unreliable and could not be trusted as a source for all knowledge.

One of Descartes's most famous arguments is *cogito, ergo sum* or "I think, therefore I am." He argued that the very act of thinking and doubting was proof of one's existence. Descartes used this argument as a foundation for his philosophy, arguing that reason and logic could be used to arrive at other certain truths about the world.

Descartes's rationalist beliefs also included the idea of innate ideas, which he believed were present in the mind from birth. According to Descartes, these innate ideas were the foundation of all knowledge. He thought that the mind could understand complex concepts and that this understanding was not dependent on sensory experiences.

The three innate ideas he believed in were the following:

(1) The idea of God who is perfect and infinite.

(2) The idea of self or mind, which he expressed in his famous phrase "*Cogito, ergo sum.*"

(3) The idea of infinity and some other mathematical truths. According to Descartes, these ideas could not come from experience but are present in the human mind from birth.

Another key aspect of Descartes's rationalist beliefs was his emphasis on the importance of deductive reasoning. He believed that by starting with fundamental truths and using deductive reasoning, one could arrive at new knowledge that could not be refuted. This approach to learning was in contrast to the sensory-based approach advocated by empiricists.

Descartes's deductive reasoning was also closely tied to the Enlightenment's commitment to the scientific method. By emphasizing the importance of starting with fundamental truths and using deductive reasoning to arrive at new knowledge, Descartes helped to lay the foundation for the evidence-based approach to science that became central to the Enlightenment's scientific and philosophical developments.

Voltaire and Rousseau: Ideas of Reason

Voltaire and Rousseau were two influential Enlightenment thinkers who championed the ancient Greek idea of reason. Both philosophers believed reason was essential to human progress and advocated for its use in every aspect of life, including politics, religion, and morality.

Voltaire, who lived from 1694 to 1778, was a French philosopher and writer best known for advocating reason, religious tolerance, and free speech. He believed that reason could be used to challenge traditional beliefs and superstitions. He also thought that reason was essential for promoting social and political progress. Voltaire was critical of the Catholic Church and its teachings, arguing they were based on superstition and fear rather than reason and evidence.

Voltaire's views on women's rights mirrored the social and cultural norms of his time. While he had some progressive ideas, such as the belief that women should have access to education, his views on women's rights were not as progressive as today. Early in his career, he believed women were inherently inferior to men physically and intellectually and that their roles should be confined to the home as mothers, daughters, and wives. His views on women changed over time. Although he held views we would see as sexist today, his thoughts on equality were revolutionary and not embraced by everyone, including other women.

Jean-Jacques Rousseau, who lived from 1712 to 1778, was a Swiss-born French philosopher and writer. Rousseau vehemently believed that reason was essential to developing an individual's mind and could be used to create a more just and equal society.

Rousseau strongly thought that individuals were equal and that everyone was born free. He believed that society must ensure everyone had access to the means to survive, live, and prosper. Like Voltaire, Rousseau also had regressive ideas about women. He believed in the natural differences between men and women. Rousseau thought women were more emotional and nurturing, making them more suitable for home life. Meanwhile, he saw men as more rational and suited for public life.

Rousseau expressed his condemnation of slavery and argued that slavery was a violation of the natural rights of man. He stated that enslaving other men went against the principles of justice and morality.

He was critical of the social and political systems of his time since he believed they were corrupt and oppressive.

We will cover these four men in more depth later in the book, but you should have a clearer picture of their core beliefs. Many Enlightenment thinkers held these same beliefs or a similar version of them. These thinkers' emphasis on reason and critical thinking helped to promote a more critical and reflective attitude toward traditional beliefs and encouraged individuals to question those beliefs and develop theories based on their own reasoning.

The Counter-Enlightenment

The Counter-Enlightenment was a movement that ran against Enlightenment thinking. It developed mainly in Europe in the late 18th and early 19th centuries as a reaction against the ideas of the Enlightenment. It was not an organized movement, and there was no single catalyst for it to emerge. Instead, it is better understood as an intellectual phenomenon that ran counter to the Enlightenment.

While the Enlightenment emphasized reason, progress, individualism, and the power of science, the Counter-Enlightenment rejected those ideas and advocated for a return to traditional values, social hierarchies, and religion.

The Counter-Enlightenment was marked by a deep skepticism toward reason and the power of the human intellect. Many Counter-Enlightenment thinkers argued that human reason was limited and fallible. They believed people could not grasp the complexities of human nature and society. In their opinion, traditional forms of knowledge, such as religion, were more reliable guides to human conduct and social organization than reason and science.

The Counter-Enlightenment also rejected the Enlightenment's emphasis on progress and individualism, arguing that these values led to moral and social degradation. Many Counter-Enlightenment thinkers believed that society needed to be structured around hierarchies of power and authority, with the upper classes exercising control over the lower classes. They also emphasized the importance of social cohesion and communal values instead of individual rights and freedoms. Some prominent Counter-Enlightenment thinkers include Johann Georg Hamann, Joseph de Maistre, and Friedrich von Schelling.

The Counter-Enlightenment's rejection of Enlightenment ideals did not find widespread acceptance among the general population, but it did impact elites. Many prominent writers, artists, and philosophers embraced the Counter-Enlightenment's critique of reason and individualism. They saw Enlightenment ideas as contributing to great upheavals in society. They did not want to mess with their traditional ways of life and advocated for a return to established values and traditional authority.

This shift in cultural and intellectual attitudes had an impact on society. The Romantic movement, which emerged in the late 18th and early 19th centuries, was a reaction against rationalism. This movement celebrated emotion, intuition, and nature instead, helping to create a cultural climate that was less receptive to Enlightenment ideas and more sympathetic to traditional values and religious orthodoxy.

Most people rejected the Counter-Enlightenment since they saw tangible benefits from the Enlightenment's emphasis on reason and progress. For example, advances in medicine, agriculture, and industry improved people's lives and made people more prosperous. The Enlightenment's emphasis on individualism and personal freedom also resonated with many people, who saw it as a way to break free from the constraints of traditional social hierarchies and allow them to pursue their own goals and aspirations.

Another reason many people rejected the Counter-Enlightenment could have been its association with religious orthodoxy and authoritarianism. The Counter-Enlightenment rejected the Enlightenment's emphasis on reason and science and sought to impose traditional values and religious dogma on society. This was seen as a threat to personal freedoms and individualism, so many people rejected the Counter-Enlightenment's ideas in favor of the more open and liberal values of the Enlightenment.

Chapter 3 – How Science Changed the World

In the early 18ᵗʰ century, coal miners in England encountered a formidable obstacle of how to drain water from the mines to extract coal safely and efficiently. Mines were frequently inundated with water, leading to serious fatal accidents. Horses and manual labor were used to pump water from the mines, but they were insufficient for the task. Miners desperately looked for more advanced solutions.

And this was when Thomas Newcomen intervened. He had been experimenting with steam power for years, and in 1712, he designed a machine that he believed would work. His steam engine employed a piston to drive a pump, and it was powered by steam that was generated by boiling water by burning coal.

Newcomen's engine was a marvel of ingenuity and quickly proved to be a game-changer for the coal mining industry. Miners could now pump water from the mines to extract coal at a faster and more efficient pace than ever before, and they could do so without risking their lives.

The Power of Science

A new beginning was on the horizon that would shake the very foundations of knowledge, truth, and reality and revolutionize everything in which people believed. That force was science.

As the Enlightenment gained momentum, science became ever more important, spreading its influence over all aspects of society. During the Enlightenment, people experienced immense transformation, as they finally broke free from the shackles of mysticism. They wielded the power of rationality and empirical evidence, enabling them to perceive the world in previously unfathomable ways.

In the wake of this transformation, remarkable discoveries and innovations emerged, altering the course of history. Science was no longer just a tool for comprehending the world; it became a way of life and a force capable of revolutionizing everything it touched.

The scientific discoveries of the time, including the laws of physics and chemistry and principles of biology, created a new framework for comprehending the world. This framework challenged the traditional authorities, namely the church.

Science also helped to cultivate a sense of optimism and progress. The belief in reason and the power of human ingenuity led many thinkers to believe that humanity was capable of achieving great things. New scientific discoveries and theories inspired writers, artists, and musicians to explore new themes and experiment with new forms of expression by using new tools developed during this era.

For example, author Jonathan Swift was inspired by science to write *Gulliver's Travels* in 1726, a popular novel that can be called proto-science fiction writing. Mary Wollstonecraft Shelley was an English writer who wrote *Frankenstein* in 1818, which is considered to be the first science fiction novel.

A scientific invention called the camera obscura was an optical device that makes images without a photographic film. This invention was used by artists like Johannes Vermeer and Canaletto to create more realistic paintings with better perspective, realistic colors, and lighting.

Artists Maria Sibylla Merian and John James Audubon painted detailed and scientifically accurate paintings of plants, birds, and other animals, which contributed to the dissemination of scientific information and also satisfied their artistic urges.

At the forefront of the "scientific revolution" of the Enlightenment was the scientific method, which emphasized the value of observation, testing hypotheses, and empirical evidence. This approach was groundbreaking, allowing scientists to delve deeper into the natural world and human nature. This method provided a rigorous and systematic way of understanding the world and helped to establish science as a legitimate and respected field of study.

Another significant facet of science during the Enlightenment era was an emphasis on rationalism. Enlightenment thinkers believed that the human intellect was capable of understanding the world through rationality and logic rather than depending on religious or traditional authorities to tell them why things worked the way they did. In science, the emphasis was on empirical observation and experimentation, which was a radical deviation from the past and paved the way for modern scientific advancements.

Enlightenment science was not only concerned with furthering people's comprehension of the natural world but also with enhancing and improving life and society. For instance, novel medical discoveries and treatments helped to boost public health and prolong life. Several Enlightenment thinkers believed the application of scientific knowledge could lead to progress in fields like agriculture and industry.

However, the changes science brought about were not readily accepted by everyone. Numerous religious and political authorities regarded the rise of Enlightenment science as a menace to their power and influence, and they endeavored to suppress or discredit scientific inquiries that challenged their authority.

Despite these challenges, Enlightenment science continued to flourish and spread throughout Europe and beyond. It inspired a new generation of thinkers and innovators who were propelled by a passion for discovery and dedication to the truth.

Scientific Advancements and Inventions

During the Enlightenment, numerous scientific advancements and inventions materialized that had a profound impact on various segments of society. We are going to cover some of the most important inventions that came out of the Enlightenment; a few might surprise you!

Steam Engine

Thomas Newcomen's steam engine, which he created in 1712, was quickly adopted by coal miners throughout England. Coal miners saw this invention as a lifesaver, as it could help them extract coal more efficiently and safely. However, Newcomen was never satisfied with his invention. He continued to experiment with different designs and techniques, trying to find ways to make his engine more efficient.

In the 1760s, a Scottish inventor named James Watt came across Newcomen's engine and saw the potential for improvement. Watt succeeded in building a steam engine that did not fail too often and was more reliable and efficient than the older models.

But Watt's work did not come without setbacks. He struggled for years to find the right combination of designs and materials, and he nearly gave up on several occasions. However, he persisted in his work, as he was driven by a fierce determination to create something truly revolutionary. In 1775, Watt succeeded in fabricating a new design of a steam engine that was more efficient than anything that had existed before.

The Newcomen steam engine used steam to push a cylinder with a piston connected to the shaft of the pump. The cylinder was then cooled by cold water, which created a vacuum. This moved the piston, and by repeating the cycle, a to-and-fro motion was achieved that operated the water pump.

The improvement that Watt made was in how the machine condensed steam. In Newcomen's engine, water was sprayed directly into the steam cylinder to condense the steam. The cylinder itself was heated and cooled continuously, which wasted a lot of steam by heating the cylinder on every stroke of the engine. In Watt's engine, the cylinder was opened to a separate chamber by a pipe, and cold water was sprayed into that chamber for cooling. That allowed the working cylinder to stay hot so that no steam was wasted reheating the cylinder on each stroke.

The steam engine was a groundbreaking invention, and it was used in the development of new industries, such as textile and other manufacturing industries. It also transformed the transportation industry since it powered the first locomotives and steamships, which changed the way people traveled and transported goods.

The steam engine had a profound impact on the economy and helped to transform society by creating new employment opportunities and increasing the production of goods. The steam engine had many applications in many different fields of industry, making it incredibly versatile. The Industrial Revolution, which started around 1760, would not have been the same without the steam engine.

Immunization

For many centuries, smallpox was a horrible disease that devastated humankind. Smallpox affected all levels of society. In the 18th century in Europe, 400,000 people died annually of smallpox. The disease began with a fever and a red rash that spread all over the body. The rash converted to mushy pustules that dried up and became scabs. When the scabs healed, they fell off, leaving behind large ugly pockmarks all over the skin, particularly the face. The disease had a fatality rate of 20 to 60 percent and left most survivors with horrible disfiguring facial scars. One-third of the survivors went blind.

Dr. Edward Jenner lived from 1749 to 1823. He was an English country physician who noticed that the general population was disfigured by smallpox while the milkmaids in the countryside had clear complexions. These ladies had smooth, flawless skin, their faces unscarred by the disease. Jenner observed that since the maids were in daily contact with the cow's udders while milking them, they had a mild disease they contracted from the cows called cowpox, which only left a single pustule on the hands with no other serious manifestations of the disease. Thus, these girls never acquired smallpox.

Jenner wondered if cowpox gave some protection against deadly smallpox. He decided to test the effectiveness of this method. In the summer of 1796, he extracted some gooey matter from a diseased pustule on the hand of a milkmaid. Using a syringe, he injected some of the pustule material into the forearm of his gardener's young son. The boy soon developed a scab on his arm and experienced some soreness and a mild fever for a day or so.

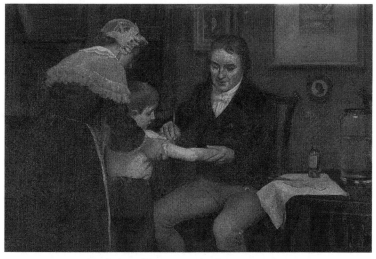

A painting of Jenner vaccinating a young boy.
https://commons.wikimedia.org/wiki/File:Jenner_phipps_01_(cropped).jpg

After about six weeks, Dr. Jenner again injected the young boy, this time with smallpox matter. As Jenner was expecting, the boy did not develop smallpox. He showed no symptoms of the disease at all. This was the first successful vaccination experiment.

Of course, such an experiment, especially one on a child, would not be allowed today. Dr. Jenner would have gone to jail had he done the experiment that way in present times. But those were different times. And thankfully for the boy (and civilization), Dr. Jenner had successfully invented vaccination. The word "vaccination" has its roots in the Latin *vacca*, meaning "cow."

Dr. Jenner published his findings about the vaccination procedure in scientific journals. Vaccination became the standard procedure for preventing people from obtaining the deadly smallpox disease.

Immunization had a significant impact on public health since it prevented many infectious diseases. As a result, the mortality rate came down drastically, and people lived healthier and longer lives.

Today, people can get vaccines against a whole host of infectious diseases, but smallpox is not one of them. Due to a global program of mass vaccination, the entire world population was officially declared free of this devastating disease in 1980.

Lightning Rod

It was a stormy day in June of 1752. Dark clouds were gathering over the city of Philadelphia. Rain was beginning to fall, and bolts of lightning streaked through the sky. People scuttled around for shelter, but not Benjamin Franklin. He was in the mood for a little kite flying. But flying kites in a storm wasn't a pastime of his; it was a scientific experiment that he had been planning for some time. He wanted to prove that lightning was indeed electricity.

He made a kite tied with two strings, one of silk and one of hemp. The silk string was for him to hold, while the hemp string would hold a better electrical charge. He also had a metal key, which he tied to the hemp string, and a Leyden jar, which is an instrument that can store an electrical charge. His son William was there to help him since he was more adept at kite flying.

They waited as the kite soared in the air. Just when they were about to call it quits, Franklin suddenly noticed that the loose threads of the hemp string were getting stiff and erect. He moved his finger near the key, and he felt an electrical spark.

The kite was never actually struck by lightning; if that had happened, Franklin likely would have been electrocuted, even though he took precautions to stay somewhat safe. Instead, the kite collected the ambient electrical charge from the wet atmosphere. The hemp string got wet in the rain and became a conductor, and the electrical charge was passed on to the key.

It is also important to note that Benjamin Franklin did not discover electricity during this experiment; electricity had already been discovered. Franklin also did not discover that lightning was electricity, although he thought he had. The same experiment had already been carried out in France a month prior. Still, Franklin's theory and experiment are the most well known, and he did demonstrate the connection between lightning and electricity. Franklin also invented the lightning rod, which was eventually used to protect tall buildings from lightning strikes.

Oxygen

Joseph Priestley was an Englishman who lived from 1733 to 1804. He was the first person to discover oxygen and describe some of its remarkable properties. Priestley discovered over a dozen other gasses as well. He also invented carbonated water and the rubber eraser. But his unorthodox religious writings and his unflinching support for the American and French Revolutions upset others. A crowd destroyed his home and his scientific equipment. He was hounded out of his town, and he eventually migrated to the United States, where he lived until his death.

But before all that happened, Priestley found that air was not an elementary substance but a mixture of many gases. In 1774, he conducted his most famous experiment using a twelve-inch-wide magnifying glass, focusing sunlight on a piece of reddish mercuric oxide to heat it and capture the emitted gas. He found that this gas caused a flame to burn intensely and kept a mouse alive about four times as long as a similar quantity of normal air. He called this gas "dephlogisticated air," which was later named oxygen by the French chemist Antoine Lavoisier.

Priestley later inhaled the gas himself and reported that he felt light and relaxed. He realized oxygen's medical and recreational use and wrote that this "luxury" gas had been inhaled by himself and two mice with none suffering any ill effects.

Of course, oxygen had important medical applications, and its discovery led to the development of new technologies, such as the oxyacetylene torch, which would change the metal-welding industry forever.

The Marine Chronometer and the Sextant

Mariners going on a long voyage needed to determine their position on the sea where no land was in sight. For this, it was necessary to know the latitude and longitude to accurately know their position on the map. Up until the middle of the 18th century, mariners were unable to determine their position at sea with accuracy, and they faced huge risks, such as shipwrecks or not reaching their destination before running out of supplies.

Navigators could determine their latitude by measuring the sun's angle at noon or by measuring the angle of Polaris or the North Star (in the Northern Hemisphere) at night. This was done by using a sextant, an instrument that could provide latitude while at sea. Of course, sailors had problems when the skies were cloudy.

Although various forms of sextants were used, British inventor and mathematician John Hadley perfected a sextant that could provide very accurate measurements in 1731. His sextant was used by mariners to find latitude at sea.

However, until the mid-1750s, accurate navigation at sea was an unsolved problem due to the difficulty in calculating longitude. To know the longitude, it is necessary to know what time it was where a ship currently was and what time it was at the port they had initially sailed from. Comparing local time with the time back home would tell the sailors how far around the earth they were from their home port. And if they knew the longitude of the port city where they started their journey, then they could more easily find the longitude of their current location.

The obvious solution to this problem was to get an accurate clock and set it to the time of their home port before setting sail. But until 1735, no accurate clock existed that could be relied upon at sea.

In 1714, the British government offered a prize of £20,000 to build a marine clock that could find the longitude at sea within half a degree. This meant the clock would be accurate to within 2.8 seconds, an accuracy that was considered unthinkable at that time.

Self-taught English inventor John Harrison took up the challenge and built various models of a clock, one of which was demonstrated to be sufficiently accurate to win the prize. The last watch made by Harrison in 1770 was even more accurate, allowing mariners to know their position very accurately wherever they were at sea.

Hot Air Balloon

Humans have always wanted to fly in the air like a bird. Two French brothers, Joseph-Michel and Jacques-Étienne Montgolfier, were prosperous paper manufacturers who were also interested in scientific experimentation. They were fascinated with the idea of seeing a balloon made of lightweight paper filled with heated air rise in the air.

The Montgolfiers built a balloon made of silk and lined it with paper that was thirty-three feet in diameter. They launched it in a crowded marketplace in Annonay, France, on June 4th, 1783. Nobody was on board. The balloon rose to over five thousand feet and stayed aloft for ten minutes, traveling more than a mile. This experiment encouraged the brothers, and they constructed a balloon about thirty feet in diameter made of taffeta and coated it with a varnish of alum for fireproofing.

King Louis XVI of France was invited to attend the demonstration. The king was so excited about the experiment that he wanted to test it for human flight by putting prisoners in a basket hung below the balloon. However, the Montgolfiers loaded the basket with a sheep, a duck, and a rooster. The experiment was successful, and the balloon flew for eight minutes and a distance of two miles, with all the passengers surviving the flight. This experiment was witnessed by the French king, Marie Antoinette, and a crowd of 130,000.

On October 15th, 1783, a balloon with a tether carried Jean-François Pilâtre de Rozier, a science teacher. The balloon soared over Paris for almost four minutes. And finally, on November 21st, Pilâtre de Rozier and a military officer made the first free flight in a hot air balloon. The pair flew from Paris, going about 5.5 miles in 25 minutes.

This was the start of human flight and ushered in a new era of human transportation. Today, hot air balloons are not used for human transportation on a large scale, but they are routinely used in scientific investigations of the atmosphere.

The Modern Thermometer

Several people attempted to perfect various types of thermometers, such as the water thermoscope by Galileo Galilei in 1593 and the air thermoscope by Santorio Santorio in 1612. However, neither Galileo's nor Santorio's instruments were very accurate.

The first modern mercury thermometer with a standardized scale was invented by Daniel Gabriel Fahrenheit in 1714. Fahrenheit used the first standard temperature scale for his thermometer. He divided the freezing and boiling points of water into 180 degrees. The number 212 was chosen as the boiling point, and 32 was chosen as the freezing point of water. This produced a scale that would not fall below zero, even when measuring the lowest possible temperatures that he could produce in his laboratory. This thermometer was very accurate.

The Celsius temperature scale is called the "centigrade scale." It was invented by Swedish astronomer Anders Celsius in 1742. Zero was the boiling point, and one hundred was the freezing point of water. The scale was divided into one hundred degrees. Later, a Frenchman named Jean Pierre Cristin inverted the Celsius scale, with zero as the freezing and one hundred as the boiling point of water. In 1948, by an international agreement, the Celsius scale was adopted as the standard international temperature scale, and it is the most widely used temperature scale today.

The Spinning Jenny and the Flying Shuttle

For a long time, the spinning of cotton into threads for weaving into cloth was a small cottage industry. The process was slow and labor-intensive. In 1764 or 1765, James Hargreaves, an English carpenter and weaver, worked on a new design of a cotton thread spinning machine.

Although he was illiterate, he understood the slow, laborious process of spinning thread. He also knew there was a shortage of sufficient thread for weavers. So, Hargreaves developed a machine that would increase the output of thread by increasing the number of spindles able to be operated by a single wheel.

A spinning jenny was a metallic frame with eight wooden spindles at one end. Eight rovings were attached to a beam on the frame. When extended, they passed through two horizontal bars. The worker would move these bars along the top of the frame, and the thread would be moved. At the same time, the spinner would turn a wheel. The spindles turned, and the thread was spun and wound onto a spindle.

Hargreaves kept the machine secret for some time, but cloth workers found out about this new labor-saving device that might threaten their jobs. They attacked his house and destroyed his machine. But Hargreaves was not deterred and continued the development and production of the machine.

In the first design, eight spindles were built into the machine, which spun the thread by turning a single wheel. This meant the operator could spin eight threads at a time just by moving a single wheel. The number of spindles was increased to 90 and then up to 120 in the newer designs, which resulted in a massive increase in the production of cotton thread.

Previously, in 1733, John Kay invented the flying shuttle, which was used in cloth weaving machines. In older loom designs, the shuttle was pushed through the threads by hand. If a wider size cloth was required, then two workers were needed to operate the loom.

Kay redesigned the loom and put the shuttle on wheels that ran on a track. The weavers used flat paddles to move the shuttle from one side to the other by pulling a cord. By using this method, one weaver could create fabrics of a larger width more quickly than before, improving the speed and quantity of the cloth.

The flying shuttle and the spinning jenny revolutionized the textile industry since a large quantity of cloth could be produced efficiently at a lower cost.

The Flush Toilet

In medieval England, people used "potties" and would simply throw the contents through a door or window into the street. The more affluent would use a "garderobe," a room with an opening suspended over a moat where waste could be dumped.

Common people relieved themselves in communal toilets at the end of the street. A huge public toilet was constructed in London that emptied directly into the River Thames. It caused massive pollution, which resulted in widespread stench and inflicted various types of diseases on the city's population.

In 1592, Sir John Harrington, a godson of Elizabeth I, was believed to have invented a toilet with a raised water reservoir connected to a pipe by which the water could flush the waste. This invention was ignored for almost two hundred years. In 1775, Alexander Cummings, a watchmaker, developed the S-shaped pipe under the toilet basin to keep out foul odors from the toilet room. This partly solved the problem of bad odors in the houses. However, sewage was still spilled into the streets, polluting the nearby rivers.

In 1858, when rotting sewage surrounded the city of London, creating a very bad stench, the government commissioned the building of a sewer system in London. The construction was completed in 1865. This resulted in a drop in deaths from cholera, typhoid, and other waterborne diseases.

Scientific Establishments

These scientific discoveries and inventions were mostly made by individuals, not groups or institutions. During the pre-Enlightenment era, new scientific establishments and associations were created for like-minded individuals to talk about ideas. The two most prominent were the Royal Society in England and the Académie des Sciences in France.

Although both institutions were founded in the 17th century during the Scientific Revolution, they continued to flourish, bringing together leading scientific minds during the Enlightenment for practical and philosophical discussions.

These establishments aided in promoting scientific exploration and nurturing a culture of scientific experimentation, research, and scholarship. They also helped disseminate scientific knowledge and encourage literacy, which, in turn, created a new breed of scientists.

Chapter 4 – Ambitious Lust for Absolute Power

There are many fables and myths associated with Catherine the Great of Russia. One gruesome tale suggests that Catherine perished while engaging in carnal activities with a stallion that went berserk and collapsed on her, causing fatal injuries. However, there is no evidence to validate this account. Most historians presume that it was likely fabricated by Catherine's adversaries to defame her and tarnish her reputation.

In truth, Catherine the Great passed away in her chamber at the Winter Palace in St. Petersburg on November 17th, 1796, at the age of sixty-seven. The reason for her demise was a stroke, which she had encountered several days earlier. Catherine the Great was one of the most triumphant and influential enlightened monarchs of the 18th century. But she was far from being the only one.

Enlightened Autocracy

Enlightened autocracy was a method of administration that emerged in Europe during the 18th century. It sought to unite the principles of autocracy, where a sovereign had complete power over their kingdom and people, with the ideas of the Enlightenment, which underlined rationality and the pursuit of knowledge.

Enlightenment thinkers believed their sovereigns should be enlightened, erudite individuals who utilized their power to bring about societal, economic, and political changes. They saw sovereigns as the ultimate authority and believed they had a responsibility to govern in the best interests of their subjects rather than simply maintain their power and privilege.

The significance of enlightened autocracy lay in the fact that it symbolized a new way of thinking about governance. Rather than regarding power as the only thing that mattered, the enlightened autocrats perceived it as a means to improve society. By embracing rationality and the pursuit of knowledge, sovereigns could (hypothetically) create a more equitable and fair society. The needs of the people would be taken into consideration, and the sovereign would be answerable to their subjects.

Enlightened despots proclaimed that their royal power emanated not from the divine right to rule but from a social contract that entrusted them with the power to govern. These despots believed the people could not improve their lives on their own and that it was their responsibility to help them. In many cases, these rulers were benevolent and did many good things, but in the end, they increased their hold over the masses and their authority. This self-serving philosophy stated that the sovereign knew the interests of his or her subjects better than they did. And if the monarch took responsibility for their subjects, then their subjects would have no need to engage in politics.

Enlightened autocracy emerged as a response to the challenges encountered by European monarchies after the Enlightenment became more popular. As mentioned before, the Enlightenment challenged many of the conventional sources of authority, including the right of kings and the authority of the Catholic Church.

Thus, some sovereigns believed that embracing the ideals of the Enlightenment would allow them to reinforce their power. They believed that by becoming enlightened, they could promote the well-being of their subjects and cement their place in history as "enlightened rulers."

Enlightened sovereigns, such as Frederick II of Prussia, encouraged economic and social reforms, including the eradication of serfdom and the promotion of education. Catherine the Great of Russia and other rulers fostered cultural and intellectual developments, sponsoring the arts and science and advocating the ideals of the Enlightenment.

Enlightened despots recognized the significance of education, both for themselves and for their people. They believed that an educated populace could better contribute to society and support the monarch's objectives. Many enlightened despots supported schools and promoted education.

Although enlightened despotism achieved some success in advocating reforms and enhancing the living standards of the subjects, it had its limitations. Firstly, enlightened despots retained absolute authority, which meant they could suppress dissent and restrict political freedoms. Additionally, many of the implemented reforms were still restricted in scope and did not address the fundamental inequalities prevalent in European societies.

Overall, enlightened despotism represented a crucial moment in European history, highlighting the tension between conventional sources of authority and the Enlightenment's ideals. Although it had its limitations, it demonstrated the possibility of using power for the greater good and advocated the notion that governments had a duty to promote their citizens' welfare. The legacy of enlightened autocracy can still be observed today, especially in the belief that governments work for the greater good and aid the people under their rule.

Frederick the Great of Prussia

A portrait of Frederick the Great.
https://en.wikipedia.org/wiki/File:Friedrich_II.,_K%C3%B6nig_von_Preu%C3%9Fen_(Frisch).jpg

Frederick the Great of Prussia (also known as Frederick II) is widely regarded as one of the most prosperous and influential enlightened monarchs of the 18th century. During his long reign from 1740 to 1786, he implemented significant reforms that helped transform Prussia into a modern, affluent, and powerful state.

Frederick made some progress in improving the conditions of his subjects. For example, he was quite successful in controlling grain prices. The government storehouses would store sufficient amounts of grain and distribute it in times of need to the people so they could survive hard times when the harvest was poor. Frederick was also a good administrator, and he improved the bureaucracy and civil service. He abolished torture, granted amnesty to political prisoners, and established an independent judiciary, which ensured fair and impartial justice.

Frederick was in favor of freedom of thought. He was also quite tolerant in religious matters, with the people being allowed to follow their religious beliefs and practices, not a state-mandated religion. Frederick was largely non-practicing, although Protestantism became the favored religion. While he protected and encouraged trade by Jewish citizens of the empire, he repeatedly expressed strong anti-Semitic sentiments. Still, he expanded the Jewish population's rights, allowing them to settle in Prussian territories and practice their religion freely. Before this, they had been largely persecuted. Frederick also encouraged immigrants of various nationalities and faiths to come to Prussia.

Moreover, he promoted education, particularly in the sciences, and encouraged cultural and artistic growth. He was a prolific writer and composer, and his court attracted many of the leading intellectuals of the era.

Frederick implemented major economic reforms. He encouraged trade and commerce, promoted agricultural productivity, and supported industry growth. He abolished serfdom and other feudal obligations, granting greater freedom to the peasantry and the middle class. He also reformed the tax system, making it more equitable and efficient, and established a centralized bureaucracy, which consolidated his power and promoted effective governance.

However, despite Frederick's numerous successes, he was not without failures and controversies. He participated in numerous wars during his reign, often to expand Prussian territory and influence, which resulted in a significant loss of life and resources. He also faced criticism for his authoritarianism, which was deemed incompatible with his professed commitment to Enlightenment values. He censored the press, restricted freedom of speech, and suppressed dissent.

Frederick the Great of Prussia was a complex and multifaceted figure. As an enlightened monarch, he embraced many of the Enlightenment's values, promoting religious tolerance, economic advancement, and cultural and intellectual growth. However, his authoritarian tendencies and military ambitions attracted significant criticism, highlighting the tensions inherent in the concept of enlightened despotism.

Charles III of Spain

A painting of Charles III.
https://en.wikipedia.org/wiki/File:Charles_III_of_Spain_high_resolution.jpg

Charles III of Spain reigned from 1759 to 1788. He was probably the most successful European ruler of his time. He provided firm, consistent, intelligent leadership. He chose capable ministers, and his personal life was rather chaste and nondramatic, which won him the respect of the people.

During his reign, he transformed Spain into a more contemporary state. His policies sought to promote economic growth and social justice. Charles deregulated the economy, established chambers of commerce, set up new industries, and promoted science.

In Madrid, Charles established a new customs house, hospital, porcelain factory, and museum of nature. He also oversaw improvements to the sewage system, street lighting, and roads. The municipal government was reorganized, and theaters were renovated.

Charles III was a patron of the arts and science. He stimulated the growth of the arts, endorsing artists and musicians and promoting the development of Spanish literature and theater. It seems as if no aspect of public life was immune from the new spirit of progress.

King Charles III implemented significant agrarian and industrial reforms aimed at enhancing productivity and advocating economic growth. He stimulated the growth of commerce and trade, eliminating trade barriers and promoting free trade within Spain and with other European countries. Reforms included a royal decree "ennobling" the mechanical trades. He established government factories, providing productive employment for the poor.

However, his reforms did not always work as planned. "Ennobling" the mechanical trades did not produce the desired results. However, the economy did experience an upturn. The population of Spain increased from eight million to twelve million under his rule, leading to an increased demand for food and a sharp rise in prices. The larger population benefited the large landowners in the south and the small farmers near growing towns, such as Barcelona. The most remarkable feature of this economic revival was the emergence of a modern cotton textile industry in Catalonia.

The obsolete iron industry in the Basque region started to slowly modernize. The fishing industry grew in Galicia, where the Catalan immigrant fishermen became quite prosperous. Catalonia also became a hub for the brandy trade.

There were also many reforms in the financial sector, with the abolition of many duties and taxes, the encouragement of local markets, and the opening of trade with America.

However, Charles III was not without his failures. His efforts to encourage economic growth often came at the expense of the lower classes, and his policies regarding the working classes were often severe and exploitative. He implemented significant tax reforms that disproportionately affected the poor, and his labor policies were frequently oppressive and restrictive. His legacy as an enlightened monarch persists in Spain, but his reign also reminds us of the contradictory nature of enlightened absolutism.

Catherine the Great of Russia

A portrait of Catherine the Great.

The reign of Catherine the Great of Russia lasted from 1762 to 1796 and was marked by significant innovations and reforms that transformed Russia into a major power on the world stage.

Catherine's ascendancy to power in a coup d'état was a theatrical and violent event in Russian history. In 1762, Catherine's husband, Peter III, became the tsar of Russia. Peter was an unpopular and peculiar ruler who had little interest in governing. He could barely even speak Russian, as he had been raised in what is today Germany. He was more engrossed in military affairs and was known to admire the Prussian king, Frederick the Great, to the extent of garbing himself in Prussian military uniforms.

Catherine, on the contrary, was popular with the Russian populace and had a strong interest in politics and culture. She had been brought to Russia from her native Germany as a teenager to wed Peter, but their union was unhappy and fraught with tension.

After only a few months on the throne, Peter's erratic behavior and unpopular policies estranged many of his supporters. On June 28th, 1762, Catherine and her supporters staged a coup d'état. The coup was swift. Peter was arrested and forced to abdicate in favor of Catherine. He was later killed under mysterious circumstances, with many believing that he was assassinated on Catherine's orders.

One of Catherine's greatest achievements as an enlightened monarch was her advocacy of education, culture, and the arts. She established schools, hospitals, and orphanages, and she championed the growth of the arts and science. She was a prolific writer and corresponded with many of the leading intellectuals of the day. She also patronized the construction of the Hermitage Museum, which became home to one of the largest and most prestigious art collections in the world.

Another one of Catherine's accomplishments was the expansion of the Russian Empire. She annexed Crimea, the Caucasus, and portions of Poland, significantly broadening Russia's borders and influence. This expansion helped to establish Russia as a major European power and laid the groundwork for its subsequent domination in the 19th century.

Nonetheless, despite her many achievements, Catherine still faced controversies. Her greatest failure was perhaps her incapability to address the fundamental issues confronting Russia's social and economic systems. She maintained serfdom, a feudal system of labor that kept millions of peasants in bondage, and failed to implement significant reforms to the country's political and economic structures. This failure led to widespread social unrest and opposition, which contributed to the eventual downfall of the Romanov dynasty.

An example of Catherine the Great's ruthlessness was her response to Pugachev's rebellion, which took place from 1773 to 1775. She ordered a brutal crackdown on the rebels, using military force to suppress the rebellion. Thousands of rebels were captured, and Pugachev was eventually captured and executed. His body was dismembered in Moscow. Catherine's retribution was severe, with widespread executions, torture, and reprisals against those believed to have supported the rebellion. Tens of thousands of people were killed during the suppression of the Pugachev Rebellion.

Catherine's enlightened rhetoric was often at odds with her actual policies and practices. She was an autocratic ruler who limited the people's freedom of the press, speech, and assembly. She also engaged in imperialistic wars, and her policies toward Poland and other territories were often merciless and exploitative.

Catherine died in 1796 in St. Petersburg, Russia. Her death marked the conclusion of a long and eventful reign that spanned over three decades and had seen significant political, social, and cultural changes in Russia.

Catherine the Great's reign was marked by achievements and progress in many areas, but it was also marred by instances of brutality, oppression, and criticism. Nevertheless, Catherine's impact on Russian history and her contributions to the country's political and cultural development cannot be denied. She remains a significant figure in Russian and world history.

Leopold I of Tuscany

Leopold I of Tuscany, also known as Grand Duke Leopold I, was one of the most prosperous and forward-thinking enlightened monarchs of the 18th century. Throughout his reign, from 1765 to 1790, he enforced noteworthy reforms that aimed to modernize Tuscany into a more effective and fair state.

One of Leopold I's accomplishments as an enlightened monarch was the introduction of significant agricultural and industrial reforms aimed at enhancing efficiency and stimulating fiscal growth. He encouraged commerce and trade by abolishing trade obstacles and promoting free trade. Leopold also instituted the first modern insurance system in Europe, safeguarding people against loss or destruction of property.

Leopold I was a sponsor of the arts and sciences. He supported the Accademia dei Georgofili, which concentrated on the study of agriculture, and also promoted the Accademia delle Belle Arti, which focused on the arts. Leopold encouraged the proliferation of the arts, sponsoring artists and musicians, and endorsed the development of Tuscan literature and theater.

Leopold abolished capital punishment and ensured smallpox vaccinations were easily obtainable for everyone. He created hospitals for the mentally ill, becoming one of the first to do so. Although these hospitals were not like the ones we have today, his doctors did not believe in torturing or punishing those who lived there.

But of course, Leopold I had his faults. And those faults mainly came to light when Leopold took over the Holy Roman Empire from his brother, becoming Leopold II. Although he continued some of his enlightened policies while ruling this vast territory, he also used brute force. He didn't want to be unpopular with his subjects, mainly the nobles. To put down a disturbance, Leopold placed thousands of people who had been freed from serfdom back under the yoke. Leopold was a politician, and he played the politician's game when his hand was forced.

Leopold I's reign helped to transform Tuscany into a more contemporary and prosperous state. But his policies, especially once he became the Holy Roman emperor, could be unjust.

Joseph II of Austria

Joseph II, also known as Joseph the Reformer or Joseph the Great, was a Holy Roman emperor and archduke of Austria who ruled from 1765 to 1790. Joseph was Leopold I's brother. Joseph was a proponent of enlightened absolutism. He is known for his ambitious and wide-ranging reforms aimed at modernizing Austria and improving the lives of his subjects. However, his reign was also marked by controversy, challenges, and, ultimately, an unfinished legacy.

One of Joseph's greatest accomplishments was his policy of religious toleration. He ended the Catholic Church's control over education, allowing for greater intellectual freedom and the proliferation of scientific inquiry. He also granted religious protections to Protestant and Orthodox minorities and promoted the rights of Jews. Additionally, he reformed the judicial system, granting greater protections to defendants and enhancing the efficiency of legal proceedings.

Joseph also reformed the economy and the social system. He implemented significant agrarian and industrial reforms that were aimed at increasing productivity and economic growth. One of his major acts was abolishing serfdom, granting greater liberties to the peasantry and the bourgeoisie. He restructured the taxation system and eliminated trade barriers, encouraging greater economic integration within the Holy Roman Empire and beyond.

However, Joseph's enlightened policies were often met with substantial opposition. His efforts to centralize power and eliminate regional autonomy were met with resistance from the aristocracy, who witnessed their traditional privileges and powers being affected by what they saw as radical moves. His attempts to reform the Catholic Church also encountered substantial opposition from conservative clergymen, who saw their influence and power being eroded. Moreover, his policies toward Hungarians and other ethnic minorities were frequently heavy-handed and contributed to nationalist sentiment and opposition.

Another captivating aspect of Joseph's life was his relationship with his mother, Empress Maria Theresa. The two were notoriously close, with Joseph serving as his mother's right-hand man and chief advisor for many years. Nonetheless, their relationship was not without its strains and conflicts, primarily over Joseph's progressive policies and his desire to modernize the empire.

Joseph II was a controversial figure whose reign was marked by both successes and failures. His promotion of religious tolerance and social modernization helped to transform the Holy Roman Empire into a more efficient and fair state, but his efforts to centralize power and eliminate regional autonomy often encountered resentment from the elite and the Hungarians, making him unpopular and isolating him politically from other nations. His legacy as an enlightened monarch remains a topic of discussion by historians today.

Absolute Rulers: Flourishing or Failures?

Absolute rulers were commonly regarded as the ultimate power in their territories, as their authority was not subject to any constraints. This could be both an asset and a flaw. On the one hand, absolute rulers had the power to make sweeping transformations and enact policies they believed were in the best interest of their subjects. However, this also meant they could act with impunity and frequently had little thought for the wishes of their subjects.

The absolute rulers mentioned in this chapter were powerful in their own right, and their reigns had an enduring impact on their individual nations and European history. While they were all absolute rulers, they also espoused the principles of the Enlightenment and sought to foster progress and reform, reflecting the evolving attitudes of the period.

Nonetheless, these rulers were just that, rulers. They wanted to retain their power and ensure that power would be passed down to their heirs. Numerous people chafed under their rule and resented the fact they had no voice in governance. In addition, the concentration of authority in the hands of a solitary ruler frequently resulted in corruption, nepotism, and abuses of power. This, in turn, weakened the legitimacy of the monarchy and led to rebellion or revolution.

All in all, the triumph and acceptance of absolute monarchs varied extensively. While some were able to employ their power to foster progress and ease the lives of their subjects, others were regarded as oppressive and corrupt, leading to widespread discontent and even revolution.

Chapter 5 – Core Pillars of Enlightened Thought

The core pillars of Enlightened thought are reason, individualism, skepticism, and progress. Other crucial concepts include the separation of church and state and constitutional governance.

Reason

The pre-Enlightenment era spans a lengthy period of history, but one of the earliest intellectuals who championed the use of reason was the ancient Greek philosopher Aristotle (384-322 BCE). Aristotle believed that reason was the key to comprehending the world and that humans could utilize it to ascertain truth and knowledge. He emphasized the significance of observation, analysis, and logic.

Aristotle's ideas about reason influenced many subsequent thinkers, including the medieval philosopher Thomas Aquinas (1225-1274), who endeavored to reconcile Aristotle's philosophy with Christian theology. Aquinas contended that people could employ reason to understand the natural world but that faith was essential to comprehend spiritual matters.

Accepting reason was a radical departure from how people contemplated understanding. Before the Enlightenment, knowledge was frequently based on teachings from authority figures, such as the church or the government. The reason was a lack of education, books, and other reliable sources of information. However, Enlightenment thinkers repudiated authority figures being used as sources of knowledge, arguing they were frequently dogmatic and superstitious, basing information on arbitrary rules instead of reason.

One of the most eminent and influential figures associated with the rise of reason to comprehend knowledge was French philosopher René Descartes, who lived between 1596 and 1650. Descartes argued that people could acquire knowledge through reason and that skepticism was crucial for testing the validity of claims.

Of course, there were opponents to the rise of reason, primarily the Catholic Church. The church saw the emphasis on reason and empirical evidence as a menace to its authority, so it actively opposed many ideas and practices associated with the Enlightenment. For instance, the church condemned Galileo for his endorsement of the heliocentric model of the solar system, which contradicted church teachings.

Some Enlightenment intellectuals were also critical of rationality and stressed the limitations of reason. The German philosopher Immanuel Kant contended that reason had its restrictions. In his opinion, there were certain aspects of the world, such as morality and the existence of God, that could not be comprehended through reason alone.

The achievement of the scientific method, the uptick of new forms of communication, the evolution of new philosophical and political ideas, and the application of reason to daily life persuaded individuals of the significance of logical thinking.

Individualism

The emergence of individualism symbolized a significant shift in reasoning about the individual's role in society, highlighting the significance of personal rights and self-rule. The idea of individualism profoundly affected the progress of modern liberal democracy and the preservation of individual rights and freedoms.

But what exactly is individualism? Simply put, individualism promotes the idea that the individual is more important than the state. Enlightenment thinkers who touted this belief wanted people to realize they had goals and dreams that deserved to be fulfilled, not shoved to the side so the government could force them to work in the fields.

One of the critical factors that contributed to the rise of individualism during the Enlightenment was new economic and social systems, such as the rise of trade, the ascension of the middle class, and the decline of feudalism. These changes created new opportunities for social mobility and economic prosperity.

Enlightenment thinkers were pivotal in promoting individualism, asserting that individuals should be free to pursue their interests and desires without interference from the state or other authorities. They stressed the importance of the right to free expression, religious freedom, and the right to possess property. They also attempted to limit the power of the state and other establishments to safeguard these rights.

One of the most influential intellectuals associated with the rise of individualism during the Enlightenment was English thinker John Locke, who lived between 1632 and 1704. Locke stated that individuals were endowed with fundamental rights and that the state should preserve these rights. He also contended that governments should derive their authority from the consent of the governed.

Another advocate of individualism was French philosopher Jean-Jacques Rousseau, who lived from 1712 to 1778. He claimed that individuals were born free and equal and entitled to certain natural rights, including the right to life and liberty. He stressed the importance of individual self-rule and self-determination, contending that individuals should be able to pursue their interests and desires without undue interference from the state or other forms of authority.

Rousseau's ideas significantly differed from traditional forms of social organization, highlighting the importance of duty, obligation, and deference to authority. His emphasis on individualism paved the way for a new understanding of the relationship between individuals and society.

Paradoxically, Rousseau, while himself a supporter of individualism, also criticized certain aspects of individualism that he saw as contributing to social inequality and injustice. Rousseau argued that individualism could lead to self-centeredness and social fragmentation. He believed it could undermine the social bonds and shared values necessary for a cohesive and just society.

Other adversaries of individualism included religious authorities and conservative political leaders who viewed individualism as threatening the traditional forms of power and the social hierarchy. They argued that individualism could lead to moral decadence, social disorder, and political instability, so they sought to promote more conventional forms of social organization and authority.

Individualism is a prominent belief today, with many countries, including the United States, South Africa, and Germany, basing their government on it. Individualism will likely continue to spread in the years to come.

Skepticism

Skepticism pertains to a discerning mindset toward conventional beliefs and practices. Enlightenment thinkers moved away from the idea of traditional authority and sought to challenge established norms and conventions. They believed in the importance of questioning information and validating ideas through empirical observation and scientific inquiry instead of being handed information from a clergyman or king. Skepticism goes hand in hand with reason, as skeptics wanted to use logic to prove old beliefs as being wrong.

One of the most significant proponents of skepticism was the French philosopher René Descartes. Descartes stressed the significance of doubt as a means of challenging accepted beliefs and assumptions. He argued that individuals should rely on their own thoughts and judgments to evaluate the veracity of various claims.

Scottish thinker David Hume, who lived between 1711 and 1776, is widely regarded as one of the greatest champions of skepticism. He argued that knowledge could only be derived from sense and experience. Hume stated that any claims that could not be verified through observation and experimentation should be treated with skepticism. In his opinion, people's knowledge of cause-and-effect relationships is based on a constant conjunction of events rather than any logical connection between them.

Hume also applied his skeptical approach to religious and ethical claims, arguing that these could not be established through reason or observation and were therefore based on faith and sentiment. Hume's skeptical views on religion and morality were contentious. They attracted widespread criticism but also contributed to a broader cultural shift toward a more critical and scientific approach to social and moral issues.

Religious institutions and figures often denounced skeptics, mainly regarding religious claims, arguing that faith was indispensable for establishing the truth of religious doctrines. Some philosophers and intellectuals were also critical of skepticism, arguing that it led to relativism or nihilism, which undermined the foundations of knowledge and morality.

German philosopher Friedrich Nietzsche criticized this skeptical approach to knowledge, arguing that it eroded the possibility of objective truth and left individuals without any moral or intellectual compass.

Nietzsche's critique of skepticism was part of a broader cultural shift toward a more subjective and existentialist approach to knowledge and truth, which rejected the notion of objective reality in favor of a more subjective and individualistic worldview. This concept is a little complex, but to put it simply, Nietzsche believed that people viewed the world based on their own experiences and that there was no one "right" way to live.

The impact of religious and political upheavals prompted many individuals to scrutinize the authority and claims of leaders. For example, the Protestant Reformation challenged the power of the Catholic Church, encouraging individuals to read and interpret the Bible for themselves, contributing to a more critical approach to religious claims.

Similarly, the political revolutions of the time, such as the American and French Revolutions, challenged the authority of traditional monarchies and aristocracies and encouraged individuals to question the legitimacy of political power.

Progress

Enlightenment thinkers believed that society could improve through reason and the application of scientific knowledge, a concept known as progress. Progress was a significant shift in how people viewed human history and society. Before the Enlightenment, people believed that the world was static and unchanging and that human history was merely a cycle of rises and falls.

Enlightenment thinkers challenged this view, arguing that society progressed and improved through reason, skepticism, and individualism. Many Enlightenment thinkers believed that progress was essential for humans to flourish and create a just society. Enlightenment thinkers produced works on topics like science, philosophy, economics, and politics, using rhetoric to persuade their readers of the importance of progress.

Some Enlightenment philosophers, such as Immanuel Kant, contended that progress resulted from man's search for logic. Others, such as Adam Smith, regarded progress as the outcome of the growth of commerce and trade, which facilitated the creation of wealth and the spread of ideas.

French philosopher and author Voltaire was one of the most influential figures in shaping the notion of progress. He was a prolific writer who created works on various topics, including history, politics, philosophy, and religion. He was a staunch advocate of reason and individualism, believing that progress was critical for human prosperity and creating a fair society.

In his celebrated work *Candide*, Voltaire ridiculed the idea that everything was for the best in this "best of all possible worlds," arguing instead that the world was full of suffering and injustice that could only be overcome through the pursuit of enlightened values. He championed religious tolerance, free speech, and the separation of church and state, all of which he believed were essential for creating a more open-minded society.

One of the key drivers of progress during the Enlightenment was the rise of science, which allowed people to understand the natural world better and develop new technologies and innovations. This, in turn, led to improvements in medicine, agriculture, transportation, and other fields, which helped to better people's lives.

The Romantic poets and thinkers who emerged in the late 18th and early 19th centuries rejected the emphasis on reason and praised emotion, imagination, and intuition instead. They were suspicious that human progress could be achieved by applying reason and technology. They criticized the Enlightenment's faith in progress as a naive and dangerous idea. They thought science, technology, and an emphasis on logic would make life dull and devoid of creativity and romance.

German philosopher Friedrich Nietzsche argued that the emphasis on reason and progress led to a loss of meaning and purpose in modern life. He advocated rejecting Enlightenment values in favor of a more individualistic and life-affirming philosophy.

The rise of progress during the Enlightenment was the product of a complex interplay of social and political factors, and it was propelled by a growing sense of optimism and a belief in the power of human reason to shape the world for the better.

The Separation of Church and State

The separation of church and state refers to the notion that the government should not be involved in ecclesiastical matters and vice versa. Individuals should also be able to practice their own religion or lack thereof of their own volition.

The idea of the separation of church and state originated as a reaction to centuries of religious strife and persecution in Europe. The idea that religion and government should be kept apart was considered a way to foster tolerance and prevent the abuses of authority that had been pervasive throughout much of European history.

The French philosopher Voltaire argued that religious leaders should have no say in government affairs. He believed that the government should be indifferent to religious matters, allowing individuals to practice whatever religion they choose without fear of retribution.

English philosopher John Locke maintained that the government should be restricted in its power and allow individuals to have the liberty to pursue their own religious convictions. Locke considered religious tolerance to be crucial in promoting social harmony and thought that the government had no right to meddle in religious belief or practice.

In the United States, the separation of church and state was formalized in the First Amendment to the Constitution, which states, "Congress shall make no law respecting an establishment of religion, or prohibiting the free exercise thereof." This principle has been a cornerstone of American democracy ever since and has helped to ensure that the government does not exhibit partiality toward any religion or use its power to suppress religious minorities.

However, some disagreed with the concept. French philosopher Jean-Jacques Rousseau opined that religion and the state should be intertwined. He argued that religious convictions and practices were indispensable for creating a sense of community and social cohesion. He also held that the state had a duty to safeguard and advance religious values.

Rousseau's views on the relationship between religion and the state directly opposed the separation of church and state. Nevertheless, his opinions ultimately did not triumph, and the principle of the separation of church and state remains a crucial tenet of contemporary Western democracies.

Constitutional Government

A constitutional government refers to a government where power is limited by a written constitution that delineates the rights and responsibilities of citizens and the government's powers. Enlightenment intellectuals held that a constitutional government was essential for safeguarding individual liberties and preventing the abuse of power by those in authority.

The Enlightenment was a period of immense political upheaval, and many intellectuals grappled with questions of how to create a just and stable society. One of the principal ideas that emerged during this time was constitutional government.

The growth in demand for constitutional governments was closely connected to the social contract theory, which held that a government should be founded on a mutual agreement between the people and their rulers. This theory emphasized the significance of individualism and the need to restrict the government's power to safeguard the rights of citizens.

One of the most influential advocates of a constitutional government was the English philosopher John Locke, who contended that government should be founded by the consent of the governed and that a constitution should restrict authority figures.

Another prominent champion of constitutional government was French philosopher Montesquieu, who lived from 1689 to 1755. In his notable work *The Spirit of Law*, published in 1748, Montesquieu advocated for the separation of powers in government and the limitation of any individual or faction holding all the power. He believed that the best form of government combined elements of a monarchy and democracy. Montesquieu also thought a constitution was mandatory to protect individual rights and hinder abuses of power.

The rise of constitutional governments was closely linked to the growth of capitalism and commerce. As trade expanded, individuals began to demand greater safeguards for their property rights and individual liberties, which led to the establishment of constitutions and other legal protections.

Several monarchs and aristocrats of the time opposed restricting their power through a constitution. Some conservative thinkers, such as Edmund Burke, argued that society's traditions and customs should lay the groundwork for a government rather than abstract principles or documents like a constitution. Burke also feared that excessive change or reform could lead to confusion and instability. He saw the importance of religious institutions for the moral stability and good of the state. He argued that the French Revolution would end disastrously because its foundations ignored human nature's and society's complexities.

The American and French Revolutions present examples of effective constitutional governments in action, which helped to spread the idea. However, the French Revolution was much bloodier and unfair, as many elites were persecuted and killed during the Reign of Terror. Ultimately, the democratic government of France fell to Napoleon Bonaparte, who created an empire that was seen as more liberal, although his power was still absolute.

The rise of the printing press and the wider availability of books and pamphlets enabled all of these Enlightenment ideas to reach a vaster audience. The essential pillars of enlightened thought stress the significance of rationality, individualism, progress, and skepticism in promoting a better understanding of the world and society.

Chapter 6 – Intellectual Titans Who Changed the Course of History

Imagine a time when the world was still in the grip of superstition, religious dogma, and monarchial rule. A time when knowledge was the privilege of the elite and dissent was met with brutal punishment. Against this backdrop, a group of radical thinkers emerged whose ideas would change the course of history forever.

From daring explorers to brilliant philosophers, from visionary economists to revolutionary writers, these great men were not content to sit back and accept how things were. They were driven by a fierce desire to understand the world around them and to make it a better place.

In the following short biographies, you will observe these extraordinary men's thrilling lives and ideas and understand their impact on their world and ours.

John Locke

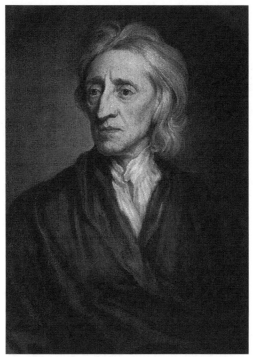

A portrait of John Locke, one of the most influential Enlightenment thinkers.
https://commons.wikimedia.org/wiki/File:John_Locke.jpg

John Locke (1632-1704) was an English philosopher and physician who is considered one of the most influential figures of the Enlightenment. He is known for his contributions to political philosophy, the theory of knowledge (epistemology), and educational theory.

As a young man, Locke was determined to pursue his dreams, despite the many obstacles in his path. He struggled to make ends meet and was constantly battling illness, but his passion for knowledge and his unrelenting spirit drove him forward. Locke's most remarkable feat was his ability to rise above the limitations imposed on him by society, despite being born into a time when social class and birthright dictated one's destiny.

Locke's father and mother came from Puritan trading families, with clothiers on his father's side and tanners on his mother's. His father earned a living as an attorney and clerk to the Justices of the Peace in Somerset. He owned some land but not enough to enable his family to live as aristocrats. However, it was enough to lead a reasonable life.

Until his mid-thirties, Locke lived a rather unexciting life. For more than three decades, he was involved with politics, but in his late fifties, he became very famous as a philosopher. He published his writings, with one of his most notable works being *An Essay Concerning Human Understanding*, published in 1689.

The theory of knowledge set out in *An Essay Concerning Human Understanding* is, in some ways, extremely skeptical. He believed humans were born as blank slates that were filled with their own unique experiences in life. In other words, people were not born with innate ideas of how to live; that was something a person gained over time. He also stated that there was a limit to the knowledge a person could gain.

As he writes in his essay, "Knowledge, say you, is only the Perception of the Agreement or Disagreement of our own Ideas: but who knows what those Ideas may be?"

Locke also famously believed that governments should be based on the consent of the governed and that individuals have a right to life, liberty, and property. He argued that the government's role was to protect these rights. If a government failed to do so, then the people had the right to overthrow it.

His philosophy obviously had a significant impact on the development of modern democracy, and his ideas were influential in the American and French Revolutions. He also wrote extensively about education, advocating for an approach that emphasized individualism and encouraged students to think for themselves.

In the last decade and a half of Locke's life, as an old, sick, and immensely distinguished man, he was at last in a position to see the scale and meaning of his achievements. Locke was a man who refused to accept the status quo and instead chose to challenge it at every turn. His ideas continue to shape the world we live in today.

Baruch Spinoza

Baruch Spinoza (1632–1677) was a rebel in every sense of the word. As a child, he attended a Jewish school and the synagogue, where he studied Hebrew and the works of Jewish and Arabian theologians. Although he was brought up in a strict Portuguese-Jewish family in Amsterdam, he challenged the traditional religious beliefs of his community and dared to think for himself. His unorthodox ideas about God and nature would eventually lead to his excommunication from the Jewish community.

Spinoza was branded a heretic and accused of trivializing God's role in the universe and human affairs. He was expelled from the Jewish community for speaking against religion and was declared a heretic. He disputed the existence of miracles and the afterlife and challenged the authority of the Bible. His book titled *Theologico-Political Treatise* was declared as an evil work inspired by the devil. His magnum opus, *Ethics*, put forward a system of breathtaking originality but was condemned by the Catholic Church. It was put on the list of banned books.

Undeterred, Spinoza continued to explore his radical philosophy, rejecting the notion of a personal God and embracing the power of reason to understand the natural world. He saw human emotions and passions as obstacles to rational inquiry and argued for a strong separation between church and state.

There is an interesting anecdote about Professor Albert Einstein, the author of the theory of relativity, who declared his belief in "Spinoza's God." In 1929, Einstein received a telegram from Rabbi Herbert S. Goldstein of the Institutional Synagogue in Germany, who asked Einstein, "Do you believe in God?" Einstein wrote back to the rabbi, "I believe in Spinoza's God, who reveals himself in the orderly harmony of what exists, not in a God who concerns himself with the fates and actions of human beings."

So, who was Spinoza's God that Einstein believed in? According to Spinoza, the church had fallen for the illusion of an anthropocentric God, an external being acting in the world of human affairs and intervening according to his whims. Spinoza claimed that the church made God similar to a king who grants rewards for submission and delivers punishments for any sins. It is interesting to note that famous philosophers, such as John Calvin and René Descartes, also used the metaphor of God being similar to a king in their writings.

Despite his radical ideas, Spinoza's works were widely read and respected during his lifetime, and he remains one of the most important figures of the Enlightenment. His works inspired other Enlightenment thinkers, including Voltaire, Kant, and Hume. His ideas were considered dangerous and revolutionary during his time, but his influence would be felt for centuries to come.

Montesquieu

Charles-Louis de Secondat, Baron de La Brède et de Montesquieu (1689–1755), was a prominent French philosopher and writer. Born to a noble family, Montesquieu quickly distinguished himself as a brilliant thinker and writer with a razor-sharp intellect and a deep passion for justice.

Montesquieu was primarily interested in politics and law. He was a proponent of a government with limited powers in which the leaders had to follow the law. Montesquieu believed the government's power should be separated into branches so that no single person or group held too much power. Montesquieu's ideas also included skepticism toward the rigid social structure of France. He was a vocal advocate for human rights, including the abolition of slavery, and his work helped to pave the way for the French Revolution and the rise of democracy across Europe.

Montesquieu's most famous work, *The Spirit of Laws*, published in 1748, was a groundbreaking contribution to political theory. In it, he argued that the best form of government was one that had a separation of powers with checks and balances. This idea would go on to become a cornerstone of modern democracy and constitutional governments.

In addition to his political philosophy, Montesquieu was a social commentator, and his writings often reflected his concerns about the state of French society. He was critical of the French monarchy, which he saw as oppressive and corrupt, and he championed the rights of individuals and the importance of personal freedom. His call for more rights was seen as dangerous by the ruling elite. His writings were often censored and suppressed.

Today, he is widely regarded as one of the greatest philosophers of the Enlightenment, and his contributions to political theory and social commentary continue to shape our understanding of the world around us.

Voltaire

A portrait of Voltaire.
Nicolas de Largillière, CC0, via Wikimedia Commons;
https://commons.wikimedia.org/wiki/File:Nicolas_de_Largilli%C3%A8re_-
Portrait_de_Voltaire_(1694-1778)_en_1718_-_P208_-_mus%C3%A9e_Carnavalet_-_5.jpg

Born François-Marie Arouet, Voltaire (1694–1778) was a French writer, historian, and philosopher who is considered one of the greatest literary figures of his time. His life was filled with dramatic events that shaped his beliefs and inspired his writing.

As a young man, Voltaire was known for his sharp wit and rebellious spirit. He was educated by Jesuits and studied law but quickly became disillusioned with the French legal system. He began writing satirical poems and plays that mocked the aristocracy and the church. As a result, he soon gained a reputation for being a troublemaker. He was frequently at odds with the authorities.

In 1717, Voltaire was arrested and imprisoned for insulting a nobleman. He continued to write and develop his philosophical ideas while in prison. About a year later, he was released, but he did not get to enjoy the sights of France for too long. In 1726, he was exiled to England, where he was exposed to the works of John Locke and other Enlightenment thinkers. He returned to France in 1729 and soon became embroiled in a series of controversies over his writings and beliefs.

Voltaire was a passionate advocate for human rights and religious tolerance, and his ideas had a profound influence on the development of modern Western thought. Part of his influence stems from the fact that he wrote far more than anyone else. The first-ever edition of his complete works, currently being undertaken by the Voltaire Foundation in Oxford, will result in some two hundred volumes!

Voltaire was a master of virtually all literary genres. His writings include poetry in many different styles, satire, plays, opera, history, short prose works, and even a scientific treatise. In addition to all that, he has the most extensive correspondence of any writer of the period.

Voltaire maintained a lifelong interest in science and philosophy, and he corresponded with some of the most influential thinkers of his time, including John Locke, Isaac Newton, and Jean-Jacques Rousseau. Voltaire's life was filled with drama, and his writing faced many controversies, but his legacy as a champion of reason, freedom, and justice continues to inspire people worldwide today.

David Hume

David Hume (1711–1776) was a Scottish philosopher, historian, and economist who played a key role in the Enlightenment. Hume's most important contributions to philosophy came in the form of his skepticism and belief in empiricism. He was skeptical of traditional metaphysical concepts, such as causality (the belief that one event causes another event to occur), and argued that people's knowledge of the world was based on sensory experience rather than abstract reasoning.

Hume grew up in a family of intellectuals and was driven by an insatiable curiosity about the world around him. As a young man, Hume studied law and even worked briefly as a merchant, but his true passion was philosophy. He spent countless hours reading and writing. In his groundbreaking work, *A Treatise of Human Nature*, Hume famously argued that there is no connection between cause and effect and that our beliefs about the world are based on habit and association rather than reason.

He proposed that traditional religious beliefs were outdated and needed to be replaced with a more scientific approach. He argued that reason and experience should be the foundation of all knowledge and that scientific inquiry should be used to understand the natural world. David Hume's philosophy is often represented as part of a movement that was started by John Locke in 1690. The main theme of this movement is that men have no knowledge of the world but what they derive from experiences, such as feelings, bodily sensations, sounds, smells, and tastes.

In addition to his philosophical work, Hume was an important historian and economist. His *The History of England* is still widely read today and is considered a classic. Regarding economics, Hume argued that a stable monetary system was essential for economic growth and that government intervention in the economy should be limited.

Jean-Jacques Rousseau

Jean-Jacques Rousseau (1712–1778) was born in Geneva, Switzerland. He was a larger-than-life figure whose ideas and writings shook the foundations of the Enlightenment. He rose to become one of the most celebrated thinkers of his time, despite facing constant adversity and personal turmoil.

Though Rousseau never received a formal education, he showed a prodigious intellect and a deep curiosity about the world around him at an early age. His studies in philosophy and literature led him to Paris in 1742, where he soon became the toast of the intellectual elite. He became a music teacher and befriended many of the leading academics of the day, including Denis Diderot and Voltaire. During this time, he began to write and publish his works, including his first essay, *A Discourse on the Moral Effects of the Arts and Sciences*, which won him widespread acclaim.

Rousseau entered an essay competition with a work entitled *Discourse on the Arts and Sciences*. His essay was in response to a question of whether progress in science and arts will improve or corrupt human morality or not. Guess who won the contest? Rousseau did, and it brought him greater recognition as a philosopher.

In his essay, Rousseau proposes that the sciences and art conflict with virtuousness and morality. He goes on to say that science often gives false information, which could be dangerous to society. When people study arts and science, they become lazy and scorn virtues. When people follow and indulge in art, people are rewarded based on their talent, which causes inequality in society. Enlightened values, if employed correctly, would make people wealthy, and in Rousseau's view, wealth destroys morality.

But Rousseau was not content to simply bask in his success over his essay, even though it was seen as controversial by many. Instead, he used his platform to challenge Enlightenment thoughts. He rejected the idea that reason was the sole path to truth and championed the importance of human emotion and intuition. He criticized the social and political structures of his time, arguing they were built on a foundation of oppression and injustice.

Despite the acclaim that his ideas received, Rousseau was constantly beset by personal problems. His relationship with his mistress, Thérèse Levasseur, was tumultuous at best, and his feelings of isolation and disillusionment seeped into his writing.

As the years went on, Rousseau's ideas became more radical and confrontational. His masterpiece, *The Social Contract*, laid out a vision for a just society, calling for the government's power to be derived from the people themselves and for individual freedom to be balanced against social responsibility.

Like any other Enlightenment thinker, Rousseau's ideas were not without critics, and he soon found himself at the center of controversy. His writings were accused of being anti-Christian, and his ideas were seen as a threat to the established order. He never went to jail, avoiding it by going into self-imposed exile in England.

Rousseau was known for his idealistic views on society and his belief in the natural goodness of man. He was also known for his rather eccentric behavior and had a reputation for being paranoid and a hypochondriac. Today, Jean-Jacques Rousseau remains one of the most enigmatic and captivating figures of the Enlightenment.

Denis Diderot

Denis Diderot (1713-1784) was a bold and courageous French philosopher and writer who fearlessly challenged traditional authorities and advocated for greater freedom of thought.

Diderot was deeply influenced by Enlightenment ideas. He believed that knowledge should be accessible to everyone, not just the educated elite. In 1745, he was introduced to Jean le Rond d'Alembert, a mathematician and philosopher who shared his views. Together, they began work on the *Encyclopédie*.

The *Encyclopédie* was a massive undertaking, requiring the collaboration of hundreds of contributors. It aimed to collect and organize knowledge on a wide range of subjects, including science, philosophy, art, and politics. Diderot served as the editor. He oversaw the project and wrote many of the articles himself.

Diderot was a prolific writer. He wrote plays, novels, and essays on many subjects. His most famous novel, *Jacques the Fatalist and His Master*, is a satirical work that challenges traditional notions of fate and free will.

In *Jacques the Fatalist*, a master and his servant ride through France, with the servant appearing to be free and master of his own will. The pair travel across the country, with the story revealing a panoramic view of 18th-century society. But while the servant seems to choose his own path, he remains convinced of one philosophical belief: that every decision he makes, however whimsical, is wholly predetermined.

Diderot's novel is playful and comic. It is also a compelling exploration of Enlightenment philosophy. Brilliantly original in style, it is considered to be one of the greatest novels of post-modern literature.

Diderot's work was often controversial and led to frequent censorship and persecution by the authorities. To avoid trouble, Diderot published his books anonymously. Soon after the *Pensées philosophiques* appeared in 1746, it was publicly burned in July of that same year. By 1749, the authorities confirmed that he was the author of these dangerous books. After the publication of *Lettre sur les aveugles*, he was jailed in the Dungeon of Vincennes for three months.

In *Lettre sur les aveugles*, Diderot argued that a blind man who could suddenly see would not understand what he was looking at. He has to perceive things to understand them. Diderot extended this argument to the spiritual realm, saying that if a person has to perceive things to understand them, then there is no universal spiritual truth.

Nevertheless, after Diderot's release from prison, he continued to write and challenge traditional ideas, helping shape the intellectual and cultural life of France.

Adam Smith

An etching of Adam Smith.
https://en.wikipedia.org/wiki/File:AdamSmith.jpg

Adam Smith (1723-1790) was a Scottish philosopher and economist who is widely regarded as the father of modern economics. From a young age, Smith was fascinated by the world around him, and he immersed himself in his studies. He devoured the works of the great thinkers of his time, such as David Hume.

Smith became interested in the ideas of free trade and the division of labor. He believed that a free market would lead to the greatest economic growth.

However, it was Smith's groundbreaking work, *The Wealth of Nations*, that made him a legend in the annals of economic thought. This monumental work, published in 1776, laid out Smith's vision of a free-market economy, one in which individuals were free to pursue their own self-interests without interference from the state. It outlined his ideas about the government's role in economic affairs and argued that government intervention in the market should be limited. Smith's ideas had a significant impact on the development of economics and political philosophy, and his legacy continues to influence economic thought today.

Smith was also a significant figure in moral philosophy. He believed that moral behavior was rooted in sympathy and empathy for others and that individuals had an innate sense of justice and morality that should guide their actions.

Immanuel Kant

IMMANUEL KANT
From a painting

An engraving of Immanuel Kant.
https://commons.wikimedia.org/wiki/File:Immanuel_Kant_3.jpg

Immanuel Kant (1724-1804) was a German philosopher whose life was defined by his unwavering dedication to reason, truth, and intellectual rigor. Kant grew up in a world that was rapidly changing, both politically and culturally. Despite the challenges of his time, Kant was a man of singular focus and determination. He studied philosophy, mathematics, and physics at the University of Königsberg and soon developed a reputation for his brilliance and original thinking.

As Kant embarked on his career as a philosopher, he was driven by a burning desire to uncover the fundamental truths of existence. He spent long hours in his study, poring over texts and working through complex problems, always striving to arrive at a deeper understanding of the world around him.

Kant's work was groundbreaking, as he challenged long-held assumptions about the nature of reality. His major works, including the *Critique of Pure Reason* and the *Critique of Practical Reason*, were among the most important philosophical texts of his time.

In *Critique of Pure Reason*, published in 1781, Kant seeks to reconcile rationalism and empiricism by examining the nature and limits of human knowledge. Kant distinguishes between *phenomena* (appearances) and *noumena* (things as they are), stating that our knowledge is limited to the realm of *phenomena*. He introduces the concept of transcendental idealism, suggesting that our perceptions are shaped by innate categories that structure our experience of the world. Kant also discusses the limitations of reason and contradictions that arise when reason tries to go beyond the limits of experience.

The *Critique of Practical Reason*, which was published in 1788, focuses on ethics and moral philosophy. In this book, Kant shifts his focus from theoretical reason to practical reason, specifically exploring the nature of morality and the foundations of ethical decision-making. Kant insists that practical reason, or the ability to make moral judgments and to act accordingly, is fundamental to human freedom. He introduces the concept of the categorical imperative, a moral principle that requires individuals to act according to maxims that can be universally applied without contradiction.

Kant lived a modest and frugal lifestyle, and his income primarily came from his work as a professor at the University of Königsberg, where he taught for most of his career. Although Kant was widely respected as a philosopher, and his works gained significant recognition, he did not accumulate a significant amount of wealth. Kant's focus was primarily on his intellectual pursuits and philosophical writings rather than financial gain.

Kant left behind a legacy that has continued to inspire and influence generations of thinkers and scholars. His ideas about reason, ethics, and human nature remain as relevant today as they were during his lifetime, and his contributions to philosophy and history will continue to be celebrated for centuries to come.

Cesare Beccaria

A portrait of Cesare Beccaria.
https://en.wikipedia.org/wiki/File:Cesare_Beccaria.jpg

Cesare Beccaria (1738–1794) was born in Milan, Italy, and became a man of fierce intellect and unwavering moral courage.

As a young man, Beccaria was interested in the ideas of the Enlightenment, which emphasized the importance of reason and liberty. He immersed himself in the study of philosophy, economics, and law. He also studied the works of the great thinkers of his time, such as Voltaire and Montesquieu.

His book, *On Crimes and Punishments*, challenged many of the traditional assumptions of criminal justice, arguing that punishments should be designed to deter crime rather than to exact revenge. Beccaria also believed the legal system should be based on the principles of equality and fairness.

These were radical ideas and put Beccaria at odds with the powerful institutions of his time. But he was undaunted by the challenge, and he poured his heart and soul into his work, spending years meticulously researching and writing his masterpiece.

In the end, Beccaria's efforts paid off. His book became one of the most influential books of his time, helping to shape the modern world as we know it today. And though Beccaria himself is long gone, his legacy lives on, inspiring generations of thinkers and scholars to push the boundaries of what is possible and explore the limits of human knowledge.

The Legacy of Great Men

The great men of the Enlightenment were pioneers who challenged the conventional wisdom of their time and ushered in a new era. Their ideas have left an indelible mark on our world and continue to inspire and guide us today.

Their contributions to philosophy, science, economics, literature, and politics continue to influence our understanding of the world. By embracing critical thinking, freedom of speech, and the value of the individual, these remarkable men laid the foundation for the modern world we inhabit.

As we reflect on the impact of these great men, we are reminded of the power of human intellect, perseverance, and courage. Their stories and ideas should inspire us to push the boundaries of knowledge, stand up for what is right, and strive for a better world. The great men of the Enlightenment remind us that progress is possible and that even in the face of adversity, we have the power to shape the future.

Chapter 7 – Women Who Defied the Limits of Their Time

Although Rousseau was a great intellectual and popular thinker of his day, he famously said that women were naturally inferior to men in terms of intellectual capacity and were better suited for domestic tasks and familial roles.

During the Enlightenment, there was a group of brilliant women whose ideas and writings challenged the traditional gender roles that had been firmly entrenched in society for centuries. Despite facing numerous obstacles and constraints, these women defied social norms and expectations. Many of their names have been lost in the pages of history, but we do know of several women whose contributions to the advancement of society and the pursuit of knowledge are undeniable.

Damaris Masham

Damaris Masham (1658-1708) was an English philosopher and writer who engaged in philosophical debates with some of the leading thinkers of her time, including John Locke. She was born into a prominent family and received a thorough education in languages, literature, and philosophy.

Little is known about her education, but she did have the advantage of being born into a family with a large library and a father who was one of the most learned men of his generation. She learned French, as was deemed requisite for a gentlewoman of the time, and she taught herself Latin.

Lady Masham wrote two books, *A Discourse Concerning the Love of God* (1696) and *Occasional Thoughts in Reference to a Vertuous or Christian Life* (1705), which were printed anonymously. Both books address philosophical issues that were topical at the time, such as love and moral virtue. Lady Masham believed that human beings are rational, social animals and are motivated by the pursuit of happiness.

She insisted on the importance of revelation and faith and denied that religion based purely on reason was possible. However, she also thought that religious belief that ignores the role of reason creates superstition. As she states, "An irrational religion can never rationally be conceived to come from God."

Lady Masham was particularly interested in John Locke's writings and corresponded with him extensively on topics ranging from politics to the nature of the soul. Her correspondence with Locke helped to shape his ideas and, in turn, influenced the development of philosophy during the Enlightenment. Lady Masham's writings on philosophy and religion were highly regarded in the 18th century, although they have received less attention in modern times.

Mary Astell

Mary Astell (1666–1731) was an English writer and philosopher. She is best known for her advocacy for women's education and her contributions to feminist theory. She can be called one of the earliest English feminists.

Astell began her writing career as a playwright. She later turned her attention to philosophy and wrote several influential works on education and equality. Her two books, *A Serious Proposal to the Ladies* (with part one coming out in 1694 and part two in 1697) and *Some Reflections upon Marriage* (1700), made her quite famous.

The first book, *A Serious Proposal to the Ladies*, is an appeal for more education for women. She urged women to do their best to gain knowledge and develop their own minds and the ability to think for themselves, all of which would guide them in living virtuous lives.

Astell had a problem with the cultural assumptions about femininity and the popular attitude about women. According to most people (women included), women did not demonstrate the same kind of intellectual ability as men because women were inherently more closely united to their bodies. Astell was worried that women were not being prepared for real-world issues and societal problems. Instead, women were being taught trivial things, such as social skills to look feminine and be nice and proper wives to their husbands. The average woman was not given an education that allowed them to develop their reasoning skills.

To overcome this, Astell proposed self-discipline and the establishment of an academy along Platonist lines, a place where women could receive proper education in religion and philosophy.

In her second book, *Some Reflections upon Marriage*, she examines women's subordination in marriage and their lack of freedom. She asked women not to marry and make promises to serve men or take vows of obedience. She considered these kinds of marriages as slavery and wanted women to choose husbands who would treat them as equals.

In her early twenties, Astell rejected a marriage proposal from a man who did not share her interests. She felt he would stifle her intellectual growth. She decided to remain single and devote herself to her writing.

Astell's ideas were radical at the time, and she faced much criticism and opposition from those who believed that women should be confined to domestic roles. However, her work inspired later feminist movements, and she has been recognized as an important contributor to the Enlightenment's legacy of advancing individual rights and freedoms.

Émilie du Châtelet

Émilie du Châtelet (1706–1749) was a French mathematician and writer who is best known for her translation and commentary of Isaac Newton's *Principia Mathematica*. She was born into a wealthy aristocratic family and received a thorough education in languages, literature, and mathematics. She married the Marquis de Châtelet, but their marriage was not a happy one, as they lived separate lives. However, she took on many lovers. One of her most prominent lovers was none other than Voltaire, who she met in 1733. He not only became her lover but also her companion and mentor.

Du Châtelet was keenly interested in the natural sciences, especially the writings of Newton, Gottfried Leibniz (a German mathematician who developed the binary system), and Christian Wolff (a German philosopher). Her advanced knowledge in physics and mathematics allowed her insight into Newton's physics that other women would not have. She helped shift France away from Cartesian physics, which was mostly conjecture drawn up by Descartes, toward Newtonian physics. Du Châtelet was also a scientist in her own right, searching for a metaphysical basis for Newtonian physics.

She set out to translate Newton's *Principia* into French, a project that took her several years to complete. Along the way, she added her own commentary and insights to the work, which helped to clarify and expand on Newton's ideas. Du Châtelet's translation and commentary helped to popularize Newtonian physics in France and beyond and had a lasting impact on the development of science during the Enlightenment.

In 1737, du Châtelet entered a competition to explain the nature of fire. She conducted experiments to disprove that fire was something material. Voltaire was also doing similar yet separate experiments to arrive at the same conclusion. Both of them published their results, and they both won prizes, along with another scientist, Leonhard Euler, who took the first prize.

Emilie du Châtelet died in childbirth at the age of forty-two in 1748. Her newborn daughter died around twenty minutes later. Her contributions to physics, mathematics, and philosophy during the Enlightenment, as well as her advocacy for women's rights, cannot be overstated. Her work has inspired generations of scholars, particularly women working in science and mathematics.

Laura Bassi

Laura Bassi (1711–1778) was an Italian physicist who became the first woman to earn a university chair in a scientific field, which was an extraordinary achievement for that time.

Bassi was the daughter of Giuseppe Bassi, a successful liberal lawyer. Bassi was an extremely precocious child. She received an excellent private education at home in very difficult subjects, such as mathematics, Latin, metaphysics, and philosophy.

In 1732, Bassi was invited by the University of Bologna to be appointed as a full professor of natural philosophy. Her incredible academic record and competence were so stellar that it did not matter that she was a woman.

About six years later, Bassi married Giovanni Giuseppe Veratti, a physician and fellow professor. The pair became a power couple in scientific circles. Bassi continued her work in physics, with a particular interest in Isaac Newton's theories of classical mechanics. Although she wrote around thirty papers, only four were ever printed.

Laura Bassi paved the way for future generations of women to enter academia. She also made significant contributions to the field of physics and advocated for women's rights and education.

Olympe de Gouges

Olympe de Gouges (1748-1793) was a French writer and activist. She is best known for her feminist writings and her advocacy for women's rights.

De Gouges began her writing career as a playwright. Her most famous work, *The Declaration of the Rights of Woman and the Female Citizen*, was published in 1791 as a response to the French Revolution's Declaration of the Rights of Man and of the Citizen, which excluded women. In her book, de Gouges writes, "Woman has the right to mount the scaffold; she must equally have the right to mount the rostrum."

De Gouges argued that women were equal to men and should have the same rights and opportunities. She advocated for women's access to education, property, and the right to vote. She also wrote about other social issues, pushing the boundaries of what was considered acceptable in public discourse.

She was not a philosopher, but she was known for her morally astute analysis of women's role in society, for her reimagining of the intersection of gender and political engagement, for her conception of civic virtue and her pacifist stance, and for her advocacy of selfhood for women, people of color, and children. She was among the first to demand the emancipation of slaves. She wrote about the rights women deserved, including those who had been divorced or were unwed mothers, and the protection of orphans, the poor, the unemployed, the aged, and illegitimate children.

De Gouges's ideas were ahead of her time, and she faced criticism and persecution for her views. Although de Gouges's ideas were not widely accepted in her lifetime, her work inspired later feminist movements. She challenged the prevailing social and political norms of her age and advocated for equality and justice for all individuals.

De Gouges was aware of the dangers of speaking out against the government, but she refused to remain silent. She wrote a letter to the revolutionary leader Maximilien Robespierre in which she criticized the violence and bloodshed of the Reign of Terror and called for an end to the executions. Despite the risks involved, de Gouges continued to speak out against the government and was eventually arrested and charged with treason. She was executed by guillotine.

Mary Wollstonecraft

Mary Wollstonecraft (1759-1797) was an English advocate for women's rights during a time when women were often relegated to the margins of society. Her writings challenged the status quo and laid the groundwork for a new era of feminist thought and activism.

Wollstonecraft began her writing career as a translator and journalist. She later turned her attention to philosophy and wrote several influential works on women's education and equality. Her most famous work, *A Vindication of the Rights of Woman*, was published in 1792 and argued for equal rights.

In her book, Wollstonecraft fearlessly argued that women were just as capable as men and deserved the same educational opportunities and political rights. Her words were a call to arms for women everywhere, inspiring them to demand their rightful place in society and fight for equality.

Wollstonecraft argued that women were not naturally inferior to men but were held back by their lack of education and opportunities. She called for the establishment of educational institutions for women and argued that women should have access to the same intellectual and political freedoms as men.

She goes on to say, "I shall first consider women in the grand light of human creatures, who, in common with men, are placed on this earth to unfold their faculties." She also insisted that it is essential for women's self-respect that they should have a right to earn and support themselves.

The book had a significant impact on the development of feminist theory and the broader social and political movements of the time. Her writings helped to inspire generations of women to fight for their rights and paved the way for the feminist movements of the 19th and 20th centuries.

In addition to her work on women's rights, Wollstonecraft was also an advocate for social justice and democratic reform. She believed in the importance of individual freedom and human rights, arguing that government should be structured to promote the common good rather than serve the interests of the ruling class.

One of the most dramatic moments in Wollstonecraft's life came when she traveled to France during the French Revolution. While there, she witnessed the tumultuous events that were occurring and became involved in radical political circles. She fell in love with an American diplomat named Gilbert Imlay. She met Imlay while living in Paris, and the two began a tumultuous relationship. Although they had a child together, Imlay proved to be unfaithful, and their relationship eventually collapsed. In a state of despair, Wollstonecraft attempted to take her own life by jumping into the Thames in London. She was rescued by a passerby and survived the ordeal.

Wollstonecraft's suicide attempt was a critical moment in her life, but it also speaks to the challenges she faced as a woman during the Enlightenment. Women of her time were often denied access to education and opportunities, and their personal lives were constrained by social expectations. Wollstonecraft's struggle to find meaning in her life serves as a reminder of the ongoing struggle for gender equality and the importance of fighting for human rights.

Mary Wollstonecraft's legacy continues to be recognized and celebrated today. Her contributions to feminism, literature, philosophy, and social reform have had a profound impact, and her ideas continue to inspire and shape modern discourse on gender equality, human rights, and social justice. Her work continues to be studied, debated, and celebrated by scholars, activists, and individuals who seek to promote equality and social change.

Sophie Germain

Sophie Germain (1776–1831) was a French mathematician who made important contributions to number theory and mathematical physics. Germain was born into a wealthy family and showed an early aptitude for mathematics. However, as a woman, she was initially excluded from formal education. Undeterred, she taught herself mathematics and began corresponding with leading mathematicians of her time.

Her breakthrough came when she discovered a way to model the vibrations of elastic surfaces, which helped to explain the phenomenon of musical acoustics. Germain went on to make significant contributions to number theory, including her work on Fermat's Last Theorem, which had remained unsolved for centuries. Despite facing discrimination due to her gender, Germain persisted in her work and was eventually recognized as a pioneer in her field.

Criticism Against These Women

Enlightenment male thinkers held a range of views on women and their role in society. However, many of these views were shaped by deeply ingrained patriarchal beliefs that saw women as inferior to men and relegated them to subordinate roles in the home and family.

One notable example of this perspective can be found in the works of Jean-Jacques Rousseau. In his work *Emile, or Treatise on Education*, Rousseau argues that women's natural inclination is to be domestic and nurturing and that they are best suited to the role of wife and mother. According to Rousseau, women's education should be focused primarily on developing their moral and emotional qualities rather than on acquiring knowledge or skills that would allow them to participate more fully in society. And Rousseau was not the only Enlightenment thinker who felt this way.

It is indeed amazing that these women went against the grain by challenging traditional gender roles and expectations, asserting their right to participate in intellectual and political spheres. These female thinkers changed the prevailing ideas of their time and helped to lay the groundwork for a more just society through their work. Their determination, courage, and brilliance helped them to leave a lasting legacy for future generations of women to build upon.

Chapter 8 – The American Enlightenment

It should not be surprising to hear that the American Enlightenment was highly influenced by the European Enlightenment. In the 18th century, colonists in the Thirteen Colonies realized their voice wasn't being heard in British Parliament. As time wore on, they realized they wanted something more than "tyranny." They wanted independence. They wanted a democracy.

Famous American Enlightenment Thinkers

But who led the charge? Who came up with the ideas of a self-representative government and the rights to life, liberty, and the pursuit of happiness? Let's take a look at some of the most influential American thinkers during this time.

Benjamin Franklin (1706–1790)

A portrait of Benjamin Franklin.
https://en.wikipedia.org/wiki/File:Joseph_Siffrein_Duplessis_-_Benjamin_Franklin_-_Google_Art_Project.jpg

Almost everyone knows the name Benjamin Franklin. He was an American scientist, inventor, and statesman. His experiments with electricity helped to further science during the Enlightenment. He also invented the bifocals and the Franklin stove, which was designed to produce more heat and less smoke.

Franklin played a pivotal role outside of the realm of science. He helped draft the US Constitution and created many civic organizations, including the first fire department in Philadelphia. Although he initially owned slaves, he later argued for abolition and sought to integrate African Americans into society.

Franklin served as an ambassador to France, and he also dealt with the British Parliament when he tried to get it to repeal the Stamp Act. Franklin has rightfully been called "the most accomplished American of his age." He believed in practical knowledge and the application of reason in everyday life, and thus, his writings and inventions reflected his Enlightenment ideals.

John Adams (1735–1826)

Another Founding Father of America was John Adams. He was known for his defense of individual rights, his advocacy of republicanism,

Before becoming a leader of the American Revolution, Adams was a lawyer who emphasized a person's right to counsel and the idea that one was innocent until proven guilty. He even defended British soldiers involved in the Boston massacre, successfully winning his case. Adams was against the Stamp Act and was also against insurrection, at least at first. As tensions grew, his opinions changed, especially when the British government wanted to pay the governor of Massachusetts instead of the colony's legislature, putting the governor deeper into the Crown's pocket.

Adams did not actively serve in the war, instead serving as a diplomat in Europe, where he sought to secure support for the war effort. He became the first vice president and the second president of the United States. He lost his reelection for another term to the presidency, partly due to accusations of becoming too despotic, as he had passed laws that restricted immigration and criminalized those who wrote negative statements about the government.

Nevertheless, Adams is remembered as an Enlightenment thinker, and it is worth noting that out of the first twelve presidents, Adams and his son were the only ones who never owned slaves. He once famously said, "I have, through my whole life, held the practice of slavery in such abhorrence, that I have never owned a negro or any other slaves, though I have lived for many years...when the practice was not disgraceful...and when it has cost me thousands of dollars for the labor and subsistence of free men."

Thomas Paine (1737–1809)

Unlike Franklin and Adams, Thomas Paine was not born in the colonies. He was born in England, moving to the colonies in 1774, just in time for the American Revolution. Paine was a political activist, philosopher, and writer, and he is best known for his influential works, *Common Sense* and *The Rights of Man*.

Common Sense, published in 1776, promoted the idea of American independence from Britain. The pamphlet became the best-selling work in America, even hundreds of years later. *The Rights of Man* defends the French Revolution, saying that a revolution should happen when a government does not support the rights of the people.

Paine promoted democratic principles, individual rights, and the need for social and political reform. His writings advocated for the overthrow of the monarchy and the establishment of democratic governments, which greatly influenced the American Revolution.

Thomas Jefferson (1743-1826)

An iconic portrait of Thomas Jefferson.
https://en.wikipedia.org/wiki/File:Thomas_Jefferson_by_Rembrandt_Peale,_1800.jpg

Thomas Jefferson is another one of those household names in America, mainly because of his work on the Declaration of Independence. Jefferson wrote many other works in which he emphasized the importance of individual liberty, religious freedom, and democratic ideals.

But let's dive into his most influential work: the Declaration of Independence. Although Jefferson was the original author of it, it was edited by the Second Continental Congress, so not all of his initial ideas made it to the final draft. For instance, Jefferson included a passage about how King George III had forced slavery on the colonies. "He has waged cruel war against human nature itself, violating its most sacred rights of life and liberty in the persons of a distant people who never offended him." The Second Continental Congress was worried Jefferson's article (which was much longer than that quote) would upset the Southern colonies, which greatly depended on slave labor. They wanted the Declaration of Independence to pass, not stall over something that even people in the North were not willing to fully give up yet.

Thomas Jefferson had a complicated relationship with slavery. He famously owned slaves, but he also believed the practice was evil. Regardless of his stance on abolition, his ideas on governance and human rights, as expressed in the Declaration of Independence, reflected Enlightenment principles and continue to influence American political thought.

James Madison (1751–1836)

James Madison is often referred to as the "Father of the Constitution," as he played a key role in drafting the US Constitution, primarily the Bill of Rights, which protects individual liberties such as freedom of speech, religion, and the press. He helped organize the Constitutional Convention, which helped bring about the revolutionary document in the first place.

Madison studied political philosophy at school, becoming entrenched in the ideas of the Enlightenment. Like the other American Enlightenment thinkers, he was outraged over the Stamp Act. Although Madison served in the American Revolution, his poor health made him sit out most of the battles. However, he was amazing with a pen, helping to create the Federalist Papers and the Bill of Rights, among many other essays and pamphlets. The Bill of Rights guarantees certain freedoms and ensures the separation of power, which are undeniably Enlightenment ideals. The First Amendment is like something pulled out of a European Enlightenment book: "Congress shall make no law respecting an establishment of religion, or prohibiting the free exercise thereof; or abridging the freedom of speech, or of the press; or the right of the people peaceably to assemble, and to petition the Government for a redress of grievances."

There were so many other American Enlightenment thinkers and Founding Fathers who had a lasting impact on American society and government, such as Ethan Allen and Alexander Hamilton. They influenced the ideals and principles that shaped the American

Revolution, the formation of the United States as a democratic republic, and the drafting of key documents, such as the Declaration of Independence and the US Constitution. Their emphasis on reason, individual rights, religious tolerance, and the pursuit of progress continues to be reflected in American political thought and the country's democratic governance to this day.

John Locke and His Impact on the American Revolution

American Enlightenment thinkers were greatly inspired by the thinkers who had come before, with John Locke perhaps being one of the most influential. Locke's political philosophy emphasized the fundamental rights of individuals and the social contract between citizens and government.

Locke's ideas were especially important when it came time to draft the Declaration of Independence. The Declaration of Independence's statement that all individuals possess certain unalienable rights, including life, liberty, and the pursuit of happiness, was a statement made by Loke, except Jefferson adjusted his statement slightly, replacing "property" with "happiness." Locke's ideas about limited governance and the necessity for citizens to have a voice in decisions affecting their lives played a role in shaping the United States Constitution.

In France, whose revolution we will briefly cover in the next chapter, Locke's ideas were embraced by the masses who desired to challenge the power of the monarchy and the aristocracy. Locke's emphasis on individual rights and the social contract provided a framework for the French demands of liberty, equality, and fraternity.

The Declaration of the Rights of Man and of the Citizen, another declaration partly inspired by Locke's philosophy, affirmed that all citizens are born free and equal and possess certain unalienable rights, including ownership of property, freedom of speech, and religion.

Social Contract Theory and the Concept of Natural Law

The social contract theory and the notion of natural law are two Enlightenment concepts that had a substantial impact on political and social thought. The social contract theory suggests that individuals should come to an agreement to establish governance and maintain social order.

According to this theory, individuals consent to relinquish some of their individual freedoms in exchange for security and protection, which would be provided by the government. The theory of a social contract is based on the belief that individuals have innate rights that are inviolable.

Similarly, the concept of natural law asserts that ethical and moral principles are innate in nature and apply to all human beings, irrespective of culture, society, or tradition. These principles are deemed self-evident and provide a foundation for developing fair social and political systems.

Both the social contract theory and natural law were pivotal ideas during the American Enlightenment, as well as the European Enlightenment. These concepts provided a framework for revolutionary thoughts and played a significant role in developing democratic governance and modern legal systems. Today, the principles of the social contract theory and natural law continue to spark debates about individual entitlements, social justice, and the role of governance in society.

But how did the American Enlightenment go from being thoughts inked on paper to actions that caused a revolution? What was the trigger? Well, there were quite a few, but one of the most well known was the idea that Britain should not tax the colonies if the colonists had no representation. "No taxation without representation" became a rallying cry against the unjust Stamp Tax, which was one of the major catalysts for the American Revolution.

The Stamp Tax

In 1765, British Parliament issued the Stamp Tax. The Stamp Tax required all colonial printers to pay a tax to the British on any paper used in printing in the colonies, including items like playing cards. As a receipt, an embossed revenue stamp was to be fixed on the document.

Colonists considered the tax to be illegal because they had no voice in Parliament, which means the law passed without them having any input on it. Protests were held throughout the colonies, threatening tax collectors with violence. The British Parliament finally backed off and repealed the Stamp Act in March of 1766, but the colonial reaction set the stage for the American independence movement.

As time passed, more unjust acts were passed, including the Townshend Acts and the Tea Act. Bostonians rebelled against the Tea Act by staging the Boston Tea Party, where they dumped over three hundred chests of tea into the harbor. The British government was outraged and passed the Intolerable Acts in 1774, which the colonists heavily resisted. That September, they formed the First Continental Congress, which drafted a measure outlining the colonists' grievances and called for a boycott of British goods. The members of the First Continental Congress also wrote a letter to the king, asking him to repeal the Intolerable Acts.

When the king didn't respond, and after hostilities broke out when British forces attempted to take stockpiled weapons and gunpowder from the colonists, the Second Continental Congress was formed. The American Revolution had begun, and the Second Continental Congress got to work on drafting a constitution.

The actions men and women took varied depending on the person. The more fervent revolutionaries, such as the Patriots, were not afraid to advocate violence and protests early on. Others preferred a more conservative route, such as drafting pamphlets and petitioning Parliament. History tends to focus on the men during this period, but women played an important role as well. For instance, the Daughters of Liberty was created in 1765. These women boycotted British goods, instead making their own goods at home. Many textiles were imported from Britain, and the Daughters of Liberty put on public demonstrations where they spun their own clothing, bringing awareness to other women and men that the colonies could survive without British goods.

We won't dive into the battles of the American Revolution in this book, but suffice it to say the colonists won. They successfully set up a democratic form of government, with three separate branches of government and a constitution that is still in use today. The colonists demonstrated to the world that it was possible to achieve liberty and personal freedoms. Of course, those freedoms didn't extend to everyone at the time, and it took quite a while for the major European monarchies to fall or transform into more constitutional ones, but the American Revolution laid another stone on the path to progress.

The Six Great Ideas

With that timeline out of the way, let's look at six ideas that made up the core of American Enlightenment philosophy. Some of these ideas are similar to European Enlightenment ideals, but others are unique to the American colonies.

Republicanism

Republicanism was a political philosophy that emphasized the importance of civic virtue and the common good. It advocated for a system of government where citizens participated in public life, and the welfare of the nation was prioritized over personal interests. The American Enlightenment emphasized the idea of a virtuous citizenry that actively participated in the political process and promoted the well-being of the community.

Conservatism

Conservatism refers to a belief in the preservation of traditional institutions and values, including religion, the social hierarchy, and the monarchy. While this idea was not as dominant as other ideas, such as liberalism and republicanism, conservatism still played a vital role in shaping American society and politics during the American Enlightenment.

Deism

Deism was a religious and philosophical belief system that rejected traditional religious doctrine and advocated the use of logic to understand the natural world. Deists believed in a distant, impersonal God who created the universe but does not intervene in human affairs. They emphasized the importance of reason and rejected religious dogma, advocating for a more rational and scientific approach to understanding the world.

Toleration

Toleration was the idea of allowing religious and intellectual diversity and promoting religious freedom and freedom of thought. During the American Enlightenment, there was a growing emphasis on religious tolerance, with many thinkers arguing for the separation of church and state and the right to practice religion without fear of persecution. This idea of tolerance also extended to intellectual diversity, as Enlightenment thinkers believed in the importance of open discourse and the free exchange of ideas.

Liberalism

Liberalism, at least in the context of the American Enlightenment, referred to the belief in individual liberty, limited government, and the protection of natural rights. American liberals of this era were influenced by philosophers like John Locke. They believed that individuals had inherent rights, such as life, liberty, and property, and that the government existed to protect these rights. They championed the idea of a social contract between the people and the government, stating that the government should be accountable to the people and should be limited in its powers.

Scientific Progress

The American Enlightenment was marked by a strong emphasis on scientific progress and the application of reason and observation to understand the natural world. Enlightenment thinkers promoted the scientific method as a means of understanding and solving problems and saw science as a way to uncover the laws that governed the universe.

These Enlightenment beliefs contributed to the formation of the principles that shaped the American Revolution and the subsequent development of the United States as a democratic republic. The American Revolution inspired other groups of people to speak out against tyranny, most notably in France.

Chapter 9 – Quest for Liberty and Equality

"Égalité, liberté, fraternité" was the battle cry that reverberated through the boulevards of Paris. It seemed as though the people of France had reached the limit of their patience in the late 18th century. The mob took to the streets, armed with little more than their fierce courage and dogged determination, and began a quest for freedom that would change the course of history in France and the world.

In the summertime of 1789, the thoroughfares of Paris were like a tinderbox waiting to explode. The atmosphere was fraught with tension and uneasiness as the people of France boiled with anger and exasperation at the despotic reign of the monarchy.

The teeming crowds of people gathered in the streets and stayed there as the evening turned into night. One could see their faces lit up by the flames of the flickering torches they carried. The clamor of their angry voices echoed off the walls of the city as they shouted vociferous slogans and called for change. It was as if they could sense change was on the horizon.

Amidst the pandemonium, there were groups of people at peace, but their hearts were filled with a profound sense of fear and uncertainty. Mothers clutched their offspring, their eyes scanning the mob for any sign of danger. Elderly men watched with a mix of acceptance and despair, while young men and women were filled with a ferocious determination to fight for their rights.

The tension was tangible, and the crowd surged forward, the people's fists raised in defiance. One could hear the explosive sounds of shattering glass and the stench of burning wood. Shuttered windows were broken open, and doors were smashed in. The smell of burning flesh and smoke filled the air as small fires turned into large bonfires in the street as the crowd moved toward the Bastille to gain weapons and gunpowder that were stored there.

As the night progressed, the chaos only increased. The shouts of scared men and women mingled with the sounds of gunshots piercing through the darkness. The forces of the monarchy clashed with the revolutionary mobs, and the streets flowed with blood.

It was a scene of absolute chaos and devastation. The people of France had suddenly woken from their cozy slumber and seemed determined to fight for their rights.

The French Revolution had begun. And the world would never be the same again.

King Louis and Marie Antoinette

King Louis XVI was the king of France when the French Revolution took place in 1789. He married Marie Antoinette of Austria for political reasons when he was only fifteen. He became king in 1774 at the tender age of nineteen. Louis was an intellectually capable person, but he lacked decisiveness and authority. However, he was still an absolute monarch, and his rule has often been regarded as corrupt and extravagant.

Still, he made sweeping reforms in all areas of the government, including religion, foreign policy, and financial matters. He signed the 1787 Edict of Versailles, which gave non-Catholics civil and legal status in France and the opportunity to practice their faith. He likely could have been considered an enlightened ruler if it were not for the crippling debt France had incurred. His financial reforms to get France out of debt were blocked by the nobles and *parlements*. Few understood the state's dire financial situation, and matters got worse by the day.

King Louis XVI and Queen Marie Antoinette lived in the luxurious Palace of Versailles, away from the problems of the masses. As discontent grew, King Louis did little to understand the economic and financial troubles of his people.

Marie Antoinette's wasteful lifestyle particularly irked the people. In 1789, after being told that the French population was facing a shortage of bread and was starving because of the poor crop harvest, Marie

Antoinette famously exclaimed, "Let them eat cake!" It is widely believed that she never uttered these words; the idea that she said them appeared decades after her death. However, the people knew she spent enormous sums on dresses and games when they could barely afford to buy bread.

The Palace of Versailles was stormed by an angry mob on October 5th, 1789. The royal family was captured and taken to Paris, where they were forced to accept their new roles as constitutional monarchs. After nearly two years of negotiations, Louis and his family attempted to flee Paris for Varennes, but their plan failed, and they were recaptured. Louis was put on trial for high treason. He was executed by guillotine on January 21st, 1793.

His wife, Marie Antoinette, was executed nearly ten months later, on October 16th, 1793. Louis's death marked the end of over one thousand years of a continuous monarchy. Many have argued it was a key moment in the radicalization of revolutionary violence.

The French Revolution

You might be wondering why we are talking about the French Revolution in a book on the Enlightenment. Well, the French Revolution might have never occurred if it were not for the Enlightenment. And it was essentially Enlightenment thoughts put into action. The cries for equality, freedom, and brotherhood reverberated through the streets of Paris and beyond as the insurgents battled to form a new society based on those principles.

At the center of the French Revolution was a profound sense of injustice and subjugation felt by the masses. The catalyst was the famine and shortage of grain due to poor crops and pests. The insurgents faced formidable adversaries, including the aristocracy, the church, and foreign powers, all of whom were resolute in maintaining the status quo. But despite the odds, the insurgents, driven by a deep sense of resolve and a conviction in their cause, persevered.

The French Revolution started on May 5th, 1789, with the summoning of the Estates General. Representatives from the three estates of French society—the clergy, the nobility, and the common people—gathered together upon orders of the king, Louis XVI, to address the growing financial crisis in the country. The Estates General had not assembled since 1614.

Although the Third Estate had been promised more representation, they soon found out the promised representation would not be enough to outweigh the votes of the First Estate, whose members held contrasting views on what would be best for France. So, instead of debating with the other two estates, the Third Estate met on its own, eventually declaring itself to be the National Assembly.

The National Assembly invited the other estates to join but also warned them that they would continue with their goals, with or without them. King Louis XVI unsurprisingly did not like this turn of events, as he could see that power was slipping out of his fingers. Although he tried to shut the National Assembly down, he could not. And as time passed, members from the other estates (mainly the Second Estate) joined the National Assembly, calling for a constitution.

The king sent out the military, hoping to rein in the people's passion. However, this move only served to upset them more. They demanded the king remove the military, but the king refused, instead offering to move the National Assembly to a safer place, one where they would be cut off from the people of Paris.

Things escalated until the storming of the Bastille occurred on July 14th, 1789. As mentioned above, the Bastille was a fortress and prison in Paris that had come to signify the tyranny of the monarchy. At the time, the prison only had seven inmates, but the people weren't there to free political prisoners. Instead, the event was supposed to be a symbolic attack on the monarchy. The Bastille also gave the mob armor, weaponry, and ammunition.

The storming of the Bastille is seen as the starting point of the French Revolution. The people wanted to reform the government, create a constitution, and provide the people with basic liberties. The idea should sound familiar, as this was something Enlightenment thinkers often wrote about. The Americans' victory over the British was also one of the catalysts for the French Revolution. The French people saw that a revolt could be successful, even against a major military power. Although the American government was new at that time, the French saw the potential for a reformed government and the promises that it could bring.

The Declaration of the Rights of Man and of the Citizen was ratified on October 5th, 1789, by Louis XVI under pressure from the riots that had broken out. This document served as the preamble to the first constitution in 1791.

The Declaration of the Rights of Man and of the Citizen was inspired by the writings of Enlightenment philosophers, such as Jean-Jacques

Rousseau, Montesquieu, and Voltaire. Other influences included the 1776 Virginia Declaration of Rights and the manifesto of the Dutch Patriot movement of the 1780s. The creators of the Declaration went beyond its sources, as they intended the principles to be universally applicable.

The Declaration has a preamble and seventeen brief articles. The first article contains the document's central statement: "Men are born and remain free and equal in rights." It states that the purpose of "political association" should be the preservation of these rights, with those rights being "liberty, property, security, and resistance to oppression." The document protects the freedom of speech and religion and also provides equal treatment of people before the law. It also asserts that taxes should be paid by all citizens in accordance with their means.

Things were fairly peaceful until Louis XVI and his family tried to escape. People were worried that spies and traitors were among them, causing distrust. Faction groups rose up, threatening the unity of the revolution. Other monarchs, fearing that the revolution would spread, declared their support for Louis. Some even hinted at invading France to help stop the revolt.

Progress needed to be made, and the French formed the Legislative Assembly in October 1791. However, this assembly was not very strong. For the most part, it ignored the people the French Revolution was fighting for: the working class, those who were the most affected by the bread shortages. There were also those who felt the French Revolution had gone too far; these people were likely shocked at how much further it would go.

The French Revolutionary Wars began in April 1792, with French forces fighting Austrians and Prussians who were situated along the border. The French were not very successful at first, but the Brunswick Manifesto, whose details were revealed in early August, angered the French. The manifesto stated that if the royal family were harmed, then civilians would be harmed. Obviously, the manifesto was supposed to intimidate the people into submission. But it had the opposite effect. Later that month, Louis was removed from the throne. About a month later, the French First Republic replaced the monarchy.

Things quickly escalated after this. For instance, in September, over one thousand prisoners in jails were executed, as they were thought to be potentially conspiring with Prussia. In January 1793, Louis XVI was condemned to death, a move that horrified the European monarchs.

It was clear by this point that the French Revolution had morphed into something that went against the "ideal" Enlightenment thoughts. It is very likely that Enlightenment thinkers would have been shocked at the brutality that occurred. But reality is often different than lofty thoughts dreamed up in some salon. The dates for the Reign of Terror differ, with some pointing to the September Massacre as the beginning or to 1793 when the Revolutionary Tribunal was formed. Regardless of when it started, it was a period of intense violence, turmoil, and political oppression. Around seventeen thousand perceived adversaries of the French Revolution were killed, while another ten thousand died in prison.

The Reign of Terror was led by Jacobin leader Maximilien Robespierre. He pointed to the ideas brought up during the Enlightenment to encourage the people, saying that a government should act for the good of the people instead of certain groups. However, Robespierre believed that the only way that could happen was by expelling those who fought against such an idea. In his opinion, terror was the only way to create the kind of France he envisioned.

Robespierre had many goals he wanted to accomplish, such as the right for people of color and Jews to vote. He wanted to end the slave trade in France and give men the right to bear arms for self-defense. During the Reign of Terror, Maximilien Robespierre gained immense power. He was brutal and caused fear, but in his mind, he was doing it for the good of his country. However, personal rivalries and clashes with other revolutionaries contributed to his downfall, resulting in his arrest and execution in July 1794.

In 1795, the Directory was established, along with a new constitution. The Directory was a five-man executive committee that brought about a period of relative political stability. However, the Directory was unable to tackle the ongoing political and economic problems of France. Some saw the group as a betrayal of what they had been fighting for. It was dissolved by a coup by Napoleon Bonaparte in 1799.

Napoleon created the Consulate, which was composed of three assemblies. Even so, Napoleon held a lot of power. In 1802, he declared himself First Consul for Life, a role that is akin to a dictator. Although the French Revolution succeeded in establishing a republic in 1792, that republic was torn down when Napoleon Bonaparte was crowned the emperor of France in 1804.

Napoleon Bonaparte

Napoleon Bonaparte is an interesting figure in history, and he is considered an enlightened autocrat, so his background is worth exploring. He was born on the island of Corsica in 1769, the same year Corsica became a French territory. Napoleon was picked on in school because of his accent and birthplace. He became very introverted, devoting himself to his studies.

And his hard work paid off. He started his career as a second lieutenant in the French Army in 1785. Because of his expertise in military matters, he rose through the ranks, and by 1793, he had become a general.

During the French Revolution, Napoleon played a pivotal role in several campaigns, and he swiftly gained notoriety as an ingenious martial strategist. In 1796, he led the French Army to triumph in Italy, and he followed this up with a sequence of campaigns in Egypt and Syria, which were not as successful.

Napoleon made sure to keep on what was happening in France while he was on campaign in Egypt. Worried that France would be lost after hearing about its defeats in the French Revolutionary Wars, he sailed back to France, even though he did not receive orders to do so. By the time he had arrived, the situation had stabilized, but it was clear to Napoleon that the Directory was not fit to lead; it couldn't even properly punish him for deserting his men.

Perhaps that is when the wheels started turning in Napoleon's mind. He met with other influential figures to discuss a coup, which happened in November 1799. He became the First Consul for ten years, but he later decided to extend that term for life. And then he went one step further and declared himself emperor.

As emperor, Napoleon enforced a sequence of far-reaching reforms that transformed France into a contemporary, centralized state. He created a new judicial system called the Napoleonic Code, which created equality before the law and secured the people's rights to property. He also changed the educational infrastructure, instituted a system of civic projects, and propagated economic expansion and growth. He created the first central bank and sought to ease tensions with the Catholic Church, whose clergymen had been targeted during the French Revolution. Of course, like any enlightened despot, Napoleon had his downfalls. One of the most notable tyrannical things he did was reinstate slavery in the Caribbean. It ultimately did not matter for the people in Haiti, who were able to rise up and create their own government without slavery in 1804. Although Napoleon later abolished the slave trade during the Hundred Days, his legacy regarding slavery is not seen in a favorable light.

Napoleon's military conquests expanded the limits of France, but in doing so, he made a lot of enemies, primarily Britain. Today, Napoleon is seen as a military genius, with his battles and tactics studied by military scholars and buffs. He did suffer defeats, but with a military career of over eighty battles and only losing eleven of those battles is pretty good. Nevertheless, he was eventually defeated in 1814 and forced to relinquish his throne. He was exiled to the island of Elba.

However, Napoleon was not content to sit still. He returned to France in 1815, where he briefly regained authority in a phase recognized as the Hundred Days. He was famously defeated in the Battle of Waterloo in June 1815, and he was exiled again, this time to the island of Saint Helena in the South Atlantic. There, he died as a prisoner in 1821 at the relatively young age of fifty-one. The end of the Napoleonic Wars is typically used as a convenient end date for the Enlightenment, although some argue that it ended earlier.

Conclusion

The Age of Enlightenment was a period of transformation, a time when rationality and personal autonomy were embraced. Enlightenment philosophers believed in the right to life, freedom, and ownership of property. They championed the concept of democracy and the rule of law. They also believed that government should be based on the consent of the governed and that laws should be created through a logical and democratic process.

The Enlightenment gave birth to a world that was completely different from anything that existed before. Inventions and discoveries were made that changed how people saw the world. Ideas about new forms of governance challenged the status quo and forced the people to think more critically. Women made a push to be seen and heard in different ways than before, laying the groundwork for future suffragist movements. The Enlightenment changed many things, but it mainly provided the foundation for a new world, a world that was secular, experimental, individualistic, and, above all, progressive.

It is rather difficult to imagine how the world would have turned out without the Enlightenment since it was a complex movement that had a far-reaching impact in many different fields. However, we can make some educated guesses.

Without the Enlightenment, the values of liberty, separate branches of government, and religious tolerance would not have been as deeply ingrained in Western culture as they are today. Religious and superstitious beliefs might have had a much greater impact on people's thinking today. Scientific progress and technological innovations might not have advanced as astonishingly as they did.

Without an emphasis on empirical reasoning and experimentation, our comprehension of the natural world might be much more limited today. For instance, we might have never discovered insulin or learned about the structure of the atom.

Without the influence of Enlightenment thinkers like John Locke and Montesquieu, many countries would likely still be ruled by dictators or monarchs, and the concept of human rights would not have gained the widespread acceptance it has today.

And the absence of fundamental rights would have meant a legal system that didn't benefit the people. This hypothetical legal system likely would not have placed importance on the protection of the accused, making it difficult for individuals to prove their innocence. Laws in many countries might have heavily tilted in favor of the state, making it easier for authorities to imprison or torture citizens and even entire families. Punishments would likely have been more severe, with people being sentenced to long, inhumane prison sentences and barbaric forms of execution.

The impact of the Enlightenment on the modern world cannot be overstated. It was a period of great excitement, where thinkers of all kinds gathered to question the old ways of thinking and created new pathways to a more reasonable, humane society.

These concepts greatly influenced the revolutions in France and the United States. After all, the Declaration of Independence was based heavily on Enlightenment philosophy, particularly the philosophy of John Locke, who believed that every individual had a right to life, freedom, and ownership of property. The French Revolution sought liberty, equality, and brotherhood. These concepts and values were directly inspired by Enlightenment thinkers like Rousseau and Voltaire.

Without the Enlightenment, these revolutions might not have occurred or might have created something entirely different. Would Thomas Jefferson have been inspired to write the Declaration of Independence without John Locke's thoughts to guide him? Would the French have rebelled just to replace their ruler with another king? These are, of course, hypotheticals, but they are interesting to think about.

While it is difficult to argue for certain what would have occurred without the Enlightenment, it is clear that the ideas and values of the Enlightenment had a profound impact on history.

If you enjoyed this book, a review on Amazon would be greatly appreciated because it would mean a lot to hear from you.

To leave a review:

1. Open your camera app.
2. Point your mobile device at the QR code.
3. The review page will appear in your web browser.

_____

Thanks for your support!

Here's another book by Enthralling History that you might like

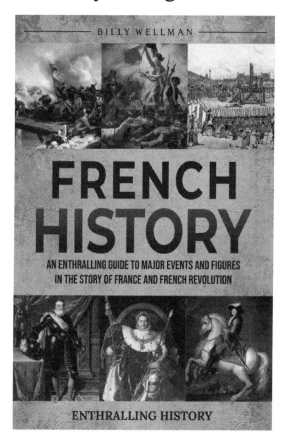

Free limited time bonus

Stop for a moment. We have a free bonus set up for you. The problem is this: we forget 90% of everything that we read after 7 days. Crazy fact, right? Here's the solution: we've created a printable, 1-page pdf summary for this book that you're reading now. All you have to do to get your free pdf summary is to go to the following website: https://livetolearn.lpages.co/enthrallinghistory/

Or, Scan the QR code!

Once you do, it will be intuitive. Enjoy, and thank you!

Sources

Boer, P. den, Bugge, P., Wæver, O., & European Association of Distance Teaching Universities. (1995). The History of the Idea of Europe. (K. Wilson & W. J. van der Dussen, Eds.) (Revised, Ser. What Is Europe?, bk. 1). Open University.

Curta, F., & Stuckey, J. (2011). Charlemagne in Medieval East Central Europe (ca. 800 to ca. 1200). Canadian Slavonic Papers / Revue Canadienne Des Slavistes, 53(2/4), 181-208. http://www.jstor.org/stable/41708339

Faust, D. R. (2018). Ancient Rome (Ser. A look at ancient civilizations ser). Gareth Stevens Publishing LLLP.

McGrath, A. (2009). Christianity's Dangerous Idea: The Protestant Revolution— A History from the Sixteenth Century to the Twenty-First. United States: HarperCollins.

Pflanze, O. (1955). Bismarck and German Nationalism. The American Historical Review, 60(3), 548-566. https://doi.org/10.2307/1845577

Roberts, J. M. (1997). The Penguin History of Europe. Penguin Books.

Rossi, D. (2007). Humanism and the Renaissance. The Year's Work in Modern Language Studies, 69, 476-490. http://www.jstor.org/stable/25834052

Rothenberg, G. E. (1988). The Origins, Causes, and Extension of the Wars of the French Revolution and Napoleon. The Journal of Interdisciplinary History, 18(4), 771-793. https://doi.org/10.2307/204824

Schedvin, C. B. (1990). Staples and Regions of Pax Britannica. The Economic History Review, 43(4), 533-559. https://doi.org/10.2307/2596734

Shirer, W. L. (1998). The Rise and Fall of the Third Reich. United States: Simon and Schuster.

Williamson, S. R. (1988). The Origins of World War I. The Journal of Interdisciplinary History, 18(4), 795-818. https://doi.org/10.2307/204825

Zoch, P. A. (2020). Ancient Rome: An Introductory History (Second). University of Oklahoma Press.

Ackerman, J. S. (1998). Leonardo Da Vinci: Art in Science. *Daedalus, 127*(1), 207-224. http://www.jstor.org/stable/20027483

Bartlett, K. R., & Bartlett, G. C. (2019). *The Renaissance in Italy: A History.* Hackett Publishing Company.

Manca, J. (1995). Michelangelo as Painter: A Historiographic Perspective. *Artibus et Historiae, 16*(31), 111-123. https://doi.org/10.2307/1483500

Marrow, J. H. (1986). Symbol and Meaning in Northern European Art of the Late Middle Ages and the Early Renaissance. *Simiolus: Netherlands Quarterly for the History of Art, 16*(2/3), 150-169. https://doi.org/10.2307/3780635

Merriman, J. M. (2010). *A History of Modern Europe: From the Renaissance to the Present* (Third). W.W. Norton.

Müntz Eugène. (2019). *Michelangelo.* (A. Borges, Trans.) (Ser. Temporis collection). Parkstone International. Retrieved May 22, 2023, from https://public.ebookcentral.proquest.com/choice/publicfullrecord.aspx?p=6006696.

Müntz Eugène. (2019). Raphael (Ser. Essential). Parkstone International. https://public.ebookcentral.proquest.com/choice/publicfullrecord.aspx?p=5930199.

Nash, & Nash, S. (2009). *Northern Renaissance Art* (Ser. Oxford history of art ser). Oxford University Press USA - OSO. from https://public.ebookcentral.proquest.com/choice/publicfullrecord.aspx?p=5751187.

Nauert, C. G. (2006). *Humanism and the Culture of Renaissance Europe.* Cambridge University Press.

Séailles Gabriel, & Leonardo. (2011). *Leonardo da Vinci.* Parkstone International

Sullivan, M. A. (2008). Bosch, Bruegel, Everyman and the Northern Renaissance. *Oud Holland, 121*(2/3), 117-146. http://www.jstor.org/stable/42712203

Wasserman, J. (2007). Rethinking Leonardo da Vinci's "Last Supper." *Artibus et Historiae, 28*(55), 23-35. http://www.jstor.org/stable/20067137

Whitford, D. M. (2016). Erasmus Openeth the Way Before Luther: Revisiting Humanism's Influence on "The Ninety-Five Theses" and the Early Luther. *Church History and Religious Culture, 96*(4), 516-540. http://www.jstor.org/stable/26382865

The Internet Encyclopedia of Philosophy

https://iep.utm.edu/

Britannica

https://www.britannica.com/

Stanford Encyclopedia of Philosophy

https://plato.stanford.edu/

Reill, Peter Hanns (2004), Encyclopedia of the Enlightenment, New York, Facts On File, Inc.

S. Pinker (2018) Enlightenment Now, New York, Penguin Random House.

A, Gottlieb, (2016) The Dream Of Enlightenment. New York, W. W. Norton & Co.

A, Gottlieb, (2016) The Dream Of Reason, New York, W. W. Norton & Co.

V. Ferrone, (2015) The Enlightenment, New Jersey, Princeton University Press

S. Fleischacker, (2013) What is Enlightenment?, New York, Routledge

R.Wokler (2001) Rousseau, A Very Short Introduction, New York, Oxford University Press

A.J. Ayer (2000) Hume, A Very Short Introduction, New York, Oxford University Press

John Dunn (1984) Locke, A Very Short Introduction, New York, Oxford University Press

Roger Scruton (1986) Spinoza, A Short Introduction, New York, Oxford University Press

Printed in Great Britain
by Amazon

41091725R10218